Dwelling in Fiction

 FLASHPOINTS

The FlashPoints series is devoted to books that consider literature beyond strictly national and disciplinary frameworks and that are distinguished both by their historical grounding and by their theoretical and conceptual strength. Our books engage theory without losing touch with history and work historically without falling into uncritical positivism. FlashPoints aims for a broad audience within the humanities and the social sciences concerned with moments of cultural emergence and transformation. In a Benjaminian mode, FlashPoints is interested in how literature contributes to forming new constellations of culture and history and in how such formations function critically and politically in the present. Series titles are available online at http://escholarship.org/uc/flashpoints.

SERIES EDITORS: Ali Behdad (Comparative Literature and English, UCLA), Editor Emeritus; Judith Butler (Rhetoric and Comparative Literature, UC Berkeley), Editor Emerita; Michelle Clayton (Hispanic Studies and Comparative Literature, Brown University); Edward Dimendberg (School of Humanities, UC Irvine), Founding Editor; Catherine Gallagher (English, UC Berkeley), Editor Emerita; Nouri Gana (Comparative Literature and Near Eastern Languages and Cultures, UCLA); Susan Gillman (Literature, UC Santa Cruz), Coordinator; Jody Greene (Literature, UC Santa Cruz); Richard Terdiman (Literature, UC Santa Cruz), Founding Editor

A complete list of titles begins on page 297.

Dwelling in Fiction

Poetics of Place and the Experimental Novel in Latin America

Ashley R. Brock

NORTHWESTERN UNIVERSITY PRESS | EVANSTON, ILLINOIS

Northwestern University Press
www.nupress.northwestern.edu

Printed in the United States of America

10 9 8 7 6 5 4 3 2 1

Library of Congress Cataloging-in-Publication Data

Names: Brock, Ashley R., author.
Title: Dwelling in fiction : poetics of place and the experimental novel in Latin America / Ashley R Brock.
Other titles: FlashPoints (Evanston, Ill.)
Description: Evanston, Illinois : Northwestern University Press, 2023. | Series: Flashpoints | Includes bibliographical references and index.
Identifiers: LCCN 2023028362 | ISBN 9780810146525 (paperback) | ISBN 9780810146532 (cloth) | ISBN 9780810146549 (ebook)
Subjects: LCSH: Experimental fiction, Latin American—History and criticism. | Latin American fiction—20th century—History and criticism. | Place (Philosophy) in literature.
Classification: LCC PQ7082.E97 B76 2023 | DDC 860.9980904—dc23/eng/20230620
LC record available at https://lccn.loc.gov/2023028362

Contents

Acknowledgments   vii

Introduction   3

1. The Case for Critical Regionalism   37

2. Embodying the Local   87

3. Dwelling in the *Travessia*   129

4. Learning One's Way around *la Zona*   165

Coda   205

Notes   217

Bibliography   265

Index   283

Acknowledgments

The research and writing of this book were made possible by financial support from the Department of Comparative Literature at the University of California, Berkeley, and the Wolf Center for the Humanities at the University of Pennsylvania. I would like to thank the Mudd Library's Manuscript Division at Princeton University for allowing me to consult Juan José Saer's manuscripts and the *Revista de Estudios Hispánicos* for allowing me to reprint in chapter 4 sections of my article: "Algo Más Que Mirar: More-Than-Looking at Regional Life in Juan José Saer's *El limonero real*," *Revista de Estudios Hispánicos* (52:1, 2018).

Books might seem to be solitary endeavors, but whatever life courses through the pages of this one is thanks to the community that helped me bring it into being. I have had the good fortune of writing it in the company of brilliant, generous, and patient people. I would like to express my heartfelt thanks to those who encouraged me early on, shared my passion for difficult novels, and guided my scattered ideas toward this topic: Natalia Brizuela, Francine Masiello, Candace Slater, Anne-Lise François, Karl Britto, Adriana Amante, David Oubiña, and Marília Librandi. My immense gratitude goes to those who have accompanied me in the writing process, offering friendship, advice, and skilled readings at every stage: Paco Brito, Emily Drumsta, Phoebe Bronstein, Julie Ann Ward, Krista Brune, Ivett López Malagamba, Camilo Jaramillo, Alex Brostoff, Yael Segolovitz, Jamille Pinhero Dias, Victoria Saramago, Carolina Sá Carvalho, Martina Bronner, Carolyn Fornoff, and Amanda

Smith. They say the last mile is the hardest, and special thanks go to those who walked it with me and offered support: Julia Chang and Manuel Cuellar for their solidarity, help brainstorming titles, and many hours over Zoom and Ramsey McGlazer for a most sensitive and timely reading of the introduction and chapter 1.

I would like to thank my colleagues in the Spanish and Portuguese Department at the University of Pennsylvania for their unfailing support and guidance: Ericka Beckman, Ignacio Javier López, Michael Solomon, Jorge Téllez, Luis Moreno-Caballud, and Odette Casamayor-Cisneros. I acknowledge with gratitude the graduate students who helped me wrestle with the ideas in this book in seminar during my first three years at Penn: Juan Pablo Cárdenas, Nancy Lee Roane, Alexandra Brown, Daniela Sánchez Russo, Juan Garceran Fructuoso, Humberto Morales Cruz, Lenin Lozano Guzmán, Meche Mayna-Medrano, Monica Veiga Puente, Michael Shea, Maria Wagner, Marta J. Sanchís Ferrer, Josué Chávez, Marco Áviles, Kathryn Phipps, and Nico Suarez Guerrero.

This book would not exist in its current form without the amazing team at Northwestern University Press. I thank the FlashPoints series editors, especially Susan Gillman and Michelle Clayton, for believing in the manuscript, Faith Wilson Stein and Anne Gendler for all the work they have put into shepherding the project through peer review and production, and the anonymous reviewers for their invaluable input.

Finally, I thank my family, who have taught me what it means to dwell: my brothers, Peter Brock and Reilly Brock, whose intelligence, humor, and compassion make them the best lifelong interlocutors I could hope for; and my parents, Maureen King and Peter Brock, for teaching me to love stories, encouraging me to tell my own, and treating my right to think for myself as sacred. Special thanks go to Josh Mathews, without whose strength, nurturing, and steadfast faith in me I could not have seen this enormous undertaking through.

Dwelling in Fiction

Introduction

What does dwelling have to do with literature? At the outset, it might seem that the two are incommensurable, that one involves our embodied interactions with the places we inhabit, and the other can at best represent but not enact the practices that go into dwelling: the cumulative encounters that render a place familiar, the care and stewardship we undertake toward the places we call home, and the sense of belonging—of entanglement with something beyond the self—that results. Other art forms—surely architecture, arguably certain forms of sculpture, installation art, cinema, and virtual reality experiences—would seem better suited than literature to convey and shape the sensorial and affective experience of place. Nevertheless, Martin Heidegger, the preeminent philosopher of dwelling, assigns a special role to the poetic in his later writings, where dwelling takes center stage.[1] For Heidegger—and for many subsequent poets, writers, philosophers, and literary scholars who diverge from him on other points—it is poetic thought and language that make dwelling possible in the modern world.

Grappling with Heidegger's legacy, including his infamously reactionary politics, is one of the tasks this book takes on, but it was not with Heidegger that this project originated. It started, instead, with an affinity for extremely and programmatically difficult texts about so-called regional spaces, those imagined as geographically and culturally removed from metropolitan centers of culture, commerce, and power.[2] Reading the most experimental works of authors such as João Guimarães Rosa, José María Arguedas, William Faulkner, Juan Rulfo, James Agee, and Juan José Saer got me thinking about how literature—and particularly literature that privileges the poetic over the communicative or representational function of language—might at once signal and seek to overcome its limitations as a means of conjuring place, engendering situated knowledge, and drawing the reader into an affective and ethical relationship with a particular locale. These texts prompted me to ask: What is literature uniquely positioned to teach us about the experience of dwelling? Who is the "we" in question when we read about regional spaces, and what makes these issues pressing for so many experimental regionalist writers in the mid-twentieth century?

In efforts to bound my investigation of these dauntingly broad questions with a degree of regional and historical specificity, I have limited this study to South American literature (my examples are drawn from Peru, Brazil, and Argentina) of the late 1950s through the early 1970s. In Latin America, this is a moment dominated by developmentalism (*el desarrollismo*) and populism, each aimed at incorporating the hinterlands and the peasant classes into the rapidly modernizing nation. The literature of this period, which proved prolific for many of Latin America's most recognized authors such as Alejo Carpentier, Gabriel García Márquez, Julio Cortázar, and Mario Vargas Llosa, is known for breaking the realist pact and inaugurating a new phase in which the relationship between aesthetics and politics would be renegotiated. *Dwelling in Fiction* focuses on authors who, though arguably at the center of this midcentury renovation, are less well known outside Latin America: José María Arguedas, João Guimarães Rosa, and Juan José Saer. Conjuring a hyperlocal world through extreme formal experimentation, this grouping of writers defies both the regionalist paradigm said to have preceded them and the interpretative lenses through which many of their peers are read: either lauded for making Latin American literature "universal"[3] or critiqued for the self-absorption of their anti-realist aesthetics. I propose in what follows that the politics of some of the most radically experimental novels of this period lies in how they handle their readers.

It is worth noting that in this historical context, the "we" that makes up the audience for formally complex neo-regionalist literature has little in common with the peasants, cowboys, backland bandits, Indigenous laborers, and migrants who populate its pages; the readership tends to be educated (*culto*), city dwelling, and more closely identified with European or *criollo* culture than Indigenous culture. For the first time, in fact, this audience is likely to be removed not only from the rural communities depicted (as is the case for the elite classes in cities such as Lima, Rio de Janeiro, and Buenos Aires) but also from Latin America writ large; thanks to the editorial phenomenon known as the boom, Latin American literature began to be published primarily on other continents.[4] *Dwelling in Fiction* shows that even texts that do not explicitly take on political subject matter often anticipate and respond through their form to the (neo)colonial power relations across which their readers encounter the rural interior of the continent, its underdevelopment, and its connection with the natural world.

The regional spaces on which I focus—the Andean highlands, the Brazilian *sertão* (interior, semiarid desert), and the inland plains of Argentina—have long been sites of material extraction and cultural appropriation. If the wealth and modernity of capital cities as well as foreign empires was built on their natural resources, so too were foundational narratives of national identity built on their types (the *gaucho*, the *jagunço*, the *indio*, the by turns noble and indolent *campesino*, etc.) and autochthonous traditions. Though I would not wish to conflate these two means of instrumentalizing the rural interior, I join those ecocritical thinkers who recognize that extractive economic models are ideologically propped up by and in turn perpetuate epistemologies that suppress local knowledge and reify local life forms.[5] It follows that to learn to dwell—to train the senses, the imagination, and the affects through prolonged inhabitation—in zones of extraction is to symbolically reclaim such spaces from and implicitly oppose the logic of extractive capitalism, which depends on producing a rift between those spaces imagined as inhabited and inhabitable and those conceived as sources of raw materials.[6] Though the most urgently needed responses to the threats faced by our planet (and its rural populations) as a result of this model of development will not come from literature alone, engendering sense of place and local belonging remains one of the major contributions the cultural sphere can make toward changing the narratives that have led us to this point.[7]

This book thus forms part of a larger turn in Latin American studies, driven primarily by ecocritical, historical materialist, and new materialist thinkers, to revisit regionalist cultural production, and the twentieth-century regionalist novel in particular, and discern a more complex relationship between this archive and the rapid, often violent modernization of the continent it registers.[8] Whereas many have traced in regionalist literature ideological justifications for and/or critiques of extractivist models of development, I am primarily interested in how the most radically experimental neo-regionalist novels might lead their readers to imagine, and, indeed, to practice alternative modes of relating to place. I underscore, moreover, the stakes of dwelling—as an ethical and political practice—in conversations concerning postcolonial geopolitics, internal colonialism, and decolonial approaches to world literature, all of whose imbrication in ecological questions is becoming increasingly unavoidable.[9]

One of the aims of the recent reuptake of regionalism in Latin American studies (one shared by the present study) is to challenge long-established but limiting views of regionalist literature: that it is historically confined to the early twentieth century, that it is more concerned with identitarian and social questions than aesthetic questions, and that it simply facilitates the ossification of rural types and customs.[10] As I go on to discuss in chapter 1, by the heyday of Latin American regionalist literature in the 1920s and 1930s, it was not uncommon for regionalist texts to grapple in complicated ways with the thorny question of how their authors and readers might relate (ethically, economically, politically) to the rural communities represented. Nor was it uncommon for regionalist writers, who were often in dialogue with if not themselves affiliated with avant-garde movements of the time, to address such concerns through literary form. As such, the ostensibly odd marriage of decolonial geopolitical consciousness and radical formal experimentation that I trace in this book predates the mid-twentieth-century moment on which I focus.[11]

At this historical juncture, nevertheless, these questions take on new urgency in many parts of Latin America, even as they become less readily legible.[12] In broad terms, this urgency has to do with three factors, which manifest in variable forms and stages in different national and regional contexts. The first is the rapid expansion of development, infrastructure, and capital into zones that had previously been difficult to access and therefore minimally impacted by such modernization projects.[13] As a regional landscapes were materially and culturally transformed at an unprecedented rate, there was a growing sense, best articulated by Ángel Rama, that regional particularity in Latin America was at risk of being subsumed by the homogenizing forces of capitalist modernity.[14] The second factor is the expansion of the middle class in many areas of Latin America and, in response, the rise of populist ideology.[15] The rural population (which increasingly migrated to the cities) was disproportionately represented and appealed to in midcentury populist discourse and propaganda, as regional identity became of renewed centrality to nationalist ideology. As I go on to argue, many of the most formally experimental neo-regionalist texts of the period— such as Guimarães Rosa's *Grande sertão: Veredas* (1956) or Saer's *El limonero real* (1974)—can be read as pushing back against this political instrumentalization of the rural interior. Finally, the boom brought Latin American literature to a wider audience and created international demand for representations of "authentic" Latin Americanness. Not for the first time, but at an unprecedented scale, exotic images of life in remote, underdeveloped places became an export commodity.

In this context, literary texts that practice what I call *critical regionalist poetics* attempt to escape the trap of fetishizing regional life by teaching their readers to exchange the outsider's gaze for the dwelling perspective, that is, to come to know a place-specific form of life from within by attending to its sounds, sights, textures, and rhythms. In short, rather than aspiring to ethnographic, testimonial (autoethnographic), or national-allegoric representation, these texts seek to conjure for the reader the experience of dwelling differently. The reader who learns to dwell must renounce the privilege associated with totalizing vision from without and embrace "the 'limited horizons' attributed to those who experience and imagine the world from some local, rooted position below."[16] Related to what Donna Haraway calls *situated knowledges*, the forms of knowledge imparted by such texts are embodied, localized, and specific, rather than abstract, transcendent, and fungible. Lest such particularity be confused with essentialism, however, these texts remind their readers of the inescapable mediation, the opacity of translation, the power dynamics of representation through which one might approach their regional subject matter. In keeping with Haraway's urgings, these texts make clear that "to see from below is neither easily learned nor unproblematic" even as they earnestly insist on the value of learning "how to see faithfully from another's point of view."[17]

Such paradoxes are held together through dialectic movement between a self-reflexive project of critique and a pedagogical project.[18] On the one hand, the formal difficulty of these texts fractures imperial ways of knowing (such as through totalizing vision), as their metadiscourse calls attention to all they cannot hope to transmit to the reader. On the other hand, they persist in offering aesthetic experience as an exercise through which the reader might slowly become literate in the local landscape, conceived not simply in visual terms but also in terms of broader phenomenological experience: the daily rhythms of work and rest, the sensorial and affective textures of life lived off the land, the increasingly precarious existence of communities on the margins of capitalistic modernity. My reading brings to the fore questions such as: Is it possible to dwell in worlds one has only read about? Is it possible to represent regional spaces to outside audiences without flattening them to snapshots of local color? I propose that the experimental narratives I analyze in *Dwelling in Fiction* recognize the urgent stakes of trying as well as the impossibility of fully succeeding in these endeavors.

In fact, often to the dismay of their authors and narrators, these texts encounter insurmountable obstacles. These are usually related to their media specificity (being bound to the written word) or to the subject positions of the intellectuals who create and consume them; the educated elite are by definition outsiders to the largely rural and working-class worlds depicted. In *El zorro de arriba y el zorro de abajo* (1971), J. M. Arguedas agonizes over the difficulty of embodying "la materia de las cosas" (the substance of things) in words, when the locale he depicts (Chimbote, Peru), is known to its inhabitants primarily through the body.[19] In *Grande sertão: Veredas* (1956), Guimarães Rosa's narrator, the *sertanejo* Riobaldo, questions how his urban interlocutor could possibly understand his story when he wasn't there: "E o senhor não esteve lá. O senhor não escoutou, em cada anoitecer, a lugúgem do canto da mãe-da-lua" ("And you were not there. You did not hear the lugubrious song of the whippoorwill at each nightfall").[20] Without the capacity to induce the sensorial and iterative experience of dwelling (in this case, hearing language-defying birdsong *every night*), Riobaldo concludes any narrative is condemned to be false.

As I aim to show, such failures are both inevitable and instructive. The ethical value of the lessons in dwelling I trace in this book does not depend on their complete (arguably impossible) success. Instead, it lies in chastening the reader who comes as a tourist in search of postcardlike images of the exotic, the quaint, or the backward and, simultaneously, in inviting them to stay with the difficult and perpetually incomplete work of learning to dwell in a textual world that is initially unfamiliar, perhaps even alienating. I propose that the narratives of Arguedas, Guimarães Rosa, and Saer that I examine in the following chapters anticipate a global readership for Latin American literature that was coming into being at the time of their writing. In light of this development as well as the stark regional divisions that internally stratified large and rapidly but unevenly developing Latin American nations in the mid-twentieth century (and in many cases, continue to do so), I argue that these texts presume their readers to be outsiders implicated in neocolonial relations with their regional landscapes. They underscore, moreover, that this position is one of inescapable exteriority as well as inescapable entanglement, one tainted by (internal) colonialism but nevertheless capable of shifting toward solidarity. In dialogue with scholars such as Luís Bueno and Laura Demaría, I propose that readers who are outsiders to the regional worlds about which they read are not condemned to remain absolute outsiders—tourists and foreigners—though neither will they be allowed to forget that they require initiation; they must *learn* to dwell.[21]

One of the contentions of this book, then, is that despite the genuine anguish or performed modesty of narrators and author figures who declare the futility of the project, literary language *can* engender, up to a point, the experience of dwelling, understood at once in the mundane sense of everyday life lived in space, time, and the body and in the Heideggerian sense of place-making: building a sense of belonging, growing accustomed to, allowing the experience of being-in-the-world to disclose itself. For the later Heidegger, dwelling is both the fundamental condition of human existence and the series of activities that render one's at-homeness in the world available to perception.[22] These activities include literal building, tending, residing, and protecting as well as less material (but no less situated) practices associated with ongoing inhabitation, such as staying with, cherishing, and safeguarding (in the sense of letting be), which are what ultimately bring forth the locale, allowing its essence and one's at-homeness there to reveal themselves.[23] In short, dwelling is "a form of being-in-the-world and making it a 'home'" carried out both through physical interaction with one's surroundings and through thought.[24]

For Heidegger, it is poetic thought specifically that enables dwelling in the modern world. If this world is characterized by homelessness and alienation, as Heidegger proposes, dwelling presents itself as the antidote: it is the way of living and thinking that allows one to perceive one's belonging to and in the world in spite of everything. As Laura Bieger argues in her updated reading of Heidegger, narrative becomes a fundamental way of engendering such belonging, of giving "meaning and mooring to life" in the modern world.[25] It is worth noting that for the Heidegger of *Poetry, Language, Thought*, the poetic is not limited to poetry per se. In "Dichterisch wohnet der Mensch" ("Poetically Man Dwells"), *dichtet* refers to the creation of literature more broadly, and poetic (*vieldeutig*) language refers to that which is ambiguous or equivocal, "possessed of a 'multiplicity' or 'richness of meaning.'"[26] Whereas ordinary language can name, represent, and communicate, the poetic is unique in its capacity for "bringing forth the unnamable" and disclosing the "'richness' of being itself."[27] Therefore, though not all writing or thought is poetic, that which activates the connotative and affective dimensions of language to reveal more than what is available to immediate perception is poetic, regardless of the form it takes (poetry, narrative, philosophy). My use of "poetics" in *poetics of place* and *critical regionalist poetics* is similarly inclusive.

Heidegger's insistence on the unity of poetry, thought, and dwelling in his later work complicates reductive readings of his philosophy that would conclude that dwelling properly is simply a matter of staying with the familiar, or, worse yet, hunkering down in one's place of origins and protecting it from foreign influence. Nevertheless, Heidegger's concern that modernity has unmoored humankind from a crucial sense of belonging to a place or homeland is often (and not erroneously) linked to his reactionary politics; it is easy to see how such nostalgia lends itself to appropriation by totalitarian and nativist discourses. Even if it were possible to set aside the philosopher's Nazi allegiances, his ontology of place is inherently retrograde in a historical moment marked by an expanding cosmopolitanism. One of the philosopher's most influential critics on this point, Emmanuel Levinas, contends that Heidegger misses the "liberating, utopian" potential of modern life, defined by movement rather than rootedness, and that his position thus proves naively nostalgic, antidemocratic, and ultimately dangerous, as it divides "the world into native dwellers and nomadic outsiders."[28] The risks of this ideology are all too apparent in an age of nostalgically inflected resurgences of nationalism and nativism (as in "Make America Great Again"). Though Heidegger's thought undoubtedly lends itself to such ideologies, there is a growing movement to recuperate a form of dwelling that "draws us out into the world" instead of isolating us from it.[29] As I lay out in chapter 1, thus revising Heidegger's philosophy to offer more progressive means of thinking emplacement in a globalized, multicultural world is one of the primary aims of critical regionalist thought.

Though not all thinkers in this conversation maintain Heidegger's interest in poetic language, this is for me one of the foremost ideas worth recuperating from Heidegger. I argue in the chapters to come that it is precisely the poetic or literary aspects of the texts I read that teach the reader to dwell. Moreover, I propose that, counterintuitively, experimental, difficult, or avant-garde texts that lean into their textuality, as opposed to aspiring to reach popular audiences or render the act of representation transparent, have an important role to play in the decolonial project of reframing relations between center and periphery, city and country, the West and the rest. This is because, rather than delivering knowledge about regional cultures to a sovereign reader, the self-consciously literary texts I analyze demand to be traversed, inhabited, and dwelled in.

THE SLIPPERY POLITICS OF EXPERIMENTAL LITERATURE

The idea that difficult, formally experimental, and conspicuously poetic novels harbor radical politics runs counter to long-standing trends (particularly in the US academy) in understanding midcentury Latin American narrative.[30] While the *testimonio* movement, which first emerged in the 1960s and turned outside of literature toward nonfictional representations of subaltern subjects, is often seen as synonymous with political commitment, concurrent trends in experimental, fantastical, and metafictional literature tend to be viewed in the opposite light. The present study contributes to undermining this narrative by focusing on highly stylized, self-consciously literary texts that nevertheless throw into question the supposed insularity and solipsism of modernist style.

Though the historical avant-gardes of the 1920s and '30s are commonly understood as combining radical aesthetic projects with radical political projects, the same view is rarely extended to the formal experimentalism of the postwar novel. In Latin America, subsequent avant-garde aesthetic movements associated with leftist and anticolonial politics, including the *neovanguardistas* of the 1960s and '70s, tend to privilege genres other than narrative: poetry, theater, film, visual and performance art. Meanwhile, the socially committed novel is generally considered to be bound to realist conventions and to have peaked with the regionalist wave of the 1920s and '30s. What follows—the emergence of *la nueva narrativa latinoamericana* in the 1940s through the 1970s—represents a widespread though far-from-monolithic movement away from naturalist aesthetics. This turn is often narrated as a coming-of-age story for the Latin American novel, wherein forms pejoratively dubbed naive, provincial, and derivative (those associated with regionalism) were superseded by techniques understood as more modern and universal (which, given the Eurocentric nature of these terms, means more similar to the modernism of Joyce, Woolf, Faulkner, Kafka, and the like).[31] Paradoxically, though the development of magical realist and transculturated aesthetics has been heralded in emancipatory terms—as the moment when Latin America finally claims an original literary voice and style, one rooted in its autochthonous cultures and experience of colonization—the turn away from realism is often understood as an abdication of politics. As Jean Franco argues, the achievements for which the authors of *la nueva narrativa* are lauded, such as the autonomy and creativity of their art, imply universal appeal and international marketability as well as "political disengagement."[32]

Much debate has been devoted to the question of whether the antirealist novels catapulted to international notoriety by the so-called Latin American boom of the 1960s represented simply an exotic (and therefore novel, revitalized, more marketable) version of European modernism, or a counterhegemonic development, even, as Mariano Siskind suggests, a proto-postcolonial critique of neo-imperialism carried out on the cultural and epistemological planes.[33] Dissenting from this view, skeptics allege that the emergence of Latin America onto the global literary stage does not even the playing field, let alone decenter Eurocentric narratives of modernity. The problem, of course, is that the recognition of parity with hegemonic forms depends on the judgment of a metropolitan readership, which tends to be biased by colonial (or what Edward Said calls *orientalist*) paradigms of consuming otherness. Rather than being read as part of a decolonial critique of positivist epistemologies, the elements of the fantastic and the irrational in magical realism are all too easily received as symptoms of a primitive and pre-rational society. Moreover, given that the boom erupted at the height of semiotic analysis and deconstructivist critical practices, Román de la Campa argues that even the more sophisticated and postcolonial readings of Latin American texts from abroad were prone to absorbing them into a universalist "utopian poststructuralist critical practice," celebrating them for their subversive potential without attending to the specific historical, material, and political realities to which these texts responded.[34] In sum, the formalist reading practices that predominated in the United States academy were ill equipped to appreciate the political stakes of formally experimental texts written in and about different geopolitical contexts, particularly those of the formerly colonized world.[35]

Within Latin America, too, it has been argued that the boom feeds into an old colonialist appetite for exoticism, now allied with the economic incentives of global capitalism. In fact, the boom has often stood accused of being an extension of the developmentalist agendas of the postwar era, one that exploits an appetite for images of underdevelopment. David Viñas writes: "Latin American developmentalism of the

1960s had sensed that novelists could be converted into commodities: 'national' commodities, exportable and lucrative."[36] Rather than taking such debates on directly, this book turns to texts that have always challenged their terms to further a different understanding of formally experimental aesthetics issuing from the Global South.

I take as my point of departure a position that has by now been widely accepted (though its implications still not fully unpacked): that the complexity of the politics of experimental form in the midcentury was for decades obscured by the dualistic logic of the cultural Cold War, which allowed for little overlap between political literature, associated with Soviet realism, on the one hand, and so-called high literature or art for art's sake, associated with international modernism, on the other. Such rhetoric was particularly charged and polarizing in Latin America precisely because the prospect of socialist revolution remained very real. The Cuban Revolution (1953–1959) nourished the hope of leftists throughout the continent even as it stoked fear in the governing class of elites, not to mention in US policymakers observing these developments from the North. The efforts of the governing elites to placate and control the working and middle classes, which were growing in size and becoming increasingly politicized, would yield a rash of national-populist and authoritarian regimes in the middle decades of the twentieth century. The United States' efforts to influence Latin American domestic politics through covert operations such as the CIA's Operation Condor are by now infamous. The ways in which anti-communist initiatives spearheaded by the CIA influenced cultural discourse in Latin America have also been well documented. These included the funding of literary journals, the direct and indirect dissemination of propaganda, and the advent of categories such as "international modernism" and "abstract universalism," used to describe and confer status on literature that was neither overtly political nor regionalist.[37] In sum, Cold War propaganda contributed to a climate in which literature dubbed "universal" in its appeal or "international" in its style garnered outsized prestige. Many of the most acclaimed Latin American authors of this period, such as Jorge Luis Borges, Carlos Fuentes, and Julio Cortázar, are celebrated within and beyond Latin America not only for the formal complexity of their work but also for its universal themes and abstract, metaphysical concerns.

For many midcentury intellectuals, the question of the rise of modernist aesthetics was inseparable from the question of the fate of regionalist literature, which was often seen as an outdated mode that would need to be superseded for Latin American literature to become modern. For example, Mario Vargas Llosa's 1968 article in the *Times Literary Supplement*, "Primitives and Creators," exemplifies many of the most problematic gestures of the narrative that seeks to celebrate *la nueva narrativa latinoamericana* by disparaging its predecessors. For Vargas Llosa, the "primitive novel" encompasses regionalism, *indigenismo*, and *costumbrismo*, all of which are dismissed as holding little literary value; while they may offer historical documentation and social criticism, Vargas Llosa insists they are aesthetically bankrupt. Indifferent to style or superficially and clumsily derivative of European forms, the primitive novel is prized only for its ability to represent distinctly Latin American subject matter: "Rustic and well-intentioned, earnest and garrulous, the primitive novel is, nevertheless, the first which can justifiably be called original to Latin America."[38] Vargas Llosa's condescending tone in this article may seem no worse than an extreme version of a pervasive sentiment among many Latin American intellectuals of the time; however, given the racial dynamics of regionalism in the Andes and Vargas Llosa's history of belittling *indigenista* authors in similar terms, his snobbery here rings of racism.[39] Notwithstanding the offensive tone of these remarks, the author must be credited with making two distinctions missed by many versions of Latin American literature's coming-of-age story: (1) he insists that the two stages of literature he calls "primitive" and "creative" do not sequentially supersede one another but exist contemporaneously; and (2) he challenges the simplistic narrative that "the change from the primitive novel to the new novel involves a move from the country to the city."[40] Though accelerated industrialization and urbanization starting in the 1950s did lead, throughout the continent, to a rural exodus and increased cultural homogenization, as Ligia Chiappini asserts of the Brazilian context, these changes did not, as many critics allege, spell the extinction of regionalist literature.[41] Thus, for all the flaws of Vargas Llosa's model, he succeeds in complicating the reductive narrative that the regionalist novel simply gives way to the urban, cosmopolitan, and avant-garde novel as the bearer of literary modernity.

Around the same time, in his essay "Literatura e subdesenvolvimento" (Literature and underdevelopment) (1970), Antonio Candido coins the term *super-regionalismo* to describe the innovative merging of autochthonous and cosmopolitan forms, themes of underdevelopment and of universal significance in the works of authors such as Vargas Llosa, J. M. Arguedas, Augusto Roa Bastos, and Gabriel García Márquez. This essay, written on the request of Candido's friend and frequent interlocutor, Ángel Rama, in many ways anticipates Rama's theory of narrative transculturation, which he would elaborate in *La transculturación narrativa en América Latina* (*Writing across Cultures: Narrative Transculturation in Latin America*) (1982), citing an overlapping cast of characters.[42] Candido developed the concept of *super-regionalismo* based in large part on his reading of Guimarães Rosa and this author's break with the realist conventions long associated with regionalist literature.[43] Candido proposes and Rama enthusiastically picks up the idea that using modernist techniques to depict the particularities of Latin America's material reality could be a politically radical, anti-imperialist gesture. Both intellectuals, notes Gabriel dos Santos Lima, thus offer a third alternative to the binary thinking of the Cold War era, in which "high art" was considered apolitical when not reactionary.[44]

For Rama's *transculturaturación narrativa* more than for Candido's *super-regionalismo*, new, hybrid forms promise to save regionalism from becoming an ossified genre and irrelevant current in Latin American literature. Rama critiques the predominant account of *la nueva narrativa* for disavowing the importance of the regional in reinventing Latin American literature and seeking to cleave modern Latin American literature from its regionalist roots. Rama acknowledges, however, that the regionalist and indigenist traditions, though once the primary driving forces of Latin American literary innovation and originality, risk becoming ossified and irrelevant in the mid-twentieth century and find themselves under "assault from the foreign modernism that entered through the ports and capital cities."[45] For Rama, the "panoply of avant-garde devices" to which Latin American writers are suddenly exposed are readily assimilated by poetry and, in prose, give rise to the genre of literature of the fantastic, but Rama sees regionalist literature as ill equipped to absorb these new techniques because it remains rooted in a "rigidly rationalizing ideology" that cannot accommodate the dynamic and fractured worldview of the avant-gardes.[46]

Though Rama's version of events condemns historical and positivistic regionalism to extinction, or at least irrelevance, he emphasizes that the most vital elements of this tradition—namely, "rural speech and popular story structures"—will be recuperated by a new generation of authors no longer bound by the ideological rigidity of regionalist literature.[47] Rama thus offers the hopeful vision that instead of being passively absorbed by Western culture, local cultures will respond creatively to intercultural contact, leading to innovative and uniquely Latin

American cultural production grounded in and inspired by autochthonous cultural materials:

> In an era of rather childish cosmopolitanism, our aim is to demonstrate that one can indeed create new art on a high level based on the humble materials from one's own traditions and that such traditions can do more than provide picturesque themes; they can also be the sources of well-designed techniques and shrewd artistic structures that fully translate the imaginaries of Latin American societies that have been crafting brilliant cultures for centuries.[48]

One of the most radical features of Rama's theory of narrative transculturation is that it succeeds in disentangling formal sophistication from novelty and cosmopolitanism, insisting that centuries-old local traditions can be similarly complex and vital. This new model of *transculturated* literature, argues Rama, allows the "continent's hinterland cultures" to participate in the modern era rather than simply being plowed under by it.[49]

In contrast to Rama's determination that formal innovation might save regional cultures from oblivion, Candido implies that *super-regionalismo* may be but a stepping stone along the way to the subsumption of regional life by urban modernity and that this may not be such a bad thing, given that "underdevelopment keeps the regional element alive."[50] As Lima points out, Candido's enthusiasm for the modernization of Latin American literature reflects the progressive, developmentalist ideology of the 1950s and '60s, when governments from the Partido Revolucionario Institucional in Mexico to those of Juan D. Perón and Arturo Frondizi in Argentina and Getúlio Vargas and Juscelino Kubitschek in Brazil were implementing large-scale modernization campaigns.[51] The optimism of the moment, which was shared by those on the left who hoped development would diminish inequality, would soon give way, as the promises of developmentalism and populism collided with the realities of economic dependency and the rise of authoritarian military regimes, which were already in place in Brazil, Argentina, Peru, and Guatemala at the time of the publication of Candido's essay.[52] In the intervening years before the publication of Rama's *Transculturación narrativa*, the full effects of capitalist development under these military regimes, as well as the bloody extremes to which they were willing to go to eliminate opposition on the left, would become apparent. These factors may account for shifts in Rama's thinking and his tempered enthusiasm for modernization, which is apparent in his choice of J. M. Arguedas as the poster child for the transculturated aesthetic he champions. As Lima points out, Arguedas emphatically rejected universality as the telos for Latin American literature and would not have embraced being called a "super-regionalista."[53] I argue in chapter 3 that despite the praise he has received for making the *sertão* universal, Guimarães Rosa (Candido's muse) is aligned with Arguedas on this matter.

In Brazil, the publication of Guimarães Rosa's *Grande sertão: Veredas* in 1956 for many literary historiographers marks the end of an era dominated by regionalism and its attendant political projects. This text also confounds long-standing classificatory systems. Throughout the mid-twentieth century, regional origins and the demographics associated with them—North (poor, rural, underdeveloped, Afro-Brazilian, Indigenous, or racially mixed) versus South (wealthy, urban, cosmopolitan, of predominantly European descent)—stood in for ideological and aesthetic designations (left versus right, committed art versus art for art's sake, etc.).[54] As a result of such conflation, texts written in and about the Northeast and other less developed regions were often considered political by definition and aesthetically uninteresting by default. *Grande sertão: Veredas* defies this model and raises new questions about the politics of avant-garde form. Though Guimarães Rosa resisted ideological labels and traditional notions of commitment, I join critics such as Rama in seeing his project as ethically and politically closer to Arguedas's than Vargas Llosa's; the Brazilian author is deeply invested in the linguistic and sensory dimensions of local belonging but refuses to reduce these to identitarian paradigms.

In contrast, Franco notes that for intellectuals like Vargas Llosa, the championing of artistic autonomy and universalism (as opposed to the aesthetics he pejoratively associates with regionalism and committed literature) becomes an explicitly conservative position and eventually "a fully fledged defense of neoliberalism."[55] In the Andes, where class politics cannot be divorced from the so-called Indigenous problem, experimental poetics had been used—as in the work of César Vallejo and J. M. Arguedas—to give form to revolutionary imaginaries and Indigenous cosmovisions, but these forms of aesthetic innovation were not always recognized as such.[56] For example, although it received belated recognition after his death, during his lifetime, Arguedas's literature was often dismissed as sociological and ideological, not worthy of detailed formal analysis. Vargas Llosa contributed to this dismissal as well as to the broader narrative that entertaining the possibility of an Andean region where Western modernity was not hegemonic could only ever be a nostalgic, retrograde project, certainly not the purview of modern literature.[57] In this context, then, the literary merit of formally innovative texts was rarely recognized unless these texts contributed to a politics of *mestizaje*, assimilation, and class harmony. The celebrated avant-garde tendencies of authors such as Vargas Llosa served these ends and, thus, the agenda of the conservative state.

In Argentina, where the racial question was less pronounced and where populism emerged earlier, the lettered elite was seen as less indispensable in achieving political stability.[58] In fact, the 1960s were marked by a mounting anti-intellectualism with regional, class, and aesthetic dimensions. In what Oscar Terán calls a "xenophobic neo-federalist turn," or an inversion of Sarmiento's hierarchy, the elite of Buenos Aires were maligned as unduly influenced by European culture and not truly Argentine.[59] The convergence of anti-imperialist and anti-intellectual sentiments in the Peronist branch of the left in the 1960s led to bourgeois classes, cosmopolitan ideas, and aesthetic *vanguardismo* being identified with Buenos Aires.[60] As progressive politics became narrowly defined as "commitment to sociopolitical reality," the space for "communication between the artistic and political avant-garde" shrank.[61] Consequently, spaces of avant-garde experimentation, such as the Instituto Di Tella, were accused of eroding national traditions, importing foreign culture, and being anti-revolutionary in their formalist frivolity.[62] Terán notes the irony of this last claim, given that Peronism has a mixed history with Marxism: though Perón's followers would eventually, after his exile, rally under the banner of revolutionary politics, the movement originally rejected the label and, moreover, embraced a populist ideology aimed at preventing the working classes from demanding a more radical revolution.[63]

At the same time that it spurned intellectual trends that rang of "lo *culto-extranjerizante*, lo *aparente-ajeno* y lo *Europeo-colonizador*" ("the highbrow-foreignizing, the apparently alien, and the European-colonizing"), Peronist national-populist ideology located the most authentic aspects of national culture in the provinces.[64] In this cultural climate, Juan José Saer, on whose work I focus in chapter 4, represents an anomaly because he writes exclusively about the provinces while embracing the formal innovations of international modernism and rejecting the ideological work of representing the nation. He likewise rejects any traces of magical realism, bristling under the demands of editors and presses that he satisfy the expectations of a foreign readership whose tastes had been conditioned by the boom.[65] Saer's disdain for the commodification of Latin American culture in many ways echoes that of Arguedas, but unlike Arguedas, whom Julio Cortázar disparagingly dubbed *un provinciano*, Saer is more often read as a modernist than a regionalist, and his work is often cited as a challenge to the traditional regionalist model. While his early champions, such as Beatriz Sarlo and María Teresa Gramuglio, worked to "rescue" Saer from the obscurity of his provincial origins and celebrate him as a great cosmopolitan writer, subsequent critics such as Pablo Heredia and Laura Demaría have centered him in their reconceptions of Argentine regionalist literature.[66] I join these latter thinkers in emphasizing the centrality of local ways of thinking and dwelling in Saer's work.

Though I discuss each of these specific dynamics in more detail in the following chapters, my aim in this book is not to provide a comprehensive account of the interplay between aesthetics, politics, and regional identity in any one of these contexts, much less on the continent as a whole. Instead, I seek to highlight a specific trend that is often missed and, in fact, actively occluded by the dominant narratives of the period (the 1950s–1970s). I propose that, in a moment known for the solipsism of late modernism, the dualism of Cold War rhetoric, and the *bestsellerismo* of the Latin American boom, radical formal experimentalism remained a vital political tool, at least in the hands of some Latin American authors, as a way of mediating the absorption of local cultures by an increasingly global literary market. At the same time, the poetic language of experimental texts makes alternative forms of dwelling and community imaginable.

What most fascinates me about the texts I analyze here is the way that their authors appear to have presciently sensed what scholars of postcolonialism and skeptics of world literature have subsequently articulated: that it is not enough to make life on the peripheries of the metropole universally visible and relatable.[67] In fact, liberal discourses of representation and empathy may reinforce rather than interrupt the power hierarchies that marginalize perspectives from the Global South.[68] The authors on whom I focus in this book—Arguedas, Guimarães Rosa, and Saer—were highly cognizant of this dilemma and, I argue, attempt to develop aesthetics grounded in local particularity while safeguarding this particularity from commodification. For reasons I discuss in the following section and more fully unpack in chapter 1, the name I give to this ethos is critical regionalism. I differentiate this term, which encompasses a wide range of interdisciplinary conversations, from my more specific key term, *critical regionalist poetics*, which I define as a set of experimental literary techniques that impart the critical regionalist ethos.

CRITICAL REGIONALISM AND
CRITICAL REGIONALIST POETICS

If, as Lauren Bieger argues, people consume narratives to "familiarize themselves with unknown modes of dwelling," might not certain narratives prepare for these visitors to their worlds, whether imagined as guests, tourists, students, invaders, or some combination of the above?[69] What measures might they take to handle their outsider-readers, to train and guide them, to keep them at bay, to govern the terms on which to invite them in?

Of course, the question of if and how literature (and the aesthetic more broadly) might close the gap between one's own lived experience and that of others is not new. Nor is the specific question of the ethics and politics of using literature to bring the elite, educated classes closer to the experience of dwelling as a peasant. The British Romantics grappled with these very questions, and, as Gayatri Chakravorty Spivak argues in *An Aesthetic Education in the Era of Globalization*, "The great experiment didn't work. The poets had no real involvement with infrastructure. Our situation is even worse because we don't even have as much enthusiasm."[70] I am not proposing that modernist-regionalist novels succeed where Romantic poetry failed, either by engendering more complete empathy between classes or by more directly impacting policy. I do not even believe the texts I examine in this book are enthusiastically invested in the Romantic project; to the extent that they return to it, they do so, like Spivak, because its failure is instructive.

According to Spivak, the (partially) misplaced faith of the Romantic poets—"Wordsworth's and Shelley's belief that you could with poetry exercise the imagination, train ethics [. . .] in the othering of the self and coming as close as possible to accessing the other as the self"—can be traced back to Schiller's misreading of Kant.[71] Schiller grants the aesthetic the capacity to fill a gap that Kant had declared unbridgeable (originally that between understanding and pure reason).[72] Nevertheless, Spivak insists that the attempt to do so is as indispensable as it is futile. On the one hand, "Radical alterity—the wholly other—must be thought and must be thought through imaging."[73] On the other:

> By definition, we cannot—no self can—reach the quite-other. Thus the ethical situation can only be figured in the ethical experience of the impossible. This is the founding gap in all act or talk, most especially in acts or talk that we understand to be closest to the ethical—the historical and the political [. . .] we must somehow attempt to supplement the gap.[74]

If the aesthetic cannot (and must not pretend to) close this gap, an aesthetic education can nevertheless train the imagination to navigate it and, perhaps, to supplement it.

In other words, writing and reading literature will never resolve what Spivak calls "the double bind at the heart of democracy": the incommensurability between the particular and the universal, the self and the other, and the need to imaginatively move between these positions anyway.[75] The tools of the humanities might, however, prepare us for citizenship in a world where this double bind remains insoluble. Spivak insists on the importance of continuing to teach and practice "deep language learning" and "literary textuality" as ways of "training the ethical reflex."[76] Yet she also cautions against mistaking the nineteenth-century "institutional practice of producing the colonial subject" or the twenty-first-century turn toward multiculturalism for the ethical and political work for which the aesthetic is uniquely equipped, which is not to close in on, represent, or speak for the other but, rather, to hold open "that figure of the experience of the impossible" as an ethical horizon.[77] In sum, the aesthetic education that Spivak claims is indispensable if we are to attend to the particularity and diversity of experiences and thus counter "the mind-numbing uniformization of globalization" entails instilling an abiding consciousness of this double bind.[78] This can be achieved in part, argues Spivak, by reading for form and not merely for content.

Critical regionalist poetics is the term that I have developed to name a particular set of formal strategies in literature that might impart such an aesthetic education (and do so, moreover, from the Global South). Whereas the aesthetic education championed by Spivak takes place primarily in the classroom, I am interested in the possibility that literary texts might educate their readers directly by discouraging certain reading practices and inviting others. In so doing, I propose, they might craftily resist appropriation by paradigms of consumption in the metropole, the *ciudad letrada*, and the Global North, even as they endeavor to train the reader's imagination and perception for different forms of engagement.

But why "critical regionalist"? Critical regionalism refers to an interdisciplinary field loosely rooted in the architectural theory of Kenneth Frampton. I detail the origins and evolution of critical regionalist thought in chapter 1, where I also give the concept my own inflection, arguing that, despite its origins in the US academy in the 1980s, many of its tenets and strategies had been elaborated in Latin American thought decades earlier. Of the plethora of critical frameworks that now exist for thinking the relation of the lettered city to its spatialized others, I privilege critical regionalism for three principal reasons: First, though inherently transnational, it is rooted in the idea that local particularity matters and is irreducible to any so-called universal language. Second, in the genealogy of thought on which I draw, critical regionalism is intrinsically dialectical in the negative, Adornian sense: it demands critical self-reflexivity on the part of the thinker, who is called on to examine the limitations of what can be thought and known from any given position and through any given language or medium. Third, despite its broad uptake across cultural studies, critical regionalism was first imagined as an aesthetic practice and one with very specific aims: evoking and shaping embodied experience of place. Critical regionalist aesthetics in any medium trains the attention of viewer/reader/occupant of the cultural object to immanently inhabit the local rather than contemplate it only from a geographic or intellectual distance. As such, the theoretical framework of critical regionalism allows me to articulate the political and ethical projects of the literary works I analyze as well as the formal means by which they attempt to realize these projects.

In the following chapter, I trace critical regionalist thought back to its roots in Heideggerian phenomenology on the one hand and Frankfurt School Critical Theory on the other and follow the meandering path critical regionalism has taken through architectural theory (Frampton, Jameson), North American regional and cultural studies (Powell, Comer, Herr, Campbell), Latin American studies (Moreiras), and transnational political theory (Spivak and Butler). I also note the places where it abuts, overlaps with, or reprises the thought of scholars who do not use the term, ranging from recent studies in phenomenology and embodiment (Ingold, Baskin, Haraway, Masiello, Librandi), to critiques of world literature and comparative literature (Siskind, Hoyos, Apter, Spivak), to ecocriticism (French, Andermann, Heffes, Gómez-Barris, Rogers, Heise, Pérez Trujillo Diniz), to classic as well as recent theories of regionalism and regionalist literature in Latin America (Rama, Candido, Kalimán,

Alonso, Heredia, Cornejo Polar, Chiappini, Bueno, Brito, Zevallos Aguilar, Tarica, Demaría).

From this broad sense of critical regionalism, I go on to develop a more specific notion of critical regionalist poetics as a set of aesthetic strategies developed in response to the heightened visibility of provincial, underdeveloped spaces on an increasingly globalized world stage. In the midcentury novels I analyze, this response takes the form of engaging the reader's senses to re-create the immersive, embodied, and temporal experience of dwelling, even as elements of negativity, opacity, and self-reflexivity check the illusion of immediacy and remind the reader of that which escapes capture. Critical regionalist poetics thus thwarts the interrelated drives for closure, for distance, and for a totalizing visual perspective on the region and reveals these drives to be bound up in ideologies in service of colonialism and extractive capitalism, thus subtly (or not so subtly) implicating themselves and their readers in these legacies. Beyond launching a by-now familiar critique of the imperial gaze shared by the conqueror, the nation-state, the foreign traveler, and the outsider-reader who comes as a tourist to behold—and thus domesticate—the alterity of the region, such texts, I argue, also invite the reader to linger in the difficult, tedious, and perpetually incomplete work of learning the lay of the land from the dwelling perspective.

Thus critical regionalist poetics is an ethos and a pedagogy—a commitment to encouraging a particular mode of perception, to training a rarified kind of attention—more than a particular literary style. Yet because this ethical education is imparted through formal means, critical regionalist texts share certain aesthetic affinities. These include the fragmentation of visual and social panoramas, the refusal of linear narrative in favor of paratactic and recursive structures, an immersive, phenomenological sensibility that calls on multiple senses at once, and a combination of metadiscursive commentary and formal difficulty (both structural and linguistic) that reinforces the elusiveness and impenetrability of the world represented.

The texts I take as my primary examples—J. M. Arguedas's *El zorro de arriba y el zorro de abajo* (*The Fox from Up Above and the Fox from Down Below*) (Peru, 1971), Guimarães Rosa's *Grande sertão: Veredas* (*Devil to Pay in the Backlands*) (Brazil, 1956), and Saer's *El limonero real* (*The Regal Lemon Tree*) (Argentina, 1974)—are notoriously difficult. Preferring recursive narrative structures to linear ones and immersive perspectives to cartographic ones, they fragment both time and space. The disoriented reader may feel compelled to read them multiple times, and even after doing this will still struggle to arrive at a coherent chronology or stable visual or social panorama. Compounding these hindrances to comprehension, their language is unlikely to be fully legible to most readers. In *Los zorros*, Arguedas includes untranslated words and phrases from Quechua as well as the nonstandard Spanish of non-native speakers and abundant slang and colloquialisms issuing from a wide range of regions and dialects, all but guaranteeing that the reader will be excluded in one moment or another. Guimarães Rosa famously invents his own version of the Portuguese language, drawing on regional dialects, archaisms, and foreign languages, similarly defamiliarizing the reader's encounter with the text wherever they hail from. The difficulty of Saer's language issues less from the "foreignness" of its vocabulary than from its style. Description-rich sentences can go on for pages at a time, and the reader is given precious little access to the interior thoughts of the characters. In all three cases, the effect is that the world related remains frustratingly opaque; the reader is systematically denied the satisfaction of having grasped it in its entirety.

For the reader willing to persevere in the face of such frustration, however, other forms of local knowledge do eventually emerge. For example, one gains greater fluency in unfamiliar languages and references (such as local names for flora and fauna) through repeated exposure to them. In the case of Guimarães Rosa, as Axel Pérez Trujillo Diniz notes, the initial opacity of a regional world conjured through descriptions dense in localisms (such as the regional, colloquial, or Indigenous names for species rather than more common names) might, over time, conjure for the initiated reader intimate and embedded local knowledges.[79] Importantly, the primary form of literacy to be gained from such texts is not semantic but, rather, sensorial and affective. Arguedas conjures the Peruvian fishing port of Chimbote through all five senses, which often merge synesthetically. He incorporates Quechua folk songs, and his text emulates the meandering rhythms of traversing the city on foot. Saer creates similarly rich, sensorial experiences of the riverbanks of Santa Fe province, Argentina. Moreover, the looping narrative structures employed by all three authors iteratively saturate these worlds with affects, which, though presumably always present for those who dwell there, only gradually become perceptible to the reader. As such, though the reader is barred from certain forms of knowledge (ethnographic, positivistic, cartographic, totalizing), they are nevertheless given the opportunity to learn about the world about which they read from an intimate and participatory vantage point.

Lest this proximity be mistaken for full access or complete belonging, however, each text contains elements of self-reflexivity that remind the reader of the mediated nature of their encounter as well as their status as an interloper in this world. Arguedas includes first-person diary entries, which frame and interrupt his third-person narration of life in Chimbote with reflections on his struggle to complete the novel in front of him. The difficulties he relates include his own lack of belonging in and understanding of Chimbote as well as his shaken faith in his ability to transmit through the written word lived experiences with which the reader will likely be unfamiliar. *Grande sertão: Veredas* contains a frame narrative in which the *sertanejo* narrator Riobaldo recounts his life story to an educated visitor from the city, who serves as a proxy for the reader. Riobaldo repeatedly interrupts his tale to apologize for narrating it poorly and to call into question his interlocutor's capacity for understanding it. The self-reflexivity of *El limonero real* is less explicit, but the way the story incessantly starts over again at the beginning suggests that the narrator struggles to keep his place in it or remains unsatisfied with the version(s) elaborated so far. The consciousness of this narrator is also marked by a degree of exteriority, which is passed on to the reader through pseudo-objectivist descriptions of surfaces that never give way to fully reveal the psychological interiority of the characters.

In these various ways, the reader is interpellated as a foreigner, what Demaría calls *un extranjero*, which is less a designation of nationality than of inability to interpret and recognize the local world.[80] But whereas *extranjeros* by definition do not dwell in the land to which they are foreign, the readers of the texts I analyze may develop some degree of literacy and belonging in the local. Readers might shift their relationship with a textual version of place over time by attending to its demands: that they synchronize their explorations to its pace and rhythm, that they tune their ears to its musicality, and that they adjust their eyes to its enduring opacity. In many cases, a character or narrator models for the reader how one might learn to dwell, up to a point, as an outsider—one who is not from this world but comes to inhabit it anyway. The key to doing so lies in engaging the senses, renouncing one's intellectual remove, and committing to living with a world one cannot hope to master.

In other words, though the heavily stylized prose of these texts and the overbearing skepticism of their narrators ensure that their appeal to phenomenological experience remains dialectical and reflexive, their authors nevertheless work toward making dwellers of their readers. It is this contrapuntal movement between immersion and interruption—generating a sense of immediacy by calling on the senses but then checking it and reinforcing the aesthetic frame[81]—that unites the diverse texts assembled in *Dwelling in Fiction*.

The result of this back-and-forth movement can be quite jarring for the reader who may alternately find the experience of the text abrasive and absorbing, intimate and alienating, demanding and off-putting. Staying with this experience, which gives aesthetic form to a version of Spivak's double bind—one cannot possibly know what it is like to dwell elsewhere and otherwise, but one must not desist from trying anyway—amounts to the ethical and imaginative training the reader is asked to undergo. In sum, even as the formal difficulty of these texts confronts the reader with the fraught nature of reading across differences—in culture, class, race, language, and lived experience—they present local belonging as a plastic, learnable, necessarily cultivated practice rather than an inherent quality or birthright. Thus a negative gesture (thwarting access, denying demands for transparency) is coupled with a pedagogical project: teaching the outsider-reader how to perceive the local and the subaltern through a less fetishizing lens.

Many of the literary techniques I have described are common in literary modernism, begging the question of what is regionally or historically specific about critical regionalist poetics. To be clear, it is not so much that I consider certain formal approaches uniquely suited to the task of depicting rural life on the peripheries of late capitalism; rather, I propose that they carry specific political and ethical freight for writers preoccupied with how representations of local particularity circulate and are consumed in an increasingly globalized cultural marketplace. The texts I examine all deal with regions that have been objects of internal colonization and respond to moments of rapid modernization that threaten to subsume the particularity of these regions. That said, exclusive focus on rural or traditional life is not a requirement for a text to be considered critical regionalist in the sense that I use the term. My first case study, Arguedas's *El zorro de arriba y el zorro de abajo*, is set in a rapidly growing city where Indigenous campesinos are but one of many kinds of immigrants attempting to make a home. I argue in chapter 2 that the critical regionalist ethos of this text lies in the way it centers the relations that bind traditional Andean cultures to urban industry and transnational capitalism in the second half of the twentieth century.

If one understands this ethos as fundamentally grounded in a commitment to subverting the ossification of regional life—its reduction to the exotic, the quaint, the backward—and foregrounding its coevalness with the metropole, its dynamism, and its relationality, then essentializing notions of unadulterated autochthony need to be abandoned.[82] In other words, critical regionalist texts are not exclusively concerned with the countryside; on the contrary, they are principally concerned with the contact zones that result when country dwellers go to the city and when urbanites go to (or even read about) the countryside. Yet I would not go as far as to say that any text that thematically represents such contact zones practices critical regionalist poetics, just as I would not say so of any text that makes use of experimental techniques such as spatial and temporal fragmentation, sensorial engagement, or self-reflexivity. It is, rather, in the convergence of these features—avant-garde form deployed to foreground the perils as well as the learning opportunities of contact zones between city and country or center and periphery—that we might look for the myriad manifestations of critical regionalist poetics.[83] These undoubtedly include texts and aesthetic practices from other places, other times, other media, and other languages. Though a full inventory of these is beyond the scope of this book, I gesture toward a couple of candidates within the Latin American context in the coda, and I hope that the critical vocabulary I develop here will also resonate with scholars working on similar questions in other parts of the world.

Finally, I believe further scholarship is necessary to realize the full potential of critical regionalist thought and poetics in our current moment, in which the economic and cultural gap between country and city has not disappeared. In the first decades of the twenty-first century, the millennial myth of a flat world, wherein globalized commerce and digital technology have made geographic location irrelevant,[84] has begun to fall away, revealing stark contrasts and raw tensions between urban and rural worldviews. Though by no means new, these tensions have only intensified and become more politically divisive in the twenty-first century, in the wake of a series of financial and environmental crises and, most recently, a global pandemic, all of which have unevenly affected urban and rural populations. I am not suggesting that the study of literature, or art more broadly, will on its own heal these divides; however, the value of critical regionalist poetics as I understand it lies in the light it throws on the disconnect between different ways of dwelling (and thus of thinking, of being) in different locales and the alternate channels of relation it opens up between worlds that have, to paraphrase Arguedas, been walled off from one another.[85] Above all, critical regionalist texts demand humility and openness to an ongoing learning process directed not simply to the intellect but also to sensory, affective, and ethical ways of being. These dispositions are as sorely needed as ever. As the Yanomami shaman Davi Kopenawa eloquently argues, the survival of peoples on the margins of global capitalism, as well as of the planet on which we all dwell, may depend on their ability to educate those at "the center"—in the metropolitan cities, in the Global North, at the helm of the destructive machine of capitalist extraction—in their ways of dwelling.[86]

In other words, the questions driving critical regionalist thought may have taken on new forms in recent decades, but they have not lost their urgency. They continue to resonate in decolonial anthropology, in the environmental humanities, and in cultural studies and literary studies. This should not be a surprise, given that the conditions in response to which critical regionalism arose at the end of the Cold War—including extractive economic models and the dawning of neoliberal globalization—continue to structure the relationship between North and South, city and country. What is more, the capacity for academic expertise and market forces to subsume voices of alterity, dissent, and resistance has only become more apparent. To be clear, I do not mean to suggest that critical regionalist texts are capable of carving out a space outside such appropriative relationships, let alone of changing their underlying structures. Though the formal difficulty and "untranslatability"[87] of texts like *El zorro de arriba y el zorro de abajo*, *Grande sertão: Veredas*, and *El limonero real* may limit their circulation and readership, these features have not hindered their canonization. In fact, these characteristics likely contribute to their cult status among scholars. If, as I propose, such texts attempt to forestall the commodification of regional cultures, their political instrumentalization, and their conversion into cultural capital, this work is complicated by these texts' own inevitable participation in such processes. Their critique must therefore be understood as immanent, targeting institutions with which they recognize their own implication.

The complicated nature of this position, I would argue, makes critical regionalist approaches all the more relevant to our current moment. Reflecting on how aesthetic markers of the Global South are appropriated by high culture, Francine Masiello argues that a rhetoric of rescue coincides with that of the neoliberal market:

It seems to me that the rediscovery of the south, so in style these days, coincides with this project of rescuing the popular and offering it as goods belonging to high culture. If the foreignness and multilingualism of the local are valued as aesthetic objects, so too does the local enter into the literary context as an object for sale.[88]

This is not a new phenomenon, but rather can be traced back to nineteenth-century ethnography, which Masiello sees as opening the way for "the future conquest and commercialization of the peripheral zone."[89] The question for our moment becomes, how do we break with this legacy? How can we afford a place of prominence to cultures of the Global South in the canon of global culture without reproducing the colonial logic of a world's fair: "the spectacle of the marginalized in the center of the great city"?[90] Critical regionalist literature may not offer a way out of this impasse, but I propose that it might, in Spivak's language, train the imagination and the ethical muscles that will be needed to live with it. It might attune us to what Anna Tsing calls the friction of a heterogeneous world: "the awkward, unequal, unstable, and creative qualities of interconnection across difference."[91]

I foreground midcentury texts that presciently plant such issues decades before they emerged in critical conversations about multiculturalism, world literature, and Latin Americanism. For practical and methodological reasons, I have limited myself to this moment and to a select few texts that represent the usual suspects in conversations around Latin American neo-regionalism, emphasizing that such texts can be read against the grain of the predominant narratives of transculturation and universalization of the particular. I hope, however, that the conversation will not end with these texts or the specific lessons in dwelling they offer. Further scholarship on critical regionalist poetics is needed, for example, to address the intersectional nature of regional belonging: how gender, age, race, class, and ability affect the way one dwells.[92] Though there is, following Haraway, an inherently feminist, ecological, and decolonial bent to the kinds of knowledge engendered in the texts I read, looking beyond the midcentury, and beyond white, male, settler authors will be necessary to unpack its full potential.[93] Moreover, given the diversity of the media landscape today, future scholarship will once again need to work out the formal qualities of critical regionalist poetics in other aesthetic practices. In this spirit, I devote the coda of this book to considering how critical regionalist poetics might manifest in experimental cinema.

METHODOLOGY AND COMPARATIVE APPROACH

Why write a comparative, transnational study about dwelling in the local? Does not generalizing about regional particularity represent, if not a contradiction in terms, at least a betrayal of the spirit of irreducibility central to authors such as Arguedas, Guimarães Rosa, and Saer? Grappling with these contradictions and risks is a fundamental part of comparative scholarship and, I would argue, of the critical regionalist instantiation of Spivak's double bind: though the particularities of local experience will never be grasped by universalizing discourses, nor can they be treated as islands in a globalized world where they are already in relation of one kind or another. Attending at once to the particularity of a given region and its enmeshment in larger historic, economic, and cultural forces is central to the critical regionalist ethos that guides my approach. Grafting the critical regionalist imperative to think the region transnationally—in defiance of both the internally homogenizing logic of the nation and the arbitrarily imposed borders between nations—onto the supranational continental sensibility invoked by Latin American thinkers from José Martí to Oswaldo de Andrade to Ángel Rama, I treat the varied regions that appear in my corpus as singular yet interrelated.[94]

Latin America's hinterlands may be varied, but they share a history of being interpellated as modernity's other. According to Pérez Trujillo Diniz, in spite of their ecological, topographical, cultural, and linguistic diversity, the Peruvian altiplano, the Brazilian *sertão*, and the Argentinian pampas are all subsumed under the category of inland plains by settler epistemologies.[95] In imagining such spaces as barren, empty, and uninhabited, travelers, prospectors, writers, and intellectuals from Europe as well as from Latin America's coastal metropoles have justified the extraction of their resources and the genocide, displacement, and exploitation of their Indigenous inhabitants.[96] In the process, a pluriverse of local and Indigenous knowledges are marginalized and delegitimized in favor of a single, dominant "cognitive empire."[97] The recent resurgence of interest in regionalism in Marxist, ecocritical, and decolonial veins of Latin American cultural studies seeks to expose such ideological agendas as well as unearth fault lines in the very narratives charged with upholding them.

In the historical moment on which I focus, diverse inland territories are recruited to play a specific role in the modernization narratives of their respective nations. In short, regions such as the Andean highlands, the *sertão*, and the pampas are all cast as internal others—recalcitrant or atavistic backlands to be domesticated and brought into the fold of the rapidly modernizing and industrializing nation. Yet, at the same time, they have each been detained in a state of perpetual underdevelopment by internal colonial relations that condemn the vast majority of their inhabitants to poverty and exploitation under neo-feudal and extractive economic models. As the riches and cosmopolitan aspirations of coastal cities such as Lima, São Paolo, and Buenos Aires are sustained by the labor and natural resources of less developed regions, these regions are imagined alternately as founts of national patrimony—places in which to root discourses of autochthonous identity—and problems to be solved—repositories for backwardness and strongholds for insubordinate factions. Historically governed by Indigenous collectives, unruly bandits and *caudillos*, or oligarchies of landowners hostile toward the involvement of the federal government in local affairs, these regions share the legacy of antagonistic or separatist regionalist sentiments, which exist in uneasy relation with their ongoing material exploitation and symbolic appropriation by nationalistic discourse.

Nevertheless, there are important differences, which I discuss in more detail in the chapters that follow, and it is important to be clear that my aim in this book is not to develop a universal theory of Latin American regionalism. On the contrary, my comparative approach allows me to underscore some of these differences. To begin with an obvious point, Latin America, though often treated as coextensive with Hispanic America, includes Brazil, which covers nearly half of the South American continent and accounts for nearly 40 percent of the Latin American economy and 50 percent of its population, but whose history of colonialism, independence, and modernization does not track with that of its Spanish-speaking neighbors.[98] Moreover, the way that racial and ethnic tensions play into regional tensions varies greatly across Latin America. Indigeneity cannot be mapped on to the rural interior to the same degree in Argentina, where the Indigenous populations were decimated by the genocidal campaigns of the nineteenth century, as in the Andes, where the majority of the population is of Indigenous ancestry.

The attitude of urban elites toward traditional and autochthonous regional cultures also varies, as these are more central to national identity formation in some places and times than others. Out of respect for such differences, I treat both *Latin America* and *critical regionalist poetics* as constellations rather than unitary and coherent objects of study. The chapters that follow spotlight three geographically, historically, and culturally specific instantiations of critical regionalist poetics in midtwentieth century Latin America, but they are not intended to provide a totalizing account.

But why bring into conversation these three authors in particular: José María Arguedas (Peru, 1911–1969), João Guimarães Rosa (Brazil, 1908–1967), and Juan José Saer (Argentina, 1937–2005)? At first glance, the differences between them might seem pronounced. Nevertheless, as I have suggested, they respond to an interrelated set of developments of the midcentury, and they are united by ethical commitments and aesthetic affinities. Figuring out the nature of these connections, which I have long intuited could not be fully accounted for by the existing literary historiography, has been the task I have set for myself in this book.

Though I conclude it is possible to speak of a critical regionalist community in which Arguedas, Guimarães Rosa, and Saer all participate, I would not wish to overstate the coherence or homogeneity of this collective endeavor. In many ways, the three are united precisely by their contrarian refusal to fit squarely into established movements, genealogies, styles, and genres (though the texts I analyze are all technically novels, they push the limits of the genre by including elements of poetry, song, autobiography, and oral tradition). These are authors who are notoriously difficult to categorize: they come too early or too late, or write in the wrong languages or styles, or lack the cultural and political affiliations to be easily assimilated to the major Latin American literary movements of the twentieth century: *regionalismo, vanguardismo, la nueva narrativa,* the boom, and so on. I propose that this marginality (when not overt hostility) reflects a collective, though not monolithic, rejection of predominant configurations of the relationship between aesthetics and politics in an age defined by the Cold War, the rise of the populist state, and the emergence of late capitalist globalization.

As Florencia Garramuño argues with regards to contemporary aesthetic practices in Latin America, such a quality, which she describes as *impertenencia* (not belonging), need not designate only lack or dislocation; it can also be a way of reimagining the common and the collective.[99] What new communities and modes of comparative study, she asks, might emerge from recognizing unlikely affiliations between those who do not properly belong to a given discipline, ideological position, or national-linguistic tradition? Echoing sentiments expressed by many critical regionalist thinkers (Spivak in particular comes to mind), Garramuño suggests that such an approach might free us from "a restrictive continuity of the national tradition and an oppressive relation between literature and territory."[100] In fact, she advocates for Kenneth Reinhard's definition of comparative literature, in which we might group and compare texts not only based on similarities and shared genealogies or "families" but also by contingent proximity and ethical encounters between them.[101] In such a model, affiliation might replace filiation and direct influence as the grounds for comparison. This is the model of comparison that guides my approach.

Nevertheless, there are several established connections between the authors featured in *Dwelling in Fiction*. As I discuss in chapter 2, Arguedas recognized an unlikely kinship with Guimarães Rosa, who, along with Juan Rulfo, is one of the few contemporaries from whom Arguedas does not distance himself. This trio of writers—Arguedas, Rulfo, Guimarães Rosa—also exemplifies narrative transculturation for Ángel Rama.[102] I engage with Rama and the similarities and differences between critical regionalism and narrative transculturation in depth in the following two chapters.

One of the previously unremarked connections I highlight is the way Arguedas, Guimarães Rosa, and Saer respond to the seismic shifts in Latin American literary production and consumption in the wake of the Cuban Revolution. Though *Grande sertão: Veredas* (1956) is published on the threshold of this new chapter associated with the boom, as I argue in chapter 3, Guimarães Rosa, a polyglot who lived for many years abroad, appears to anticipate (and fret over and deflect) an outsider readership in ways that would only become more pronounced in critical regionalist poetics in the decades to follow. Arguedas was roughly Guimarães Rosa's contemporary, but I focus on his last novel, *El zorro de arriba y el zorro de abajo*, posthumously published in 1971 but written in the late 1960s, nearly contemporaneously with Saer's *El limonero real* (published in 1974 but written over ten years). In this sense, there is a contemporaneity between the late Arguedas and the early-to-mid-career Saer: in both cases, their most radically experimental work takes shape in the late 1960s and is characterized by a growing awareness and suspicion of the boom and its impact on Latin American cultural production.[103] Additionally, though Saer ostensibly belongs to a later generation of neo-regionalists than Arguedas and Guimarães Rosa, one could argue that the regionalist paradigm is revised later in Argentina than in other parts of Latin America, owing to the entrenched duality between *la capital* and *las provincias* and the particular role that regionalist discourses played in Peronist populism.[104] In this sense, Saer is on the vanguard of a new paradigm, much as Arguedas and Guimarães Rosa were in their respective contexts.

This constellation of authors, organized around a shared commitment to teaching the art of dwelling, also brings into focus new dimensions of these well-studied writers, allowing them to be read against the grain or freed from the pigeonholes to which they have been consigned. For example, the avant-garde dimensions of Arguedas's work have often gone unappreciated, but they become more apparent when he is placed alongside Guimarães Rosa and Saer. Inversely, Saer is often championed as a cosmopolitan writer who swore off regionalism, but reading him with Arguedas and Guimarães Rosa makes his abiding investment in a revised version of the regionalist tradition harder to ignore. Finally, while Arguedas and Guimarães Rosa are often celebrated as transculturators, as translators of alterity, reading them alongside Saer makes the recalcitrant strain of their experimental poetics more legible; it becomes easier to see them as safeguarders of particularity.

In short, considering Arguedas, Guimarães Rosa, and Saer at once on their own terms and alongside one another makes it possible to identify among ostensibly singular and anomalous achievements a trend that defies dominant models of reading Cold War–era literary production in Latin America, such as binaries between regionalism and universalism, political commitment and *l'art pour l'art*. Though generally avoiding direct ideological engagement, Arguedas, Guimarães Rosa, and Saer all practice a form of social commitment grounded in recognizing not simply the dignity and humanity of the rural poor but also their modernity and dynamism, their ethical and creative agency, and the inalienable entanglement of their lifeways with place, oral tradition, and, increasingly, global capital. It is by training the reader to perceive such connections from an immersive vantage point, I argue, that critical regionalist poetics combats the commodification of rural life.

Crucially, this ethical and political commitment cannot be reduced to message or critique; the desired response is instead brought about in the reader through a process of aesthetic education.[105] Even as they represent communities that are in the process of being decimated, disbanded, and driven out of existence, the texts I analyze do not abandon this educational project. The practice of dwelling doggedly persists: the characters and narrators model for the reader the ongoing work of learning to (poetically) perceive and nurture one's at-homeness (in the sense of affective entanglement with place and community, rather than the traditional Heideggerian sense of belonging) in a world undergoing momentous transformations.

Undoubtedly, there are other neo-regionalist writers who could be brought into this conversation, but I have chosen to focus on a few key examples, rather than paint a panorama of a moment or a movement, so that I might linger on each one, providing my reader with an immersive encounter of the kind I believe each text merits and, in fact, demands. If, as I propose, reading can be a form of dwelling, this can only be the case when one reads closely rather than distantly, when one stays with, lives with a given textual world over a long duration. I can attest that this methodology—committing to inhabiting and revisiting a single text over the course of years, thinking and theorizing from the specificity of its form outward in hopes of eventually making contact with wider conversations and other texts—is an inefficient way of practicing comparative literature. But I have become convinced that there is no other way possible, at least not in keeping with the critical regionalist ethos these texts have taught me. The prolonged encounters that lead to dwelling in a textual world not only allow the reader to come to know this world from within; they also shape the reader as a reader, and it is not an overstatement to say that the texts I analyze in this book have made me the scholar I am.

The key concepts of *Dwelling in Fiction*—dwelling, critical regionalist poetics, aesthetic education—emerged from my encounters with my primary texts before I knew the names others had called them by. Only much later did I find the critical vocabulary that has helped me to refine these ideas and articulate their relevance to a broader scholarly landscape. My hope is that in the end, these readings tell a passingly coherent, though by no means totalizing story of a series of interrelated places, moments, and aesthetic turns. This is the story of how literature helps us dwell in—and not simply document, categorize, remember, or eulogize—place-specific worlds in the throes of rapid transformation. It is also the story of how textual form conditions intercultural encounters between city and country, North and South, and how the concept of belonging is reimagined in the process. Finally, it is a model for what an affiliative mode of comparison can look like and an exploration of what new forms of commitment and collectivities it might make visible. As the extensive bibliography on each of the authors I spotlight makes clear, none of them is simply a critical regionalist; each has other commitments and affiliations. But in calling them all critical regionalists, a new form of transnational community emerges.

CHAPTER I

The Case for Critical Regionalism

WHAT WE TALK ABOUT WHEN WE TALK ABOUT REGIONALISM

I am far from the first to point out that the texts I read in the chapters that follow—José María Arguedas's *El zorro de arriba y el zorro de abajo* (*The Fox from Up Above and the Fox from Down Below*, Peru, 1971), João Guimarães Rosa's *Grande sertão: Veredas* (*Devil to Pay in the Backlands*, Brazil, 1956), and Juan José Saer's *El limonero real* (*The Regal Lemon Tree*, Argentina, 1974)—are not regionalist texts in any traditional sense of the term. Nor is Latin American regionalist literature a singular, well-defined entity, as the plethora of critical studies devoted to the topic attests.[1] It is beyond the scope of this book to give a full account of the historic and ongoing debates surrounding this deceptively slippery category, but it is important to provide a general idea of how the term *literatura regionalista* is used in order to make sense of the paradoxical fashion in which it is invoked in discussions of J. M. Arguedas, Guimarães Rosa, and Saer, as both as an umbrella category under which these writers might be included and a foil against which to celebrate their accomplishments.

In broad strokes, Latin American regionalist literature can be traced back to the national-identity-building projects of the nineteenth century and is said to come to full fruition in the early decades of the twentieth century with movements such as *la novela de la tierra*, *la novela social, la novela indigenista, la novela de la Revolución Méxicana,* and *el ciclo nordestino* in Brazil. Though diverse in many ways, these movements are united in their focus on rural life and are generally described as stylistically realist and ideologically committed to the articulation of a uniquely American identity and, later, to social reform. The long-underappreciated complexity of the literature associated with these movements is itself a vast topic, but I am primarily interested in the distorted lens through which historical regionalism tended to be viewed during the Cold War period. In many accounts, it stands in for all that would be superseded with the rise of *la nueva narrativa latinoamericana* in the mid-twentieth century: the inherited forms of romanticism, naturalism, and *costumbrismo*; the ideologically driven treatment of autochthonous themes, and the naive ignorance of "high" literary concerns (often inaccurately) ascribed to writers distant from the metropole.[2] There is a perplexing disconnect here. On the one hand, as Mary Louise Pratt observes, "In the Americas, North as well as South, modernity produced a flourishing of experiments in nonurban aesthetics, artistic projects anchored not in the city but in the countryside, the jungle, the mountains, border regions, and the heterogeneous ex-colonial social order."[3] On the other hand, throughout the latter half of the twentieth century and into the twenty-first, regionalist literature is persistently dismissed as passé.

In the face of this prejudice, a growing number of critics have recognized—intermittently and often in isolation—that regionalist literature, far from having been abandoned sometime in the 1940s, is still with us and continues to evolve. Yet many historiographies that emerged to account for this evolution, from the tripart schema devised by Antonio Candido in *Formação da literatura brasileira* (1960) to that more recently developed by Friedhelm Schmidt-Welle, follow a progressive model that dismisses previous waves of regionalism in order to celebrate the most recent.[4] In other words, there is a pervasive tendency to narrate the history of literary regionalism as the gradual overcoming of its romantic, positivist, and ideologically determined origins in order to arrive at something new—*neo-regionalismo, super-regionalismo, regionalismo no regionalista, regionalismo no nostálgico.*[5]

In order to understand the political valences of these ostensibly terminological debates, it is necessary to appreciate the degree to which regionalist literature throughout Latin America has been historically recruited to support nationalist agendas. It is precisely the purported realism or documentary nature of the genre that allows it to pass off ideologically driven portraits of the region and the nation as neutral, transparent representations. In the nineteenth century, for example, romantic regionalist literature claimed the interior of the continent as the autochthonous core of a distinctive national identity at the same time as it reinforced the nation-state's claims to emerging modernity. These seemingly incompatible ends are reconciled using rhetorical tools learned from the *crónicas*, or travel writings, of foreign conquerors, speculators, scientists, and tourists: the positivist, ethnographic, and nostalgic gaze denies the coevalness of the least developed regions (imagined as unruly and backward) at the same time that it domesticates them and renders them potentially productive.[6] Graciela Montaldo observes of the Argentine context that transposition into the past is precisely what allows the rural to be reclaimed as a site of national origins: "The moment when the rural becomes archaic it tends to become common and desirable heritage."[7] Similarly, in other parts of the continent, marginalized populations—Indigenous communities, rural laborers working under pseudofeudal conditions, and backland bandits and outlaws—who would pose a threat to the legitimacy of the state were their demands for rights, social mobility, and self-determination acknowledged head-on, are reduced to figures in innocuous folklore and bearers of local color.[8] Thus, much as Raymond Williams describes the pastoral mode as whitewashing social conflict and economic exploitation in Europe during the Romantic era, early regionalism in many cases reimagines zones of extraction and underdevelopment like the Argentine pampas, the Brazilian *sertão*, or the Peruvian highlands not as hot spots of factiousness and insubordination or stains of backwardness on the nation but instead as spatial repositories for nostalgia on a national level.[9]

Though the politically committed regionalist literary tradition of the 1930s is known for its searing social critique, its most renowned works are easily absorbed by nationalist discourses because they engage in this temporal displacement. Texts that laud the nobility or decry the exploitation of those who work the land, such as Graciliano Ramos's *Vidas secas* (Brazil 1938) and Ciro Alegría's *Los perros hambrientos* (Peru 1939) often wax elegiac in tone. Their projects of social criticism are thus compatible with nationalistic campaigns of progressive reform and modernization in which peasants are praised for embodying the best of the national spirit at the same time that the systems that condemn them to misery and perpetuate their euphemistically "quaint" way of life are either romanticized as relics of a bygone era or condemned as backward, vestiges of colonialism that the young nation must purge.

In the mid-twentieth century, the populist state proves adept at co-opting representations of the rural poor crafted in the spirit of critique. The continental tide of populism of the 1940s to 1970s[10] comes in reaction to rapid urbanization and industrialization, which created a ballooning working class that demanded political representation. The economic and social instability wrought by the global economic depression of the 1930s, and later, the ongoing prospect of socialist revolution in the context of the Cold War and the Cuban Revolution made it imperative for those in power to secure the legitimacy of the government by showing it to be of the people and for the people.[11] The symbolic inclusion of marginalized groups in the national image (still crafted and disseminated by elites) was therefore paramount. Moreover, constructing the national origins myth around rural archetypes—the *gaucho*, the *jagunço*, the *campesino*—enabled a convenient sleight of hand: a heterogeneous populace that often included immigrants, forced immigrants (the enslaved), and their descendants was said to cohere around shared roots in the land and in a way of life that could be slyly displaced into the rearview mirror by forward-looking regimes. The midcentury texts on which I focus push back against such co-optation of rural iconography by the state and directly or indirectly question the centrality of the nation to regional belonging. As I go on to argue, it is precisely their experimental form that allows them to do so.

To be clear, earlier waves of regionalist literature were often more formally innovative than is generally acknowledged. Fully unpacking the limiting stereotypes that emerge about classical regionalist literature is beyond the scope of this book, but I find it instructive to examine a few of them. Doing so reveals telling differences as well as surprising continuities between periods and regions. I am particularly interested in the resonances between different versions of the story of how the most innovative (neo-)regionalists of the midcentury—including Guimarães Rosa, J. M. Arguedas, and Saer—are said to have broken with or revised earlier regionalist paradigms.

We might begin with Brazil, where, relative to the Hispanic Latin America, the potential for regionalist literature to be at once formally and politically avant-garde was recognized early on, even if it was frequently obscured in subsequent decades. The sociologist Gilberto Freyre first codified the regionalist movement, convoking in 1926 the Primeiro Congresso Regionalista do Nordeste (The First Northeastern Regionalist Conference) and publishing the "Manifesto regionalista" ("Regionalist Manifesto") in response to the Semana de Arte Moderna (Modern

Art Week), which had taken place in São Paulo four years earlier. Freyre's Recife-based regionalist movement is characterized by a complex relationship to Brazilian *modernismo*, the avant-garde movement associated primarily with the coastal cities of the Southeast.[12] Even as Freyre upbraided the *modernistas* for neglecting northeastern traditions and contributions to the national culture, he claimed that the *regionalismo* he championed shared many of the same political and aesthetic principles of *modernismo*, such as renovating Brazilian literature by calling on autochthonous tropes, forms, and languages and rejecting cultural dependency on European models. In fact, his primary criticism of the *modernistas* of São Paulo and Rio de Janeiro was that they did not take their own principles of originality and autonomy far enough, that their identification with the cosmopolitanism of the European avant-gardes compromised their authenticity.[13] Not to be confused with separatism, parochialism, or the fetishization of autochthony, however, the regionalism espoused by Freyre and practiced by writers such as José Lins do Rego and Graciliano Ramos was informed both by the Brazilian *modernistas* and European and North American modernisms.[14] Though strongly denunciatory of "false modernisms" that superficially mimic European styles, Freyre's manifesto advocates a new understanding of regionalism as inherently hybrid and cosmopolitan; in fact, Freyre insists that its practitioners are "in their way modern and even modernist."[15] Indeed, regionalist writers of the 1930s—including not only Lins do Rego and Ramos, but also José Américo de Almeida, Raquel de Queiroz, and Jorge Amado—were deeply influenced by the linguistic experiments of the *modernistas* and explored how such innovations might lend themselves to capturing oral and traditional cultures as these increasingly confronted the impact of modernization.[16]

Nevertheless, the modern and even avant-garde features of the Brazilian regionalists of the 1930s were often ignored or denied, particularly by the urban *modernistas*, who saw their regionalist counterparts as driven by social commitment to representing common people and social crises rather than aesthetic innovation.[17] In fact, in the midcentury, it became common to characterize this generation of writers as a retrograde movement, interrupting the experimental trajectory initiated by the *modernistas*, which in many accounts is taken up again only in the 1950s and '60s with the work of Guimarães Rosa and Clarice Lispector.[18] In short, both the continuities between the historical *regionalistas* and *modernistas* and those between the generation of the 1930s and the renewed regionalism of Guimarães Rosa are often overlooked.

In "Literature e subdesenvolvimento" ("Literature and Underdevelopment"), for example, Candido claims that *Grande sertão: Veredas* exemplifies the new category of *super-regionalismo*, which leaves behind the exoticism, documentary quality, and picturesque local color of earlier regionalisms and gives form instead to a universal human story located in the paradigmatic setting of Brazilian regionalism: the *sertão*.[19] It must be noted that Candido does not completely flatten the landscape of regionalist literature. In *Formação da literatura brasileira* (*The Formation of Brazilian Literature*), he draws distinctions between three earlier phases of regionalism, and in "Literatura e subdesenvolvimento" he holds certain writers he esteems, such as Graciliano Ramos, apart from the general category of regionalism that he declares exhausted. Nevertheless, Candido's account of *super-regionalismo* forms part of a continent-wide trend in which the celebration of the new and "universal" nature of *la nueva narrativa* contributes to the creation and cementation of unfavorable stereotypes about previous waves of regionalism, which fall into disrepute in the second half of the twentieth century.

The strength of the stigma that developed around Brazilian regionalist literature is evident in the difficulty of overturning it. Twenty-first-century scholars continue to make the case that, contrary to beliefs that have become entrenched, regionalism is neither retrograde nor dead. As literary scholar Ligia Chiappini writes, "Many times the end of regionalism was decreed, and even today there are those who do so, but there are also those who affirm that it renovates itself and persists."[20] In defiance of those who declare the end of this or that version of regionalism, scholarship by the likes of Chiappini, Luís Bueno, Maria Arminda do Nascimento Arruda, and Herasmo Braga de Oliveira Brito has underscored the continuities between classical regionalist literature and neo-regionalist literature such as that of Guimarães Rosa and the generations that follow him. Moreover, such scholarship has established that the former was never simply a symptom of underdevelopment nor a reflection of a social reality but rather an aesthetic project whose aims included reaching and affecting a readership that hailed from outside the region. I join these thinkers, whom I identify with the critical regionalist turn, in their insistence that innovative regionalist texts like *Grande sertão: Veredas* are best appreciated as extending and critiquing, rather than completely breaking with earlier regionalist traditions in Brazil.

In Argentine literary criticism as well, the designation of *regionalismo* has historically carried a negative connotation that has been hard to overcome: to be called a regionalist was (and in some circles still is) to be accused of dealing in *folklorismo*, *costumbrismo*, local color, and romanticized myths of national origins and thus to be stripped of any real literary prestige.[21] The descriptive fallacies of this pejorative designation have been repeatedly pointed out, but its staying power reflects the entrenched nature of the *capital* versus *provincias* dichotomy in Argentina, which Laura Demaría describes as "fix[ing] these spaces in a fixed and unchanging scheme," wherein Buenos Aires is always the center and everything else reduced to the periphery.[22] Even in a work as recent as Noé Jitrik's 1999 *Historia crítica de la literatura argentina*, the critics Hebe Beatriz Molina and María Moreno Burlot note, regionalism is written off as "a past phenomenon, surpassed by new forms, even though it is never defined, nor is its initial historic position established."[23] For Molina and Burlot, the persistence of this tendency reflects not only the ongoing dominance of the urban biases but also the problematic, ambiguous nature of the term "regionalism" itself; it has never mapped cleanly onto geographic origins (not all writers from the provinces are branded regionalists) or stylistic characteristics (though the term is often used as shorthand for "realism," the works to which it is applied are in truth diverse).

The pejorative sense of regionalism as a positivistic discourse with little literary value has proven even more intractable in Argentina than in other parts of the continent, in the absence of a great midcentury modernist-regionalist writer to defy these stereotypes. Argentina had no Guimarães Rosa, Arguedas, or Rulfo in the 1950s, and it was not until the emergence of a new generation of writers in the late 1960s and early 1970s that the country saw a boom of neo-regionalist literature, including the work of Heraldo Conti, Héctor Tizón, and Antonio Di Benedetto, on whose heels Daniel Moyano, Juan José Hernández, and Saer would follow. In addition to underscoring the literary merit of the new regionalist literature, scholars such as Victoria Cohen Imach and Pablo Heredia have attributed its ascendance in part to Peronism and the revalorization of "authentic," modest, and provincial life (over the supposedly foreign and colonial influence of the capital city and its elites) in national-populist rhetoric.[24] They have also signaled the importance of the Latin American boom, which stoked European and North American interest in exotic Latin American locales and, as if reproducing this phenomenon in microcosm, rekindled a national search for identity in the provinces.[25] Interestingly, however, at least in the case of Saer, on whose work I focus in chapter 4, the formal innovations of the new regionalism react against rather than further enable the appropriation of regionalist tropes by nationalistic ideology and international markets.

The new Argentine regionalism defies the traditional use of the term, which was used to designate sociologically inflected literary texts invested in representing the region as a referent.[26] In fact, many writers including Saer reject the label of regionalism, understanding it in this reductive sense.[27] Saer writes:

> Practically all my stories take place in the Argentine littoral, the region that's found between the eastern edge of the pampa and the large rivers, the Paraná and the Uruguay. [. . .] But the objective of my literature is not to speak about the region; I prefer to leave that work to the more pertinent discourses of geographers, sociologists, and historians.[28]

As Julio Premat notes, Saer's frequent references to scientific ways of knowing—anthropology, ethnography, psychoanalysis, historiography, philosophy, and so on—seem designed to underscore the insufficiency of these disciplines as means of accounting for reality.[29] To read *El limonero real* (the novel that most directly takes on regionalist subject matter) as a regionalist novel, notes Heredia, it is necessary "to leave aside all nineteenth-century categorizations of 'realism' as an aesthetic school"; here, in contrast, the region is configured "through its sensory aspects."[30] As I argue in chapter 4, for Saer, it is only through the proliferation of meanings afforded by poetic language, through the sensorial richness of subjective experience, and through the material dimensions of local knowledge (*conocimiento*) that the real can be known. The literary and metaphysical sophistication of an author like Saer has not, however, categorically redeemed regionalist literature in Argentina. On the contrary, for decades, he, much like the experimental regionalists of Guimarães Rosa's generation, was celebrated as having successfully broken with this tradition and ascended to the ranks of "high" literature, "universal" subject matter, and cosmopolitan writer.

The terms of this conversation are necessarily different in the Andes, where it is impossible to talk about regionalism without also talking about *indigenismo*, so closely are racial questions mapped on to geographic questions in the region. Similarly to many discourses of regionalism in other parts of the continent, in the Andes, Estelle Tarica writes, "Twentieth-century *indigenismo* draws from the tellurism characteristic of nineteenth-century Romantic nationalisms" but centers ethnic identity: "to be Indian involves, essentially, to be of the national land, and vice versa: if one is of the land, then one is essentially an Indian."[31] The Andean counterparts to the *novelas de la tierra* are generally considered to be the *indigenista* novels of the 1920s to 1940s penned by authors such as Alcides Arguedas, Jorge Icaza, and Ciro Alegría.[32] Andean indigenist discourses and literature have, moreover, played a parallel role to that of regionalist discourses elsewhere on the continent: "From the colonial period to the modernizing national-populism of the twentieth century, *indigenista* discourses have contributed to the consolidation of state power."[33]

If Andean *indigenismo* historically promoted *mestizo* nationalism and the exploitation of rural and Indigenous labor, in Peru, a new wave of twentieth-century regionalist writers took up the banner of José Carlos Martiátegui's Marxist-inflected *indigenismo*. Mariátegui reclaimed the term for "anti-colonial, socially progressive, even revolutionary" projects, including those that pushed back "against Lima's centralizing tendencies" and the state's capitalist vision of modernity.[34] As Ulises Juan Zevellos Aguilar argues, for the past century, regionalist writers from Luis E. Valcárcel to J. M. Arguedas, to contemporary Quechua poets such as Fredy Roncalla, Odi Gonzales, and Chask'a Anka Ninawaman have proposed alternative solutions—grounded in provincial and Indigenous points of view—to the series of crises that have accompanied Peru's modernization process. These suggestions have generally gone unheeded, however, as the provincial origins of their authors allows them to be dismissed as mere regionalists in the pejorative sense.[35] Nevertheless, the vein of regionalist and *indigenista* literature inspired by Mariátegui has persistently challenged Peru's internal colonial relations as well as the racist and centralist views about Indigenous communities held by urban elites, who tend to be descendants of settlers. For example, such texts often combat the view that Indigenous values and practices are backward, a relic of an earlier era, by revealing the coevalness of Indigenous and non-Indigenous cultures.[36]

Though these regionalist texts are generally considered realist novels on account of their political commitment to representing social problems, their form often bears the influence of the historical avant-gardes and later, of the modernist techniques associated with the boom.[37] In fact, as Tara Daly notes, early twentieth-century *indigenismo* and *vanguardismo* were often so closely linked so as to be indistinguishable.[38] In this sense, the formal experiments of J. M. Arguedas, much like those of Guimarães Rosa, are more properly viewed as the continuation of an avant-garde vein in regionalist literature than as unprecedented in-novations. One of the most noteworthy features of Arguedas's *El zorro do arriba y el zorro de abajo*, which I discuss in chapter 2, is that the author's lifelong political commitment to revalorizing Indigenous cul-ture and denouncing exploitative systems here coincides with radically avant-garde form.

Another important shift that I trace in Arguedas's last novel is that the author's nonbelonging to the communities he represents goes from being simply an unremarked structural condition of *indigenista* litera-ture to a central thematic and formal concern. This is one of the senses in which I consider this text a work of *critical* regionalism or *indigenismo*. In addition to being written for a non-Indigenous audience, up until and well into the twentieth century, Andean *indigenista* literature was con-sidered by definition "a discourse by non-Indians about Indians," one that was orientalist, paternalist, and positivist by nature.[39] *Indigenistas* in the wake of Mariátegui, however, occupy a more complex position. Though many of the writers in this tradition, including Arguedas, are still outsiders in the sense of not being themselves Indigenous, they are celebrated for practicing a hybrid or transculturated aesthetic rooted in Quechua and Aymara cosmovisions. As in the other regional contexts I examine, however, it can be hard to disentangle the "straight" *indi-genismo* or regionalism of the Andes from its more politically radical counterparts. One does not strictly speaking supersede the other; a sin-gle text may, in fact, participate in a nationalist ideological project and reveal its limits.

Nevertheless, there is a general consensus among scholars of Andean literature that regionalist and *indigenista* literature undergoes a trans-formation in the mid-twentieth century, and that J. M. Arguedas is at the center of it. Arguedas takes it upon himself to revalorize a part of Peruvian culture that had long been stigmatized. This is not dissimilar to how the Argentine neo-regionalists of the 1970s were understood: as reclaiming part of the national identity that had always been kept in the shadows and deemed inferior to the "civilization" represented by the capital city. There is in both cases an epistemologically decolonial im-pulse behind this movement. As Martin Lienhard argues of the first case and Victoria Cohen Imach of the second, this new *indigenismo*, or new regionalism, manages to subversively insert itself into the lettered city, making use of the master's tools to undermine the master's hierarchies.[40]

In this turn, Mariátegui's sanctioning of violence to combat the op-pression of internal colonialism is reflected in the radical sundering of traditional literary forms. Rather than reconciling cultural differences through formal hybridity, the experimentalism of the new *indigenismo* expresses what Antonio Cornejo Polar calls *heterogeneity*. Cornejo Polar argues that the politics of this aesthetic turn lies in exposing the unreconciled differences of the nation and, thus, "the failure of the dominant half of Peruvian society—its urban, coastal, lettered, Spanish-speaking, occidental half—to provide an undistorted and realistic account of the subordinate half of the country—its rural, Andean, oral, Quechua-speaking, indigenous half."[41] This is another way in which the new Andean regionalist literature embodied by J. M. Arguedas might be considered a form of *critical* regionalism rather than simply a break with regionalism and *indigenismo* in the traditional, pejorative use of the terms.

In spite of the many differences between these regional contexts, in all three cases (Brazil, Argentina, Peru), midcentury experimental regionalists and the scholars who study them undertake the work of over-turning entrenched stereotypes about what regionalist literature is and can be. The formal innovations of these writers break the mold of tra-ditional regionalism, but they do not transcend this category so much as revise it for new political ends. The politics of this shift may be more immediately legible in some cases, such as Arguedas's intervention into the *indigenista* tradition, than in others, such as Guimarães Rosa and Saer's apparent flight into "universal" philosophical questions. Never-theless, I propose that even in the latter cases, evading the ideological demands that the nation has historically (and once again with the rise of midcentury populism) put on representations of the region is in itself a politically radical move. In fact, I argue in what follows that such texts anticipate post- and transnational thought more often associated with the era of neoliberal globalization and challenge their readers to con-ceive of community and belonging in terms we might, anachronistically, call critical regionalist.

WHY CRITICAL REGIONALISM?

Critical regionalism is an interdisciplinary field that was first developed in architectural theory in the 1980s as a reaction to postmodernist aes-thetics (Frampton, Jameson) but that has since migrated into US cul-tural studies (Powell, Campbell), Latin American studies (Moreiras), and transnational political theory (Spivak and Butler). These diverse approaches cannot be said to coalesce around a single, coherent theory or prescription for aesthetic and critical praxis, but they collectively pose questions such as: How can local cultures resist the homogenizing forces of modernization without clinging to ossified traditional forms? How can we, as readers, critics, and theorists, break from narratives that diametrically oppose the local and the traditional to the global and the modern—whether nostalgically pining for the former or triumphantly declaring the arrival of the latter—and instead recognize the contemporaneity and co-constitutive relationship of the two? How does formulating a less essentialist understanding of the regional compel us to move beyond categories such as ethnic, national, or linguistic identity and conceive of community, belonging, and ethical responsibility in terms better suited for a world where our individual and collective selves are increasingly constituted by movement—in the form of migration, dislocation, exile, travel, and translation—rather than rootedness? How might we grapple with the fluidity and hybridity of culture in a postcolonial world while still attending to the specificity of place and materiality of lived experience—the ways that one's social and economic conditions, one's immediate environment, and one's embodied interactions with it shape one's subjectivity, relationships, and political agency?

In privileging critical regionalism, which was not developed until the 1980s, I knowingly bring an anachronistic theoretical framework to bear on the literature of the midcentury, but this does not mean that the theory undergirding my argument would have been unknown to the authors about whom I write; on the contrary, the phenomenology and Critical Theory in which critical regionalism is rooted circulated widely in Latin America in the 1950s to 1970s.[42] Moreover, critical regionalism as I understand it is inherently backward facing.[43] In fact, one of the reasons I am attracted to this theoretical approach is that, in spite of being particularly attuned to the globalized world of the late twentieth and twenty-first centuries, critical regionalist thought emphasizes the continuity between past and present. Many critical regionalist projects turn back to previous moments in time, to seemingly traditional cultural production, to demonstrate that the region has always been relationally constructed.[44] In this way, critical regionalism offers an alternative to the diachronic taxonomies that separate literary production into say, first, second, and third waves of regionalism or that otherwise cordon off "traditional regionalism" from neo-regionalism, postregionalism, or what Antonio Candido has called "super-regionalism." This insistence on continuity rather than rupture with the past character-izes my approach as well: I am reading mid-twentieth-century texts as both continuous with an earlier tradition of regionalist literature whose experimentalism has often been underrecognized and as anticipating more recent conversations about the importance of the local and the particular as sites of resistance to the cultural and experiential flatten-ing that accompanies globalization.[45] The beauty of the model, then, is that rather than hinging on the novelty of its own approach, it allows us to read any number of earlier literary and critical works as already engaged in critical regionalism. For example, what Fernando Rosenberg calls the "critical cosmopolitanism" of avant-gardes like César Vallejo might also be considered a form of critical regionalist poetics.[46]

In describing Arguedas, Guimarães Rosa, and Saer as critical region-alists, I am not suggesting that they were simply ahead of their time, though in certain respects they undeniably were. Instead, I propose that critical regionalism was already part of the midcentury zeitgeist, though its presence in this moment may be obscured by the very ideologies against which it reacts: national-populism, Cold War dualism, and un-bridled developmentalism and cosmopolitan longing.[47] Unequivocally, what I am calling *critical regionalist poetics* was being practiced long before critical regionalism was named and theorized as such.

What is more, I propose that, despite the term's coinage in the United States, critical regionalism was being practiced in geographically diverse places united by their peripheral status. I thus join thinkers from Fred-ric Jameson to Alberto Moreiras in considering critical regionalism a response to modernization from the Global South.[48] As Moreiras has suggested, critical regionalism, as a framework that dialectically nego-tiates the autochthonous and the "universal," may be more properly Latin American than North American; at least, it contends with many of the most vexing problems faced by modern Latin American cultural studies.[49] Going a step further, I propose that it is possible to read the critical regionalist discourses that took hold in US cultural studies in the early 2000s as a belated rendition of debates that have long been ines-capable in Latin America: How to ground imagined communities in the autochthonous without reverting to essentialism? How to speak of col-lectivity, of ways of saying "we" in the face of ethnic, linguistic, regional, and cultural heterogeneity? How to embrace the flux, dynamism, and multiculturism that characterize modernity while still centering the sin-gularity of regional belonging? In reclaiming this framework as always already Latin American (rather than simply imported from the North), I seek to emphasize what Latin American thought contributes to broader debates surrounding the role of the local in a globalized world.

In other words, though critical regionalism was first named in the United States, critical regionalist poetics as I understand the term did not originate there (at least not exclusively). As the following chapters affirm, decades before Frampton began theorizing critical regionalism, a number of Latin American authors had already been independently working out a critical regionalist literary aesthetic grounded, like Frampton's architectural aesthetic, in repudiating the dominance of visual representation and foregrounding embodied experience of place. Moreover, theorists of Latin American cultural production had long been grappling with the same questions that underlie Frampton's critical regionalism.

In what follows, I provide a brief genealogy of critical regionalist thought in the Americas, including thinkers who have explicitly claimed the term as well as those who have developed their own terminology. Critical regionalist vocabulary has not been widely adopted in Latin American studies or in literary studies. Nevertheless, my understanding of the concept is largely informed by scholars of Latin American literature whose work, in my view, embodies the tenets of critical regionalism. Beyond suggesting that the writings of José Martí, Gilberto Freyre, Ángel Rama, Ligia Chiappini, Luís Bueno, Ricardo Kalimán, Laura Demaría, and others might be considered examples of critical regionalism practiced under other names and, in many cases, *avant la lettre*, I propose that dwelling on the contributions of these thinkers stands to deepen and nuance what has been a largely Anglocentric conversation. As I propose at the end of this chapter, a version of critical regionalism anchored in Latin American thought also offers promising possibilities for reimagining the discipline of comparative literature for the twenty-first century and from the Global South.

A BRIEF HISTORY OF CRITICAL REGIONALISM

Architectural theorist Kenneth Frampton first articulated critical regionalism as an aesthetic strategy to resist the placeless aesthetics popularized by modernist and postmodernist architecture. In "Towards a Critical Regionalism: Six Points for an Architecture of Resistance" (1981), Frampton champions designs grounded in "a place-conscious poetic," which might include responsiveness to local topography, climate, and light conditions or use of site-specific building materials.[50] He is careful, however, to differentiate critical regionalism from a straightforward, nostalgic return to vernacular forms and autochthonous traditions. Critical regionalist architects, among whom Frampton includes Tadao Ando, Alvar Aalto, and Oscar Niemeyer, do not sentimentally reconstruct styles from the past; instead, they design structures that engage the local environment and culture in nonrepresentational, avant-garde terms. Rather than citing visual elements from a local tradition (such as a thatched roof in the tropics), critical regionalist architecture attends to the phenomenological experience of a specific space (such as orienting windows so as to keep a building cool in a tropical setting). Critical regionalist architectural aesthetics thus redirects the attention of the building's occupants away from the purely visual and toward the tactile or synesthetic experience of the locale.

The embodied nature of one's interaction with architecture is central to Frampton's articulation of critical regionalism. He emphasizes "the capacity of the body to read the environment in terms other than those of sight alone" and the "complementary sensory perceptions" that allow a body to register place: "the intensity of light, darkness, heat and cold; the feeling of humidity; the aroma of material; the almost palpable presence of masonry as the body senses its own confinement; the momentum of an induced gait and the relative inertia of the body as it traverses the floor; echoing resonance of our own footfall."[51] Though Frampton's attention to embodiment (and, for that matter, the aesthetic) has not always been central in subsequent discourses of critical regionalism, I seek to recuperate it as a central component of critical regionalist poetics.

Frampton's critical regionalism drew the attention of thinkers beyond the field of architecture, including Jameson, who in an essay devoted to the topic in *The Seeds of Time* (1994) wrote that the "non- or antirepresentational equivalent [of Frampton's architectural aesthetic] for the other arts (or literature) remains to be worked out."[52] This book is, among other things, a belated response to Jameson's call and an attempt to work out critical regionalist poetics as a literary aesthetic. Though the formal solutions involved in creating an embodied experience of place through architecture—an art form that quite literally dictates how we inhabit space—may seem far removed from those available to literature, at the heart of Frampton's critical regionalist aesthetic lies a shift from *showing* us what the local looks like to inducing the *feeling* of what it means to dwell there. The experimental texts I go on to analyze evince this shift toward imparting the multisensory experience of dwelling.

Over the past several decades, critical regionalism has evolved into a multifaceted and interdisciplinary mode of inquiry united by the insistence on the contemporaneity and the dynamism of peripheral regions that tend to be fetishized as objects of nostalgia or as vestiges of an earlier stage in a teleological modernization narrative, whether understood in terms of economic development or the conquest of *barbarie* by civilization.[53] Though still grounded, albeit loosely at times, in Frampton's architectural theory, this broader sense of critical regionalism grows primarily out of conversations in US regional studies in the early 2000s, when scholars of the North American West such as Krista Comer, Gerald Vizenor, José E. Limón, Stephen Tatum, Ramón Saldívar, and Nathaniel Lewis begin to challenge the idea of the region as a "coherent and unitary space."[54] With an increasing emphasis on migration, border studies, and transnational cultures, these scholars advance a paradigm of regional studies with theoretical underpinnings in Mary Louise Pratt's contact zones, James Clifford's structures of place-d feeling, and Gloria Anzaldúa's hybrid Borderlands. For Neil Campbell, for example, critical regionalism depends on seeing the region in contact and dialogue with the globalized world and is marked by the "desire to bring the outside into the frame" as opposed to resorting to any "narrow definition or 'rootedness.'"[55] A recurrent trope in North American critical regionalist scholarship is, following Clifford, the need to think in terms of routes rather than roots, eschewing essentialist accounts of authenticity and local belonging "in order to better account for shifting and unfixed place of regions in late capitalism."[56]

Most critical regionalist scholarship today shares a commitment to redrawing the area studies map, challenging Cold War–era Eurocentric paradigms, and developing transnational approaches that attend to shifting borders and fluid movement of people and cultures. Many approaches are explicitly Deleuzian, seeking to replace discrete and binary categories with models of networks and webs of influence. (Though Édouard Glissant does not use the term *critical regionalism*, I would include his emphasis on rhizomatic and nomadic *relations* rather than singular, stable roots in this vein of theory.) Distancing themselves from critical regionalism's Heideggerian origins, these contemporary approaches are almost all poststructuralist, understanding local identities as discursive constructs rather than ontological categories, thus interrogating conventional notions of authenticity and autochthony and treating local identity as contingent and performative.

For example, although Chiappini does not use the term, her work is paradigmatically critical regionalist in conceiving of the region not as the positivistic notion of a place that can be found on a map but rather as a fictionally constituted idea that simultaneously refers to and evokes subjectively lived experience of particular parts of sociohistorical reality.[57] This way of thinking the region eludes simplistic binaries like city/province, progress/backwardness, modernity/tradition, vanguard/regionalism, universalism/regionalism.[58] Likewise, Demaría's scholarship on neo-regionalism in Argentina complicates the duality of the *capital* and the *provincias* and advances an anti-identitarian model for understanding the region that fits well within the critical regionalist paradigm. She proposes understanding *las provincias* in terms of negativity and difference, putting emphasis on the instability of an enunciatory position that is at once within and without (*adentro/afuera*), "a being present without belonging."[59] Demaría argues that this more fluid relationship to place frees neo-regionalist authors from the identitarian logic nationalist discourses have long imposed on the region and from the sense that being from the provinces is "una fatalidad" ("a fated misfortune") or a restrictive, immutable determinant.[60] Demaría draws on Kalimán's (also arguably critical regionalist) assertion that regions do not exist as objective and essential spaces. For Kalimán, the region is a way of thinking that generalizes based on the particular. Given that regions are always thought from somewhere (generally the academy, the metropole, often from imperialist powers), they tend to be inventions that facilitate the control, exploitation, exclusion, and marginalization of others.[61] The decolonial dimensions of the critical regionalist paradigm thus become pronounced in Kalimán's work, as in Glissant's.

In fact, one might say that in its cultural-studies incarnation, critical regionalism can be understood as a decolonial corrective to the positivism of colonial ways of knowing: ethnography, orientalism, area studies. As Latin Americanists of diverse stripes—from Walter Mignolo to Nelly Richard to Macarena Gómez-Barris[62]—are quick to point out, area studies derives from imperial relations of knowledge and power and tends to treat so-called peripheral regions as objects of knowledge to be observed and analyzed from global centers of culture. In contrast, critical regionalism by definition attends to the imbrication of the Global North in the Global South, of the city in the country. In Powell's words, the goal of this critical practice is to "make visible the forces that intersect and intercede to create a network of places, not to isolate them from the larger movements of culture, politics, and history but to enmesh them in these movements intricately and inextricably."[63] Critical regionalism thus expresses the historical materialist injunction to demystify the economic and power relations that produce an objectified, spatialized region: "Instead of seeing each map as a discrete definition of the region, we need to see the historical and contemporary interactions of these definitions—convivial or agonistic—as constituting the definition of the region."[64] Inherent in any critical regionalist project, then, is the restitution of the presentness, or coevalness, of underdeveloped regions that tend to be reduced to objects of nostalgia or vestiges of primitivism and seen as antecedents to urban modernity.

Though the connection has rarely been made explicit, critical regionalism also has an intrinsic affinity with ecocritical discourses that seek to contest the ideology of "nature as a resource."[65] Foregrounding local knowledge and "submerged perspectives"—as the texts I read do—reveals that regional spaces, far from being untouched Arcadias or uninhabited deserts, are traversed by social, economic, as well as ecological relations.[66] This recognition, according to many ecocritical and decolonial thinkers, is the first step in contesting the process through which "*inhabited* land becomes *occupied* land, as capital provokes a process of deterritorialization and displacement of local people, their economies, and social fabric."[67] As I mention in the introduction, regionalist cultural production is, with good reason, beginning to be centered in this movement in Latin American studies.

One of the few scholars to have explicitly adopted the framework of critical regionalism in Latin American studies is Alberto Moreiras, whose elaboration of the concept forms part of his deconstructive critique of identity politics and area studies. Moreiras invokes critical regionalism as a non-Eurocentric aesthetic and epistemology for Latin America.[68] As a form of locational thinking that resists recommodification, critical regionalism appears to answer Moreiras's call for a third space "that resists both cultural imitation and any type of identitarian reaction."[69] Like Frampton and Jameson before him, then, Moreiras understands critical regionalism as a fundamentally negative and antirepresentational practice. Rather than countering the hegemony of false universalisms (e.g., Eurocentrism or *criollismo*) by foregrounding the subaltern identities they exclude, critical regionalism guards against any and all essentializing identities: "It does not point to the production of any kind of counteridentity; rather, it moves beyond identity as well as difference in order to interrogate the processes of their constitution."[70] Nowhere does Moreiras specifically discuss critical regionalism as a literary practice, but it is clear that its aims and strategies align with those of the literature he associates with *el segundo latinamericanismo* and the postboom. If the boom belonged to the first *latinamericanismo*, which is organized by identiarian projects, national allegories, and developmentalist ideologies, then postboom literature (which does not necessarily come sequentially later) can be distinguished by the way it registers negativity and mourns the failures of the capitalist model of modernization. In Moreiras's understanding, postboom literature is committed to unmasking the false promises of developmentalist projects as well as the ideologies that prop them up (including transculturation) and revealing the hidden costs of these, which include the exploitation and disenfranchisement of subaltern sectors of the population as well as their fetishization in the very discourses that promise them visibility.[71]

Still, the critical regionalist turn in Latin American literary scholarship might be said to begin much earlier than Moreiras's adoption of the term, arguably in the 1980s, concurrently with the emergence of the term in North American architectural studies but decades before its elaboration in cultural studies. It is in the 1980s, near the end of the Cold War and at the dawn of global neoliberalism, that the prejudices surrounding regionalist literature begin to be critically examined by scholars like Rama and Chiappini. I want to suggest that this is in part because regional particularity begins to appeal as a tool in anti-imperialist discourses. Nevertheless, the literary works to which these scholars turn are from the preceding decades, revealing the degree to which previous moments of contact and interchange between Latin America and the Global North, including the burgeoning cosmopolitanism of the historical avant-gardes and the boom, had already heightened concerns about how Latin American culture would be viewed and consumed from without.

In literary studies, the critical regionalist project includes revalorizing regionalist works that have been consigned to the dusty attics of literary historiography and redefining regionalist literature. In this sense, Freyre might be considered a critical regionalist: he was determined to correct the misperception of literary regionalism as anachronism, a bygone chapter with which no modern writer would wish to be associated. Why, he wonders in his manifesto, does no one remark on the fact that Cervantes was a regionalist?[72] In fact, I propose that Brazil has one of the strongest critical regionalist traditions in the Americas. A recurring principle in this vein of thought is that the problems grappled with by regionalist literature are always bigger than the region or even the nation. As Humberto Hermenegildo de Araújo claims, the conundrums of Brazilian regionalist literature are those of Brazilian literature and arguably those of the literatures of the colonized world more broadly; the difference between how center-periphery questions play out within the nation and globally is primarily one of scale.[73] For these reasons, he argues, doubling down on regional specificity in Brazilian literature is not a conservative gesture but, rather, a "reaction to the imposition of a uniform order present in the cultural marketplace" and an "agent of resistance in the fight against the nonspecific in globalized culture."[74] These insights, which embody critical regionalist thought, are particularly poignant in the globalized, post–Cold War world, but they can be traced much further back in Brazil's intellectual tradition.[75]

The list of scholars developing versions of critical regionalist thought in the Hispanic American literary tradition is likewise long and historically deep, including the likes of Martí, Mariátegui, Cornejo Polar, Rama, Kalimán, Heredia, Cohen Imach, Leinhard, Moreiras, Tarica, French, Demaría, Molina, and Burlot. I dialogue with many of these thinkers in the chapters to come but perhaps none in such a sustained and explicit fashion as Rama. As I have already mentioned, Rama is one of the great champions of renewed regionalist impulses in Latin America. His work is particularly germane to this study, given his emphasis on the role of experimental form in this renaissance and the corpus he discusses. What is more, Rama's narrative transculturation, like Frampton's critical regionalism, is conceived at the dawn of the neoliberal era in the early 1980s and is grounded in a Frankfurt School critique of capitalist modernity.

To my knowledge, the only scholar to have brought narrative transculturation and critical regionalism directly into dialogue is Moreiras, who understands the two frameworks in oppositional terms.[76] I find it useful, however, to linger on the affinities between them. Both can be understood historically as responses to the rapid industrialization and urbanization spurred in the interwar years and continuing in the wake of the Second World War, and both are particularly attuned to the vulnerability of underdeveloped regions in the face of the unequal relations that shape geopolitics and market forces in late capitalism. As such, their emphasis on new interconnectivity between previously isolated regions does not share the unadulterated optimism of discourses of cosmopolitanism; these frameworks underscore instead the susceptibility of local particularity to being subsumed by capitalist modernity. In response to the impending threats facing local cultures in an age of accelerated development and globalization, both Frampton and Rama focus on aesthetic means of resistance (architectural and literary, respectively). Recognizing that local cultural forms cannot remain vital either by sealing themselves off from cosmopolitan trends or by giving in to their homogenizing pull, both thinkers place their faith in hybridized forms that arise in direct response to this dilemma. Each sets out to elaborate a novel (architectural or literary) sensibility that is grounded in the specificity of local experience while also incorporating the latest technical innovations of the international avant-gardes.

Implicitly and explicitly, Rama's theory of narrative transculturation makes the case that Latin American authors need not abandon local perspectives nor social engagement in order to participate in cosmopolitan literary culture. Instead, he argues that by deliberately and selectively adopting modern literary techniques and inflecting them with autochthonous forms, a new generation of Latin American authors is able to revitalize local traditions without assimilating to the dominant, Eurocentric culture (a process that the Cuban anthropologist Fernando Ortiz called *acculturation*). Unlike Ortiz, who first coined the term *transculturation* as a name for an alternative to acculturation and considered it an organic social process, Rama defines narrative transculturation as an intentional act of mediation carried out by the author.

My corpus includes literary figures who are central to Rama's notion of narrative transculturation, such as J. M. Arguedas and Guimarães Rosa, but I read these authors against the grain of Rama's thesis, focusing on their poetics of recalcitrance and opacity. In addition to treating the encounter between disparate cultures as a site of creative fusion, these texts turn the negativity of avant-garde poetics into an ethical resource to highlight the necessary impasses, fissures, and moments of failed translation that accompany any such cross-cultural dialogue. Oftentimes this is accomplished through the formal difficulty of the text, which may deliberately alienate and disarm the reader as a way of calling attention to, if not completely dismantling, the disparity in power between the subaltern subjects represented and the presumably educated, middle-class reader who consumes their images and stories. By directly or indirectly staging encounters between urban intellectuals and "native informants" fraught with friction and breakdowns of communication—untranslated and untranslatable Indigenous words (Arguedas), language rendered nearly unintelligible by archaisms and vernacularization (Guimarães Rosa), a moment when language degenerates into meaningless babble and eventually a black box on the page (Saer)—these texts call attention to the incommensurability of the world and the word, and, more specifically, of the largely oral cultures depicted and the text-based media through which the reader encounters these worlds. In other words, I read the experimental form of these texts as underscoring the distance that separates the reading experience of the metropolitan audience from the local lifeways represented *and* raising the questions of whether and how aesthetic experience might bridge this divide.

I thus join thinkers such as Adam J. Shellhorse in making the case that transculturation does not go far enough and that radical negativity and formal experimentalism are necessary tools for breaking with the state-centered, identitarian literary regime and pushing back against the demand that literature serve "as a translation device of cultural alterity."[77] My primary interest, however, lies in the reparative or educational project that might follow in the wake of such a refusal. How do these same experimental techniques teach the art of dwelling?

In other words, though my intervention in this book forms part of the critique of transculturation, I consider it an immanent critique, one aimed at revitalizing Rama's framework by reading critical regionalist tenets into it. Whereas transculturation is often understood as a process in which a cultural translator confers universal legibility and thus longevity on local cultural forms, in what I call *critical regionalist poetics*, literary discourse mediates this encounter not by producing transparency but rather by making palpable the friction and opacity of (neo)colonial encounters.[78] Much like Julio Prieto's notion of *escribir mal*, *critical regionalist poetics* calls attention to that which is negotiated in the contact zone—asymmetries, antagonisms, discontinuous temporalities and imaginaries, the meeting of different modernities and social orders—thus making visible the heterogeneity and mediation that have been willfully invisibilized in less experimental treatments of alterity.[79] Conceived as such, mediation is not simply a matter of translation but, equally, a matter of running interference or buffering the local from the reader eager to understand and appropriate it. On this point, I follow scholars such as Cheryl Temple Herr who understand critical regionalism as grounded in the negative dialectics of Theodor Adorno. Rama, like Frampton, was a reader of Adorno, and I argue in chapter 2 that recuperating a more Adornian version of transculturation might make Rama's framework both more relevant today and more recognizable as a form of critical regionalism.

THE PEDAGOGY OF CRITICAL REGIONALIST POETICS

> When practiced correctly, negative dialectics will render the static buzz of nonidentity into a powerful reminder that "objects do not go into their concepts without leaving a remainder" and thus that life will always exceed our knowledge and control. The ethical project par excellence, as Adorno sees it, is to keep remembering this and learn how to accept it. [. . .] Negative dialectics is, in other words, the pedagogy inside Adorno's materialism. This pedagogy includes intellectual as well as aesthetic exercises.[80]

There is nothing new about the idea that regionalist literature might educate the reader of an urban and elite background about country life. In fact, Latin American regionalist literature has long been conceived in pedagogical terms. The educational project of classical regionalist texts is most often understood either as that of imparting information and local color (as in regional customs and vocabulary) or as that of raising the political consciousness of the reader by revealing conditions of inequality and exploitation. What sets *critical* regionalist texts apart, I argue, is that they educate primarily through aesthetic experience, and the lessons they impart cannot be reduced to information or ideological message. Instead, they practice a form of pedagogy that leaves the student empty-handed. As in Adorno's negative dialectics as glossed by Jane Bennett, the education offered by critical regionalist texts is in how to live with that which we cannot fully grasp.

I understand this pedagogy as an outgrowth of rather than a complete rupture with the educational projects of the regionalist writers of the 1920s and '30s, such as those associated with the Hispanic American *novela de la tierra* and the Brazilian *ciclo regionalista nordestino*. As Chiappini argues, regionalist literature in Brazil ought to be understood not simply as a genre defined by rural setting, thematic content, or autochthonous origins but, rather, as "um modo de formar" ("a way of forming or educating") that operates by way of introducing elements usually banished from high culture.[81] In this understanding, regionalist literature has always contained a pedagogical mission directed at an outside audience. It was not uncommon for writers associated with historical regionalism to indirectly suggest, with the inclusion of glossaries and annotations, that the reader might require an education to dwell properly in the textual world presented. Regionalist authors from José Eustasio Rivera to José Américo de Almeida to Ricardo Güiraldes to Rosario Castellanos confronted the reader with the maladjusted, bumbling nature of the elite classes in the country setting, underscoring their illiteracy in the natural landscape and in local and Indigenous ways. What is more, as Carlos J. Alonso has argued, the *novelas de la tierra* already contained the gesture of self-reflexivity I trace in critical regionalist texts, although it was not always so obvious because, despite the avant-garde tendencies of some of its practitioners, the historical regionalist novel stayed within the bounds of the realist novel and did not recruit experimental form for its pedagogical endeavor to the degree that critical regionalists texts do.

To illustrate this contrast, it is helpful to compare Güiraldes's *Don Segundo Sombra* (1926) with Guimarães Rosa's *Grande sertão: Veredas* (1956). These two novels are rarely read side by side owing to their vast stylistic differences: the first is a pastoral bildungsroman and the second a wildly experimental modernist feat.[82] Yet their plots display remarkable similarities. Both novels are related in the voice of a narrator-protagonist who, unbeknownst to him, is born the illegitimate son of a wealthy landowner. Both Güiraldes's Fabio and Guimarães Rosa's Riobaldo are formally educated with their fathers acting as their benefactors but soon defect, seduced by the romance of the life of the cowboy (the *gaucho* and the *jagunço*, respectively). Upon running away into the backlands, each young protagonist undergoes a journey of *apprentissage*, learning through experience the ins and outs of a way of life that is already on the verge of extinction. Instead of fully and permanently becoming a *gaucho* or *jagunço*, however, each discovers his true parentage when he inherits his father's ranch and assumes his position as member of the local oligarchy and as lettered subject whose role as a mature man will be to narrate rather than live adventures in the backlands.

There are three principal formal differences between the novels. First, *Grande sertão* is not narrated in chronological order and, in fact, defies the teleological logic of the novel as a genre,[83] thus complicating its relationship to the bildungsroman and, ultimately, the very notion that the experiential education imparted by the land can ever be complete. Second, *Grande sertão* includes a frame narrative wherein Riobaldo tells his tale to an unnamed interlocutor from the city, who serves as a stand-in for the reader; it is rife with metacommentary on the difficulty of narrating life in the *sertão* and making an outsider understand. Third, Riobaldo's language, to which Guimarães Rosa's novel knows no outside, is so far removed from standard Portuguese (and for that matter, from any specific regional dialect) that it unavoidably strikes the reader's ear as foreign, not fully comprehensible, at least until they acquire a degree of fluency in it, which happens slowly and immersively over the course of the novel. Rather than simply reading about a journey of *apprentissage*, then, the reader must themself undergo one. They must confront, moreover, the unlikelihood that this journey will ever yield definitive knowledge of the *sertão*.

As Alonso has argued, awareness of the gap between the pampas on the page and the real pampas was already present in *Don Segundo Sombra*. Though Fabio's experience of *apprentissage* among the *gauchos* ought to legitimate his claim to the land, just as Güiraldes's experience on the ranch serves to authenticate his novel, the most interesting feature of *Don Segundo Sombra* may be the way these claims to genuine belonging are subtly undermined.[84] Alonso points out that the most common critique of the novel—that the attempt to authentically represent the life of a *gaucho* is undercut by the author's upper-class background—is also in a sense the plot of the novel. The elegiac tone of Fabio's narrative reflects the irremediably eccentric position of both narrator and author in relation to this world. While the process of *apprentissage*—of living among the *gauchos*—may induct a member of the landowning class into their world, in Alonso's reading, the very act of writing represents a fall from such "a state of ontological grace."[85] Importantly, for Alonso, as for Williams, pastoral nostalgia in literature is not a longing for a specific and foreclosed historical moment (a less industrialized, more agrarian mode of existence), for, from any point in history, the imagined prelapsarian Arden is projected further into the past. Instead, Alonso argues that this nostalgia is a longing for a state of prediscursive, unmediated oneness with the land, which tends to coincide in regionalist-nationalist projects with a longing for an authentic, unadulterated sense of identity, a collective myth of origins. It follows for Alonso that autochthony is the discursive construct that attempts to fulfill this longing but that, by virtue of its very discursivity, can only reflect the impossibility of doing so. It is this self-reflexive, allegorical (in the de Manian sense) gesture of signaling an always already irrecuperable moment of anteriority that makes *las novelas de la tierra* "very modern texts even in spite of themselves," according to Alonso.[86]

In the midcentury critical regionalist texts I analyze, in contrast, the quintessentially modernist gestures of self-reflexivity and negativity become glaringly central. The reader of *Grande sertão*, to return to this example, is incessantly reminded of their outsider status both by Riobaldo's metanarrative comments and by their inevitable struggle to follow his meandering narrative and idiosyncratic expression. They are, moreover, never rewarded with totalizing explanations or definitive answers to the many questions Riobaldo plants, as the novel remains defiantly ambiguous and open ended. What they do learn, however, is how to become a better reader of Riobaldo's world, how to attend to the details that are meaningful to him, such as the sound of birdsong or the eddying rhythms that interrupt the ostensibly forward-moving currents of rivers, of narrative, and of history. Though some readers may be more predisposed to this mode of reading than others (and, as such, perhaps, more likely to persevere), I argue in chapter 3 that even those who are not are encouraged to practice and to learn.

LEARNING TO DWELL: AN EMBODIED PRACTICE

It bears repeating that the pedagogy of critical regionalist poetics is not abstract or didactic; on the contrary, it is situated and embodied. What is gained in reading a critical regionalist text is not knowledge per se but rather a mode of attention or perception that I, following Tim Ingold, call the *dwelling perspective*. An anthropologist by training, Ingold arrives at a neo-Heideggerian notion of dwelling from an interest in how cultural formation shapes one's perception of the environment. While a long tradition of anthropology—including the work of Émile Durkheim and Clifford Geertz—claimed that sensation, conceived as universal, precedes conceptualization, conceived as culturally determined, Ingold instead follows the model of Pierre Bourdieu, whose concept of *habitus* collapses the separation between sensations and knowledge. In dialogue with Bourdieu as well as the ecological turn in cognitive science, led by James Gibson, Ingold arrives at the conclusion that one learns to perceive in a manner appropriate to a given culture,

> not by acquiring programmes or conceptual schemata for organizing sensory data into higher-order representations, but by "hands-on" training in everyday tasks whose successful fulfilment requires a practiced ability to notice and respond

fluently to salient aspects of the environment. In short, learning is not a transmission of information but—in Gibson's (1979: 254) words—an "education of attention." As such, it is inseparable from a person's life in the world, and indeed continues for as long as he or she lives.[87]

If people from different cultures experience the same sensory input differently, Ingold reasons, it is not because of "alternate cultural models or cognitive schemata" but because, due to their previous bodily training, their senses are differentially attuned to the environment. If we are formed as perceiving subjects through interactions with the environment rather than by receiving (genetically or culturally) a script for how to process our environment, it follows that there is room for a great deal of plasticity. Cultural specificity and upbringing shape how we perceive the environment, but the relationship is not deterministic. We relearn, for example, when we travel or migrate to a new location or culture, how to "read" our world. In fact, Ingold argues that this learning process never ceases; we are forever recalibrating our perception of the environment, whether this means fine-tuning our interactions with a familiar landscape or adjusting to a new or transformed one.

I propose in this book that literary texts can retrain our perceptions in ways that formally resemble the lessons in dwelling we continuously receive from our lived environments. The leap from the material environment, which literally engages all our senses, to the textual environment may seem far-fetched to some readers, but as thinkers from Walter Benjamin to Michel Collot have argued, the value of literary texts may be precisely the way they demand to be traversed and dwelled in rather than instrumentally consumed as vehicles for information.[88] In fact, Wolfgang Iser's description of reading as a phenomenological process, which he develops in dialogue with Maurice Merleau-Ponty, closely echoes Ingold's description of how one learns to read the environment: "The way in which this experience [of reading] comes about through a process of continual modification is closely akin to the way in which we gather experience in life."[89] If this idea is not new, neither is the idea that poetic language can actually transmit somatic experience; we might think back to Susan Sontag's 1964 call for "an erotics of art" in place of a hermeneutics: "We must learn to see more, to hear more, to feel more."[90] This idea has gained new traction in recent conversations surrounding affect and embodiment. Literary scholars such as Jason Baskin, Marília Librandi, and Francine Masiello have argued not only that certain written texts create aural and tactile experiences for the reader but also that this capacity to activate the senses holds the key to the ethical and political work of literature: building affective community across differences, listening to long-silenced voices, and learning to perceive situations of oppression and exploitation for what they are.[91]

If, as Jacques Rancière claims, the politics of aesthetic experience lies in retraining the senses (intervening in the distribution of the sensible), in critical regionalist poetics, this pedagogical project has a notable anti-occularcentric bent. Nevertheless, critical regionalist poetics counteracts the reification of regional life not simply by moving away from the visual representations that predominated in the *costumbrista* and realist regionalist traditions but also by reintegrating vision into a broader sensorial experience of place.[92] Instead of configuring the local as the object of an exterior gaze, critical regionalist texts construe it phenomenologically as an ecosystem of sensations, affects, and repeated and embodied movements through space. Learning to perceive this environment lies, in Ingold's words, "not in the ascent from a myopic, local perspective to a panoptic, global one, but in the passage from place to place, and in histories of movement and changing horizons along the way."[93] As I argue in chapter 2, Arguedas expresses his commitment to this perspective "de adentro, muy de adentro" ("from inside, from well inside") in his emphasis on the sonic and olfactory specificity of place and on *listening* as the ethical skill his reader must hone in order to enter into a relationship with the local that is neither superficial nor exploitative.[94] In chapter 3, it is by rejecting the totalizing vision of the cartographic perspective in favor of the blind, immersive experience of traversing the landscape that Guimarães Rosa invites the reader to experience the *sertão* from the dwelling perspective. In chapter 4, I propose that Saer's prose engages the languages of photography and cinema negatively to draw attention to that which cannot be represented in visual terms. Rather than disavowing visual poetics, Saer takes verbal ekphrasis to extremes in order to foreground the impossibility and undesirability of beholding rural landscapes through visual means alone.

These texts do not, then, repudiate visual knowledge *tout court*; they do, however, refuse what Haraway calls "the god trick": the illusion of being "from everywhere and so nowhere, to be free from interpretation, from being represented."[95] They thus question epistemologies grounded in the exceptional status vision is afforded in Enlightenment thought. In this tradition, vision, unlike the other senses, creates the illusion of being able to grasp the world intellectually and from a distance, eliding one's corporeal participation and mutual imbrication in it.[96] In addition to furthering a sense of domination and lack of reciprocity, in which the viewing subject is completely separate from and unaffected by the object beheld, visual representations are capable of obscuring the temporality of perception and reducing their objects to static, spatial entities. For all these reasons, visual technologies and the epistemologies they engender have been integral to the colonial enterprise.[97] The project of consolidating the young Latin American nation in the nineteenth century likewise relied heavily on visual technologies (such as cartography and photography) and visual rhetoric (such as ekphrasis and visual metaphors) to symbolically apprehend distant territories and assimilate cultural difference.[98] In the mid-twentieth century, however, the visibilization of traditional, largely rural ways of life acquires new dimensions and new stakes: during this period, the saturation of the cultural imaginary by the visual languages of photography and cinema coincides with the heightened visibility of provincial, underdeveloped spaces on an increasingly globalized world stage. As a result, the turn from conceiving of the regional landscape as a space to be *seen* to conceiving of it as an environment to be *dwelled in* acquires new urgency for writers living through this moment. The ecological and decolonial stakes of this shift have only recently begun to be recognized in Latin American literary criticism.[99]

In calling for a shift from in visu knowledge to in situ knowledge, critical regionalist texts form part of a larger turn away from visual landscape[100] as the predominant mode of representing nonurban spaces and the natural world. Jens Andermann has thrown this trend into relief, tracing its manifestations in Latin American cultural objects—including literature, film, architecture, the visual arts, and performance pieces—from the 1920s to the present.[101] In terms resonant with but distinct from my own, Andermann asks how aesthetic objects impart "un proceso de aprendizaje" ("a learning process"), leading viewers from beholding the landscape, as sovereign subjects with a claim to dominion over it, to inhabiting the landscape.[102] How might the gaze be reclaimed from its legacy of participation in the violence of (neo) colonial projects of occupation and extraction and restored as a mode of sensorial participation in one's surroundings? What new forms of collectivity might come into being as a result of this shift? Andermann answers these questions by drawing on posthumanist thought and signals the utopian potential of postsubjective modes of relation with the natural world that might allow for "the possibility of returning to a reciprocal mode of relating to the land, based on use rather than exchange."[103] Similarly, in the texts on which I focus, the line between the human and the nonhuman is often treated as porous or irrelevant, and the viewer is encouraged to come to know these worlds through the senses and affects, which favors relation over mastery. Yet, as I have already emphasized, critical regionalist texts do not lead their readers to an undialectical immersion in or merging with the worlds they conjure, what Andermann describes as "trance": "In trance, there are no longer any subjects and objects: on the contrary, trance is the time and space of the one being possessed by, and becoming co-extensive with, the other."[104] Such states arguably occur in the novels I go on to analyze, but they are, importantly, always fleeting or intermittent.

Like Andermann, I home in on texts that dismantle the sovereign position of the idealist subject, but critical regionalist poetics as I define it retains the phenomenological subject in Merleau-Ponty's sense.[105] Never escaping the condition of immanence and bound to the material world in a porous and mutually vulnerable relation, this subject remains, nevertheless, a singular individual formed and limited by the sum of their embodied experiences in the world. In other words, although I share Andermann's interest in how aesthetic experiences affect (and perhaps even disrupt) the subjectivity of the reader or viewer, the end of critical regionalist pedagogy as I understand it is not the dissolution of the boundary between the self and the other.[106] This possibility is less than desirable in the texts I analyze precisely because they imagine their readers to be outsiders with neocolonial ambitions. As such, they actively check Western "fantasies of becoming," which Sara Ahmed argues can be traced back to "the classical nineteenth-century narrative of 'going native.'"[107] These texts give formal expression to Ahmed's concerns that in many cases "narratives of becoming other reconstitute rather than transgress the integrity of the Western subject who becomes."[108] In other words, it matters who is doing the becoming. Acts of mimesis and creative appropriation, celebrated as subversive and liberatory from Oswaldo de Andrade's *Manifesto antropófago* to Homi Bhabha's notion of colonial mimicry, do not read the same when carried out by one in a position of relative power; they become acts of appropriation continuous with the history of colonialism.

For this reason, critical regionalist texts remind the reader not simply of the plasticity of the phenomenological subject—the fact that the self is continuously being shaped by encounters with the environment—but also of the difficult-to-overcome differences between subjects that afford them differential access to the experience of dwelling in a particular landscape—the fact that this landscape may not (yet) disclose to the reader what it discloses to a native dweller. As Emily Apter has argued, we should not assume we all have equal access to the affective experience of cultural groups whose history and backstory we may not share.[109] The same applies to sensory experience, for, as Laura U. Marks reminds us, far from being universal, one's sensorium is always cultivated within a cultural context.[110] In the chapters to come, I follow the leads of Apter and Marks and read for moments of opacity, untranslatability, and formal difficulty that mark differential experiences of dwelling, thus dialectically complementing the sense of proximity afforded by the dwelling perspective.

In short, critical regionalist texts mark the reader's status as an interloper in the world narrated and, simultaneously, challenge the reader to undertake the ethical work of learning to experience this world from the perspective of those who dwell there. These two seemingly contrary impulses prove oddly compatible as both are rooted in the recognition of the situatedness of our perspective. If embodiment is, as Baskin argues, what draws us into community with those outside our identity groups, it is also, according to the phenomenology of Merleau-Ponty on which he draws, what denies us the transcendent view from nowhere and everywhere at once. In other words, it is because perception is embodied that it is limited. Baskin connects the humbling recognition of one's situatedness demanded by Merleau-Ponty's thought with the lesson of Adorno's negative dialectics: that the world always exceeds our conceptual categories. There is always more than we can perceive or comprehend directly and, therefore, we must infer it. Though we must not lose sight of the speculative nature of the imaginative, intellectual, ethical, and aesthetic exercises through which we infer the existence of other perspectives, such exercises may nevertheless expand the horizons of the collectivities in which we participate. In fact, Baskin locates the social or political commitment of certain modernist texts written after 1945 precisely in their evocation of an affiliative community through embodiment: "Embodiment becomes the basis for a sociality that extends beyond the particularity of group identity."[111] Baskin's methodology, which weds phenomenology with historical materialism, partially inspires my own, which makes similar use of this confluence between the thought of Merleau-Ponty and Adorno to explain how critical regionalist poetics resists and contests the reification of regional lifeways.

THE IMMANENT POLITICS OF
CRITICAL REGIONALIST POETICS

Critical regionalist poetics as I understand it is inherently political, not because it denounces the exploitation of the rural poor (though it may) but rather because it restores the temporal dimensions of regional life that are often elided in ethnographic and folkloric representations and, in doing so, renders perceptible historical processes and social and ecological relations that are immanent in the phenomenological experience of daily life. Though using a very different idiom, Ingold's notion of dwelling shares with historical materialist approaches to space (such as Henri Lefebvre's concept of practiced space, Neil Smith's theory of uneven development, and what Hosam Aboul-Ela calls the *Mariátegui tradition of dependency theory*) the conviction that differential spaces such as the city and the country are produced rather than naturally occurring and, as such, are inalienably dynamic and historical.[112] In blunt terms, the representation of space as fixed and timeless is for the Marxist tradition the result of mystification and therefore remedied through demystification (the revisibilization of occluded social and economic relations), and for the phenomenological tradition on which Ingold draws, it is the result of limited perception and therefore remedied through an education of attention and the senses. Most of the texts on which I focus lend themselves better to being read through the second lens than the first, but they also reveal the two to be interrelated. Though my authors do not all engage in explicit materialist critique, I contend that formal properties of their texts cast a critical light on—and, beyond that, attempt to redress—the ossification and othering of underdeveloped spaces. They do so by focusing on the phenomenological experience of inhabiting such spaces, which as Baskin suggests may lead to the perception of an immanent social totality.

To be clear, I consider critical regionalist poetics a Marxist aesthetic practice only in an extremely heterodox sense indebted, above all, to Adorno.[113] With the exception of *Los zorros* by Arguedas, the texts in my corpus are only indirectly concerned (at the level of thematic content) with how capital produces differential spaces and how the production of space allows for the continued survival of capital. This is not to say, however, that they neglect the material conditions that shape local life. The class dynamics of Arguedas's Chimbote are clearly on view in his portraits of fishermen, factory workers, sex workers, and union leaders, but the author appears equally interested in capturing these subjects' embodied experience of place. Less obviously, Saer includes the underlying economic forces that structure the world of the peasants in *El limonero real*—the market where they struggle to sell their crops and the draw of the city's wealth, which lures the younger generation into dangerous lines of work like construction and sex work—but, although these forces lie at the novel's thematic core and drive its plot, they are latent rather than explicit in most scenes and descriptions, which tend to foreground the sensory dimensions of daily life. Similarly, the socio-economic and political implications of Guimarães Rosa's pseudomythic fictional worlds are far from immediately apparent; in fact, the Brazilian author always insisted his texts should not be read politically. Nevertheless, as Willi Bolle argues compellingly, *Grande sertão* can be read as an allegory for the cost of social and economic advancement at both the individual and national levels: one joins the landed class by abandoning one's solidarity with the precarious life of the common *sertanejo*, just as the nation becomes modern and cosmopolitan by invisibilizing and excluding exploited sectors of society.[114]

In all these cases, perceiving spatialized class politics is a matter of honing our attention so that "the very objects would start talking under the lingering eye."[115] As Héctor Hoyos proposes, there may be cases when attending to the material reality of objects, landscapes, and phenomenological life may be as or more politically radical and even "more materialist than the party-line historical materialists."[116] His call for "the cross-fertilization of materialisms" in *Things with a History* shares with this study the belief that attending to the materiality of cultural objects may also harbor the potential to "repair the suture that Cartesianism has made in Western rationality," to counterfetishize and rehistoricize that which has been objectified in other discourses.[117] The social as well as ecological stakes of this convergence of old and new materialisms are particularly pronounced in Latin American (neo-)regionalist literature. In fact, Andermann emphasizes that "Regionalist literature and thought"—with their ability to generate and critique the ideologies undergirding extractive capitalism as well as to reveal the entanglements of human and nonhuman worlds—"deserve to take pride of place" in this turn.[118]

Dwelling in Fiction is premised on this same conviction, though my focus is more narrow, homing in on the role formal experimentation in midcentury narrative plays in counterfetishizing and rehistorizing the region. Moreover, whereas Hoyos professes ongoing loyalty to many aspects of historical materialist methodology—"demystification, suspicion, analysis of the superstructure, and so forth"[119]—I embrace meth-odological cross-pollination with the turns toward affect, new ethics, and new formalism, particularly insofar as these turns recognize the text as pedagogical agent acting on and shaping the reader.[120] Nor do I understand this methodological shift as abandoning materialist imper-atives, at least not in their Frankfurt School incarnations. If the mecha-nism of reification or "thingification" that Lukács decries in "Narrate or Describe" involves mystifying the processes and relationships through which things and characters alike are constituted and presenting these as finished "products," then, following Ingold and Baskin, this process might be stalled and even reversed through a particular pedagogy of perception.[121] I propose, moreover, that it is the formal and affective qualities of critical regionalist texts that equip them to carry out this pedagogical task.

This view of the social content of art as immanent in its form stems from the aesthetic theory of Adorno, for whom "artworks become el-oquent with wordless gesture. In expression they reveal themselves as the wounds of society."[122] In this vein of theory, artistic autonomy, like everything else, must be understood dialectically. Though it may mean de-emphasizing communication and political messaging, formalism (as both aesthetic and critical practice)[123] does not necessarily amount to an abdication of politics because, for Adorno, "the unsolved antago-nisms of reality return in artworks as immanent problems of form."[124] In fact, he believes that "real denunciation is probably only a capac-ity of form, which is overlooked by a social aesthetic that believes in themes."[125] In a contemporary uptake of this idea, Ellen Rooney insists that "to read past or through this formal work is not to misread but to dismiss reading as such" and fall into a fetishistic relationship with content and theory alike: "In such a process, all of our texts are reduced to banalities, that is, to the already known. Finally, even our ideology critique misses its mark, because we have forgotten the critical fact that ideology too is a matter of form."[126] In my elaboration of critical regionalist poetics, it is the act of reading itself—understood as grap-pling with form and thick textuality—rather than theme or message that prompts a radical change in perspective. In other words, political content need not be explicit.

In order to discern latent political stakes, the reader must learn to look with what Baskin calls "soft eyes." In a piece that comes as a re-joinder to the call for surface reading, Baskin turns to phenomenology to defend Marxist literary criticism from the implicit allegation that it ignores what is manifest in the text—including but not limited to literary form—in its quest to root out hidden ideology. Like many skeptics of surface reading, Baskin insists that surface and depths cannot be separated from one another. "Soft eyes" is the phrase he uses to describe the gaze attuned to this interrelation, a gaze that looks beyond the surface without ceasing to attend to it in its own right. Baskin reminds us that, for Merleau-Ponty, "Depth provides the very thickness and texture that allow surfaces to be perceived."[127] Far from being superficial or deceptive, then, the surfaces of the textual world are our only point of contact with its depths. They are the visible faces of something much bigger, something that Baskin, following Raymond Williams, calls the *social totality*. This totality remains largely unavailable to direct perception. In similar terms, I propose that critical regionalist poetics challenges the reader not to blow past the surface but to dwell there until they learn to perceive what is not directly visible in addition to what is: the depths, the negative spaces, the intricate relations, and the sedimented histories that make up the world that meets the eye.

As I argue most directly in chapter 4, this approach to the political would not have been immediately legible as such in midcentury Latin America. Though continental theory circulated widely, it was Jean Paul Sartre's phenomenology, rather than Merleau-Ponty's (or Heidegger's) that gained the most traction. Not unlike Ernesto "Che" Guevara's vision of *el hombre nuevo*, Sartre's model of commitment, which was nearly hegemonic among Argentine leftists in the 1950s and into the 1960s, depends on the freedom of the sovereign subject.[128] Revolutionary politics at this historical juncture needed the construction "human will," which would be eroded by structuralist and poststructuralist thought and to some degree by Merleau-Ponty's phenomenology, which for many leftists represented the worst of Sartre's philosophy.[129] Nevertheless, Baskin's materialist rereading of Merleau-Ponty is helpful in unearthing another approach to politics, one that I argue critical regionalist authors had already developed half a century earlier.

WHY SO DIFFICULT?

For the Adornian tradition in which I locate critical regionalist poetics, the ethical and pedagogical value of aesthetic experience is closely related to formal difficulty. The difficulty, estrangement, and frustration that accompany the reading of formally avant-garde texts can spur

Brechtian defamiliarization and demand that the reader participate more actively in their education. As Ramsey McGlazer argues, modernist texts that "block our narrative interest and impede our understanding [and] cause us to chafe against the limitations they impose" may develop in the reader a more critical (and thus more politically radical) relationship to education.[130] Rather than leading the reader to unwittingly internalize the ideology of the author or narrator (as in the sentimental education of the bourgeois novel), critical regionalist texts make the reader aware of the fact that they are being educated. It follows that to persist in reading is to actively accept the work of being educated and, by extension, to accept the fact that one *needs* additional education to approach the world about which one reads.

As emphasized in the new ethical turn, furthermore, formal difficulty may serve to curb (or at least complicate) projection, thus reframing the encounter with otherness staged by the text: "As Butler describes it, we come to self-consciousness about our pretended certainty through the confrontation with alterity, an experience of the other that surprises us in its intractability, its refusal to conform to what we imagine we know."[131] Judith Butler compares the demanding and uncomfortable nature of "passing through the unfamiliar" and "passing through difficulty" in the act of reading to being immersed in a foreign landscape, culture, or language; this exercise is discomforting and humbling; it requires a willingness to be disarmed.[132]

Instilling humility in the reader is not the only ethical or political value of difficult form, however. If difficult regionalist texts merely chastised their metropolitan readers for their inability to relate to regional life, they would relieve these readers of the work of forging community across differences. Following Gayatri Chakravorty Spivak's notion of aesthetic education, one might say that critical regionalist texts also train the metropolitan reader to attend ethically to the experience of those who have not been the victors of history, colonialism, and capitalism, thus breaking with a fetishistic relationship to the other and shifting "toward ethical practices—care of others as care of the self— that were defective for capitalism."[133] The texts I analyze model and encourage in the reader such forms of care for elements of experience that are harder for capitalist logic to grab hold of, such as the value of birdsong for Riobaldo or the slow, recursive descriptions of "nonproductive" daily activities in Saer—petting a dog, taking a swim, watching others dance. These experiences are conjured through a multiplicity of senses but are all "tactile" in the sense that Frampton uses the word:

rooted in the ontological experience of place, resisting circulation or being reduced to information that can be commodified.[134]

These texts themselves are also "defective for capitalism" in the sense that their formal difficulty, recalcitrant attitudes, and discernment about which readers might be willing and able to take them on assures they will never be bestsellers. These same features undoubtedly limit their reach, but they also introduce ethically valuable friction into the act of consuming cultural production from the Global South. As such, critical regionalist poetics as I define it is a dialectic of obstruction and education, along the lines of what Doris Sommer once called the slaps and embraces that subalternist texts strategically deliver to the reader.[135] This emphasis on the reader—as a culturally situated and embodied subject who encounters the text from somewhere—is one of the central differences between my approach and other recent reevaluations of the politics of difficult, experimental style in Latin American literature, such as those of Shellhorse and Prieto.[136]

Nevertheless, both Shellhorse's conception of "anti-literature" and Prieto's of "escribir mal" resonate profoundly with my argument, given their emphasis on the necessary failure of translation when representing alterity and their compelling cases for the political power of a literary style marked by this failure. Shellhorse privileges antirepresentational (often self-reflexive) aesthetics as a way of disrupting identitarian paradigms and, simultaneously, creating new affect-based forms of community and solidarity. Meanwhile Prieto develops a notion of "productive illegibility" as a way of manifesting the impossible drive to bring the outside (the extraliterary, the popular, the political) into the text. It is the instability of the resulting position—existing neither fully in the world nor fully in the text—that makes such aesthetic strategies radical according to Prieto, who distinguishes the aesthetic of "escribir mal" from the hypertextuality of European and Anglo-American modernism:

> It is as distinct from the textualist poetics that promote an indefinite residence in the text or a stable habitability of the literary, as from the political practices and discourses of *testimonio* that position themselves tendentially or programmatically on the outside of the literary. In practices of *mala escritura* it would be about trying to inhabit the contradictory nature of this in-between, that which circulates between text and world, that which shuttles between the aesthetic and the political.[137]

The question of the habitability (or lack thereof) of the textual world is central to the notion of dwelling in the text that I have put forth. I concur with Prieto that, following Adorno, if a literary text is to be political, it must not be permanently and comfortably inhabitable (it must also direct the reader back to the world). Nevertheless, I maintain that the political strategy of the texts I analyze (including Arguedas's *Los zorros*, which Prieto also reads) hinges on being at least intermittently inhabitable and that this habitability is not simply the result of the suspension of disbelief or intellectual engagement but also of activating the senses. In other words, the detour into the text is necessary (and politically justifiable) only insofar as something is learned on the journey, and this something cannot be reduced to information or even ideology critique; what is learned is learned experientially by trying out or rehearsing (*ensayar*) new ways of being in a particular place, of dwelling.

Each of the novels I analyze contains an immanent critique of the way literature appropriates regional particularity and packages it for consumption at the national or global scale. Yet, as I have been arguing, the political project of critical regionalist poetics does not end with critique. These initially recalcitrant or abrasive texts also extend an invitation to the reader who is willing to learn the art of dwelling. As readers of critical regionalist texts, part of what we learn to perceive over time is our own forever-evolving and forever-limited capacity to see the regional worlds about which we read. The difficulty of deciphering what we behold attunes us to our outsider status and our limited vocabulary in this local world, as well as our ability learn its ways, up to a point. Thus, the negativity of critical regionalist poetics constitutes at once an ethical call to keep challenging ourselves to be more attentive readers and a humbling reminder that, heeding Adorno's warnings about the hubris of Western epistemologies, we should not expect to ever fully close in on that which we are trying to grasp.

Here it is important to remember that aesthetic experience for Adorno confronts us with the limits of conceptual thought, but its pedagogy does not end with this negative gesture; running up against such limits is also an invitation to imagine beyond them. As Bennett emphasizes, in negative dialectical thought, obstructions and points of opacity serve as invitations to cultivate one's utopian imagination: "The negative dialectician should imaginatively re-create what has been obscured by conceptualization."[138] In this act of imagination lies the ethical work prompted by difficult, avant-garde texts.

When understood in pedagogical terms, moreover, aesthetic experience—encompassing grappling with thick textuality, difficulty, and opacity as well as activating one's imagination to reach beyond apparent impasses—may perform political (in addition to ethical) work in postcolonial contexts. Along these lines, Spivak argues that a revised version of Schillerian aesthetic education remains crucial to keeping alive the promises of radical politics in the age of global neoliberalism. Putting her faith in "aesthetic education as training the imagination," Spivak claims that "an imagination trained in the play of language(s) may undo the truth-claims of national identity, thus unmooring the cultural nationalism that disguises the workings of the state."[139] An imagination thus trained is equipped for carrying out important political work beyond the aesthetic realm, such as the "re-invention of the civic state in the so-called Global South, free of the baggage of nationalist identitarianism."[140] It is this reinvention that lies at the core of Spivak's notion of critical regionalism. Crucially, aesthetic, ethical, and political work cannot be separated in Spivak's pedagogical theory.

Similarly, for Adorno, in Martin Jay's gloss, far from offering a retreat from the world or a "safe haven from history," aesthetic experience demands "an openness to the unexpected with its dangers and obstacles" and provides "a reminder of the encounters with otherness and the new that await those who, despite everything, are willing and able to embark on the voyage."[141] Though Adorno's thought, with its privileging of high art forms and those who are "willing and able" to engage them, is often seen as elitist, its pedagogy, like that of the difficult texts I analyze, remains democratic in the sense that the ethos of openness and perseverance in the face of the unknown is cultivated in the act of reading and therefore available to any reader committed to staying with the text, to dwelling in it.

NEW WAYS OF SAYING "WE"

My emphasis thus far has been on the education proffered by critical regionalist texts to the metropolitan reader. This emphasis reflects the probability that the texts I study were, at least initially, most often consumed by the urban elite, given not only their formal difficulty but also the low rates of literacy in rural Latin America in the midcentury as well as the economic forces governing the publication and distribution of literature. Nevertheless, I do not want to discount the possibility that critical regionalists texts also telepoetically anticipate and summon a more heterogenous readership. For example, critic William Rowe claims that Arguedas writes for a bilingual (Spanish and Quechua), bicultural (*mestizo* and Indigenous) readership in his last novel.[142] Understood in this vein, Arguedas, like the North American Indigenous artists studied by Dylan Robinson, writes "for a readership yet to come, for future generations of fluent [. . .] readers and speakers, of which there are currently few," thus willing the existence of "the future many."[143]

As such, it is important to emphasize that these texts may offer different kinds of aesthetic education to—and demand different kinds of imaginative engagement from—different audiences. As I have underscored, in the hands of the metropolitan intellectual, the difficulty of the critical regionalist text can render bidirectional limits to access that have traditionally barred subaltern subjects from full participation in the dominant culture, underscoring that the urban intellectual, too, may be barred from certain forms of understanding and participation. Just as importantly, however, in the hands of the colonized subject, a text that requires imagination in addition to comprehension through the epistemological systems of the colonizer may be a valuable tool for perceiving otherwise occluded experiences of inhabitation.[144]

It should be noted, moreover, that the real or hypothetical reader who is also an inhabitant of the region in question does not necessarily, for this reason, cease to be an outsider. On the contrary, once such a reader assumes the position of reading or writing about one's home in order to understand it better, one necessarily becomes internally divided. In other words, provincial subjects, too, must learn to dwell without fully belonging. For Haraway, in fact, it is only the "split and contradictory self," rather than the self-identical subject, who might practice situated knowledges because the latter does not truly exist except as a projection, either the unmarked, transcendent subject of knowledge or the essentialized other ontologically locked into a gender, race, ethnicity, place of origin, and so forth.[145]

This splitting is thus not merely a loss, though it may be experienced in a melancholic or guilty register as a form of exile, failure, or betrayal, as is the case for many of the narrators in the texts I discuss. This split or migratory positionality, what Demaría calls at once "within and without," in but not of the provinces, is also what makes the regional subjects depicted in these texts dynamic subjects and agents, rather than "passive and inert" objects of another's knowledge.[146] Arguedas's author figure in *Los zorros* is distraught and paralyzed by his sense of nonbelonging in Chimbote, but as I argue in chapter 2, this is precisely what necessitates the dialogic form of the novel so central to the text's ethics. Guimarães Rosa's narrator, Riobaldo, occupies the unusual position of being a *jagunço letrado*, at once of the *sertão* and detached from it as a retrospective narrator. This divided subjectivity, I argue in chapter 3, is inseparable from his fear that he has sold his soul, but it is also what makes him a true interlocutor and teacher for the reader rather than merely a native informant. Saer famously projects his internally divided self on to two twins who appear as recurring characters in his fiction: one who stays and one who leaves, as Saer did when he went into self-imposed exile in France. In chapter 4, I trace the ways that this divided subjectivity manifests in the narrator of *El limonero real*, who is at once intimately close to and removed from the world of the characters, rendering their world in scintillating images that are sensorially rich, temporally dynamic, and intractably opaque.

If the reader recognizes themself in such subjects, it is likely on account of this divided state, rather than simply a shared identification with a given place, culture, language, or set of traditions. Rather than granting authentic access to the perspective from within, then, being from the community represented may raise a host of other issues for the reader regarding the nature of their belonging. Because these texts posit belonging as an activity, a practice rather than a stable ontological state, all readers, regardless of where they hail from, will be called on to learn to dwell, which means negotiating the push-pull of two equally illusory poles: complete belonging and complete sovereignty. The reader's challenge will necessarily be different depending on how closely they identify (or long to identify) with each of these two extremes: one who simply dwells and wholly belongs and one who knows transcendently from everywhere and nowhere at once. It is precisely because neither of these positions can truly be inhabited that lessons in dwelling—understood as lessons in "living within limits and contradictions—of views from somewhere"—are available and vital for all, as are their rewards, which do not amount to knowledge per se but rather the "connections and unexpected openings" born of embracing one's partial view and, therefore, one's entanglement with that which one seeks to know.[147]

One of the most important ends of critical regionalist poetics is to engender community, new ways of saying "we." As Spivak proposes, the telepoetic creation of new collectivities may be one of the most politically radical offerings of literature.[148] From at least as far back as Kant, the social function of aesthetic experience has been theorized as bringing forth: "a virtual *sensus communis*, an intersubjective community that is to be made, not simply found."[149] Taking this premise in a more pointedly political direction, Adorno likewise underscores the futurity of such a community: "Aesthetic experience, Adorno argues, expresses a collectivity that does not yet exist because it would be the result of a future social transformation."[150] Critical regionalist texts differ from their regionalist predecessors in projecting the collectivity they construct into the future instead of the past. Another important difference is that, whereas the latter located collective belonging in the nation, in the former, regional belonging is, as Spivak and Butler suggest, liberated from nationalist discourses.

In fact, one of the most salient differences between classical regionalist discourses and critical regionalist discourses is that the latter dissolve the link between the region and the nation that the former reinforced. In the literary texts I go on to analyze, in stark contrast to the midcentury political discourses amid which they arise, the nation is not the primary frame through which the region is understood. In this respect, they anticipate postnationalist ("post" in an aspirational rather than purely descriptive sense) veins of critical regionalism. For example, in *Who Sings the Nation-State?*, Spivak and Butler understand the stakes of critical regionalism to include recognizing and fostering modes of regional solidarity and political agency that go "over and under nationalisms."[151] They define critical regionalism as the pursuit of a "rigorously non-nationalistic" mode of belonging, a new way of saying "we" that pries the concept of citizenship loose from birthplace and language.[152] For critical regionalists, then, the region need not be limited to a single geographic or political territory and might include transnational and diasporic communities.

Challenging nationalism as a basis for communal belonging not only allows critical regionalism to articulate collective identities more appropriate to today's world of dislocation and mass migration; it also combats the exclusionary logic of the nation. One of the ways I conceive of critical regionalism, then, is as a way of recuperating the Heideggerian concept of dwelling from Heidegger's nativist politics. Critical regionalism is explicitly grounded in Heidegger's thought; both Frampton and Paul Ricoeur, whose work serves as Frampton's point of departure, were readers of Heidegger. Frampton cites "Building, Dwelling, Thinking" directly, crediting Heidegger with offering him "a critical vantage point from which to behold this phenomenon of universal placelessness."[153]

How does one square this debt to Heidegger with the ostensibly progressive, anti-nationalistic project for which critical regionalism has been appropriated? As I allude to the introduction, Heidegger's ontology of place is famously out of tune with the opportunities afforded to build new forms of belonging and community in a postcolonial world characterized by mobility and intercultural exchange.[154]

As Laura Bieger recognizes, however, returning to Heidegger's writings in *Poetry, Language, Thought* allows for a less reactionary and Romantic reading of the German thinker's phenomenology.[155] It is here that Heidegger reminds us that we *"must ever learn to dwell,"* that dwelling is "a staying with things," and that the root of the word (in *wohnen*) means "to grow accustomed to, or to feel at home in, a place."[156] If we understand belonging, as these essays encourage us to do, as achieved through the ongoing activities of dwelling and learning to dwell, it ceases to be a birthright, an intrinsic status that separates insiders from outsiders, and becomes instead an ethos, a way of being in the world that is available (even if not readily or easily arrived at) to anyone committed to practicing it. It is this latter sense of dwelling that this book seeks to recover.

The project of recuperating a more useful, progressive notion of dwelling from Heidegger goes hand in hand with the project of rescuing regionalism from the notion that it is inherently retrograde. For example, when Guimarães Rosa rejects the term "regionalista," he explains (somewhat inaccurately) to his German interviewer, Günter Lorenz, that being called a regionalist in Brazil is like being called a *Heimatschriftsteller*: one who writes about his native land.[157] Guimarães Rosa, who along with his wife helped grant Brazilian visas to those fleeing the Nazis, was sensitized to the connotations of this term in Germany, which imply a Romantic, agrarian, and anti-modern ideology that fed into National Socialism.[158] The question for critical regionalists such as Guimarães Rosa is how to valorize dwelling in regional particularity while rejecting the most problematic parts of Heidegger's legacy: "his reactionary longings to return to an Arcadian place untouched by modernity."[159] One of the arguments of this book is that the aesthetics devised by the likes of Guimarães Rosa anticipate a new approach to dwelling, at which theorists have only recently arrived via transnational, postcolonial, and queer approaches to issues of migration, diaspora, and discrimination.[160] In fact, I propose that such authors recognized, far ahead of their time, what Bieger calls "the tenuous, quintessentially performative nature of belonging."[161] What this mode of dwelling takes directly from Heidegger, however, is the imaginative or poetic nature of the thought that brings one into dwelling: "It is, indeed, the ability to think that enables both building and dwelling. Yet this notion of thinking is by no means coolly rational and disembodied; rather, it is tied to an affective, sensual, and quintessentially imaginative perception of the world."[162]

Perhaps counterintuitively, the alarming trends of neo-nationalism and nativism taking hold around many parts of the world make recuperating a neo-Heideggerian notion of dwelling or place-building of renewed urgency. We cannot address these threats without acknowledging the phenomena to which they react. These include not only large-scale migration and displacement spurred by political instability, climate crisis, and uneven gradients of economic opportunity but also a generalized sense of deracination, a loss of local identity and tradition that is the result of decades of neoliberal globalization: "The more that global interconnections increase, the more local roots tend to matter—for better or worse."[163] These are the very problems anticipated by thinkers from Ricoeur to Frampton to Rama at the dawn of the neoliberal era, although these thinkers did not generally consider the way discourses of regional resistance could be, would be, and in fact already had been, appropriated by the Right.[164]

From the vantage point of the twenty-first century, characterized by the convergence of humanitarian and ecological crises, the challenge of how to be critical of "late capitalism's dislocating effects" without becoming suspicious of "dislocated peoples themselves" animates debates about how to reconcile environmental and postcolonial discourses.[165] Such a reconciliation is urgently needed, according to Glissant, to heal relations with the land that have been damaged for colonized peoples subject to forced migration, displacement, territorial and economic imperialism, and the collapse of spatial differences by the circulation of capital.[166] The problem, however, is that when conceived in nostalgic or mystic terms—going back to the land or fetishizing premodern ways of life—"An aesthetics of the earth seems, as always, anachronistic or naïve: reactionary or sterile."[167] Critical regionalist texts, I contend, anticipate some of these problems and, through their thickly textured, sensorial, and affective evocations of place, respond with "an aesthetics of belonging through language and literature."[168] This sense of belonging does not stem from being firmly rooted in a place, tradition, or identity; instead it is cultivated through aesthetic experience, through poetic, relational, and situated thought.

In short, contending with nativism requires a shift wherein dwelling is no longer seen as the rarefied privilege of those who are "at home."

In fact, as Sara Ahmed points out, "Home is implicitly [and problematically] constructed as a purified space of belonging in which the subject is too comfortable to question the limits or borders of her or his experience."[169] In contrast, the concept of *learning* to dwell presupposes that one is not "at home" to begin with, either because one has traveled or migrated or because "there is already strangeness and movement within the home."[170] "Dwelling" in the sense that I am using it is more a matter of building a home, making oneself at home, than already being at home.

WHAT IS ASKED OF THE THINKER: CRITICAL REGIONALIST METHODOLOGY

"How can we learn to dwell properly without succumbing to a highly problematic ideology of place that turns many of us into strangers and outsiders?"[171] How do we build a collective sense of belonging without othering? How might we conceive of citizenship untethered from the nation-state? How do we uphold "the goal of place-conscious and place-sensitive culture" while recognizing that it "need not dictate a place-bound, stationary lifestyle of monogamous relationship to just one place"?[172] When we formulate and answer such questions, there is always a contrapuntal play between, on the one hand, insisting on the value of the idea of place, home, and differential identity and, on the other hand, deconstructing or disrupting these concepts before they become reductive, limiting, or exclusionary.

For this reason, critical regionalists such as Herr have called on Adorno's negative dialectics as a counterweight (or dialectical corrective) to Heidegger's ontology. Although Heidegger's place in Adorno's thought has received relatively little attention, Samir Gandesha understands Heidegger to be one of Adorno's primary interlocutors, the former's thought serving as a foil for the latter's.[173] Gandesha points out that in spite of the apparent antagonisms between the two, "Adorno and Heidegger [. . .] approach the same constellations of problems, though from opposite sides."[174] Both are deeply suspect of positivist thought and abstract philosophical concepts that purport to transcend the particularity of language, form, and lived experience, though they express this reduction of experience in different terms—forgetting for Heidegger and reification for Adorno—and both turn to the aesthetic as the realm where the specificity of experience might be preserved.[175]

For both, moreover, what the work of art renders perceptible is precisely the failure of philosophical thought to grasp its object and the need to think differently.[176] Where the two thinkers diverge, however, is that Heidegger holds out greater faith that thinking poetically can solve the problem; he suggests that dwelling beyond metaphysics is enough, whereas for Adorno, the aesthetic realm does not offer a satisfactory solution to historical problems; being at home in language can never be enough. Negative dialectics is, among other things, a way of constantly reminding oneself of this inadequacy, of rousing "the dreamer from the dream," and vigilantly deferring the resolution of having arrived.[177] Adorno writes: "Today we should have to add: it is part of morality not to be at home in one's home."[178] Statements such as these distance Adorno's thought from Heidegger, bringing him closer to Levinasian ethics with its emphasis on dislocation and the importance of encountering and welcoming alterity.[179] It is no coincidence, of course, that Adorno and Levinas both wrote from the experience of exile.

Whereas Heidegger's notion of dwelling is, on its own, ill-equipped to account for the kinds of communities that need to be imagined and built in a world increasingly defined by dislocation, migration, and cross-pollination of ideas and cultures, Herr, noting the debt to Adorno in critical regionalist thought, claims that "Adorno provides a framework within which cross-cultural, interdisciplinary, and subnational readings necessarily find a home."[180] In fact, she offers Adorno's injunction for the thinker to be "both within things and outside them" as a possible definition of critical regionalism.[181] In *Minima Moralia*, Adorno writes that "the morality of thought lies in a procedure that is neither entrenched nor detached, neither blind nor empty, neither atomistic nor consequential. [. . .] Nothing less is asked of the thinker today than that he should be at every moment both within things and outside them."[182] This dialectical movement between immanence of experience and critical distance is one of the defining characteristics of Adorno's philosophy. For the critical regionalist thinkers in his wake, moreover, it follows from this dialectical imperative that dwelling in and with the local, far from amounting to provincialism, is the only way to think beyond it: "Knowledge can only widen horizons by abiding so insistently with the particular that its isolation is dispelled."[183] This dialectical notion of abiding with the particular in order to think at once with and beyond it guides the aesthetic projects at the heart of this study as well as my own methodology, which is grounded in close reading even as it engages broad theoretical conversations, and which seeks to attend to the local historical context and critical reception of each text even as it draws connections between different places and times.

In fact, the way I have come to understand it, critical regionalism offers an alternative to humanistic conceptions of world literature, from Goethe to Wellek to more recent Habermasian articulations, in which, according to Mariano Siskind, "What seems to be lost is the opaqueness of cultural otherness and the intermittent failures of communication and global translation."[184] Along the lines of the approach Hoyos has advocated, critical regionalism as a methodology for literary study is bottom-up and skeptical of universal legibility, of "the transparency of the novel as an instrument of cultural translation."[185] Such an approach would require, as both Spivak and Chiappini urge, that we pay attention to the aesthetic construction of particularity, especially when dealing with non-Western literatures, those that have traditionally been read as vehicles for cultural content.[186]

One of the political and ethical functions of critical regionalist poetics as I use the term is the preservation of what Glissant calls the "right to opacity" of formerly colonized cultures.[187] Importantly, in Glissant's theory of poetics of relation, opacity engenders rather than forecloses relation with the cultural other by separating out solidarity and affective relation from forms of comprehension that border on mastery and possession: "To feel in solidarity with [the other] or to build with him or to like what he does, it is not necessary for me to grasp him."[188] Similarly, Apter values literary style for its ability to mark differences, aporia, and modes of experience that are necessarily lost in translation at the same time as she insists we must continue to translate and to read about other cultures anyway. The value of staying in relation with the other who remains opaque and ungraspable lies at the heart of Levinasian ethics, but along with new ethicists like Butler and Spivak, Glissant and Apter emphasize the particular freight of such ethical relations in postcolonial contexts.

To be clear, the renunciation of the impulse to grasp in this vein of theory ought not to be confused with liberal shrinking in the face of difference, what Ahmed calls the "assumption that 'we' in the West cannot encounter [those] who live elsewhere."[189] On the contrary, the ability to recognize and learn from the local knowledge and situational consciousness of others even when one does not and cannot fully understand them requires dialectical thought in Adorno's sense: it requires both cultivating critical awareness of one's inability to grasp and continued commitment to staying with, living with this challenge.

A critical regionalist approach takes regionalism to be, as Chiappini suggests, a particularist view of the whole world.[190] In concert with thinkers such as Kalimán and Demaría, Chiappini proposes that the local and the provincial are not places to be contrasted with the universal and the metropolitan but, rather, ways of thinking, ways of giving form to particular perspective.[191] Where Chiappini's work stands out from most cultural-studies approaches to the region, however, is the attention she pays to *literary form* in shaping thought and engendering the experience of the particular. Following Adorno's view that the lyric makes the general perceptible through the particular, Chiappini points out that literary studies is always, in a certain sense, a regionalist endeavor: it is how we think from the specificity of a text outward toward larger concepts without ever fully abandoning, transcending, or betraying the particularity of our starting point.[192] For these reasons, she argues, it is time that regionalist literature assumes its spot at the center rather than the periphery of comparative literature and, crucially, that it be studied *as literature*.[193]

Yet not only are the old, Eurocentric models of comparative literature inadequate for the task but new multiculturalist approaches also have their pitfalls, such as being excessively celebratory of fusion and fluidity, without taking into account the losses that accompany hybridity in a world of (often forced) migration.[194] As Jennifer Wenzel observes, the problem with many world literature approaches in the twenty-first century is that "they often imagine a world of circulation without friction, where unresolved histories of economic ecological, and epistemological violence are elided, naturalized, or euphemized."[195] This critique, though emerging only recently in debates over comparative and world literature, has long been familiar to scholars of Latin America.[196] For Chiappini, for example, Habermas's approach simply repeats at a global scale what Freyre's model of regionalism had done at a national scale in Brazil in the 1920s and '30s.[197] In other words, it is the ideology of *mestizaje* all over again. What we need instead, writes Chiappini, is to imagine "the possibility of a literature of the region, and also a literature of the world" that helps us better understand "the economic-touristic literarization of regional space," including the hawking of "clichés of authenticity."[198] In other words, regionalist-cum-world literature needs to be self-reflexive about how the region is produced through literature. This is precisely the critical gesture of critical regionalist poetics as I understand it. Yet, as I have been emphasizing, critical regionalist poetics is not merely a mode of critique; it is also a pedagogical mode invested in situated knowledges. Its contribution to comparative literature, then, would be to remind us that "the only way to find a larger vision is to be somewhere in particular."[199]

If we take critical regionalism as a model for a renewed comparative literature, the discipline would necessarily need to go beyond national and philological studies, but it would also have to go beyond the deconstruction of such categories to account for the way that "regionality is anchored also in the senses, in the gaze and in the skin, in hearing and in smell, in the voice and in silence, in the stomach and in the heart."[200] It is the phenomenological roots of dwelling that I find missing in the deconstructivist vein of critical regionalism in cultural studies. As such, though I join thinkers such as Moreiras in understanding critical regionalism as an anti-identitarian practice insofar as it reveals the contingent and relational nature of categories that have historically been treated in essentialist terms, this is not all critical regionalism is for me. On the contrary, I find the original aesthetic-pedagogical project of Frampton's critical regionalism—teaching one to attend sensorially to one's local surroundings—equally valuable when it comes to appreciating what some midcentury writers understood all too well: that if safeguarding local particularity cannot be a matter only of gaining visibility and representation, nor can it be a matter only of deconstructing stereotypes and reified images; it must also be a matter of turning more outsiders into local dwellers, or at least challenging them to imagine this perspective, even if they are, as they must be, persistently woken from this dream.

The texts to which I turn my attention in the chapters to come do not allow their readers to indulge for long in the fantasy of merging with the world related—of going native—but nor do they allow them to turn away from the work of learning to dwell. This would be to take the easier route, which Benjamin describes as soaring above the text as if in an airplane, rather than traversing it and submitting to its landscape.[201] In this way, these critical regionalist texts safeguard the worlds they imagine from being reduced to concepts or passive objects of knowledge. They demand instead that the reader remain in close, protracted relation with that which cannot be reduced or grasped. In this sense, they not only shape the reader but also, potentially, if we heed them, the discipline of comparative literature.

CHAPTER 2

Embodying the Local

In "No soy un aculturado . . ." ("I Am Not an Acculturated Man . . ."),
the speech José María Arguedas gave upon receiving the Inca Garcilaso
de la Vega prize in 1968, he describes Peru as "an infinite source of
creativity" whose diverse landscapes have much to teach their would-be
colonizers:

> The warm valleys of the coast and the sierra, agriculture
> at an altitude of more than 13,000 feet, ducks who speak
> in highland lakes where all the insects of Europe would be
> drowned, and hummingbirds who rise up to the sun to drink
> in its fire and to flame over all the flowers of the world.
> Being here and imitating others would turn out to be rather
> shameful. In technology they will surpass us and dominate
> us, for how long we do not know, but in art we can already
> oblige them to learn from us and we can do it without even
> budging from right here.[1]

What begins as a description of unique Andean landscapes, flora, and
fauna gives way to a critique of the absurdity of the charge that the
cultural forms of this region are merely derivative of those of metropol-

itan centers. Arguedas alludes here to his position in a well-publicized polemic with Julio Cortázar:[2] although the Peruvian writer feels technically inferior to his more cosmopolitan contemporaries, he finds the idea of imitating them or relocating unthinkable. Instead, using the first-person plural, he suggests a radical mission for Andean authors: planting one's feet firmly in the local landscape and obliging the world to come close, to learn from "nosotros." As suggested by the images of the ducks who *speak* at altitudes where European insects could not breathe and the hummingbirds who soar to the sun and return unharmed to share its blazing light with the flowers, the education this world has to offer to outsiders is not reducible to information or technique. It consists instead of the opportunity to acclimatize one's body to new landscapes, attune one's ears to new forms of speech, and expose one's psyche to new cosmovisions.

Shortly before committing suicide in 1969, Arguedas wrote to his Argentine editor, Gonzalo Losada, requesting that this speech appear as a prologue to the novel he was working on, *El zorro de arriba y el zorro de abajo* (*The Fox from Up Above and the Fox from Down Below*), which would be published posthumously in 1971. Although Losada included it as an epilogue rather than a prologue, the effect of placing the two texts together under one binding has often been that *Los zorros*, as Arguedas referred to his last project, is read in terms of its success or failure at realizing the goals articulated in the speech. These include innovating based on local forms and languages and finding ways to make Andean realities transmissible to outside audiences through literature. Here it is clear that Arguedas saw serving as an intermediary between the Quechua-informed Andean culture in which he was raised and the Westernized culture from which most of his readers hail as his life's mission. Although born to *misti*[3] parents, Arguedas was brought up by Quechua-speaking servants. His bilingualism and his deep identification with Indigenous (what he calls *indio*)[4] culture are central to his work as an anthropologist and writer of fiction. Whereas Indigenous cultures have historically been marginalized, spurned, and seen as a source of shame by Peruvian elites, Arguedas aims to amplify and valorize Quechua components of the national heritage. His hope is that fortifying the connections between *indio* and *misti* cultures in Peru will not result in the imposition of Western values on Quechua culture, requiring that the latter "renounce its soul [. . .] that is to say, that it should become acculturated."[5] Instead, Arguedas aims to instill Indigenous values and forms in the dominant culture.

The mission articulated in "No soy un aculturado . . ." contains many of the key elements of the theory of transculturation that Ángel Rama develops in *La transculturación narrativa en América Latina* (1982), citing Arguedas as the exemplary transculturator. Yet one of my contentions in this chapter is that the long shadow cast by Rama—more specifically by the predominant, "tame" understanding of his theory of transculturation[6]—on the reception of Arguedas's work leads to a reductive understanding of the project Arguedas articulates in "No soy un aculturado . . ." and attempts in *Los zorros*. Although both ideas are present in Rama's *La transculturación narrativa*, neither the aesthetic-pedagogical mission—"in art we can already oblige them to learn from us"—nor the importance of teaching in situ—"we can do it without even budging from right here"—alluded to by Arguedas is fully captured by the common understanding of transculturation as an act of cultural translation or hybridization. In this chapter, I take these tenets as central to the mission Arguedas undertakes in *Los zorros*.

I contend, moreover, that the form of the novel imparts to the reader from the metropole an ethical education in how to dwell amid alterity. The notoriously difficult text demands that the reader navigate cacophonous heterogeneity, untranslated or untranslatable languages, and selective opacity: ideas, images, and sounds that will be recognizable and legible to some readers but not others. In asking the reader to grapple with what they cannot (yet) understand and relate to, the novel recasts belonging as *learnable* ethos: a way of dwelling in the phenomenological sense of moving through and attending to one's environment. This intimate and embodied relationship to the Andean landscape is implicitly and explicitly valorized in *Los zorros*. Though it is not universally accessible nor readily acquired, neither is the possibility of achieving it through the act of reading completely foreclosed. The text thus sets an ethical challenge for the reader from the metropole: that they, against all odds, learn from a book how to hear the songs of an unfamiliar world. At the same time, the task of the Indigenous, bicultural, or bilingual reader is just as urgent: that they draw on their embodied memories to make these songs resonate in the present.[7]

I consider this pedagogy grounded in embodied experience a form of critical regionalist poetics, and I propose that foregrounding it casts Rama's theory of transculturation in a new light. Rama argues that Latin American authors have the best chance of preserving local traditions if, instead of defensively clinging to rigid forms, they *selectively* and *deliberately* incorporate modern forms. The role of the mediator, then, is not simply to translate (to make the local universally legible), but rather to buffer the uneven encounter between local and cosmopolitan cultures. This tenet, though often overlooked in the reception of Rama's work, is central to Frampton's articulation of critical regionalism: "The fundamental strategy of Critical Regionalism is to mediate the impact of universal civilization with elements derived *indirectly* from the peculiarities of a particular place."[8] As I laid out in the previous chapter, this concept of mediation-as-buffering lies at the heart of both critical regionalism and narrative transculturation as I understand them. This subtle point, which is missed in the most reductive interpretations of transculturation as simply a model of fusion or hybridity, is harder to overlook if one attends to Rama's reading of Frankfurt School Critical Theory.[9]

Like Paul Ricoeur, whose seminal (for the field of critical regionalism) essay, "Universal Civilization and National Cultures" (1961), gave voice to the anxiety that burgeoning consumer culture, mass industrial production of goods, and widespread dissemination of new media and technologies threatened to flatten cultural differences between regions, Rama was a reader of Walter Benjamin.[10] Unlike Ricoeur, who saw the threat of "being swallowed up in a vague syncretism" as applying equally to European cultures as to those of their former colonies, Rama understood that Frankfurt School critiques of the reification of experience resulting from industrial modernization had specific implications in postcolonial contexts.[11] Among the sources of alienation with which Latin American subjects had to contend in the postwar years was living in an environment inundated with imported technologies and cultural forms.[12] Rama saw lucidly that if regionalist and indigenist authors wanted to break free from cultural dependency, they could not continue to passively adopt European bourgeois forms such as the realist novel as if these were neutral techniques.[13] José Eduardo Gonzáles thus discerns in Rama echoes of "Benjamin's warning about traditional forms of art nullifying the new political content being expressed."[14] In the wariness of reproducing old ideologies by reproducing old forms, which underlies Rama's reading of Benjamin as well as Frampton's critical regionalism, moreover, lies a debt to Theodor Adorno's theory of avant-garde formal experimentation as indispensable to radical thought.

To be clear, I do not mean to undercut the originality or the Latin Americanness of Rama's work by suggesting it is merely derivative of Benjamin's or Adorno's thought. Rather, the Uruguayan critic performs the transculturating process he describes by combining elements of continental Critical Theory with the particular material and cultural history of Latin America. It is precisely in the unusual marriage of Adornian thought and "proximity to Latin American cultural texts" where Román de la Campa locates the originality of Rama's work.[15] Underscoring this influence is important, not for its own sake but because it allows us to recuperate a version of Rama's transculturation that is more resilient in the face of twenty-first-century critiques.

One of the most salient critiques of narrative transculturation is that its emphasis on harmony over dissonance, translation over opacity, and reconciliation over betrayal does not allow it to fully grapple with the violent colonial legacy that colors cultural heterogeneity in Latin America.[16] This critique centers on the way transculturation upholds the ideology of *criollismo* or *mestizaje*, which subsumes Indigenous and European heritage into a unified if hybridized identity for the individual nation or the Latin American region writ large. Introducing instead a more conflictive notion of heterogeneity, Antonio Cornejo Polar finds fault with the way such discourses present a false vision of harmony and unity, mystifying "that which is obviously fractured and belligerent, proposing figurations that are ultimately pertinent to those with an interest in imagining our societies as smooth and not at all conflictive spaces of coexistence."[17] Foremost among those served by "the great homogenizing discourse" was the newly independent nation of the nineteenth century, which had to invent and project "a community integrated enough to be recognized—and to recognize itself—as an independent nation."[18]

As Gareth Williams has argued, by the mid-twentieth century in many parts of Latin America, this mantle is taken up by the populist state attempting to define *el pueblo* as a unified social body. The task of consolidating the modern Latin American nation-state in the era of national populism (1940s–1970s) required the successful integration of the working classes and the peasants into the nation.[19] According to Williams, the narrative of transculturation serves to placate and interpellate these sectors of society, granting them representation while simultaneously demanding their assimilation and denying their self-determination. Williams emphasizes, however, that this is not the only possible version of transculturation; attending to and articulating cultural heterogeneity also has the potential to produce "a persistently and recalcitrantly violent collision."[20] Yet, according to Williams, Rama's "tamed" version of transculturation stays "firmly within the horizons of national (capitalist) modernization and its discourses of cultural integration and development" and thus contributes to a hegemonic notion of *criollismo*.[21] Cornejo Polar shares these concerns but distinguishes between Rama's notion of transculturation and the afterlife of the term, writing that that "the idea of transculturation has become more and the most sophisticated cover for the category of *mestizaje*."[22] As a discourse that is ideologically expedient for the state seeking to manufacture national unity, this "tamed" transculturation ignores what Silvia Spitta calls "the dystopic, discordant side" of mediating a multicultural heritage rooted in colonial violence and trauma.[23]

Rama's *La transculturación narrativa* may exude optimism, emphasizing harmony, successful translation of difference, and resolution of conflict, but it is not without ambiguity and nuance. Rama stresses that transculturators must select techniques that "translate exactly the imaginary of Latin American peoples" and that, instead of simply accumulating diverse source materials, they must "unitarily bind" the differences among these and "assume [*asumir*] the discordances and the problems of cultural collision."[24] It is worth noting first of all that Rama does not ignore the fissures and conflicts inherent in Latin American cultural heterogeneity. Furthermore, the last turn of phrase I have cited is not as unambiguous as the first two. *Asumir*, to assume, accept, or take on (as in to assume responsibility), does not connote "to absorb or transcend" so much as "to face or grapple with." In this chapter, I probe this ambiguity and propose that if we are to understand José María Arguedas as an exemplary transculturator, as Rama claims, then we must consider the tension between striving for communication and harmony on the one hand and contending with difference, conflict, and failure on the other as fundamental to the process. We must reconceive of the work of the mediator as a self-reflexive and negative process whose goals include visibilizing what Anna Tsing calls the friction that arises out of "heterogenous and uneven encounters."[25] In this view, the impossibility of achieving exact translation and seamless unity is not the undoing of transculturation but rather is integral to its operation; the transculturator's inevitable failure is a feature, not a glitch.

Though I believe this negativity is latent in Rama's elaboration of narrative transculturation, neither Rama nor the majority of his readers has emphasized it. Scholars have recognized, however, that this negatively inflected conception of transculturation more accurately describes how many of the authors Rama cites approached their roles as mediators. In fact, Spitta finds that the works Rama offers as examples of transculturated texts often belie what she calls Rama's "easy and reconciliatory syncretism" and that they are able to register the disconnects suppressed in the most reductive versions of transculturation because of their avant-garde form.[26] Among the techniques Spitta highlights is the self-reflexivity of the text on the difficulty—if not the impossibility—of narrating stories of upheaval and trauma. Together with linguistic experimentation and the sundering of novelistic conventions, this meta-textual self-interrogation is a fundamental structural component of *Los zorros* as well as the other works I consider exemplary of critical regionalist poetics.

As such, I propose that Arguedas's last novel might prompt us to reread Rama against the grain. Rama's exposition of his theory of transculturation centers on Arguedas's earlier novel, *Los ríos profundos* (1958), and largely ignores *Los zorros*. Following Rama's lead, many subsequent critics have concluded that the posthumous novel, when not chalked up to a failed or aborted project, represents a departure from or renunciation of the author's earlier mission.[27] Alberto Moreiras, for example, argues that *Los zorros* represents the apotheosis of the transculturating project pursued throughout the writer's career.[28] Curiously, however, others have read it in a nearly opposite sense, as demonstrating the radical potential of the framework. For example, in *Cultura Andina y forma novelesca: Zorros y danzantes en la última novela de Arguedas* (*Andean Culture and Fictional Form: Foxes and Dancers in Arguedas's Last Novel*), Martin Lienhard argues that whereas Arguedas's treatment of Andean aesthetic and cultural forms such as orality, music, and dance in earlier novels may be read as a politically innocuous form of transculturation, *Los zorros* radically subverts dominant discursive practices.[29] In this avant-garde novel organized by an Andean cosmovision, Lienhard argues, the form of the novel is thoroughly infiltrated by oral culture, and the dominant culture is represented from an Indigenous perspective.[30] Building off of Lienhard's reading, William Rowe locates the politics of *Los zorros* in an epistemological shift away from rational knowledge grounded in sight, language, and abstract reason and toward a more intimate form of *conocimiento* grounded in sound, music, and nature.[31] Rowe's reading of musicality and sonority in Arguedas in many ways guides my attempt to recuperate the congenital hopefulness of Rama's model even as I draw out the negative side of transculturation.

Moreiras implicitly refutes the readings of Lienhard and Rowe—and any that grant *Los zorros* the power to resist and subvert the dominance of Western culture—by taking Rama on directly and arguing that *Los zorros* reveals transculturation to be no different from acculturation, ultimately a renunciation of cultural difference rather than a means of preserving it: "Both appropriation and transculturation are purchased at the price of service to historical hegemony: not so much an over-coming of modernization as a submission to it."[32] Moreiras reads *Los zorros* as staging an "implosion of meaning" that calls into question the politics of difference celebrated not only in Arguedas's earlier novels but also in Latin American magical realism writ large.[33] Beyond testifying to the impossibility of the redemptive project of transculturation, Morei-ras claims, the novel unmasks the more sinister side of transculturation-as-acculturation: the erasure or silencing of that which does not enter squarely into the dominant system.[34] As such, Arguedas's accomplish-ment in *Los zorros* is for Moreiras a negative one: "The novel triumphs in its very failure" by bringing the machine of transculturation to a stop.[35] While Moreiras focuses on the negativity of the novel and Rowe on its sensory epistemology, I move between these approaches to attend to the education of the reader that follows in the wake of the collapse of communicability and identity.

In other words, though I join Moreiras in emphasizing the break-down of identitarian categories in *Los zorros*, I do not join him in de-claring transculturation exhausted, full stop. On the contrary, I attempt to rehabilitate an understanding of Rama's transculturation as already containing the negativity manifest in Frampton's version of critical re-gionalism. Unlike Gonzáles, though, I draw out the Adornian influence on Rama not by attending to the Uruguayan critic's reading of continen-tal theory but rather by taking a closer look at Arguedas, particularly the Arguedas of *Los zorros*. Reconstructing a model of transculturation from *Los zorros* demands that we temper Rama's celebratory tone, but it also allows us to recuperate elements of Rama's theory that have been overlooked. These include the model of commitment Rama identifies in Arguedas, one that is grounded in immersion in material life and community, and the suggestion that the ultimate end of transculturation might not be simply to represent the rural subaltern in terms legible to the reader from the metropole but rather to impart an affective and sensorial education to the latter.

One of the characteristics Rama emphasizes in the writers he calls transculturators is having "been strongly affected by the specific situ-ation of the cultures to which they belong and the patterns by which those cultures modernize."[36] Though it is worth putting pressure on the question of to what degree Arguedas does belong to the cultures he represents (and what it means to belong), few scholars have attended to the affective relationship (in the Spinozean sense of affecting and being affected) between writer and region as Rama has. Rama emphasizes, for example, that rather than expressing his social commitment in ideological terms as many of his contemporaries did, Arguedas expressed political views and a sense of justice that were grounded in and elaborated through lived personal experience. This principle of "becoming immersed in real, concrete life and [. . .] vividly sharing in the life of a community" is the ethical lodestar of the works featured in *Dwelling in Fiction*.[37] Specifically, it is the phenomenological experience of dwelling that underpins these authors' sense of place, and it is this sense of place that they endeavor to pass on to their readers. As I have argued in the introduction, the political and ethical work of these texts thus lies in inciting in their readers a sense of concern for, entanglement with, and (albeit necessarily incomplete) identification with local places and communities. This ethos is engendered by asking the reader who comes as an outsider to share in the rhythms and sensations that characterize daily life for those who dwell there.

In what follows, I argue that rather than breaking with the author's previous oeuvre, Arguedas's posthumous novel becomes even more explicit, if less self-assured, in modeling for the reader how to ethically relate to local forms of life—namely, by cultivating an embodied and affective relationship to landscape and language. Though I concur with those who argue that *Los zorros* offers a critique of the essentialism and false harmony from which many versions of transculturation do not fully escape, in my reading, the novel's intervention does not end with critique.

JOSÉ MARÍA ARGUEDAS AS CRITICAL REGIONALIST

The reader who encounters *El zorro de arriba y el zorro de abajo* prefaced by "No soy un aculturado" or, for that matter, by Arguedas's previous oeuvre, might reasonably expect a novel set in the Andean highlands. Instead, *Los zorros* portrays the rapidly industrializing port city of Chimbote, which became the central hub of the global fish meal economy in the 1960s. The highland landscape appears only as evoked by the memories and songs of Indigenous migrants. Far from a straightforward representation of Chimbote, moreover, *Los zorros* is a self-critical reflection on the task of representing a space to which neither the author nor the presumed readership belongs. Complicating things further, the vast majority of the characters are immigrants and foreigners, throwing into relief the degree to which belonging in Chimbote is an activity rather than a birthright.

The novel contains five chapters, sections, or *hervores*, which elaborate a fictional version of Chimbote and trace the interactions between the diverse populations that make up its social fabric: highland *indios* who have migrated to the coast to work as fishermen, sex workers, and open-air market vendors, capitalist industrialists running the fish meal plant, mafiosos facilitating the exploitation of the former group by the latter group, and union organizers, foreign clergymen, and nonprofit workers struggling to make sense of and intervene in this intricate web of economic and power relations. The *hervores* depicting life in Chimbote are interspersed with *diarios*, autobiographical diary entries written in the voice of an author figure who chronicles his suicidal thoughts, his embattled attempt to complete what he feels to be an impossible project (the novel), and his fraught relationship with prominent intellectual figures of the Latin American boom.

The two eponymous foxes, minor deities from Andean mythology, make appearances in both the *hervores* and *diarios*. According to pre-Columbian myths collected by the seventeenth-century priest Francisco de Ávila, translated into Spanish by Arguedas, and published in *Dioses y hombres de Huarochirí*, these two foxes have met for centuries to exchange perspectives on their respective worlds: the highland *sierras* and the lowland *yungas* and coast. These two regions have been historically marked by cultural, racial, and economic difference: the world up above governed by a feudal *gamonalismo*[38] system reliant on the labor of peasants of Quechua and Aymara descent, who make up the majority of the rural population, and the world down below organized around urban centers such as Lima, and populated by *criollo* elites of Spanish descent. By the time *Los zorros* was composed, however, these categories were becoming destabilized. During Arguedas's career (1930s–1960s), the world up above was rocked by the collapse of the hacienda system and expulsion of Indigenous peoples from the traditional agricultural communities known as *ayllus*, while the world down below was transformed by the increasing presence of international capitalism and industry in the port cities and by the mass migration of displaced peasants to the coast. Whereas the Peruvian population was 80 percent rural and 20 percent urban at the beginning of the twentieth century, this ratio was inverted by the end of the century.[39] Lima saw its population triple between 1940 and 1961, and in the 1960s, the boom of the fish meal industry triggered a massive wave of migration to the coast, a wave that landed in large part in Chimbote, whose population grew from 2,400 to 170,000 inhabitants between 1940 and 1970. As *serrano* immigrants arrived from the highlands to the coast in droves to seek opportunity in the fish meal boom, they brought Indigenous languages, songs, and customs with them. Representing the collision of cultures to be found in Chimbote in the 1960s would, then, require moving beyond binary discourses of the country and the city, above and below, *indios* and *mistis*.

In spite of often being viewed as regionalist and indigenist writer who focused exclusively on the traditional cultures of the highlands, Arguedas was uniquely prepared to represent this new landscape, as he had always understood the Andean region as a site of conflict between cultural universes.[40] Arguedas's literary representations of Indigenous culture differ from traditional Andean *indigenismo* in at least two important respects: whereas *indigenismo* was historically written "from without, from afar, from above, from Lima," Arguedas seeks to provide a perspective from inside Quechua culture, and whereas *indigenismo* tended to focus exclusively on autochthonous communities, Arguedas seeks to depict a complex and heterogeneous Peruvian social reality in which Indigenous people play a central role.[41] From as early on as *Yawar Fiesta* (1941), rather than representing the Indigenous population as a monolithic group existing in isolation from other ethnic groups, he conjures a multifarious social panorama. In other words, Arguedas never offered up a fetishized or essentialist version of autochthonous cultures. According to Estelle Tarica, he gives us instead the intersection of "multiple ethno-racial categories often shading ambiguously into one another," revealing "the porousness of racial boundaries."[42] Such a pluralistic approach, argues Tarica, proves more relevant for understanding the demographic shifts that come with rural–urban migration, globalization, and increased social mobility.[43] This tendency is taken to extremes in *Los zorros*, which challenges the stability and separateness of the categories of above and below, *indio* and *criollo*, *serrano* and *costeño* and foregrounds the difficulty of representing the diverse and ever-evolving social landscape of Chimbote.

These are the very attributes that make Arguedas a critical regionalist writer. As I laid out in the previous chapter, the turn toward understanding regional life as relationally constituted and always imbricated in larger networks of culture, commerce, and power has become a hallmark of critical regionalist studies. In the critical regionalist spirit, *Los zorros* challenges essentialist notions of identity and foregrounds the interactions between what are generally thought of as segregated social and ethnic groups and separate regions. Subtract such interactions, in fact, and nothing would be left of Arguedas's Chimbote; the novel is composed almost entirely of exchanges—at turns intimate and spiritual, at turns conflictive and exploitative—between worlds. This is not only true of the plot of the *relato*, which is made up in large part of dialogue between characters from different backgrounds, but also of the form of the novel, which brings disparate languages, discourses, and forms into a cacophonous, at times barely comprehensible chorus. As Julio Ortega observes, even the diary sections, which initially appear to be written in the monologic voice of the author, are also contaminated by dialogue: in addition to the dialogues between the foxes, the diaries contain multiple sustained instances of direct address, where the author figure appears to dialogue with other writers, principally Juan Rulfo and João Guimarães Rosa.[44]

Another defining feature of critical regionalism reflected in *Los zorros* is its placement of the region within a transnational world and its emphasis on the ability of local communities to generate critiques of the global geopolitical and economic relations in which they find themselves caught up. Breaking the national frame that had defined his previous work, Arguedas includes the Global North within the horizon of Chimbote.[45] The rapid but uneven modernization of Chimbote is presented as bringing its most affluent residents and neighborhoods closer to the global metropolis. The wealthy sector where the foreign priests live is described as a "comunidad millonario que se llama Estados Unidos" ("a millionaire community called the United States"), and the center of the city is described as "limeñizado," "yankizado" ("Limafied," "Yankified").[46] In addition to the looming presence of global capital, in the form of the fish meal plant and its foreign owner, Braschi, non-Peruvian characters, including North American priests and Peace Corps volunteers, play central roles in the narrative. The foreignness of these characters is not presented as categorically different from that of the other non-natives to Chimbote. Whether they be Indigenous migrants who remain connected to the *sierras* like Astro, Antolín Crispín, and Hilario Caullama; transplants from Lima like Balazar who has forgotten how to speak Quechua; or foreigners like Cardozo, a United States–born Latino who speaks the stilted Spanish of a gringo, and Maxwell, a former Peace Corps volunteer who appears to have "gone native," all these outsiders contribute in equal measure to the cultural heterogeneity and Bakhtinian heteroglossia that characterize Arguedas's rendition of the port city.

Notwithstanding the integration of foreigners into this cultural landscape, distrust of *yanki* influence is rampant in Chimbote. Moncada, the sometimes-mad street preacher, rails against the presence of foreigners. Hilario Caulluma, a unionist described as a noble descendant of Incas, claims to mistrust all gringos and asks Padre Cardozo, a proponent of liberation theology, why he doesn't go home and make his revolution there, where it is more urgent. Those who support the foreigners are forever trying to quell conspiracy theories and rumors: that Cardozo works for the CIA or that a godparents' program that pairs indigent children with financial sponsors in the United States secretly kidnaps these children, taking them north to become servants, animal feed, or cannon fodder in the Vietnam War. Although some of these concerns are presented as outlandish and unfounded, Hilario Caullama's critique of Cardozo's mission (and liberation theology as practiced by North American priests in Latin America more generally) is amplified by other characters in the novel. Don Cecilio finds Cardozo insincere, and Maxwell compares the latter unfavorably to Madre Kinsley, a former nun who has abandoned her mission in Chimbote and renounced her Catholic order. Instead of attempting to influence cultures abroad, an undertaking she calls "pathetic," she returns to the United States to educate people there of the spiritual error of imperialism:

> Se dedicaría hasta su muerte a tratar de hacer entender a los norteamericanos que están embruteciéndose en camino de la podredumbre. El dominio y el desprecio directo o meloso sobre las naciones de medio mundo los pudre y los embrutece, porque en lugar de aprender de los viejos pueblos como éste, sólo quieren fomentar rencillas y el caos en ellos y entre ellos con el propósito insensato e imposible de meterlos en un molde y bebérselos después como si fueran una botella de coca-cola.

> She'll devote the rest of her life to trying to make the Americans understand they're becoming stupider all the time and are on the road to decadence. Their control over half of the countries in the world and the fact that they are treating them with direct or honeyed contempt is rotting the Americans and making them stupid because instead of learning from ancient peoples like this one, all they want to do is promote chaos and contention inside them and among them

with the senseless and impossible objective of pouring them
all into one mold and drinking them up afterward as if they
were a bottle of Coca-Cola.[47]

This searing critique is delivered in the voice of Maxwell, who has been
read as a figure for Arguedas.[48] Maxwell, himself a student of Andean
culture, underscores the missed opportunity to learn from ancient cultures rather than demand their assimilation and commodification.

Though Arguedas does not make the explicit connection between the
North American appetite for downing foreign cultures like bottles of
Coca-Cola and the boom, his engagement with prominent and prolific,
internationally read authors in the diaries suggests that he was concerned with the role literature played in stoking this appetite and selling
out Latin American cultures.[49] Given the groundswell of international
readership of Latin American literature in the 1960s, how was Arguedas
to ensure that his own work would not package Andean life for such
facile consumption and instead compel the foreign reader to learn from
its difference?

EMBODIED DIALOGUES

Even if the binary schema suggested by the dialogue between the foxes
from above and below proves too simplistic to account for the pluralistic reality Arguedas depicts, the fundamental question begged by
this dialogue—whether (and how) different worlds can commune and
communicate—still lies at the heart of *Los zorros*. On the one hand,
individuals from different backgrounds regularly dialogue and form al-
liances. In addition to the exchanges between the two foxes, there is
the dialogue between Diego, the mysterious visitor, and don Ángel, the
manager of the fish meal plant (chapter 1), the friendship between the
serrano don Esteban de la Cruz and the *zamba* Moncada (chapter 4),
and the partnership forged between Maxwell and don Cecilio Ramíréz,
a highland immigrant and carpenter who takes Maxwell on as his assis-
tant (part 2). On the other hand, the formal difficulty of the text, characterized by a fragmented narrative structure, ever-shifting focalization,
and a discordant blend of discourses, dialects, and languages, drives
home for the reader the obstacles in the path of cross-cultural communication. As Julio Prieto observes, the dialogues between characters
are not unobstructed either—individuals from different worlds must

learn to communicate despite speaking different languages and having different references—but certain interactions, such as the conversation between don Diego and don Ángel, yield a form of mutual contagion if not total comprehension.[50] Nevertheless, the ability of the novel to facilitate such communion is less assured.

Underscoring this point, the author of the diaries, a fictionalized version of Arguedas,[51] claims that as an outsider to Chimbote, he will never be able to understand this world, let alone communicate it to his audience. His eventual decision to take his own life before finishing the novel seems to cement this impossibility. Remaining consistent with the public image he crafted of himself throughout his career,[52] Arguedas positions himself as an outsider not to the Indigenous community that has migrated to Chimbote but rather to the urban environment itself. In the second diary, he admits that although he has spent over thirty years in cities, he has never understood them, identifying as he does with the *indio* culture of the rural highlands: "Yo soy 'de la lana,' como me decías; de 'la altura,' que en el Perú quiere decir indio, serrano, y ahora pretendo escribir sobre los que tú llamabas 'del pelo,' zambos criollos, costeños civilizados, ciudadanos de la ciudad" ("I am 'de la lana,' as you used to tell me; that is, from 'the high country,' which in Peru means an Indian, a highlander, and now I'm attempting to write about those you used to call 'del pelo,' talking about *criollos zambos*, civilized coastal people, citizens of the city").[53] He stresses, moreover, that his inability to feel at home in urban environments, to understand them, contributes to the difficulty he experiences trying to complete the novel.

Much like the Fox from Up Above, then, the author figure depends on dialogue with the other to learn about the urban, coastal world. In fact, the project that would eventually become *Los zorros* began for Arguedas as an anthropological project that involved quite literally listening to residents of Chimbote. Arguedas conducted and recorded lengthy oral interviews with two highland immigrants: Hilario Mamani (who appears in the novel as Hilario Caullama) and Esteban de la Cruz (who appears under his own name as a former coca grower and mine worker who is dying from the carbon he has accumulated in his lungs). As Fernando Rivera observes, the novel is thus born of the same type of encounter between intellectual and native informant that yields ethnofiction, *testimonios*, and testimonial novels like Miguel Barnet's *Biografía de un cimarrón*, Elizabeth Burgos-Debray's *Me llamo Rigoberta Menchú y así me nació la conciencia*, and Roldolfo Walsh's *Operación Masacre*.[54] Nevertheless, Rivera points out a consequential difference in Arguedas's approach. Beyond transposing these oral accounts into writing, Arguedas transposes them into fiction and introduces the self-reflexive element of the diaries. He thus brings increased scrutiny to the act of mediation carried out by the intellectual, begging the questions: Under what circumstances does cross-cultural dialogue yield successful communication and when does it falter? When does it lead its participants to learn from one another and when does it devolve into exploitative consumption or flattening of difference?

In *Los zorros*, the fundamental difference between the encounters that generate affective and ethical communion and those acts of communication that seem doomed to fail (including the novel itself according to the author of the diaries) is that the former involve embodied interaction and cohabitation whereas the latter rely on the disembodied word to breach societal divides. The relationship between writing and embodiment in Arguedas is a vast topic to which a great deal of scholarship has been devoted, but the important takeaway for this chapter is that Arguedas refuses to accept that writing is irredeemably alienated from bodily presence. Unlike Derrida, however, he does not question the primacy of speech over writing.[55] Instead, in the face of a long tradition that declares writing a fallen form of speech complicit in creating and maintaining hierarchies of power and mechanisms of oppression, Arguedas dedicates his career to forging a written language whose connection to embodied experience of place and community remains intact; he seeks to make of the written word "un vínculo vivo" ("a living link").[56] Rama describes this pursuit as the quest to negate the Saussurian concept of the sign.[57] Rather than treating the word as an arbitrary signifier, Arguedas seeks to rehabilitate the organic relationship between words and things that Foucault associates with premodern epistemes.

As critics from Rowe to Tarica have pointed out, the key to this endeavor lies in Arguedas's use of the Quechua language and its propensity for onomatopoeia. Tarica argues that it is this integration of sound and meaning, rather than oral culture in general, that Arguedas seeks to translate into Spanish.[58] Rowe, in turn, contends that it is Arguedas's recourse to the sonority, musicality, and use of onomatopoeia in Quechua that allows the materiality and animism of the world to saturate the written word, thus infiltrating the Western forms of both the Spanish language and the novel with an Andean cosmovision.[59] In other words, creating "a sonic space" in writing becomes how Arguedas counters the graphic world associated with the conquest and its systems of power and, at the same time, trains the ears of the reader to attend to the

Andean world.[60] This approach yields a "conocimiento vivo" ("living knowledge"), which Rowe sees as reaching its zenith rather than faltering in *Los zorros*.[61]

The paradigmatic example of how the voice of the text becomes a *living connection* to the world in Arguedas's literature is the way that *huaynos*, or Quechua folk songs, conjure distant natural landscapes.[62] In *Los ríos profundos*, these songs carry on their melodies memories and affects that the protagonist Ernesto associates with the rural highlands. Nonhuman songs such as the calls of frogs and insects share this evocative power. These bring solace and fortitude to the young narrator who, like Arguedas, identifies with the highlands and feels alienated from the more urban, Westernized world in which he must live. Song plays a similar role for the migrants in *Los zorros*. The blind beggar and musician Antolín Crispín frequently summons through song the highland landscape he left behind when he migrated to the coast. For example, the song he plays for Florinda and Tinoco conjures Andean mountains and waterfalls in great detail: "Después tocó la introducción al huayno, acordes y melodías improvisadas que describían para Florinda y el cholo cabrón, las montañas y las cascadas chicas de agua, las arañas que se cuelgan desde las matas de espino a los remansos de los ríos grandes" ("Then he played the introduction of the *huayno*, improvising melodies and chords that described for Florinda and the *cholo* pimp the warm Andean foothills and the little waterfalls, the spiders that hang down from thorny bushes towards the pools on the big rivers").[63] Note that it is the chords and melodies, rather than the lyrics, that undertake this work of description.

For Arguedas, the evocative and transformative powers of song, both human and nonhuman, stem from its *voice*, which is by definition in excess of its message.[64] Listening to the voice, as opposed to the message, means attending to tone, timbre, rhythms, and silences and discerning traces of embodied presence in these acoustic attributes. As scholars such as Francine Masiello and Marília Librandi have recently argued, the act of listening for voice in a literary text need not be merely figurative. On the contrary, reading, like listening, is an embodied act. Following Jean-Luc Nancy's affirmation that in order to be heard, the voice must resonate in the body of the listener, Masiello argues that poetic language addresses itself to the reader through its rhythm, tempo, and voice, all of which reverberate in the body as one reads.[65] Not all literature affects the body in equal measure; Masiello argues that poetry does so more than prose. Meanwhile Librandi extends this capacity to certain novels, which she dubs "aural novels"; in these, she argues, both the author and the reader become embodied listeners who register the voices of nonliterate subjects. *Los zorros* is a paradigmatically aural novel in Librandi's sense.

In his last novel, Arguedas reflects explicitly on his career-long ambition to make his language sing, to engage the reader's ear and body, and thus, as Cornejo Polar argues, to return to the written word "its primordial sense of voice."[66] Foremost among the challenges with which the author figure in *Los zorros* grapples is the fear that he has lost this way of using language, which has been called magic, epiphanic, and shamanistic, and even compared to alchemy.[67] In the first diary, he writes that it is only when he is able to recuperate "el roto vínculo con todas las cosas" ("the broken link with all things") that his writing is successful: "Cuando ese vínculo se hacía intenso, podía transmitir a la palabra la materia de las cosas" ("Once that link was strengthened, I was able to put the substance of things into words").[68] Between the challenge of writing about the unfamiliar urban world of Chimbote, his struggle with mental illness, and mounting insecurities exacerbated by ungenerous exchanges with other intellectuals,[69] the author figure begins to fear that those moments of strong connection between the word and the world lie only in his past. It is in part the inability to sustain this vital connection that leads him to suicidal thought.

The novel's preoccupation with the challenge of transmitting the world through the word becomes explicit once again in the dialogue between the two foxes at the end of chapter 1. In this scene, the Fox from Down Below positions himself as the novel's narrator, who has been relating the interactions of fishermen and sex workers in Chimbote, and asks if his highland counterpart has understood:

EL ZORRO DE ABAJO: ¿Entiendes bien lo que digo y cuento?

EL ZORRO DE ARRIBA: Confundes un poco las cosas.

EL ZORRO DE ABAJO: Así es. La palabra, pues, tiene que desmenuzar el mundo. El canto de los patos negros que nadan en los lagos de altura, helados, donde se empoza la nieve derretida, ese canto repercute en los abismos de roca, se hunde en ellos se arrastra en las punas, hace bailar a las flores de las yerbas duras que se esconden bajo el *ichu*, ¿no es cierto?

EL ZORRO DE ARRIBA: Sí, el canto de esos patos es grueso, como de ave grande; el silencio y la sombra de las montañas lo convierte en música que se hunde en cuanto hay.

EL ZORRO DE ABAJO: La palabra es más precisa y por eso puede con-
fundir. El canto del pato de altura nos hace entender todo el ánimo
del mundo.

THE FOX FROM DOWN BELOW: Do you fully understand what I say and
tell you?

THE FOX FROM UP ABOVE: You mix things up a bit.

THE FOX FROM DOWN BELOW: That's the way it is. Well, then, the word
must shatter the world. The song of the black ducks that swim in icy
highland lakes where melted snow is collected—that song re-echoes
from the rocky abysses, and sinks down into them; it's swept over
the bleak high country, making the flowers of the tough herbs hidden
under the *ichu* dance, right?

THE FOX FROM UP ABOVE: Yes, the song of those ducks is deep-toned,
like a large fowl's; the mountain's silence and shadow transforms it
into music that sinks down into everything there is.

THE FOX FROM DOWN BELOW: The word is more precise, and that's why
it can be confusing. The highland duck's song makes the whole spirit
of the world understandable to us.[70]

Though this exchange is often cited as signaling the impossibility of
translating "la materia de las cosas" ("the substance of things") into
words, it is in fact a successful act of communication, one that ends
in the affirmation of a collective "nosotros." The account of the Fox
from Down Below may be hard to follow (for the Fox from Up Above
and for the reader), but the two foxes from different worlds *are* able to
communicate, as evidenced by their agreement that the preceding narrative is muddled by its reliance on words. They arrive at this agreement,
moreover, because they share a common point of reference: the sound
of the duck song. They can both describe its tone and timbre, meaning
that they have both heard it before; they share this auditory memory.

What is more, they share the understanding that when they hear this
music, they are hearing not only the ducks but also the "rocky abysses,"
"the mountain's silence and shadow"—an entire landscape through
which this sound must resonate in order to be heard. Both foxes also
recognize that the world formed through this holistic, embodied, and
auditory way of knowing is "shattered" (*desmenuzado*: shredded, crum-
bled apart, scrutinized, analyzed) by the word, whose precision, abstraction, and cultural specificity introduce alienating distance into our way
of knowing and our way of describing. What allows the foxes' commu-

nication to overcome the damning precision of words is the shared auditory memory of the song of the ducks. This musical way of knowing can be evoked by words because it has been heard before, has resonated in the body of each of the foxes (and, perhaps, too, in some of the readers).

Slightly later on in this same exchange, it becomes clear that in order to communicate his world to one who does not know it, the Fox from Down Below will have to use not only language but also his body and his voice; his account must become like the song of the ducks. Near the conclusion of their conversation, the Fox from Up Above addresses the Fox from Down Below in Quechua:

> *Yanawiku hina takiykamuway atispaqa, asllatapas, Chimbotemanta. Chaymantaqa, imaymanáta, imaynapas, munasqaykita willanakusun ¡Yaw! yunga atoq.* [Como un pato cóntame de Chimbote, oye, zorro yunga. Canta si puedes, un instante. Después hablemos y digamos como sea preciso y cuanto sea preciso.]

> Like a duck tell me about Chimbote, you hear, *yunga* fox! Sing, if you càn, for a moment. Afterward let's talk and just tell me as much as is necessary for as long as is necessary.[71]

The Fox from Up Above suggests that an instant of song will suffice to form a channel of communication that will enable subsequent dialogue. It would seem that slipping into Quechua is also part of what enables the connection in this moment. The Fox from Down Below replies, also in Quechua, describing the diverse odors of Chimbote, those of men and the sea and the fish meal plant, which "se mezclan, hinchan mi nariz y mis oídos" ("[are] mingling, making my nose and ears swell").[72] This synesthetic image recalls the way the blind musician Antolín Crispín conjures all of Chimbote—its sounds, smells, and moving bodies—in the melody of his guitar.[73] Jannine Montauban proposes that smell in *Los zorros* becomes the privileged sense as "a means to access more profound knowledge."[74] Curiously, here, however, the Fox emphasizes his ears as much as his nose as the receptive organs that allow him to perceive all these smells: "Todo ese fermento está y lo sé desde las puntas de mis orejas" ("All that ferment is here, and I know it by the tips of my ears").[75] This encounter thus frames the project of the novel not simply as one of listening and translating, as Rivera has argued, but of synesthetically registering the sensorial experience of a specific locale and transmitting it through the voice for another to hear, thereby forging a shared phenome-nology of place among individuals from different backgrounds.

Taken as a whole, this scene draws attention to two important if subtle features of how Arguedas conceives of such embodied acts of communion: negativity and audience. First, the success of such encoun-ters must be measured not by how completely they fill silences and gaps in communication but rather by their ability to register the effects of resonant negative spaces. Second, the same landscapes will be heard dif-ferently by different listeners, depending on the acoustic and embodied memories of the individuals involved. These differences do not, how-ever, completely preclude the formation of community.

NEGATIVITY

I invoke negativity in the formal rather than the affective sense: negative space as a structuring principle of design, silence as an integral part of musical and poetic rhythms, empty cavities as that which make reso-nance audible. In the above-cited exchange about the duck song, such negative space is figured as the "rocky abysses" in which the song "sinks down" and "reechoes," and as the "mountain's silence and shadow" that transforms sound into music. One hears this landscape *because* it is riddled with negative spaces. If one listens well, moreover, one registers the silences between the sounds, including the silence of what is neces-sarily lost in translation when the landscape is rendered in words. Thus, unlike Rowe and Rama, who each discuss the musicality of Arguedas's novels at length, I am primarily interested not in what can be perceived directly through the sonority of his language but, rather, in that which becomes perceptible without being fully recovered.

Reading for negativity, silence, and that which defies discursive cap-ture in *Los zorros* yields a version of transculturation inflected with Adorno's aesthetic theory. In the predominant understanding of trans-culturation, success means that dialectical synthesis—of the Indigenous and the Western, of the archaic and the modern, of the oral and the written—yields a hybrid text that fully captures that which is alien to its form, medium, and language. In contrast, Adorno's conception of negative dialectics (which any true dialectic is for him) posits an abiding consciousness of the nonidentity between thought and its object, of the insufficiency of the abstract concept to exhaust the particularity and materiality of the world "without leaving a remainder."[76]

By alternating between attempts at conjuring the world of Chimbote in sensory terms and metadiscursive reflection on the insufficiency of the word as a vehicle for embodied experience, *Los zorros* exhorts the reader to approach this world dialectically. Even as the reader is asked to imagine its sights, sounds, and smells, they are made cognizant of their inability to ever close in on it. As such, in spite of, or perhaps because of its obsession with its own failure, *Los zorros* affirms Adorno's conviction that the aesthetic is "the last repository of this sensuous dimension of human experience. Specifically, only modernism's negative, dissonant aesthetic forms can reconnect knowledge and sensuous experience."[77] Turning to Adorno thus allows us to see that Arguedas is up to something far more specific than troubling Western epistemologies with elements that might be dubbed magical realist (e.g., magical toys and talking foxes). Just as Adorno recognizes that the philosophical concept is constitutionally unable to recover that which is alien to it, there is a sense in *Los zorros* that the world will not be made fully present in the word, but that, nevertheless, in the negative spaces between the words on the page and in the dissonance of discourses and languages colliding, the reader might perceive resonances of that which escapes. This negative presence may be, like the song of the ducks, the echo of a sound or experience they have stored in their sensory memory, or it may be, like a utopic community projected into futurity, something neither the author nor the reader has ever known but that a "we" constituted in the act of reading, or listening together in embodied copresence, might someday encounter.[78] It is in this sense that negativity is not simply annulling for Adorno. Beyond signaling the inadequacy of a unifying language or concept, contradictions and silences reveal, without defining, the existence of possibilities that have not been exhausted by this language or concept.

In Moreiras's work, for example, the insufficiency of discourses of transculturation and *criollo* identity reveals the possibility of a different form of collectivity, which he associates with critical regionalism. Drawing on Adorno's negative dialectics, Moreiras imagines a collective identity that does not absorb the cultural other, reduce him to the same, reify him as a type, or negate his existence but, rather, practices solidarity with "the voices or the residual silences of Latin American otherness" by holding space for their absence in hegemonic discourses.[79] Moreiras does not, however, fully take into account this generative side of negativity in his analysis of *Los zorros*. At least, Moreiras sees the utopian potential of Arugedas's last novel as lying beyond it, after Arguedas's death, which he reads as announcing "the end of the anthropological paradigm," as ethnofiction "is epistemologically shattered because it is revealed to be inexorably dependent upon the subordination of Indigenous cultures to an always already Western-hegemonic machine of transculturation."[80] The "implosion of meaning" staged in *Los zorros* thus marks the apotheosis of transculturation as well as the "beginning of an alternative system of writing: a 'defiance of disappropriation.'"[81] As I have been arguing, however, *Los zorros* does more than defy hegemonic ways of knowing; it also teaches alternative ways of knowing.

In this sense, my reading of negativity in *Los zorros* aligns more closely with that of Julio Prieto than that of Moreiras or Cornejo Polar, both of whom emphasize that which is foreclosed by the incomprehensibility of the novel and the author's eventual suicide. In contrast, for Prieto, the "unintelligibility" and the "inconclusion" of the text open out, in Adornian fashion toward new possibilities:

> It also implies a productive dimension of opening out to the undetermined and a vector of cognitive stimulus where "not understanding" brings forth an epistemic faith and the desire for or the promise of an "other" way of coming to know [. . .]—a knowledge of survival practices, popular imagination and solidarity—that would have the potentiality to radically transform the social and literary system, overcoming the "mortifying" elements of the learned system that historically contributed to perpetuating a regime of inequality, exploitation, and misery in the Andean countries.[82]

This "apertura" gestures beyond the text, calling for action on social and political issues, but part of the revolutionary nature of what Prieto calls "*poiesis* política" is the epistemological shift it brings to bear on the very idea of what the literary is, what a text is. These two forms of political praxis—one material and political, the other epistemological and affective; one in the world, the other in the text—cannot be separated. Though Arguedas is well aware that the act of writing or reading such a text alone will never be enough to address the legacy of colonialism, he does not accept that the revolution can wait—until he completes the project, until after his death, until political change arrives in Peru. On the contrary, the alternative (nongraphocentric, non-Western, affective, and embodied) ways of knowing, dwelling, and thinking toward which Arguedas steers his readers are not only projected into an indefinite future but also learnable (for characters and readers alike) in the novel itself. If its negativity disrupts meaning and blocks (or at least complicates) cultural translation, it also reminds readers to attune the mind's ear to all that cannot be directly captured by the words on the page: the intonations of a voice speaking Quechua, the songs (both human and nonhuman) of the Andean landscape, the experience of the illiterate peasant who cannot speak directly in literature.

As a diverse body of scholarship has underscored in recent decades, negativity, opacity, untranslatability, and silence acquire a particular political valence in postcolonial contexts where the act of representation is always bound up in dynamics of unequal power.[83] Actively attending to the absence, silence, or illegibility of the subaltern voice in so-called universal cultural forms constitutes ethical work for the reader not simply because it instills humility but also because it represents an attempt to register one's copresence with those who have been silenced. In her elaboration of the concept of *reading by ear*, for example, Librandi stresses the importance of reading not only for sounds but also for silences, especially in (neo)colonial contexts, on the margins of European traditions, and in places where "literacy is the exception and not the rule."[84] The political work of writing and reading by ear lies in the creation of "a space of listening in which traces of disappeared or minor cultures, as well as voices and histories, survive in the weavings of writings."[85] Often these survive as negative spaces, that which cannot be directly named, narrated, or translated, but whose absence nevertheless makes itself felt. Learning to stay with the challenge of listening for such resonance in silence, dissonance, and in the cacophonous babble of Chimbote's landscape is part of the task Arguedas sets for the reader in *Los zorros*.

Unlike Rowe, then, I do not believe Arguedas's engagement with sonority allows silenced experiences to be fully recovered and universally heard. Rowe describes music as harmoniously transcending the cacophony of cultural heterogeneity to create

> a space in which certain experiences become visible, narratable. What was previously unnarratable in Peruvian literature, because it did not form part of the story of the nation, now *appears in the ear that has been prepared by Andean music*. This music is no longer only folklore—the expression of ethnic groups—but rather a field of vibrations in which everything can be heard. This (alternative) universality is

only fully reached in *The Fox from Up Above and the Fox from Down Below.*[86] (my emphasis)

The idea that it is the sound of Andean music that trains the ear to hear what was previously silenced directly informs my reading of the dialogue of the foxes, but the conclusions Rowe draws are more optimistically humanistic than my own. In the end, Rowe's reading proves continuous with those that see Arguedas as a successful translator (Rama) and as infiltrating the lettered city and its cultural forms with Andean ways of knowing (Lienhard). In each of these readings, the particular (in this case, Quechua culture) can be integrated into (and even subvert) "universal" (Western) forms and be received and understood by any audience.

In contrast, I do not read the voices of the novel as universally understandable to all potential readers, but because the ability to listen to them properly, to hear all that they contain, depends on one's embodied experience, on having one's ear "prepared by Andean music," on one's literacy in Andean languages, landscapes, and cultures, it is universally *learnable*. This learning process will necessarily be marked by what Anna Tsing calls "productive friction."[87] While those marked as outsiders are barred from certain forms of auditory recognition and participation, one is only an outsider until one is not, until one attunes one's ears to the local soundscape. In other words, in writing and reading across cultures, the (forever-incomplete) work of adaptation and assimilation belongs not only to the subaltern voice striving to be heard but also to the reader who is an outsider. As Aymará de Llano proposes, "The act of reading situates the Spanish speaker at a crossroads homologous to that which the Quechua speaker encounters when trying to communicate and, even more so, when trying to insert his vision of the world in the hegemony of the central cultural system."[88] The text thus disarms rather than catering to the monolingual Spanish-speaking reader. Instead of translating for readers who lack the linguistic competency or broader literacy in the local, the text asks such readers to come close to the Andean world, to listen to it, to be affected by it, to learn from it.

AUDIENCE

At the risk of stating the obvious, it matters greatly in this discussion who the reader is. Rama saw Arguedas as writing for those in "la otra banda" ("the other side"), not for the popular subjects—*indios* and *campesinos*—depicted in his works but rather for *mistis* and educated urbanites.[89] Rowe argues, however, that *Los zorros* seems to anticipate a bicultural, perhaps even bilingual readership—a fully heterogeneous community—that had not yet come into being at the time of its writing.[90] One could argue that only such a readership could grasp all the references and understand all the languages and dialects in the text. Put another way, if we take the exchange between the foxes as our model, it would seem that the ideal reader of Arguedas's work would have embodied memories of the Andean landscape and the Quechua language. The music evoked by the text would resonate in the body of such a reader the way that, once evoked, the ducks' song resonates in the bodies of the foxes, allowing them to listen together, in the mind's ear, to a sound they have both heard before. Yet, it would also seem likely that the vast majority of Arguedas's readers will not share this auditory memory and thus will not be prepared to hear this song in the text.

Arguedas, who was skilled at gauging audience and writing for multiple readerships with varying degrees of familiarity with the Andean world, anticipates this inevitability.[91] In *Los zorros*, more so than in his previous fiction, the author signals the audience's differential sensory literacy without attempting to remediate it or even the playing field. In the first diary, the author figure describes the way the delighted groan of a pig having its head scratched conjures for him the entirety of an Andean landscape:

> La alta, la altísima cascada que baja desde la inalcanzable cumbre de rocas, cantaba en el gemido de ese *nionena*, en sus cerdas duras que se convirtieron en suaves; y el sol tibio que había caldeado las piedras, mi pecho, cada hoja de los árboles y arbustos, caldeando de plenitud, de hermosura incluso el rostro anguloso y energético de mi mujer, ese sol estaba mejor que en ninguna parte en el lenguaje del *nionena*, en su sueño delicioso. Las cascadas de agua del Perú, como las de San Miguel, que resbalan sobre abismos, centenares de metros en salto casi perpendicular, y regando andenes donde florecen plantas alimenticias, alentarán en mis ojos instantes antes de morir. Ellas retratan el mundo para los que sabemos cantar en quechua; podríamos quedarnos eternamente oyéndolas.

The high, extremely high waterfall that flows down off the unreachable rocky peak was singing in the deep tone of that *nionena*, in his stiff bristles, which softened; and the sunshine that had heated the stones, my chest, and each leaf on the trees and bushes, warming with plentitude and beauty even my wife's angular and forceful features—that sun was more present in the *nionena*'s language, in his delicious slumber, than anywhere else. The waterfalls of Peru, like those of San Miguel, where waters slide down into abysses hundreds of feet deep, dropping almost perpendicularly and irrigating terraces where food plants flower, will comfort my eyes moments before dying. They portray the world for those of us who know how to sing in Quechua; we could go on listening to them forever.[92]

Though the synesthesia through which a landscape becomes visible in the squealing of a pig might at first seem an element of the fantastic or magical, the speaker's ability to hear a beloved natural landscape in a pig's voice is not due to any supernatural ability; it is the product of his having lived in this world, of the way his sensorial and affective experiences of it intersect with one another. It is, then, a form of literacy or learnedness that cannot be gained from books alone. It is a knowledge that is shared by those who have dwelled in this world but is imperceptible to the uninitiated ear. So, too, is the ability to hear an expansive world in the sound of a waterfall limited to a specific in-group, those who speak Quechua, or more specifically, know how to sing in Quechua. The use of the first-person plural here creates an ambiguous inclusivity; the speaker addresses his own community, with which the reader will or will not identify depending on their familiarity with Quechua and Andean music. Thus readers who do not belong to this community are made aware that what is meaningless noise or silence to them is song and landscape to others.

Perhaps counterintuitively, this differential legibility is due to rather than in spite of the text's recourse to embodied experience of place. As Masiello underscores, sensory experience is not universal, in spite of frequent claims to the contrary: "Although we all see and hear, touch and taste—universal activities that might define us as one—the specific example of culture or context alters the nature of these perceptions."[93] In other words, both the cultural conditioning and the lived experience or sensory memories of an individual inform sensory perception: "The ways in which we see or hear, touch or taste the world are driven by constructions of selfhood that are formed in local contexts; social norms cross with our daily experience of pleasure and pain."[94] It follows that the way a given text resonates in one's body varies according to the specificity of one's locatedness, where one is, where one has been. Moreover, as Laura U. Marks writes in the context of intercultural film, confronting the limits of one's own sensory knowledge is a valuable experience: "The bafflement in the face of the representation of unfamiliar sense experiences is an aspect of intercultural relations that is unavoidable and salutary: it provides the ground of respect for cultural differences that must precede intercultural learning."[95] The pedagogical function of this move, then, has to do with reminding the reader or viewer that their own sensory experience is not universal but rather particular to the geographic and cultural locales in which they have been formed.

Importantly, however, one's local formation is not the same as one's origins, much less one's ethnic or national identity.[96] In fact, Marks points out that navigating multiple culturally specific sensoria is one of the defining conditions of diasporic and intercultural experience.[97] This is the case, too, for Arguedas and the migrants and expatriates who take center stage in his version of Chimbote. Arguedas's fluency in Quechua and intimate familiarity with Andean landscapes reflect his upbringing rather than his filiation. It might be shared with non-Peruvians who have dwelled for sustained amounts of time in Andean communities (such as the character Maxwell) as well as with Indigenous people who feel strong ties to the highlands, but it is not (presently) shared with those who have fully assimilated to coastal life (such as the character Bazalar).[98] This sense of affiliative community lies at the heart of Estelle Tarica's notion of intimate indigenism, which is informed by Arguedas's work, as well as critical regionalism in the sense that I am using the term.[99]

Sense of belonging (to a place or community) is never stable or fixed in Arguedas; rather, it can be learned and unlearned depending on how one attends to the natural and social landscape. For example, in *Los ríos profundos*, belonging tracks with auditory recognition. The narrator Ernesto describes listening to the music of toads and crickets on the patio of his boarding school in Abancay:

> Los sapos caminaban cerca de la pila, croaban vigorosamente. Advertí mejor, entonces, que esas voces eran más gra-

ves que la de los sapos de altura, a pesar de que en el fondo del coro de los grillos, la voz de los sapos de las regiones frías tiembla como el tañido lento de las campanas. Los de Abancay croan con cierto júbilo y ternura. En estos hondos valles los grillos no forman coros, vuelan y gimen casi solitarios. Son otros insectos, los que vibran en mantos, y con voz incierta, mezclada, en una vibración que confunde al forastero, lo fascina y lo aturde, infundiéndole sueño.

The toads were jumping about near the fountain, croaking vigorously. I noticed, then, that they had deeper voices than the highland ones, although in the background of a chorus of crickets, the voices of the toads from the colder regions reverberate like the slow tolling of bells. Those from Abancay croak with a certain joy and tenderness. In these deep valleys the crickets do not sing in chorus; they fly and chirp almost singly. There are other insects that buzz in swarms, with uncertain voices that blend in a droning that confuses the stranger, fascinating and bewildering him and making him drowsy.[100]

Ernesto can discern the regional differences among the songs of the toads and crickets because he is a migrant, having come to Abancay after living in the highlands, and because he pays attention to such things. He notices the tone and timbre of these voices and the habits of those who emit them. He has trained his ear to the way a chorus is formed by the converging songs of different animals and thus hears markers of place—different ways of dwelling—where others might hear only crickets: background noise, or empty space between legible human utterances and actions.

Perhaps most interesting is the way Ernesto ambiguously identifies with the *forastero*, the outsider or stranger, to whom this vibration is confusing. Ernesto is an outsider to Abancay; while he can describe the nuances of the night chorus in the highlands in great detail, he cannot parse the buzzing of the "otros insectos" in the valley where he is currently sitting. When he invokes the *forastero* who is fascinated and bewildered or deafened (*aturdido* can mean both) by this noise, is he describing his own experience? Or is the use of the third person here a way to distance himself from this position? Shortly afterward, he writes, "Por primera vez me sentí protegido por los muros del Colegio, comprendí lo que era la sombra del hogar" ("For the first time I felt protected by the walls of the School, I understood what the shadow of home is").[101] Is it possible that Ernesto's newfound sense of being at home in Abancay is a result of having learned to listen to the local soundscape and discern its affects and, thus, having transitioned from being a foreigner to this world to one who can truly hear it? Such a reading would redefine belonging as sensory literacy in one's surroundings.

Obviously, such sense of belonging is not immediately, if ever, available to all readers of *Los zorros*. In fact, for most, it will exist only as a possibility toward which one strives knowing that one will not fully achieve it. More so than in Arguedas's previous works, most readers will (at least initially) be alienated by this text's seemingly impenetrable form.[102] Whereas *Los ríos profundos* contains footnotes and glossaries that explain local terms and traditions, *Los zorros* makes no effort to deliver the local reality it depicts in easily digestible form. Its fragmented, nonlinear form and its dense, nonstandard Spanish, difficult for even most Peruvians to understand, require that the reader pay close attention yet relinquish any ambition of mastery. Arguedas's language descends on the reader like a *lloqlla* (the liquefied landslides he describes as endemic to the Andes), forming a nearly unbroken torrent of dialogue and interior monologue that gathers heterogeneous materials from the cultural landscapes over which it courses: Quechua words and turns of phrase, urban slang and obscenities, the broken Spanish of illiterate peasants, and the malformed Spanish of gringos. The partial legibility of this language inevitably produces discomfort and insecurity in the reader, but as de Llano argues, following Umberto Eco, the resulting readerly crisis might be considered "a productive anxiety that opens up the necessity to expand one's 'competence.'"[103]

Learning to follow the movements of this world does not require erudition in the traditional sense of training in canonical literary traditions, but it does require patience, focus, and a willingness to yield to the alterity with which nearly any reader will be confronted in the multicultural, multilingual landscape of Arguedas's Chimbote. The education the text imparts to the diligent reader is not, then, an abstract or didactic one: there are no succinct takeaways, very little to be gleaned in terms of information per se. Instead, it is what Masiello calls an "education of the senses," one that must be delivered in situ through sensorial and affective experience.[104] Even as the novel trains the reader in this form of knowledge by inviting them to engage their senses and to attend to the materiality of the language, in the moments of illegibility and in the metadiscourse of the diaries, the text signals its limits as a means of transmitting embodied knowledge and literacy in the landscape. It will not be able to impart these lessons in equal measure to all its readers, and this failure, too, is one of its lessons.

LEARNING TO LISTEN AS AN OUTSIDER

This model of education stands in stark contrast to the pedagogical model with which Arguedas was more commonly associated during his lifetime: that of purveying ethnographic knowledge about Indigenous cultures in the Andes. Readers have often observed an anthropological or documentary quality to Arguedas's work.[105] This is no coincidence, as Arguedas was a professional ethnologist.[106] Many scholars have noted that it is hard to disentangle Arguedas's ethnological work from his fiction and conjectured that writing literature was for him an alternate way of practicing anthropology, one that freed him from some of the constraints of the discipline.[107] His fiction can thus be seen as at once a continuation of and a corrective to the ethnographic tradition, whose positivist roots make it unduly schematic and dependent on the illusion of the universality of the Western gaze.[108] In contrast, the form of ethnology Arguedas practices in his fiction is one that pursues, in Tarica's words, "the possibility of penetration without violence and of intimate knowledge without power, in short, of ethnography without its colonizing function."[109] One might even say it is a decolonial, anti-ethnography intent on disrupting the power relations that allow one subject to position himself as a sovereign observer of another, who is reduced to a passive object of knowledge. As we have begun to see, this critique functions in part by shifting to a sensory epistemology that confronts the reader with the limits of their perceptions. As Marks writes, "Trying to understand somebody else's sensory organization, I must acknowledge the bluntness of my sensory instruments."[110] Yet this humbling gesture is only one of the ways in which Arguedas inscribes negativity into his project.

The other prong of the author's strategy in *Los zorros* is explicit self-reflexivity on the act of mediation attempted by the text. In what Rivera argues is an extremely modern gesture that structurally resembles Velásquez's painting *Las meninas*, Arguedas expands the frame of the novel to include its author and the act of its composition.[111] In other words, *Los zorros* is a novel about *how subaltern experience becomes*

literature. In this way, argues Rivera, Arguedas does not simply represent Andean culture in positivistic terms but, instead, interrogates the
systems of representation that underlie anthropology as well as most
indigenista literature.[112] Importantly, however, in spite of its profoundly
fatalistic tone, *Los zorros* does not merely mount a critique of the appropriation inherent in such representations nor resign itself to the impossibility of breaking from this legacy.

On the contrary, Rivera argues, the novel also performs its ethical
obligation to the other. This obligation, which Rivera claims is rooted
in the Andean economy of reciprocity, includes listening to the other, re-
ciprocating with one's own confessions, seeing oneself through the eyes
of the other, and ultimately ceding one's voice to the other, using one's
own body to register "the voice, the spirit, the body of the other."[113]
Beyond consisting in large part of dialogues between characters, Rivera concludes, *Los zorros* is itself structured as a dialogue with or act
of listening to its source materials, which include the oral testimonies
Arguedas recorded in Chimbote as well as the pre-Columbian myths he
translated for *Dioses y hombres de Haurochirí*. The author's role is thus
that of "spokesperson for other voices and other texts."[114] This description comes very close to Librandi's account of the ethical act inherent in
listening: the "listening body" serves as a "resonant chamber" in which
the voices of marginalized subjects echo and are amplified.[115] As distinct
from ventriloquizing through the voice of the other, this form of listening is profoundly corporal and requires that the author, intellectual, or
mediator fall silent. In fact, Rivera reads Arguedas's eventual suicide as
the ultimate act of ceding the word to the other.[116] If Arguedas simply
effaced his own subjectivity from the beginning, however, we would be
given the illusion of immediacy, of transparent documentary representation of Chimbote. Instead, the dialogic form achieved by the back-
and-forth between the *diarios* and the *hervores* foregrounds the scene of
mediation that is invisibilized in most *testimonio*. It forces the reader to
confront the subjectivity of the mediator so that when he does remove
himself, whether to cede chapters on end to the voices of his characters
or to eliminate his presence for good, this silence becomes legible as an
ethical act.

If we consider that the reader, too, enters into this dialogue and is
asked to listen to the voices that people Chimbote and to allow them to
resonate in the body, then the novel acquires yet another ethical dimension. The same demands that are made on the author when he listens to
the voice of the other—Rivera identifies these as demands for love and

justice—are also made on the reader.[117] Rivera argues that Arguedas's oeuvre as a whole, never more so than in *Los zorros*, upholds this act of listening and letting the other speak as a model for ethical relations in a culturally heterogeneous environment.[118] I would add that the novel also serves as a training ground for the reader in this mode of ethics, as they are asked to listen to—that is, to attend to the rhythms, sounds, and affects of—a torrent of language whose message is extremely unlikely to be consistently or fully legible to them. As the reader sinks deeper into sensory participation in this world, they are asked to forgo the illusion of mastery from a distance and to cultivate instead the mindset of the dweller, one who learns through immersive experience how to listen to and eventually become more literate in the material and linguistic landscape.

In *Los zorros*, the ability to listen well—and thus, to dwell—is not innate but cultivated. This distinction is most evident in the example of Maxwell, a former Peace Corps volunteer from the United States. Unlike the author figure, who feels at home among the highland Indigenous communities but not in Chimbote, Maxwell is depicted as a cultural chameleon capable of merging with the local culture wherever he is. After living among the Indigenous community of Paratía on Lake Titicaca, he takes on the lifestyle of the *serrano* immigrants to Chimbote. Upon leaving the Peace Corps, he goes into business with the carpenter don Cecilio, takes up permanent residence in the impoverished *barriada* La Esperanza Baja, which he claims is "mi lugar, mi verdadero sitio" ("my place, my true place"), and plans to wed a neighborhood woman.[119]

In many ways, Maxwell achieves what Arguedas, who feels himself to be an outsider to Chimbote, cannot. Whereas Arguedas comes to Chimbote as an anthropologist, Maxwell learns local culture by immersing himself in it and embodying it. It is as a musician that Maxwell has proved most adept at assimilating, and he emphasizes the time and personal connections that have led him to this point. He explains that he apprenticed with a famous *charangista* "en muchas horas y semanas, mientras bebíamos pisco y cerveza" ("for many hours and weeks, while we drank pisco and beer").[120] Similarly, when he describes the music that accompanies the *Ayarachi* dance, he attributes his authority to do so to the time he has spent working, eating, and sleeping alongside the dancers:

Y dije esto no porque haya estudiado musicología. Tú lo sabes. En la Casa de la Cultura de Lima pude tratar direc-

tamente con los bailarines; pasé noches enteras en el inter-
nado del Colegio Militar Leoncio Prado donde estuvieron
alojados. Me aceptaron bien desde el principio. [. . .] Estuve
con ellos seis meses. Pastores de alpacas, trabajé en lo que
trabajaban, comí lo que comían, dormí en las *puñunas* en
que dormían.

And I didn't say this because I had studied musicology. You
know that. In the Casa de la Cultura in Lima I was able to
deal directly with the dancers; I spent whole nights in the
dormitory at the Leoncio Prado Military School, where they
were staying. They accepted me from the very beginning.
[. . .] I spent six months with them. They were alpaca herd-
ers, I did the same work they did, ate what they ate, and slept
on the *puñunas* [adobe benches] they slept on.[121]

In short, Maxwell makes clear that he has arrived at his deep knowledge
of traditional music through *living with* its practitioners as opposed to
studying the subject academically.

At one point, Maxwell brags to Padre Cardozo about having mostly,
though not fully, gone native: "Yo he dejado de ser yanki en un treinta
o noventa porciento" ("I've stopped being Yankee by about 30 to 90
percent").[122] There is something absurd, almost parodic of the social sciences, in this statement, as Maxwell draws on the language of numerical
precision yet leaves himself a very wide margin of error, thus suggesting
the impossibility of quantifying one's assimilation. It is as if Maxwell
is trying to translate into rational, Western terms (taking into account
his audience) the intimate process of *becoming other* that Sara Castro-
Klaren has traced in the more magical transformations in the novel.[123]
What Maxwell makes clear is that "yanki" is not an indelible identity;
depending on how one inhabits one's landscape and participates in one's
community, one can become (possibly up to 90 percent) something else.

Nevertheless, the novel underscores the limitations as well as the
transgressive nature of Maxwell's assimilation. He is the first to admit
that his musical abilities do not completely close the gap between himself and the Indigenous communities whose traditions he has studied:
"No las interpreto [las canciones] como los nativos, pero ya en muchos
de esos cantos yo me vivo, yo me hago" ("I don't play them [the songs]
the way the natives do, but now in much of that singing I come alive; I
make myself").[124] The authenticity of Maxwell's musical performance,

then, does not lie in faithfully imitating Indigenous musicians; instead it lies in remaking himself in the act of playing by fully embodying the music. His musical abilities are, moreover, limited to the charango, a *mestizo* instrument. He never learns to sing or to play Indigenous instruments such as the *quena*, nor does he sing in Quechua, meaning that even he, the most successfully assimilated outsider in this world, does not belong to the in-group Arguedas names: "los que sabemos cantar en Quechua." In the end Maxwell will be murdered by El Mudo in an act of violence that seems to punish the foreigner for knowing the local community too intimately, too corporeally.[125] Still, Maxwell's dedication to Andean music does earn him acceptance by some of the locals, such as the blind musician Antolín Crispín, who allows the gringo to accompany him.

Perhaps most revealingly—and surprisingly—Maxwell *sounds* less like a foreigner than a highlander: as both the narrator and Padre Cardozo observe, he speaks Spanish not in the stilted way of gringos but with musical intonation, displaying perfect fluency in popular speech. This impressive feat owes to his musician's ear for the *voice* of language and correlates with a deeper capacity for cultural understanding than that attained by Cardozo, who speaks with a heavy Anglo accent and is fluent in Marxist discourse but not in the local culture. Maxwell unrelentingly points out that Cardozo continues to relate to Chimbote as an outsider who does not and cannot understand this world. After describing an exchange with an Indigenous man in Puno, whom Maxwell claims to have heard "en la sangre y en la claridad de mi entendimiento" ("in the blood and clarity of my understanding") in spite of not speaking the same language, Maxwell insists that Cardozo would not understand:

> Tú no puedes comprender esto.
> —¿Por qué?—preguntó Cardozo—¿Por qué no puedo? Entiendo. Te oigo bien.
> —No; bien no entiendes. Tú andas nadando en las cáscaras de esta nación. No lo digo con desprecio. En Paratía aprendí a usar bien las palabras. Estás en la cáscara, la envoltura que defiende y oprime.

> "You won't be able to comprehend this."
> "Why not?" asked Cardozo. "Why won't I understand? I do understand. I hear you well."

"No, you don't. You don't understand me well. You go swimming around in the outer layers of this country. I'm not saying that contemptuously. In Paratía I learned to use words well. You're in the outer layers, the shell that defends and oppresses."[126]

In spite of claiming not to make these remarks with contempt, Maxwell accuses Cardozo's approach of oppressing that which it attempts to liberate. In this comparison, Maxwell alleges that, unlike him, Cardozo has not learned how to use words well. Later on in the same conversation, he elaborates that this skill entails listening: "Oír la misa es entender a la gente en lo que tienen de particular; oír y saber lo que ellos oyen, saben y obedecen o niegan. 'Cavar el corral' es trabajar, por ese entendimiento, al modo y manera de ellos, nativo" ("To hear mass is to understand people—what's special about them; to hear and know what they hear, know, and obey, or deny. 'To dig the yard' is to work for that understanding, in the natives' manner of doing and being").[127] Learning to use words well includes mastering idioms like "cavar el corral," but it also entails *hearing* people. Whereas Cardozo focuses on *speaking*— saying mass, pontificating about liberation theology—Maxwell seeks to approximate the position of those *listening* to the mass. In addition to serving as a double of sorts for Arguedas, Maxwell thus serves as a proxy for the reader and models the receptivity required to learn to dwell.

Maxwell in many ways embodies the figure of the *forastero* (outsider) as elaborated by Laura Demaría. This kind of outsider, "who is in a place to which he does not belong" is distinct from the *extranjero* or foreigner. The *forastero*

> shares certain codes with this "way of being" [*estar*] to which he does not belong, and, as such, comes to belong but in his own way and in spite of his foreignness. The "extranjero," in contrast, never assembles a "way of being," because he is always somewhere else and not interested in understanding or participating in this "way of being": the *extranjero* doesn't build a dwelling [*morada*] (home) [*asilo*].[128]

In short, the *forastero* is an outsider who, through a process of "acercamiento" ("coming near") and participation in the local, learns to dwell there. In contrast, the foreigner never engages in these processes, never recognizes oneself in the place nor learns its ways and thus remains in a state of "absolute unbelonging."[129] In Demaría's examples, the *forastero*, unlike the *extranjero*, relates to the region with the critical distance of the outsider but also with personal identification, eventually accepting "certain relations of kinship."[130]

What Arguedas's Chimbote make bracingly clear is that the relations that bind the *forastero* to the region are forged through affiliation rather than filiation. Birthplace, culture of origin, and ethnic identity do not determine who can dwell as an outsider. Maxwell, like Arguedas, has not been born into the Indigenous culture with which he identifies, but this does not stop him from attaining a high degree of literacy in this culture. Cardozo, a North American Latino, struggles far more than Maxwell, a "true," ethnic gringo, to attain cultural and linguistic fluency in the Andean communities of Chimbote because he does not truly dwell there. Though he has taken up residence in Chimbote, he has not made it his home as Maxwell has; he does not traverse and listen to its streets the way Maxwell does or the way the reader is asked to do. In this contrast, Arguedas thus suggests that one's ethnic identity counts for less than one's willingness to immerse oneself in the local culture. Following a similar logic, Arguedas suggests in the diaries that being Latin American by birth does not alone qualify one to write authentic Latin American literature. It is, instead, the commitment to writing *from within* the world represented that Arguedas identifies with the writers he most admires.

REDEFINING ERUDITION AND BELONGING

In the first diary, Arguedas distances himself from many of the most celebrated practitioners of *la nueva narrativa latinoamericana*—he names Alejo Carpentier, Carlos Fuentes, and Julio Cortázar among others—whom he accuses of artifice and professionalism. Arguedas makes little attempt to veil the sense of insecurity and defensiveness from which these comments issue: he admits he lacks the technical genius of these globally renowned authors and senses that they perceive him and his work as provincial. Nor is this slight imagined. In Cortázar's article in *Life*, written in response to Arguedas, the Argentine author belittles those he calls "flag- and rosette-brandishing intellectuals," among whom he includes Arguedas, and claims that regionalist literature is the domain of those who fail to achieve a more totalizing view of global culture.[131]

In turn, Arguedas targets Cortázar, the Argentine writer living in exile in France, as representative of an entire cadre of Latin American intellectuals whose authenticity and commitment he calls into question. The ensuing public polemic dramatized an ongoing debate that divided the Latin American Left: whether Latin America was best represented on the global literary stage by a cosmopolitan, urban, and "planetary" style exemplified by Cortázar, which avoids reinforcing primitive stereotypes of Latin America but stands accused of reproducing the hegemony of Western modernity, or by works grounded in local and national tradition, as exemplified by Arguedas, which have the potential to give voice to the experiences of colonized peoples but stand accused of exoticizing their subject matter and propagating parochial regionalist and nationalist allegiances.[132] Needless to say, this dualistic schema mischaracterizes the work of both authors, which is further caricatured in the heated exchanges of this debate. The personal nature of this public polemic and its deleterious effects on Arguedas's mental health have received a great deal of attention. What is not always emphasized, however, is that in the process of defending himself and praising the privileged few writers with whom he aligns himself (principally Juan Rulfo and João Guimarães Rosa), Arguedas articulates an ethos of writing in situ and redefines erudition as a matter of local and embodied knowledge.

The preceding reading of *Los zorros* suggests that the primary grounds on which Arguedas criticizes "los cortázares" is their ignorance of and lack of concern for *what it feels like*, on an affective and corporeal level, to immersively inhabit the communities they represent.[133] In the third diary, Arguedas responds to Cortázar's latest attack in *Life*:

> Don Julio ha querido atropellarme y ningunearme, irritadísimo, porque digo en el primer diario de este libro, y lo repito ahora, que soy provinciano de este mundo, que he aprendido menos de los libros que en las diferencias que hay, que he sentido y visto, entre un grillo y un alcalde quechua, entre un pescador del mar y un pescador del Titicaca, entre un oboe, un penacho de totora, la picadura de un piojo blanco y el penacho de la caña de azúcar: entre quienes, como Pariacaca, nacieron de cinco huevos de águila y aquellos que aparecieron de una liendre aldeana, de una común liendre, de la que tan súbitamente salta la vida. Y este saber, claro, tiene, tanto como el predominantemente erudito, sus círculos y profundidades.

> Don Julio has tried to trample me underfoot and make a nobody out of me; he is extremely annoyed because in the First Diary of this book I say—and I repeat it now—that I am one of the provincial people of this world, that I have learned less from books than from the differences that exist—differences I have felt and seen—between a cricket (a loquacious dandy) and a Quechua staff-bearing leader, between a deep-sea fisherman and one from Lake Titicaca, between an oboe, the plume of a *totora* reed, the bite of a white louse, and the feathery plume of the sugar cane, between those who, like Pariacaca, were born from five eagle eggs and those who appeared out of a village nit, a common nit, from which life so suddenly springs. And indeed, this kind of knowledge has its circles and depths, just as the predominately erudite lore has.[134]

Arguedas here displays his own erudition, redefining the term to apply not only to Western culture but also to Andean cosmovisions. Beyond opposing Cortázar's bookish knowledge to a knowledge rooted in the natural world as Rowe has suggested, the contrast Arguedas underscores here boils down to differences in how closely one attends to one's local surroundings, both material and cultural.[135] The reader who does not know that "grillo" is slang for a dandy or who cannot conjure the image, much less the tactile feel, of a *totora* reed will not be able to comprehend the differences of which Arguedas speaks. In spite of his polemical tone, then, Arguedas makes an earnest case for the importance of situated knowledge: it is only from inhabiting a place that one learns to discern between the feel of insects and vegetation on the skin or, Arguedas implies, between what is sacred and what is profane, what is revered and what is mocked in a given culture. The arrogance for which Arguedas cannot forgive "los cortázares" lies in what he perceives as their unconcerned ignorance of these differences.

As such, Arguedas challenges the authority of "los cortázares" not on artistic nor intellectual grounds but, rather, on ethical grounds: his own authority lies in his decision to live amid Andean culture and to take the subtle differences between local plants, between insect bites, between linguistic variants as serious objects of study. In this gesture, Arguedas radically upends identity-based notions of authenticity by positing willingness to immerse oneself—linguistically, bodily, spiritually—in a given culture as that which allows one to understand it and become an authority on it.[136]

While he maligns Cortázar for "sus solemnes convicciones de que mejor se entiende la esencia de lo nacional desde las altas esferas de lo supranacional" ("his solemn convictions that the national essence is better understood from the high spheres of the supranational"), he contrasts this form of mastery from without, which he associates with living in exile and belonging to the cosmopolitan literati, to the forms of knowledge generated from a position of intimate proximity by writers such as Juan Rulfo and João Guimarães Rosa, whom he addresses in the second person in the diaries.[137] He addresses Rulfo, for instance, when contrasting Carpentier to the provincial writers with whom he identifies:

> ¡Es bien distinto a nosotros! Su inteligencia penetra las cosas de afuera adentro, como un rayo; es un cerebro que recibe, lúcido y regocijado, la materia de las cosas, y él las domina. Tú también, Juan, pero tú de adentro, muy de adentro, desde el germen mismo.

> He's really different from us! His intelligence penetrates things from the outside inward, like a ray of light; his is a brain that takes in, lucidly and gladly, the stuff of which things are made, and he dominates them. You do, too, Juan, but you do it from the inside, from well inside, from the germ itself.[138]

The "we" that emerges from the diaries thus coheres around a shared ethos of inhabitation rather than mastery from without. In this "we," I propose, lies an early articulation of a critical regionalist community among Latin American writers. The sense of community Arguedas claims with Rulfo and Guimarães Rosa allows us to understand the affinity between these three authors, who are frequently compared, in a novel light. Where Rama saw transculturators and where many subsequent critics see neo-regionalists or modernist-regionalists following the path forged by William Faulkner,[139] Arguedas sees writers invested in what I am calling an ethos of dwelling. It is this learnable, transmissible ethos, rather than birthright, that determines belonging for him.

If, as Butler and Spivak have contended, critical regionalism is at its core an endeavor to articulate new forms of collectivity—new ways of saying "we"—that are not bound by the nation-state or by ethnic identity, then *Los zorros* offers just such an alternative, a "nosotros" constituted by a shared commitment to attuning our ears to the songs of a place. What is more, it invites the reader, wherever they hail from, to aspire and work toward belonging to this community. The improbability of ever fully realizing this goal does not undermine the ethical education the text imparts; on the contrary, trying and failing and persisting nevertheless is precisely the ethical work with which the reader is tasked. Arguedas's posthumous novel thus anticipates Emily Apter's call for intellectuals working in the intercultural space she calls the *translation zone* to recognize both "the singularity of untranslatable alterity" and "the need to translate *quand même.*"[140]

The skills that lead one to belonging—such as the ability to speak Quechua or the ability to *hear* the songs evoked in the text—are not universally shared, but neither are they the unique purview of some and not others. On the contrary, the learnability of such embodied *conocimiento* emerges as one of the most hopeful possibilities in the novel, although this hope should not be confused with the triumphalism for which transculturation has been critiqued. In *Los zorros*, the intermediary figure of the transculturator is ultimately incapable of producing synthesis, harmony, or even coherence. Yet, as Adorno suggests, it is in the very fissures and conflicts in the discourse that other forms of community might be glimpsed. The reader is invited to participate in the formation of a nonidentitarian, affiliative, critical regionalist community by striving asymptotically toward belonging to this world. Like the readers of the texts described in the following chapters, they are asked to undertake a journey of *apprentissage* that is by definition difficult, uncomfortable, and unlikely to yield complete knowledge. In the process, however, they may learn how to perceive, though not fully understand nor master, the songs that resonate in the negative spaces in the text.

CHAPTER 3

Dwelling in the *Travessia*

JOÃO GUIMARÃES ROSA: THE WORLDLY REGIONALIST
AND HIS POETICS OF RECALCITRANCE

What if we, like José María Arguedas, were to turn to the Brazilian author João Guimarães Rosa rather than his more widely read Hispanic
American counterparts for a model of how to navigate the promise and
the threat of global visibility in the historical moment that produced
the Latin American boom? Guimarães Rosa is one of the authors Ángel Rama cites as an example of a transculturator, and his work has
often been read through this lens.[1] Yet the difficulty, self-reflexivity, and
untranslatability[2] of Guimarães Rosa's masterpiece, *Grande sertão: Veredas* (1956), demand a particular understanding of transculturation,
one aligned with the Adornian inflection of the term I have put forth
in the previous chapters: dialectical, negative, and pedagogical in the
sense of teaching the reader to stay in relation with alterity that cannot
be domesticated. What Guimarães Rosa offers to contemporaries such
as Arguedas, as well as to subsequent generations of Latin American
writers, then, is not simply a model of hybridity or translation between
the traditional and the modern, the local and the global; it is instead the
dual move that lies at the heart of critical regionalist poetics: withholding universal legibility and, at the same time, inducting the reader into a
different way of knowing the local.

Owing to his erudition and worldliness, Guimarães Rosa may seem an unlikely confidant and muse for Arguedas, who, as we have seen, was put off by cosmopolitan airs. Though originally trained as a doctor, Guimarães Rosa joined the Brazilian foreign service and spent much of his professional life living abroad as a diplomat. He studied more than twenty languages and spoke half a dozen or more fluently. His polyglotism famously drives his innovations in the Portuguese language, which include neologisms and atypical syntactical patterns drawn from other languages, both modern and ancient. Guimarães Rosa's experiments with language evoke those of Arguedas, who infuses the Spanish language with Quechua words, concepts, and syntax. Yet, whereas Arguedas's bilingualism made him more likely to be read as a regionalist writer, Guimarães Rosa's polyglotism contributed to his reception as a cosmopolitan intellectual. Often called the Brazilian James Joyce and unanimously nominated to the Academia Brasileira de Letras in 1963, Guimarães Rosa attained a level of prestige among literary elites that Arguedas would not know in his lifetime. Despite these differences, in the diary sections included in *El zorro de arriba y el zorro de abajo*, Arguedas identifies intimately with the Brazilian author and addresses his most personal confession to him.[3]

Rather than assuming that Arguedas looked up to Guimarães Rosa for successfully rendering regionalist material in universal terms (the accomplishment for which Guimarães Rosa is most widely celebrated), I am interested in the inverse possibility: that the affinity the narrator of the diaries expresses for Guimarães Rosa owes to the latter's implicit repudiation of the *bestellerismo* for which many "boom" authors have been imputed. Despite his fiction being translated into most major European languages during the height of the Latin American boom,[4] Guimarães Rosa never acquired the international name recognition or widespread readership of authors such as Mario Vargas Llosa, Julio Cortázar, or Gabriel García Márquez. Though a handful of his stories are widely read and taught, *Grande sertão: Veredas* (1956), arguably the most readable and translatable of his book-length works, is comparatively unknown outside Brazil except in academic circles.[5] The relative obscurity of this work reflects the way that Brazil in general was overlooked by the boom as well as the length and stylistic difficulty of this particular novel.[6] Yet I propose that it also owes to the attitude of the text, which Silviano Santiago has described as "acerbic, caustic, chiefly harsh."[7] It is the novel's recalcitrant stance toward readability, and not simply its difficulty or the difficulty of translating it, that sets *Grande sertão* apart from better-known works of its moment.[8] After all, other radically experimental texts, such as Cortázar's *Rayuela* (published nearly contemporaneously with the Seix Barral translation of *Grande sertão*) were much more widely read and circulated. This difference is due in part to the way *Grande sertão* is less of a puzzle or a game than an unresolvable enigma; it guards its incomprehensibility to the end.[9]

The European reception of *Grande sertão* is telling. Many reviewers commented on the way the novel keeps the reader at arm's length, obstinately refuses to give them what they are looking for, and discriminates between trifling readers and those willing to make a more serious investment. In 1962, the French critic Marcel Brion wrote that "the book refuses to convey its message to the superficial reader."[10] The Dutch reviewer Willem Kuipers noted, "The book wouldn't give itself. Only later [. . .] I understood that the translator had had the same experience. The sertão doesn't give itself easily."[11] As these comments indicate, this recalcitrance does not arise only upon reading *Grande sertão* in translation; it is intrinsic in the text. In fact, Brazilian readers have faced many of the same challenges foreign readers encounter, especially when it comes to grappling with obscure regional vocabulary and Guimarães Rosa's prolific neologisms.[12] It is significant, moreover, that Kuipers attributes this reticence to the *sertão* itself, as this space has long been construed as one that resists epistemological capture.[13]

The term "sertão" refers to the vast, semiarid central plains that span much of the Northeast of Brazil and parts of the central states of Minas Gerais and Goiás. Yet as the history of the word reveals, to speak of the *sertão* is not simply to reference a specific location but also to speak of the way geographically and culturally distant areas are figured by the metropolitan imagination. "Sertão" derives from "desertão," meaning "big desert," but rather than simply describing a particular biome, the term is inherently relational, connoting inaccessibility and distance from the coast and, thus, from central power.[14] For the young Brazilian nation (the historical setting of *Grande sertão*), as for the Portuguese empire before it, the *sertão* signified the unruliness that always hovers at the outer reaches of the power of the sovereign or the state. As an internal other in nascent discourses of Brazilian national identity, the *sertão* would persist long past independence as a symbolic space of resistance and opacity, a space not yet domesticated, not yet civilized, not yet fully known. With good reason, then, the elusiveness of Guimarães Rosa's text is often understood as an expression of the indomitability of the *sertão* itself.[15]

Yet as Piers Armstrong astutely observes, the text's hit-and-miss reception abroad also reflects its failure to conform to the demands of the international readership, which had learned to expect essentialist projections of regional and national identity from "peripheral cultures."[16] *Grande sertão* is far from the only work of Latin American literature to challenge this paradigm: *la nueva narrativa latinoamericana* writ large was heralded for doing exactly that, though many of its best-known works, ironically, have been internationally marketed and read as representations of exotic and underdeveloped societies. What sets Guimarães Rosa's novel apart is not simply the degree of its formal difficulty (which is considerable) but also the way it self-reflexively draws attention to its own illegibility and foregrounds, almost accusingly, the demand for knowability that it rebuffs. The defiant complexity and contrariness of Guimarães Rosa's text can thus be read as a direct repudiation of the outsider's expectation of essentialism and exoticism.

Such a gesture is not without precedent in Brazilian letters; Esther Gabara has noted Mário de Andrade's "refusal to feed the appetite for an exotic Brazil" in his travel writings and photography, which he anticipated would "enter the global market of goods and ideas," and describes his figuration of rural Brazil as meeting the traveler "with its arms crossed."[17] Guimarães Rosa follows in this tradition but dialectically tempers the contrariness of his writing with a pedagogical gesture that is harder to locate in the ironic distance characteristic of Andrade's writing: an invitation to learn to dwell, affectively, sensorially, temporally in the local. I propose that this is what makes Guimarães Rosa a critical regionalist.

Though he does not employ the terminology of critical regionalism, Luís Bueno has laid the groundwork for this argument by positioning Guimarães Rosa at the center of one of the most persistent problems in Brazilian regionalism: the tourist-like relationship that the lettered elite inevitably have to the exoticism of the local.[18] Bueno argues that far from being unique to Brazilian regionalist literature, this problem is endemic to literature of the formally colonized world, regardless of whether its subject matter is rural or urban. In fact, he proposes that if we view the regionalists of the 1930s primarily as class tourists, little fundamentally changes when, in the second half of the twentieth century, writers begin focusing on urban slums.[19] Bueno thus emphasizes the continuities rather than the breaks between phases of Brazilian literature that have often been viewed as distinct (as in Antonio Candido's model): the historical regionalism of the 1930s, the modernism of Guimarães Rosa and Clarice Lispector, and the (urban and rural) regional-ists who come afterward. In this sense, Guimarães Rosa's innovations do not mark the end of classical regionalism but, rather, a self-reflexive turn in a long tradition of representing alterity from the perspective of a tourist: "What Guimarães Rosa practices, in this perspective, is a form of tourism with an extremely acute awareness of the problem involving alterity and identity."[20] According to Bueno, the underlying problem at the center of Brazilian literature continues to be how the intellectual fascinated with the popular can be more than a tourist, can do some-thing other than hawk exoticism or spurious claims to authenticity.[21] One difference in recent years, however, is that increasingly the outsider-narrator may originally be from the region in question and return in a different role—that of an urban émigré or exile—who must work to claim "an internal point of view" to legitimate their narrative.[22] The split subjectivity of Guimarães Rosa's narrator, Riobaldo, anticipates this turn, foregrounding the ambivalence that often accompanies the gesture of offering up a world in which one has dwelled for consump-tion by outsiders.

In what follows, I argue that the refusal of visual, chronological, and moral clarity in *Grande sertão: Veredas* has everything to do with the refusal of distance and exteriority for which Arguedas praises authors such as Rulfo and Guimarães Rosa. By failing or declining to position himself at a spatial or temporal remove from his story, Riobaldo spurns the role of the transculturator as it is commonly (if reductively) under-stood. That is, he refuses to translate his experience into a form recog-nizable to and assimilable by the reader who is not from this world. Instead, he offers to guide us *into* the *sertão*, provided we are willing to learn it on its own terms. The form of access to the *sertão* that can be gleaned from the text is the intimate familiarity of the dwelling per-spective, which, in sharp contrast to the totalizing knowledge presumed by the map or the retrospective knowledge presumed by historical nar-ratives, discloses itself only to those who surrender to what Guimarães Rosa calls the *travessia*: the immanent experience of inhabiting and end-lessly traversing this landscape.

It is easy to recognize the illusion of spatial domination achieved by the visual map as an imperial technology, but as thinkers from Dipesh Chakrabarty to the Latin American dependency theorists remind us, the illusion that history is a straight, unidirectional, and unbranching arrow is also a tool of subjugation.[23] In *Grande sertão: Veredas*, these two illusions are revealed to be intimately intertwined. Fracturing the cartographic perspective and forestalling the forward motion of teleo-logical narratives are techniques Guimarães Rosa employs in tandem to encourage, instead, the dwelling perspective. As Axel Pérez Trujillo Diniz observes, the twin gestures of "disrupt[ing] the panoramic gaze of the land through the naming of things inside it, not over and above it" and "suspend[ing] the story and linger[ing] in the details" of the place have profound ecological implications.[24] The stakes of these narrative choices are also ethical and political, demanding changes in the terms on which the reader engages with rural underdevelopment and the human and nonhuman inhabitants of the *sertão*. In this chapter, I pursue the question of what other forms of knowledge maps and teleological nar-ratives eclipse and occlude and how these are recuperated in Guimarães Rosa's text. What does one sacrifice to attain the view from without or the view from afterward? Is it still possible to rehabilitate and relearn local knowledges after the life forms of the *sertão* have been literally and metaphorically paved over by the national narrative of modernization?

BETWEEN BIRD'S-EYE AND BIRDSONG

"Sei o grande sertão? Sertão: quem sabe dele é urubú, gavião, gaivota, esses pássaros: eles estão sempre no alto, apalpando ares com pendurado pé, com o olhar remedindo a alegria e as misérias todas."

"Do you know the great *sertão*? The ones who know it are the vultures, hawks, kites, and birds like that: they are al-ways high up there, feeling the air with lowered feet, sizing up at a glance all joys and sorrows."[25]

"A qualquer narração dessas depõe em falso, porque o ex-tenso de todo sofrido se escapole da memória. E o senhor não esteve lá. O senhor não escutou, em cada anoitecer, a lugúgem do canto da mãe-da-lua. O senhor não pode estabe-lecer em sua ideia a minha tristeza quinhoã. Até os pássaros, consoante os lugares, vão sendo muito diferentes. Ou são os tempos, travessia da gente?"

"Any narration of this sort bears false witness, because the full extent of all that was endured escapes memory. And you were not there. You did not hear the lugubrious song of the whippoorwill at each nightfall. You cannot form an adequate idea of the extent of my sadness. Even the birds become very different, in keeping with their surroundings. Or is it the times through which we pass?"[26]

Grande sertão: Veredas is an infamously beguiling novel that has been declared unreadable, unanalyzable, untamable.[27] Difficulty—the difficulty of narrating, of knowing, of transmitting experience—is also one of its central themes. On the one hand, the narrator, Riobaldo, laments the impossibility of telling and seeing his story clearly. On the other, the form of the text, from its experimental language to its irresolvable contradictions and ambiguities to its elliptical, recursive narrative structure, resists comprehension and ensures that the process of making sense of this story and coming to know Riobaldo's world will be arduous and time consuming, ultimately leaving the reader with more doubts than certainties. In short, the text does not reward those who approach it as one would a realist novel, those who read for the plot, who seek the dénouement or the overview of the world depicted. It demands a different mode of engagement and the cultivation of a different kind of attention. Embodying what Adorno calls the "enigmaticalness" of the artwork, *Grande sertão* defies those who would squeeze a message out of it; the truths it contains reveal themselves only in the activity of shuttling back and forth between complete immersion in lived experience and fraught, guilt-laden attempts to transcend it and reflect back on it. In the end, what it means to dwell in Guimarães Rosa's *sertão* is not so different from what it means to dwell in the aesthetic according to Adorno: to work to perceive what is not manifest and what cannot be rationally grasped, to pursue a form of understanding that is not an abdication or betrayal of the experience one seeks to understand.

Guimarães Rosa's only novel takes the form of a one-sided dialogue in which the *sertanejo* Riobaldo recounts the exploits of his youth as a *jagunço* to a visitor known only as "O Doutor."[28] This scene of oral conversation serves as a frame narrative, providing the impetus for Riobaldo to narrate his life story, but unlike most frame narratives, it does not fully recede into the background while the principal narrative unfolds. Instead, Riobaldo frequently interrupts himself to address his interlocutor and appears to be periodically interrupted by the latter's questions. The speech of O Doutor is not reproduced in the text, so we must infer his interjections from Riobaldo's responses. Because O

Doutor is never heard, he is less of a character than a placeholder; the reader is invited to step into the role of the anonymous, learned urbanite whose help Riobaldo solicits in the overwhelming task of making sense of his life as a *jagunço*. Thus the reader, too, is hailed when Riobaldo addresses his listener in the second person, using the formal "o senhor." This setup self-reflexively foregrounds the challenges inherent in the attempt to transmit the particularities of a place-specific lifeway to an outside audience.

In this chapter, I trace the deep ambivalence in Guimarães Rosas' text toward the possibility and desirability of representing life in the *sertão* from and for an exterior perspective. Riobaldo, who describes O Doutor as "fiel como papel" ("true like paper") and repeatedly asks him to write down what he is saying, values his interlocutor for his ability to faithfully record his story and help him process it. He explains: "O senhor me ouve, pensa e repensa, e rediz, então me ajuda. Assim, é como conto" ("Listen to me, think and think again, and repeat it. Then you will be helping me. This is the way I tell it").[29] Because Riobaldo turns to O Doutor to reflect his experience back to him with more clarity, the central question is not simply whether an urban intellectual can understand and empathize with the life of a *sertanejo*. More specifically, the novel begs the question of what stands to be gained and what stands to be sacrificed if Riobaldo allows his life story, which he experiences as an overwhelming sea of "materia vertente" ("sloping-dizzying material")—affective vicissitudes, moral confusion, contradictory impulses, and temporal fluidity—to be viewed from without, to be judged by an objective gaze and fixed in place on the pages of a book.

As the two epigraphs at the start of this section suggest, the outsider status of Riobaldo's interlocutor is one of the difficulties that plague Riobaldo's attempt to convey his lived experience of the *sertão*, but it is not the only one. In the second of these quotes, Riobaldo names the fact that O Doutor was not there as an insurmountable obstacle to communicating his affective experience, but in the first, he also claims that the *sertão* can be known *only* by those who contemplate it from without, through the (quite literal) bird's-eye view of the great raptors who soar above it. Questioning his own ability to know the *sertão*, Riobaldo grants this capacity to the birds of prey that can visually size up (*com o olhar remedir*) not only the territory but also the affects of its inhabitants (*a alegria e as misérias todas*). It is to attain such a distant perspective that Riobaldo seeks the help of O Doutor; he hopes the latter's wisdom, education, and willingness to transcribe his account into writing will allow him to interpret its key events and, most crucially, lay to rest the question of whether he has sold his soul to the devil. Yet, in these lines we can also detect a kernel of the ambivalence that laces Riobaldo's attempt to procure an outsider's judgment on his life. The birds he names are majestic, but they are predators and scavengers. What is their relationship to the land and the lives they visually survey? *Remedir*, to remeasure or regauge, suggests a precise, instrumental relationship continuous with the techniques of mapping, but it also resonates with *remediar*, to remedy or make up for. Is the comprehension outsiders bring to the *sertão* predatory or compensatory? Is reproducing this landscape through a cartographic perspective and thus conferring legibility on it a way of reifying it or of saving it? Of killing it or redeeming it? Bearing in mind these questions and the history of colonial and neocolonial mapping practices they conjure in Brazil and in Latin America more broadly,[30] I join the likes of Santiago and Willi Bolle in understanding the text's difficulty as protecting the unfathomability of the *sertão* by thwarting the very process of elucidation that motivates Riobaldo's narrative.

Sensing that the cartographic view he hopes O Doutor will reflect back to him will necessarily constitute a falsification, reduction, or betrayal, Riobaldo emphasizes in the passage about the *mãe-da-lua* all that escapes capture from this distant visual perspective: sensorial perceptions, affect, and temporality.[31] Riobaldo insists that without having heard the melancholy song of the *mãe-da-lua* every night as he has throughout his life in the *sertão*, there is no way O Doutor can grasp his cumulative sadness and loss, feelings whose depth is inseparable from their duration and iterative return. A number of readers have pointed to the birds of the *sertão* as the heart of Riobaldo's affective connection to this space.[32] It was his beloved, Diadorim, who taught him to appreciate their beauty and identify their calls. Significantly, this form of connection to place, what we might call intimate familiarity with the bioregion, is mediated by sound before sight, especially in the case of the *mãe-da-lua*, which is nocturnal and therefore heard far more than it is seen. In another moment, Riobaldo emphasizes the importance of smelling the land: "Respirar é que era bom, tomar todos os cheiros. Respirar a alma daqueles campos e lugares" ("It was good to breathe deep, to take in all the smells, to inhale the soul of those fields and places").[33] The kind of attention that Riobaldo has learned from Diadorim involves not only engaging senses beyond the visual but also patience, stillness, and tenderness. In addition to teaching him to identify birds by their songs and plumage, Diadorim tells Riobaldo, "É preciso olhar para esses com um todo carinho" ("You can't help liking them," or more literally, "You have to look at them with total affection").[34]

Riobaldo fears his narrative is constitutionally unable to train the attention and affects of his interlocutor the way the *sertão* has trained his. In lamenting this impossibility, Riobaldo signals the limits not only of the detached bird's-eye view but also of narrative form: "A qualquer *narração* dessas depõe em falso." Like maps, narratives betray and fail to capture the temporality of lived experience. As Riobaldo suggests, this failure may have to do in part with the time that has passed and with lapses in memory, although at other points he insists that he has forgotten nothing.[35] Even more fundamentally, however, this failure is due to the linear structure of narrative, which is at odds with the iterative temporality responsible for sedimenting Riobaldo's affective relationship with the *sertão*.

Finally, when it comes to capturing a lived sense of place, narratives and maps alike falter because places change with the times. Riobaldo, who narrates his youth during Brazil's First Republic (1889–1930) from a point in time many decades later, emphasizes that the landscape has been transformed: the names of towns have been changed by successive governments, new technologies and infrastructure have arrived, and a more modern, tamer *sertão* has replaced the rugged setting of his adventures as a *jagunço*. Moreover, the figures who once gave meaning to this *sertão* for Riobaldo—Joca Ramiro, Hermógenes, and, most importantly, Diadorim—are dead. Though narrative may seem the ideal vehicle to track such diachronic change, it is hard-pressed to simultaneously convey the *sertão* that once was, the *sertão* that is now, and the relation between them: the way that, in the manner of Bergsonian *durée*, "the present is sustained by the coexistence of the past that it falls into and reconfigures."[36] Linear narrative structure, like Walter Benjamin's homogenous, empty time, demands that one time and one state of things supersedes the previous one "like beads of a rosary" and that past events remain inert in their pastness.[37] This is emphatically not how Riobaldo's melancholic relationship to the past works.[38] Critic João Adolfo Hansen aptly encapsulates the narrator's relationship to time: "Riobaldo denies the pastness of the past."[39] Riobaldo is skeptical of narrative because he intuits it knows no way around consigning concluded events to a reified past. Governed by perpetual forward motion, the pursuit of telos, it is ill equipped to capture simultaneity and attend to the branching, heterogeneous nature of the present.

Michel de Certeau writes, "What the map cuts up, the story cuts across."[40] Though de Certeau generally sees narrative as a subversive counterpart to the disciplinary function of maps, this observation suggests that narrative, too, violently rends holistic experience for the sake of legibility. Ironically, it is the aspiration toward totality that leads both forms to dismember what they reproduce. In drawing neat lines, whether they be territorial boundaries or the arrow of history slicing through events, cartographic maps and linear narratives miss the branching *veredas*, or tributaries, that give life to the *sertão*. In fact, maps and narratives present many of the same problems in *Grande sertão: Veredas*: principally, their mastery depends on the spatial (in the case of maps) and temporal (in the case of narratives) separation of the knowing subject from the object of knowledge, on denying Merleau-Ponty's imbrication of noema in noesis and instead postulating a transcendent knowledge uncontaminated by immanence.[41] Contrary to this view, and to Riobaldo's explicit assertion that the *sertão* is known only from the bird's-eye perspective, *Grande sertão* insists at every turn that knowledge of the *sertão* cannot be cleaved from the immanent experience of the *travessia* or what Tim Ingold calls the *dwelling perspective*.[42]

IMAGINING THE LANDSCAPE
FROM THE DWELLING PERSPECTIVE

"Places are fragmentary and inward-turning histories, pasts that others are not allowed to read, accumulated times that can be unfolded but like stories held in reserve, remaining in an enigmatic state."[43]

What linear narrative misses is the palimpsestic (for de Certeau) or sedimented (for the phenomenological tradition in which Ingold works) temporality of places as they are known to those who dwell there. Ingold writes that for native dwellers as well as for those trained to read in their material surroundings the story of how these came to be, such as geologists and archeologists, the landscape enfolds past times but not in narrative form. Accessing this past is a matter not of recalling an internally stored memory but, rather, of "engaging perceptually with an environment that is itself pregnant with the past."[44] Learning to perceive what Ingold calls *the temporality of the landscape* involves "an education of attention" that allows us to see each object as "a 'collapsed act,'" and the landscape as a whole as the embodiment of a "taskscape": "a pattern of activities 'collapsed' into an array of features."[45] These activities—the daily movements, labors, and interactions of the landscape's human and nonhuman inhabitants—are what constitute the place.

From this perspective, the landscape is a temporal form. Not only does it bear the traces of past activities but it *is* the sedimentation of such activities, and it is continuously being shaped by the "rhythmic pattern of human activities" in concert with biological, geological, and astrological rhythms.[46] Viewing the landscape through this lens changes how we measure, map, and narrate it. When conceived of as the material embodiment of dwelling activities, the landscape cannot be rationally measured in spatial terms nor segmented into discrete territories such as nations, states, or properties. In parallel fashion, what Ingold calls the *taskscape*—the totality of these dwelling activities—cannot be measured in or segmented by abstract clock time. On the contrary, the taskscape is governed by a cyclical temporality whose boundary markers—social rituals and repeated events such as nightfall or the harvest—do not constitute definitive breaks between one period and another:

> Thus the present is not marked off from a past that it has replaced or a future that will, in turn, replace it; it rather gathers the past and future into itself, like refractions in a crystal ball. And just as in the landscape, we can move from place to place without crossing any boundary, since the vista that constitutes the identity of a place changes even as we move, so likewise can we move from one present to another without having to break through any chronological barrier that might be supposed to separate each present from the next in line.[47]

Just as it defies rational mapping, the landscape defies chronological narration because dwelling activities are by definition ongoing, cyclical affairs and because they are inseparable from the places where they occur and into which they iteratively weave themselves. In this model, the landscape is a time-space where past, present, and future times resonate within each other, interpenetrate one another, and cohabitate in the same space.

Guimarães Rosa's *sertão* is such a landscape: it defies rational measurement in space or time and refuses the imposition of breaks, whether of the landscape traversed (such as the borders between political states) or of the narrative itself (such as the division into chapters or analytical schemas). In it, argues Ettore Finazzi-Agrò, we are not confronted with two times or two spaces, one modern and one archaic, but, rather, with the impossibility of delineating between them; we encounter the coexistence of "backwardness and progress, the past and the future, the interior and the city, the dryness of the *sertão* and the flourishing of the *veredas*."[48] More specifically than creating a space of temporal hybridity or fluidity, however, Guimarães Rosa creates an aesthetic that Marli Fantini Scarpelli describes as "an archeology of the surface": in the surface of the perceptible world, other times can be read.[49] Only the trained or habituated gaze, however, will perceive this temporal dynamism.

Before continuing, is worth pointing out that Ingold uses the term "landscape" in a sense that is diametrically opposed to the way landscape has traditionally been defined: as a timeless visual tableau beheld by one who does not participate in it. This latter sense of the term, as it has been developed by thinkers from Denis Cosgrove to Raymond Williams to W. J. T. Mitchell, construes landscape as a codified discourse stemming from the European visual arts and as an ideological tool that serves to naturalize social constructs.[50] In the words of Jens Andermann, "Landscape, in short, represents a key ideological apparatus of capitalism and colonialism that naturalizes what are in fact violent and uneven social and political (as well as, we should add, ecological) relations."[51] In colonial contexts, moreover, visual landscape's function is not unlike that of the map: both serve to consolidate and domesticate vast and unruly territories under the gaze of an outsider. I refer to this traditional sense of landscape, which, according to Andermann, is "predicated on the possibility of distinguishing a subject of perception from the thing it perceives," as "visual landscape" to differentiate it from Ingold's phenomenological landscape as the time-space of dwelling.[52] Nevertheless, it is worth noting the continuity between these two seemingly opposite uses of the term. As Andermann argues, "All landscape [. . .] also gestures toward a moment when the gaze will once again coincide with the sensorial and affective capture of the land from within."[53] As such, the temporality of landscape for Andermann is not simply nostalgic—yearning for oneness and wholeness with the land that has been rent in the modern age—but also messianic, gesturing to other possible (less alienated, more ethical) modes of relation and *convivencia* between humans and nonhumans, between individual and community, between oneself and one's environment.

Although Ingold conceives of landscape ontologically rather than discursively and is not specifically interested in the relationship between landscape and literature, his work forms part of a larger phenomenological turn in landscape studies, in which we might include the work of Michel de Certeau, Michel Collot, and Anne Whiston Spirn, among others. These thinkers all conceive of landscape phenomenologically in Merleau-Ponty's sense of the term, meaning that it is made known not from above or without but, rather, from the immersive experience of traversing it.[54] It is no coincidence that this shift corresponds with the uptake of the concept of landscape in literary studies.[55] As the term is expanded to encompass verbal forms such as itineraries and poetry, it becomes less a way of visually organizing space and more a way of conjuring through language the embodied experience of inhabiting space. For Collot, it is precisely with the passage into literature from visual media that landscape ceases to be an external scene and becomes a subjective experience with unseen temporal depths.[56] Collot conceives of literary language as a form of experience that is located in the sense that it always takes place within the bounded horizon of context: "Far from being able to dominate it like a territory one flies over, the speaker finds himself engaged in language as in an encompassing horizon. The relationships between words are thus redefined with each speech act according to a singular point of view."[57] If the context-contingent valences of literary language thwart efforts at abstraction and domination, this is particularly true of Guimarães Rosa's language, which is notoriously difficult and regionally inflected. It epitomizes the literary as that which cannot be glossed or paraphrased but must be painstakingly traversed. The ethical value of approaching texts in this way—as immersive landscapes through which we move, producing meaning relationally as we pass through them—has been recognized by thinkers from Walter Benjamin to Donna Haraway to Judith Butler.[58]

As recent ecocritical scholarship has shown, in zones of extraction in Latin America, thwarting the conventions of cartography and visual landscape while opening space for local knowledge and what Macarena Gómez-Barris calls *submerged perspectives* can be a powerful political gesture as well.[59] Amanda M. Smith argues that literary texts with their "messier and more affective rendering of space" can serve as "countermaps," challenging cartographic ways of knowing by foregrounding what these exclude—the complexity of subjective, embodied, in situ experience, living assemblages that encompass human and nonhuman life, and abuses and wrongdoings that have been naturalized—thus undermining justifications of capitalist extraction.[60] Moreover, Andermann proposes that aesthetic works that operate in a postlandscape mode, denying the sovereignty and suspending the judgment of the viewing subject and demanding a mode of engagement closer to cohabitation (*con-vivir*), have a humbling effect and may upend hierarchies both social (between classes, cultures, races) and ecological (between the human and nonhuman world).[61]

In a postcolonial context, when the reader is figured as an outsider to the local landscape conjured, this dual gesture—thwarting the gaze from without while foregrounding what Gómez-Barris calls "forms of life that cannot be easily reduced, divided, or representationally conquered or evacuated"—is pointedly decolonial.[62] Historically, the Brazilian *sertão* is an underdeveloped and impoverished region, which, like much of the Global South, "has long been constructed as a region of plunder, discovery, raw resources, taming, classification."[63] From Euclides da Cunha's 1902 *Os sertões* to the classic films of Cinema Novo in the 1960s, it has been figured as a space of misery, backwardness, and superstition; these discourses serve to justify the violent imposition of modernization campaigns, even as they preserve the image of the *sertão* in the national imaginary. As Pérez Trujillo Diniz notes, the repetition of such tropes also serves to impose a single narrative on places like the *sertão*, thus condemning to oblivion a pluriverse of local knowledges.[64]

Guimarães Rosa is often credited with bringing new dynamism to this overdetermined space, freeing it from the grip of reifying regionalist and nationalist discourses, and rendering it a stage on which universal philosophical questions play out. As I have been arguing, however, Guimarães Rosa breathes new life into the myths of the *sertão* not simply by translating them into universal terms but, conversely, by revitalizing local perspectives and, in fact, demanding that the reader inhabit them. In submitting to the text as an immersive landscape to be experienced from within, the reader relinquishes the position of mastery the cartographic perspective has furnished to outsiders throughout the *sertão*'s history as a target of conquest and a zone of extraction. It is important to note, however, that the alternative position, which I am calling the *dwelling perspective*, is not one of innocence or redemption. As Andermann reminds us, letting "go of the distance [of] landscape [. . .] means assuming the risk of immersion" and accepting "multiple entanglements."[65] Though this is important work in ethical terms, recognizing one's entanglement with regional landscapes often means recognizing one's involvement in its exploitation. As I go on to argue, asking the

reader to incessantly shuttle between these interior and exterior positions, never simply or comfortably inhabiting either one, is the crown-
ing ethical achievement of *Grande sertão*.

While the novel self-reflexively calls attention to the violent and illusory nature of the totalizing gaze to which the reader guiltily aspires,
it also highlights the difficulty and duration of the process of *apprentissage* through which the dwelling perspective might be pursued. This
process can be understood as gaining literacy in the local landscape.
As Spirn notes, landscapes are not equally legible to all who traverse
them: "A person literate in landscape sees significance where an illiterate
person notes nothing."[66] Though Riobaldo openly expresses his admiration for O Doutor's book learning, he also subtly but persistently draws
attention to the latter's lack of literacy in the *sertão*. From the opening
lines, when Riobaldo corrects O Doutor—"Nonada. Tiros que o senhor
ouviu foram de briga de homem não" ("It's nothing. Those shots you
heard were not men fighting")—he signals that his learned interlocutor
does not know how to interpret this world.[67] Conditioned by the lore of
the *sertão* to hear conflict and violence when in reality it is only target
practice, O Doutor is prone to misreading this landscape and therefore
needs a local's guidance in making sense of the sensorial input of the
sertão. The reader, too, encounters in *Grande sertão* an invitation to
train or initiate their ear and, thus, to begin to hear poetry and philosophy in a landscape that has long been depicted as a void of culture.[68]

RIOBALDO AS GUIDE AND TEACHER

Although Riobaldo serves as O Doutor's guide to the world of the
sertão, he does not simply conform to the role of a translator or native
informant. Instead, by carefully meting out his tale, withholding secrets
until the end, and marking the limits of his interlocutor's capacity to understand, Riobaldo refuses what Doris Sommer calls the demand for the
native informant's sincerity, transparency, and "authenticity."[69] In other
words, he does not efface himself to offer up his story as raw material
for his listener to shape. In fact, the hierarchical relationship between
native informant and intellectual that structures classical ethnographic
texts is inverted, as it is O Doutor whose voice is absent from the text.
As Santiago notes, "The intellectual, city-bred and master of Western
culture, becomes merely a listener and scribe, inhabiting the textual
space—not with his enormous and inflated *I*—but with his silence."[70]

This distinction has far-reaching implications for the ethics of reading *Grande sertão* from the metropole. Santiago has read the novel as a reflection on and critique of "the memorialist discourse of the dominant class" wherein "the intellectual only serves to reap the discourse of the non-city-bred individual."[71] Following the logic of Bueno, it is but a short leap to the conclusion that the novel reflects on how subaltern experience is appropriated by national and world literatures.

More specifically yet, I contend that Riobaldo's account demands to be read as Sommer, several decades later, reads Rigoberta Menchú's *testimonio*: as a performance of the speaker's agency.[72] This agency includes the capacity for duplicity, equivocation, and willful silence or obscurity, but the authority Riobaldo wields in his encounter with O Doutor is also that of a patient teacher. Zé Bebelo, Riobaldo's onetime employer and later war chief, refers to Riobaldo as "professor" because Riobaldo served as his tutor and taught him to read. As a *jagunço letrado*, Riobaldo is not naive about the power that comes with discursively controlling his encounters with outsiders like Zé Bebelo and O Doutor.[73] On the contrary, in both relationships he leverages his superior literacy (whether in book learning or in the *sertão*) to his advantage even while deferentially playing the part of subordinate.

I am particularly interested in the way that Riobaldo exercises his power in his relationship with O Doutor to demand the latter's patience. Riobaldo convinces him to stay longer than he has planned and advises him that if he truly wants to know the *sertão*, he will have to undertake a "viagem mais dilatada" ("more extensive journey").[74] After claiming that if he were in better health, he himself would serve as O Doutor's guide into the depths of the *sertão*, he goes on to lead O Doutor on just such a dilatory journey without leaving the comfort of his porch. One of the requirements of this journey, or *travessia*, through Riobaldo's story is that we slow down to the pace he sets. As Santiago notes, the text "obliged the reader to progress, if there was progress, at a snail's pace."[75] Though frequently apologizing and deprecating his abilities as a narrator, Riobaldo nevertheless chastises the impatience of his listener when he (presumably) presses for information: "Senhor, senhor—o senhor não puxa o céu antes da hora! Ao que digo, não digo?" ("Sir, sir–don't you put the sky before its time! About what I say, don't I say it?").[76] In another moment, when he admits to equivocating, Riobaldo frames his failure to deliver what his audience seeks less as a lapse in memory or intellectual ability than as a recrimination of our expectations: "Falo por palavras tortas. Conto minha vida, que não entendi. O senhor é homem muito ladino, de instruída sensatez. Mas não se avexe, não queira chuva em mês de agosto. Já conto, já venho—falar no assunto que o senhor está de mim esperando. E escute" ("I speak with twisted words. I narrate my life, which I did not understand. You are a very clever man, of learning and good sense, but don't get impatient, don't expect rain during the month of August. I'll soon tell you, I'm coming to the subject that you are waiting for").[77] Still maintaining his deferential posture, Riobaldo suggests that our expectations are foolishly out of step with the reality we seek to close in on (as in hoping for rain in the dry season). In other words, our impatience is a symptom of our illiteracy in this landscape.

Yet in signaling his interlocutor's inferior capacity to navigate this landscape, Riobaldo does not simply enforce a barrier to access; he also promises that this barrier can be at least partially overcome. Many times over, he repeats that O Doutor does not yet understand but that he will, with phrases like "Ao quando bem não me entender, me espere" ("And whenever you don't understand me clearly, just wait") and "O senhor entenderá, agora ainda não me entende" ("You will understand me, sir, though you don't yet").[78] These comments, often made in reference to his confusion and guilt over his attraction to his fellow *jagunço* Diadorim, foreshadow the revelation that Riobaldo withholds until the end of his story: that Diadorim, whom Riobaldo always knew as a man, has the body of a woman. I believe, however, that this is not the only way to read such remarks. It is true that we do not yet have all the information we need to understand and judge Riobaldo's tale when he is in the middle of telling it, but it is also true that the clarity Riobaldo promises never fully arrives. As I have argued elsewhere, the unveiling of Diadorim's "true" identity is an unconvincing act of closure, one that fails to lay to rest the questions, ambiguities, and contradictions that animate Riobaldo's tale.[79] Those who want definitive answers are left empty-handed, even at the very end.[80] Riobaldo admits as much, stating paradoxically that the understanding he promises is not understandable: "O senhor por ora mal me entende, se é que no fim me entenderá. Mas a vida não é entendível" ("For the moment, you do not understand what I am talking about, and you may not understand me at the end either. But life is not understandable").[81] I propose that we might read Riobaldo's insistence that we do not *yet* understand him not as a promise of future information to be revealed and holes in the narrative to be filled but, instead, as an expression of his intent to gradually induct us into a different relationship with the *sertão*: "O senhor vá me ouvindo, vá mais me entendendo" ("The more you go on hearing me, the more you go on understanding me").[82] This promise when fulfilled will not yield the mastery of the overview; instead, undertaking the journey—listening until we become more literate in the landscape—will require patience and a posture of submission.

Riobaldo's other pupil, Zé Bebelo, never learned this lesson. To Riobaldo's awe and dismay, Zé Bebelo demonstrates an insatiable appetite for knowledge, a drive that is related to his quest to transform the *sertão*. As Riobaldo observes of Zé Bebelo, "Aquele queria saber tudo, dispor de tudo, poder tudo, tudo alterar" ("He wanted to know everything, to decide everything, to be all-powerful, to change everything").[83] As a student, Zé Bebelo demonstrates a rapacious, almost jealous relationship to knowledge: "O que ele queria era botar na cabeça duma vez, o que os livros dão e não. Ele era a inteligência! Vorava. Corrido, passava de lição em lição, e perguntava, reperguntava, parecia ter até raiva de eu saber e não ele" ("What he wanted was to cram into his head, all at once, all that books give and do not give. What intelligence he had! He was ravenous. He raced from lesson to lesson, asking questions and more questions. It even seemed to make him mad because I knew and he didn't").[84] Santiago has called this drive "irascibility" and argued that it characterizes both Zé Bebelo's desire to tame the *sertão* and the critic's desire to tame the "monster" that is Guimarães Rosa's text. Santiago sees this as a disciplinary and authoritarian gesture that the text radically rejects, as the *sertão* repels the Republican troops who seek to domesticate it.[85] Zé Bebelo seems to represent these modernizing forces. A champion of civilization and progress, he claims he was born to abolish the system of *jagunçagem* and reform the *sertão*. He speaks of bringing industry, infrastructure, education, and public health programs to the *sertão* and even signs his letters "Ordem e Progresso." If, as Santiago argues, Joca Ramiro represents the old order of the *sertão* associated with the quasi-feudal *coronelismo* system, then Zé Bebelo represents the forces of progress championed by not only the First Republic, the historical backdrop of Riobaldo's adventures, but also, subsequently, by Getulio Vargas's Second and Third Republics and Juscelino Kubitschek's ambitious developmentalist plan that promised fifty years of progress in five.[86]

These progressive impulses, which inevitably imply the end or death of the old *sertão*, are treated with profound ambivalence in Guimarães Rosa's text. When Zé Bebelo is captured by Joca Ramiro's gang and put on trial, for example, the offenses of which he is accused include being paid by the government and seeking to change the traditions that govern the *sertão*. Joca Ramiro explains to him: "O senhor veio querendo desnortear, desencaminhar os sertanejos de seu costume velho de lei" ("You came to sow confusion, to turn the people of the *sertão* from their old ways").[87] At a later point, Riobaldo observes that Zé Bebelo seems to want to push the *sertão* itself into retreat, naming his desire "para o sertão retroceder, feito pusesse o sertão para trás!" ("to attack it, as one would an enemy, to push it back!").[88] Riobaldo's gravest misgivings about Zé Bebelo have to do with the latter's association with the government troops intent on conquering the *sertão*. At the same time, though, Riobaldo respects Zé Bebelo and often appears to share his "civilizing" impulse. In his attitude toward Hermógenes, who represents the most brutal side of the *sertão*, for example, Riobaldo is unequivocal: he yearns to live in a world free of Hermógenes, just as he notes that nowadays, in the moment from which he narrates, "o mundo quer ficar sem sertão" ("the world wants to be without a *sertão*").[89] The contradictions and reversals that characterize Riobaldo's relationship with Zé Bebelo thus mirror his doubt-ridden relationship with the *sertão*: he is never sure if he fully belongs there and identifies with it.

Riobaldo's ambivalent relationship with Zé Bebelo also has many similarities with Riobaldo's reverential yet wary attitude toward O Doutor. Riobaldo respects both men for their refinement and intelligence and hopes that their wisdom and level-headedness might alleviate him of his inner conflicts and tumult. Importantly, both are outsiders who come to the *sertão* seeking knowledge of it, and in both cases, Riobaldo is aware that sharing his knowledge of the *sertão* with such an outsider could constitute a betrayal. When he is still working for Zé Bebelo, Riobaldo considers telling his pupil what he knows about Joca Ramiro's gang but decides against it: "calei a boca [. . .] Porque eu estava achando que, se contasse, perfazia ato de traição" ("I shut my mouth [. . .] for at that moment it struck me that if I told any more I would be committing an act of treachery").[90] In this case, the hypothetical act of betrayal would entail revealing strategic information that could be used against the *jagunços* in war, but as Riobaldo's criticism of his pupil's learning style belies, Zé Bebelo's rapacity for knowledge in itself represents a desire for control and mastery that Riobaldo finds repugnant (though impressive).

In short, in the person of Zé Bebelo, who starts out fighting the *jagunços* on their own terms but longs to become a government deputy and ends up becoming a lawyer, the quest for knowledge, order, and progress proves inseparable from the violent subjugation of the *serta-nejos* in the name of eliminating their "backward" ways. This drive to "civilize" by imposing Western reason on an "irrational" space reflects the Brazilian state's approach to assimilating the *sertão* as well as that of the Portuguese empire before it; the project of subduing the *sertão* has always been carried out as much through epistemological activities or mapping practices, as through military force, although the two strategies work in tandem.[91] Riobaldo's ambivalence toward Zé Bebelo is the ambivalence of one who regrets the violence and destruction wrought by this undertaking but also knows himself to be complicit in it, for Riobaldo, too, seeks the end of the *sertão* and, as a retrospective narrator who looks back on it, risks reifying it as an object of knowledge. As Hansen observes, the narrator Riobaldo, like Zé Bebelo, is in the position of attempting to impose linear, historical time on a world that resists this endeavor: "His telling consists principally in the possession of his own story, which he petrifies as linearity [. . .] in telling, Riobaldo frees himself from mythic time, or from the repetition of the past, and petrifies himself in historic progressive time."[92] Riobaldo both yearns to free himself from the *redemoinho*, or whirlwind of mythic time and repetition, and, I argue, feels the violence of "petrifying" his tale—and himself—in the linear time of historical progress.

I will return to the guilt borne by Riobaldo's account of the *sertão*, but in the conversation of the frame narrative, the figure who most shares Zé Bebelo's irascibility (to use Santiago's term) is not Riobaldo but O Doutor (and by extension, the reader). Though always cordial to his guest and often expressing gratitude and sometimes even affection, Riobaldo subtly implicates O Doutor and his quest for knowledge about the *sertão* in the demise of the way of life of his youth. Near the beginning of the novel, Riobaldo tries to fathom O Doutor's motives: "Mas, o senhor sério tenciona devassar a raso este mar de territórios, para sortimento de conferir o que existe? Tem seus motivos" ("But, are you seriously planning to launch out on this sea of territory, to find out what it contains? You must have your reasons").[93] The phrase Riobaldo uses to describe the intentions of his interlocutor, "devassar a raso este mar de territórios," echoes Riobaldo's description of Zé Bebelo's ambition to "liquidar mesmo, a rás, com o inferno da jagunçada!" ("really wipe out that hell of bandits to the last man!").[94] The former turn of phrase is highly unconventional but suggests there is an element of violence or depravity in the quest for totalizing knowledge. The neologism "devassar" makes a verb of the adjective "devasso" (immoral or wanton), which Florencia Garramuño and Gonzalo Aguilar translate into Spanish as "revelar" (to reveal).[95] It also evokes "devastar" (to devastate), which in conjunction with "a raso" (flat, level, shallow) suggests razing or ironing out the topography of these territories and draining the ocean as metaphors for O Doutor's knowledge-gathering mission.

As is often the case with Guimarães Rosa's poetic prose, the rich multiplicity of connotations entangled in each phrase includes intertextual references. Beyond gesturing to the expansiveness and diversity of the *sertão*, calling this landscape "a sea of territories" evokes the comparison between the "desierto" of the Argentine pampas and the ocean first made by Alexander Von Humboldt and later taken up by Domingo F. Sarmiento, as well as the *litoral-sertão* dichotomy in Brazil, which can be traced back at least as far as Euclides da Cunha's *Os sertões*.[96] Both Sarmiento's and Euclides's projects deploy positivistic ethnographic description as a tool to epistemologically penetrate and domesticate the unruliness and *barbarie* associated with the backlands, and both, under the influence of natural determinism, begin with the topography of the land itself as that which shapes the "backward" cultures of the nation's interior and thwarts attempts by coastal elites to "civilize" them. Da Cunha, for example, opens his report with a description of the mountain ranges that make viewing or reaching the highlands of the *sertão* from the coast a hard-won accomplishment. Bolle argues that da Cunha's text, which includes a number of maps and aspires to provide a discursive overview of these territories, effectively flattens this topography, granting the reader the bird's-eye view of the *sertão* that Guimarães Rosa strategically withholds.[97]

As Bueno argues, Guimarães Rosa is sensitized to the loss inherent in the violent, rationalizing, flattening conquest of the *sertão* and proposes through his novel that it is not the only way to reconcile this landscape with modernity.[98] Of the characters who attempt to traverse the *sertão*, it is Riobaldo, guided by the sensibilities of Diadorim, who best intuits this alternative path, and his success comes from his learned literacy in the natural landscape.[99] The intimate familiarity with the *sertão* that Riobaldo gains is not something that can be grasped; on the contrary, it leaves the traveler empty-handed but transformed.[100] It is this kind of journey, this kind of vulnerable and open-ended pursuit of situated knowledge, I propose, that Guimarães Rosa also asks the reader to undertake: to know (*conocer*) the *sertão* from within rather than seek to epistemologically conquer it or remove oneself from it.

THE DUBIOUS PASTNESS OF THE *SERTÃO*

The epistemological conquest of the *sertão* involves mastery not only through spatial mapping but also through temporal displacement. As I have outlined in chapter 1, projecting regional landscapes into the archaic past is convenient for nationalistic discourses that seek on the one hand to disavow their backwardness and underdevelopment and on the other to mine them for mythic origin stories and autochthonous roots, but doing so mystifies the presentness of such regions and blinds us to their temporal dynamism as living landscapes (in Ingold's sense of the term).

By Guimarães Rosa's time, the *sertão* had been imaginatively populated with myths of *cangaceiros* like Lampião, atavistic religious leaders like Antonio Conselheiro, and archetypes harking back to medieval times like the *caballero errante* and the disguised woman warrior-worker in *Luzia-Homem*.[101] Overlaid on this mythic landscape is also the social critique of regionalist writers from Graciliano Ramos to Jorge Amado to José Lins de Rego who underscored the misery and exploitation of northeasterners. Guimarães Rosa does not cast off any of these versions of the *sertão*, but he does suggest that with the exception of poverty, which is a constant, many of the features of the *sertão* we imagine belong to the register of folklore. Early on, Riobaldo subtly accuses O Doutor of coming in search of an archaic version of the *sertão*:

> Agora—digo por mim—o senhor vem, veio tarde. Tempos foram, os costumes demudaram. Quase que, de legítimo leal, pouco sobra, nem não sobra mais nada. Os bandos bons de valentões repartiram seu fim; muito se foi jagunço, por aí pena, pede esmola. Mesmo que os vaqueiros duvidam de vir no comércio vestidos de roupa inteira de couro, acham que traje de gibão é feio e capiau. E até o gado no grameal vai minguando menos bravo, mais educado: casteado de zebu, desvém com o resto de curraleiro e de crioulo. Sempre, no gerais, é a pobreza, à tristeza.

> But you have come late. The old days are gone, habits have changed. Of the real things of the past, few or none are left. The bands of mad men have been broken up; many a former jagunço is having a tough time of it, goes about begging. The herdsmen nowadays are reluctant to come to market

in their leather garments—they think a leather jacket is ugly and countrified. Even the cattle in the scrubland are becoming less wild, better behaved. Crossed now with zebu, they look strange beside what is left of the old domestic breeds.[102]

The changes Riobaldo describes—*sertanejos* abandoning traditional dress out of shame, the domestication of cattle through crossbreeding, and the taming of the landscape itself—reflect the success of reformers such as Zé Bebelo who wish to put an end to the old ways of life. Riobaldo suggests that by the time he tells his story, decades after it takes place, the old *sertão* has been superseded by a more modern version. It is not just that roads have been built and cars have started to replace carts (Riobaldo tells us all of this has happened too); an older order, epitomized by Joca Ramiro, has been lost.

Yet, in his characteristically contradictory speech, Riobaldo comments on this inevitability even as he calls it into question: "Ah, tempo de jagunço tinha mesmo de acabar, cidade acaba com o sertão. Acaba?" ("Ah, the times of *jagunçagem* had to end, the *sertão* ends with the city, does it? End?").[103] The line "cidade acaba com o sertão" can be read as "the city puts an end to the *sertão*" or "the city ends at the *sertão*." Both of these delineating borders—the temporal border marking the death of the *sertão* when it is civilized by the city and the spatial border that divides the *sertão* from the city—are thrown into question when Riobaldo undermines the finality of this statement by asking, "Acaba?" Can a landscape defined by its boundless expanse ever be said to end?

The implication that the *sertão* does not give way historically to the city throws into question not only the success of the modernization campaigns of the First Republic, when the adventures Riobaldo recounts take place, but also the promises being made by Kubitschek's government at the time *Grande sertão* was written. The construction of the new, modernist capital of Brasília in the heart of the *sertão* (inaugurated in 1961) was seen by many as the belated fulfillment of the progressive dreams of previous reformist campaigns: to once and for all put an end to the backwardness represented by the *sertão*.[104] As we have begun to see, this end (in the sense of teleological conclusion: the achievement of modernity) cannot be separated from the end (in the sense of termination or eradication) of the *sertão*. From Riobaldo's perspective, the *sertão* condemned to end is not only the *sertão* of Hermógenes (brutal, violent, morally repulsive) but also the *sertão* of Joca Ramiro and Medeiro Vaz (noble, romantic, governed by chivalric codes of honor and solidarity among marginalized subjects) and the *sertão* of Diadorim (enchanted with natural beauty, saturated with tender affect, appealing to the loyalty of those who have dwelled there).

One could argue, and in fact many have, that Riobaldo's narrative ensures the *sertão* never does end.[105] Recursivity and nonlinear forms (Rowland), *saudade* (Kampff Lages), melancholia (Carmello), and recourse to mythic time (Hansen) are among the strategies critics have identified as challenging teleological narrative structures and thus allowing the past to live on in the present. Guimarães Rosa's *sertão* is governed, as Hansen argues, by the cyclical time of myth and repetition, in which the present and future are prefigured in the past. Any attempt to impose linear, progressive temporality collides again and again with the cyclical time of the *sertão*, which inevitably subsumes them.[106] Deise Dantas Lima points out that the "errant" temporality of the novel has political implications, as it challenges the predominant narrative of Brazilian modernity, revealing that the linear path of progress that has long promised to lead the nation out of the *sertão* does not correspond with the real Brazil: "rural Brazil, wandering through the torturous *veredas* of modernization."[107] In this way, a number of readers have argued, Guimarães Rosa makes room for "the forgotten ones of history" in a historical moment when there is great pressure to exclude these marginalized subjects from the official vision of modern Brazil.[108] The novel thus defiantly breaks with the silencing of subaltern experience in the construction of the nation.[109] Along these lines, Bolle contrasts Guimarães Rosa's approach with that of Euclides da Cunha in *Os sertões*, which depicts "a culture considered definitively conquered and henceforth tolerated only in the innocuous registers of regionalismo and folklore."[110] Bolle argues that in refusing the elegiac tone of Euclides, Guimarães Rosa paints a living portrait of the very subjects and ways of life whose death is demanded by Brazil's modernization narrative (the conquest of *barbarie* by civilization).[111]

In sum, for Riobaldo, as for the reader, the past, like the *sertão*, is not something to be left behind but rather something that lives on "dentro da gente" ("within us").[112] In asking us to perpetually (at least for the considerable duration of the novel) dwell in the *travessia*—the act of crossing the *sertão*—Riobaldo's narrative denies the reader not only the view from above (the cartographic perspective) but also the view from afterward (the retrospective perspective). In the following section, I go on to explore the chronotope of the *travessia* and what it reveals about the confluence of spatial, temporal, and cultural distance in the mapping

practices that Guimarães Rosa's text ambivalently repudiates. I stress
that this relationship is ambivalent, dialectical, or diabolical (in Guimarães Rosa's sense of the word: two-faced, internally divided) because
I do not believe that the positivistic ambitions that Bolle attributes to
Euclides's text can be fully separated from the urge to resist or subvert them that he traces in Guimarães Rosa's text.[113] On the contrary, I
read the guilt borne by Riobaldo's narrative simultaneously as the guilt
of complicity with reifying mapping practices inherited from colonial
discourses (the guilt of betraying the *sertão* in order to document and
master it from without) and the shame of failing to fully transcend the
sertão (a shame induced by having internalized the hegemonic narrative
of modernization that demands that the *sertão* be abandoned to the
past).[114]

THE CRIME OF CLOSURE AND
THE CHRONOTOPE OF THE *TRAVESSIA*

> "Digo: o real não está na saída nem na chegada: ele se dispõe
> para a gente é no meio da travessia."

> "I mean, the truth is not in the setting out nor in the arriving:
> it comes to us in the middle of the journey [*travessia*]."[115]

> "Eu atravesso as coisas—e no meio da travessia não vejo!—
> só estava era entretido na ideia dos lugares de saída e de
> chegada."

> "I go through an experience, and in the very midst of it [the
> *travessia*] I am blind. I can see only the beginning and the
> end."[116]

Despite invoking the map and the book as forms that might help contain his experience and render it comprehensible, Riobaldo's narrative
perennially resists the imposition of such forms.[117] Though prone to
prolepsis, the narrator generally keeps his listener aligned with the perspective of the young *jagunço* Riobaldo rather than allowing his account to be colored by his retrospective knowledge. In other words,
instead of positioning himself as an omniscient narrator who might
provide O Doutor (and the reader) with a spatial and temporal over-

view, he takes us down winding *veredas*; we are asked to walk alongside the character Riobaldo, knowing only what he knows in a given moment.[118] The reader thus encounters a landscape in Ingold's sense of the term, or to use Guimarães Rosa's vocabulary, a *travessia*: the chronotope of an immersive journey. Similar to the labyrinth, to which Guimarães Rosa's text has also been compared, the *travessia* is by definition that which can only be experienced from within.[119] The word "travessia"—crossing, journey, passage—appears as a refrain of sorts throughout *Grande sertão*; it is also the famously enigmatic last word of the novel: "Existe é homem humano. Travessia" ("It is man who exists. The Passage").[120] Exemplifying the slippery multivalence for which Guimarães Rosa's language is known, the leitmotif of the *travessia* is associated with the *sertão*, rivers, danger, Diadorim, the devil, courage, repetition, temporal duration, the difficulty of narrating the past, and life itself. This seemingly all-encompassing term can be said to definitively exclude only two things: the beginning and the end—the *travessia* is by definition what lies between departure and arrival.

I propose that through the multivalent concept of the *travessia*, Guimarães Rosa theorizes a predominant strategy in his fiction: narrating from the dwelling perspective, understood in spatial and temporal terms. This is no easy feat. The problem Riobaldo runs into again and again is that while beginnings and endings are relatively easy to tell, the *travessia* is by its nature turbulent, opaque, and often uneventful. Though this is where Riobaldo insists the truth is to be found, it cannot be grasped from within the *travessia*, for in this time-space of immanence one is blind. Paradoxically, once the journey is concluded, clear hindsight becomes available, but hindsight is not true to the experience of the *travessia*. This creates a serious problem for the judgment Riobaldo seeks from O Doutor. He recounts his tale in part to learn an outsider's perspective on whether he has sinned or sold his soul to the devil, but as he declares during Zé Bebelo's trial, "Julgamento é sempre defeituoso, porque o que a gente julga é o passado" ("A judgment is always faulty, because what one judges is the past").[121] As such, it is not simply that we cannot fully understand Riobaldo's tale because we were not there but also because we are necessarily hearing it from its conclusion.

Riobaldo's solution to this dilemma is vexed: he largely tells his story from the temporal vantage point of within its unfolding, but doing so makes it harder for him to achieve his goal of giving definitive form and meaning to the narrative he relates. As Susana Kampff Lages writes, "Riobaldo would like to be able to master, to survey the totality of the past, of the lived, giving his speech a determined order. But the ductile material of memory doesn't submit itself to exterior ordering."[122] It torments Riobaldo that the past refuses to hold still and perpetually "escapes being turned into an object of narration."[123] Yet, at the same time, in the position of guide into the past he narrates, Riobaldo deliberately denies his listener the exterior, ordering perspective that would hold the past in a stable gaze. Instead, he plunges us again and again into the time-space of the *travessia*: the distance that would separate the narrator Riobaldo from *o jagunço* Riobaldo continually collapses, submerging the story in the perspective of one immersed in the events as they unfold and renouncing the temporal remove of being, in Riobaldo's words, "despois das tempestades" ("after the storm").[124] As Patricia Carmello points out, however, we are not submerged in this perspective of within-time *all the time*: the self-reflexive commentary of the narrator Riobaldo and his references to the time of narration introduce temporal play. Toggling back and forth between immersive and more distant perspectives allows Riobaldo to keep the past open and dynamic, animating it as a dance.[125]

In *A forma do meio*, Clara Rowland argues that Riobaldo's narrative resists the drive toward closure in order to forestall the deaths brought by the ending: the literal death of Diadorim as well as the figurative death of the *sertão*. According to Rowland, Riobaldo's reluctance to abandon the openness and fluidity of the *travessia* is reflected in the expansiveness of the text as well as its recourse to the cyclical and nonnarrative forms of poetry and song and its perennial invitation for the reader to double back and reread or reevaluate what they have already read. In dialogue with Peter Brooks, Rowland proposes that Guimarães Rosa stages a push-pull between the death drive, which in Brooks's narratology entails the desire for legibility provided by a proper ending, and the resistance to closure, which "appears to have death as its price."[126] According to Rowland, this tension is sustained by the equilibrium between two oppositional forces: the reader's desire for "closure, a form that delimits the story" and the narrator's reticence or resistance to completion, which "doesn't allow the extinction of the story."[127] By withholding information and negating closure, Riobaldo keeps his story perpetually open and defends it from those who would bring it to a premature end, including O Doutor and the reader.[128]

What makes Riobaldo's narrative even more complicated than Rowland's reading takes into account, however, is that this tension exists not only between the narrator and his interlocutor but also *within* the narrator. Riobaldo, too, longs for an ending and for the ability to transcend the *travessia*. In fact, his remarks about the *sertão* being knowable only by the birds that soar above it follow directly from an admission that, weary of the life of a *jagunço*, he seeks closure:

> Também eu queria que tudo tivesse logo um razoável fim, em tanto para eu então poder largar a jagunçagem. Minha Otacília, horas dessas, graças a Deus havia de parar longe dali, resguardada protegida. O tudo conseguisse fim, eu batia para lá, topava com ela, conduzia [. . .]. Sensato somente eu saísse do meio do sertão, ia morar residido, em fazenda perto de cidade.

> I was also hoping that everything would be over fairly soon, so I might then give up my life as a jagunço. At that hour, thanks to God, my Otacília was far from that place, sheltered and protected. As soon we wound up everything, I would fly to where she was, meet and escort her [. . .]. The only sensible thing would be for me to get out of the *sertão* and go to live on a fazenda near town.[129]

The proper ending Riobaldo dreams of includes leaving behind the precarious life of *jagunçagem*, marrying the properly feminine love object Otacília, and getting as far away as possible from the *sertão* and its violence. In short, it means abandoning not only Diadorim but also the openness and uncertainty of the *travessia*. This neatly packaged ending, it turns out, is very close to what Riobaldo has achieved for himself by the time he tells his story to O Doutor: no longer a *jagunço*, Riobaldo has inherited a *fazenda*, married Otacília, and generally settled into a respectable life.

Following the leads of Rowland and Walnice Nogueira Galvão, I read Riobaldo's cardinal sin as that of sacrificing the openness of the *travessia* for the closure and certainty of this proper ending. Regardless of whether the devil exists or whether Riobaldo has sold his soul to him, it is evident that he has committed an act of betrayal and that his narrative bears the guilt of this crime. Yet it is extremely difficult to pinpoint the moment of Riobaldo's transgression. One of the questions he asks his listener to settle is, "*Quando* foi que eu tive minha culpa?" ("*When* did I acquire my guilt?").[130] The impossibility of locating this guilty act in time, and thus expiating it, torments Riobaldo: "Comigo, as coisas não têm hoje e ant'ôntem amanhã: é sempre. Tormentos. Sei que tenho culpas em aberto. Mas quando foi que minha culpa começou?" ("With me things have no today or yesterday or tomorrow, but exist always. Torments. I know that I am outwardly to blame. But when did my fault begin?").[131] The nonlinear *durée* of lived experience that Riobaldo describes here is one of the reasons it is so hard to locate the moment of his transgression. Another is that his "crime" does not take place in a single scene or a single transaction. The scene of the dubiously consummated pact with the devil at Veredas Mortas is infamously ambiguous and anticlimactic. Other scenes that Riobaldo builds up, such as the final battle against Hermógenes, are similarly opaque, forcing the reader to look elsewhere (and in other times) for the moment when Riobaldo transgressed. Much like the slow violence of environmental destruction or the "atmospheric" violence of colonialism and white supremacy—institutions that even when disavowed as part of a concluded past continue to weigh down the present[132]—Riobaldo's guilt does not stem from a single event.

Instead, the guilt that weighs on his narrative issues from a more diffuse sense of transgression and betrayal, that of crossing over from the dwelling perspective—the blind, immersive perspective of a participant in the landscape, a traveler embarked on a boundless *travessia*—to the external (in spatial and temporal terms) perspective of a spectator and retrospective narrator. This betrayal cannot be separated from Riobaldo's betrayal of Diadorim, his solidarity with his fellow *jagunços*, and the space of the *sertão* itself. In other words, if on the sentimental plane Riobaldo's crime is the betrayal of his beloved, it is on the social plane the selling out of the common *jagunço* for individual social advancement, and on the ecological plane, the abandonment of submerged and relational modes of perception for the extractive view.[133] On a more formal, narratological level, his betrayal is the trading of the uncertainty, contingency, and openness of the *travessia* for the certainty, definiteness, and closure that put an end to it.

Galvão argues that in *Grande sertão*, certainty is conceived as a destructive force associated with death, given that "the essence of life is movement and change."[134] She concludes that the drive to arrest the incessant movement, flow, and changeability of life and replace it with something "crystalized, hardened" is the work of the devil and that this certainty is what Riobaldo bargained for in making a pact: "The pact, as a crime, is something that makes an attempt against the nature of existence, in its fluidity, in its permanent transformation. It's the attempt to have certainty within the uncertainty of living."[135] In pursuing the "the guarantee of certainty," Riobaldo also pursues death, the death not only of his archenemy Hermógenes but also of his beloved Diadorim (the two perish in a mutually fatal knife duel), the errant life of *jaguçagem*, the openness and ambiguity of lived experience, and the *travessia* itself.

Taking Galvão's reading together with Rowland's, it is possible to understand the ambivalence in Riobaldo's narrative toward fixing his life in an exterior and retrospective gaze as a desperate attempt to undo or at least forestall the closure that he himself has willed and set into motion. If there has been a pact with the devil, it has been made out of impatience to escape the *sertão*, which Riobaldo describes as "uma espera enorme" ("just one long wait"), and to trade the suspension of the *travessia* for the arrival of the ending.[136] Telling his life story is the consummation of this betrayal insofar as it represents an attempt to bind the meaning of lived events into a self-justifying narrative. Simultaneously, though, the ambivalence and self-annulling drive of this narrative represent an attempt to undo this transaction by thwarting its teleological impulses and suspending the story, once again, in the *travessia*. Riobaldo thus repents for his own impatience for closure as a young man, an impatience he understands as causing, or at least accelerating, the death of the *sertão* and of his beloved.

Indeed, the scene of Diadorim's death is one moment, though not the only one, in which we might locate Riobaldo's crime or betrayal. Riobaldo impotently watches the events unfold from a safe remove until, at the crucial moment, he loses consciousness. The narrator retrospectively describes this moment as one of transcendence and crossing over: "Subi os abismos. . . . De mais longe, agora davam uns tiros, esses tiros vinham de profundas profundezas. Trespassei. Eu estou depois das tempestades" ("I rose out of the abyss. . . . I could hear firing in the distance, shots coming from great depths. Then I passed through. I have outlasted the storms").[137] Hansen reads this scene as the death of the *jagunço* Riobaldo as character and the emergence of Riobaldo as retrospective narrator.[138] I would nuance Hansen's account by pointing out that the slippage from character to narrator, from *jagunço* to O Doutor's interlocutor, from one who lives the precarity of *jagunçagem* to one who looks back on it and analyzes it, does not happen in a single moment. It is a betrayal of which Riobaldo has always been guilty.

Understood as the act of transcending the dwelling perspective, this act of betrayal is intimately related to Riobaldo's social ambitions and to the quest to produce a stable narrative. Bolle reminds us that, as the (albeit illegitimate) son of a landowner, Riobaldo has never fully belonged to the world of *jagunçagem* and has always possessed the latent capacity to transcend this world.[139] This capacity is also related to his status as a *jagunço letrado*, which, following the argument of Carlos Alonso glossed in the introduction, has always already introduced a gap between him and the "state of ontological grace" of inhabiting rather than narrating the *sertão*.[140] Long before he first met O Doutor, Riobaldo began narrating his experience—to himself, to Quelemem, to Zé Bebelo—in an attempt to make sense of it. This act of narration necessitates gaining the critical distance from which to make judgments, abandoning the immanence of the dwelling perspective, and attempting to objectify his experience from without. Returning to Hansen's terminology, the risk is of "petrifying" his past self. This past self is cleaved from the present self through what Leo Bersani calls the *model of the divided subject*, wherein the conscious mind in the present is perceived as separate from the past (as well as the unconscious) and therefore as capable of objectifying, knowing, and judging it. Memory in the traditional, narrative sense depends on the model of the divided self, which "allows us to sequester the past in the past."[141] Nevertheless, Guimarães Rosa's *travessia* defies this model.

For Riobaldo, the process of separating himself from the *sertão* and from the past is perennially and perhaps willfully suspended. He is tortured by his failure to maintain this critical distance from his lived experience; for this reason he solicits the help of O Doutor. Yet in doing so, he also projects the desire for objective, distant knowledge and for closure onto his interlocutor, as if in this way he could cast himself back on the other side of the breach between living and knowing. One of Riobaldo's cleverest moves as a narrator, in fact, is the way he draws his interlocutor into this back-and-forth, essentially casting O Doutor as the devil impatiently pushing for closure so that he can play the role of resisting this drive and forestalling the death of the *sertão*, the *travessia*, and his narrative. At one point, he implores O Doutor: "Eu conto; o senhor me ponha ponto" ("I tell; you put the final point on my story").[142] Riobaldo thus outsources the violent job of imposing closure on his narrative. As Santiago writes, O Doutor becomes a coprotagonist whose role is to domesticate Riobaldo's narrative, explaining and judging it from a superior position.[143] In this godlike role, he provides the structure that makes Riobaldo's exploration of uncertainty possible. By casting his interlocutor in this role, Riobaldo not only looks for reassurance but also casts himself in the opposite role, rebelling from the authority and structure he seeks out in O Doutor's gaze.

As a result, there is a subtle antagonism between Riobaldo and O Doutor that recalls the relationship Armstrong describes between Guimarães Rosa and his translators: the career diplomat knows how to treat his interlocutor as "both partner and adversary."[144] Bolle, in turn, writes that Riobaldo's dialectic and antagonistic relationship with O Doutor expresses the tension between classes in Brazil.[145] Whether we read O Doutor as a stand-in for the urban intellectual class in Rio de Janeiro and São Paulo or for the international publishers, translators, and literary market that would bring his story to a global audience, it is clear that Rosa sees the act of collaboration as a delicate diplomatic relationship rife with the potential for betrayal. Importantly, however, it is also an opportunity to educate his interlocutor, making him feel the guilt, violence, and futility of the very undertaking with which he is tasked: imposing legibility and form on the *sertão*.

In sum, Riobaldo fears he has made a Faustian pact in the sense of trading the chaos and intimacy of lived experience for the all-knowing perspective of the gods or, perhaps more aptly in Guimarães Rosa's world, the birds. The act of narrating his life to an outsider is for Riobaldo both the apogee of this sellout and a desperate bid to undo it by strategically denying his listener the vantage point from without and from afterward, thus entangling us, too, in the *travessia* and making it impossible for us to do exactly what he asks us to do: bring his story to a close and judge it through a retrospective lens.

In the historical context of the *sertão*, the exterior perspective Riobaldo denies his listener corresponds with the violently reifying perspective of the cartographers, the ethnographers, the geologists, and the prospectors—in short, the colonizers, the settlers, and the extractive capitalists. In becoming both a landowner and a relator of local lore, Riobaldo eventually joins this class. His divided subjectivity thus expresses what Andermann calls the "radical form of alienation" often apparent in regionalist literature, wherein urban migration in the wake of "boom-and-bust" extractivist development "forced inhabitants into becoming agents of the destruction of their own lifeworlds."[146] The tension of the dialogue with O Doutor, through which the narrator Riobaldo attempts to re-create a world prior to this betrayal while passing the blame for seeking its death on to his interlocutor, gives external form to this internal alienation.

At the same time, the outside vantage point the text ambivalently rejects aligns with the perspective of the educated elite in Brazil (a class of which the author was a member) and of the burgeoning international readership for Latin American literature, of which Guimarães Rosa had to be aware as a world-traveled diplomat and an active collaborator with his international translators. As a *jagunço letrado* who relates life in the *sertão* to an outside audience, Riobaldo is a go-between spanning these worlds, but unlike the figure of the conciliatory transculturator or the cooperative native informant, he does not simply advance the cause of universal legibility of the particular.

Granted, the structural conceit of the dialogue between Riobaldo and O Doutor has been read as "very successfully bridg[ing] the imaginary gap between the educated, intellectual world of Brazilian cities and the universe of the still remote, rural backlands" with "a harmonious epic structure constituted by the most heterogeneous of elements."[147] Nevertheless, this same dialogue, according to Bolle's reading, manifests the incomprehension, strained communication, and tension between these diverse sectors of Brazil. My analysis in this chapter has been aimed in part at showing why and how the latter reading is more compelling. Furthermore, I have sought to trace the reader's complicated implication in this dynamic. Because O Doutor is a stand-in for the reader, *Grande sertão* calls on the reader to grapple with the tensions, contradictions, and what Mary Louise Pratt calls the "perils" of writing and reading in the contact zone.[148] However, as I have noted, Riobaldo is every bit as culpable as O Doutor or the reader in his urge to know and thus to reify, to put an end to, the *sertão*. As I have been emphasizing, moreover, the text does not simply rebuke or chastise the irascible reader; it also invites them to undertake a *travessia* and, thus, imposes its terms of engagement on the reader who is willing to surrender to this immersive perspective.

At this point, I would like to return to the question with which I opened the chapter: what does J. M. Arguedas take from Guimarães Rosa? It is hard to verify if Arguedas had read *Grande sertão*, but he was familiar with the Brazilian writer's short stories; he mentions "A terceira margem do rio" ("The Third Bank of the River") in the diaries of *Los zorros*. In this fable-like story, the narrator's father enigmatically disappears in a canoe not to reach the far bank of the river but, rather, to remain indefinitely suspended between the two banks in "a terceira margem" ("the third bank"). Fantini Scarpelli postulates that the appeal of this story for Arguedas lies in its refusal to explain, to narrate, which amounts to a suspension of the work of narrative transculturation; yet she sees Guimarães Rosa's act of narrative suspension as less pessimistic than Arguedas's in *Los zorros*, which may be precisely why it offered Arguedas valuable inspiration during his struggle to complete his last novel.[149] In the end, however, Fantini Scarpelli focuses less on the generative negativity of Guimarães Rosa's *terceira margem* (the refusal of arrival and resolution) than on its figuration as a third path of hybridity and heterogeneity, one that ends up sounding a lot like Rama's narrative transculturation.[150] Fantini Scarpelli is not alone in this regard—the *terceira margem* has often been taken up as an alternative to the dichotomies that fail to fully account for Brazilian social reality (and for that matter, the dichotomies of Latin America more generally): civilization and *barbarie*, the European and the Indigenous, the universal and the regional, the modern and the archaic.[151] I want to propose instead understanding the *terceira margem* as informed by the notion of the *travessia* that Guimarães Rosa elaborates in *Grande sertão*. Such a conception would be thoroughly rent with negativity: the ungraspable expanse suspended between two banks of a river or between the beginning and the end of a journey or a narrative; the interminable dialectical negotiation between two positions equally impossible to hold: immanence and exteriority.

For Guimarães Rosa (and Arguedas), however, the affective and moral valence of these two positions is quite different. Whereas the fixed and transcendent view from without and from afterward is revealed as epistemologically and ethically bankrupt, the immersiveness of the *travessia* is presented as something to be cherished, cared for, and safeguarded. To be clear, being in the *travessia*, which implies being always in motion, cannot be reduced to a static sense of belonging or at-homeness. Instead, to be in the *travessia* is to be in open-ended relation. According to Finazzi-Agrò, the knowledge to be gleaned from the *travessia* depends on *o convívio* (cohabitation), and Riobaldo's world is made known to us through an incessant and invasive "being in relation": "In fact, in *Gs:v*, the reader is invited to let oneself be totally invaded by the *sertão* and, on the other hand, to invade it with the immeasurable complexity of the self."[152] This relationship of interpenetration with and participation in the text would seem to be diametrically opposed to the posture of critical distance.[153] Yet the reality is, as always in Guimarães Rosa's world, messier.

As I have argued, Riobaldo needs O Doutor to play the role of the outside knowledge seeker (a role continuous with the reformer and colonizer) in order to expiate the guilt of aspiring to such a position of exteriority himself. I have suggested, moreover, that the narrator's ambivalent disavowal of the distant, cartographic, retrospective perspective he might claim over his story is a form of allegiance to the world he narrates: an attempt to atone for having outlived this world and willed its end. At the same time, the dialogue with O Doutor allows Riobaldo to occupy the role of teacher and to model for his listener the renunciation of the totalizing and retrospective gaze in favor of the dwelling perspective. The latent antagonism of this relationship reflects the way Riobaldo needs O Doutor to play his adversary even as he ensnares him into experiencing the *sertão*, in Arguedas's words, "de adentro, muy de adentro" ("from inside, from well inside").

CHAPTER 4

Learning One's Way around *la Zona*

HABITUATING OUR EYES TO JUAN JOSÉ SAER'S WORLD

Juan José Saer's short story "El viajero" recounts the slow, nonlinear movement of a British traveler named Jeremy Blackwood, who appears to be hopelessly lost on the Argentine pampa. From the first glance, it is clear that this is no conventional narrative. The layout on the page, full of breaks and spaces, visually expresses the halting rhythm of the journey traced by its breathless and exhausted protagonist. The story begins:

> Rompió el reloj   el vidrio que protegía el gran cuadrante
> en el que los números romanos terminaban en unas filigra-
> nas prolijas   delicadas   lo diseminó sobre el montón
> de ceniza húmeda que noches atrás había sido la hoguera
> temblorosa que él mismo había encendido

> Estuvo acuclillado un momento   entregado al trabajo
> pueril de espolvorear de vidrio la masa grisácea y pegoteada
> de la ceniza   después se paró y miró a su alrededor

> La llovizna seguía   impalpable lenta   adensándose
> pareciéndose más y más a la niebla a medida que se alejaba
> hacia el gran horizonte circular

He broke the watch   the glass that protected the great
face in which the roman numerals ended in prolific delicate   filigrees   He disseminated it on the pile of wet
ash that nights before had been the trembling fire that he
himself had lit

He was kneeling a moment   given over to the puerile work
of sprinkling the grayish and sticky mass with glass   then
he stopped and looked around him

The drizzle continued   impalpable slow   densify-
ing increasingly resembling the fog as it withdrew toward
the great circular horizon[1]

Why does Jeremy Blackwood break his watch? How did he end up
here, alone and lost? Is he condemned to die on the pampa? These are
questions Saer leaves open, but the final line of the story, "A Jeramías
Blackwood que no dejó ni rastro de su viaje" ("To Jeramías Blackwood
who left no trace of his journey"), suggests that he has been claimed by
his surroundings.[2] Does the switch from Jeremy to Jeramías mean that
he has gone native, or has he been fatally swallowed up by the pampa?
Again, these questions prove unanswerable. What Saer makes clear,
however, is that Jeremy Blackwood, as distinct perhaps from Jeramías,
is exceedingly ill equipped to navigate the landscape in which he finds
himself. The expanse of the pampa, bounded by the circular horizon
and shrouded in mist, is as meaningless as the face of the broken watch;
it reveals to him no information. The gray, mottled textures of drizzle,
broken glass, and ash that make up his field of vision become almost
indistinguishable forms of illegibility.

The reader of this tale is likely to be just as thoroughly confused in
these opening paragraphs but, I would argue, not condemned to remain
so. First, what dooms Blackwood is that the ostensibly blank disk of
the *llanura* signifies nothing to him; to a reader with minimal familiarity with Argentine literature, in contrast, these descriptions evoke
the well-worn trope of *el desierto*. Since Domingo F. Sarmiento's *Facundo* (1845), the pampa has been figured as a desert, a formless void of
culture and reason that deterministically taints the Argentine national
character, both urgently requiring and perennially resisting intervention
from the state in the form of military campaigns, modern infrastructure,
and Western education.[3] The iconography of the pampa thus serves

both as a metonym for the nation and, in Graciela Montaldo's words, "a hole where specificity and meaning disappear."[4] Second, the cyclical structure of the story, though initially disorienting, provides the reader with the opportunity to learn its patterns, to become familiar with its internal logic, rhythms, and refrains. As Noé Jitrik argues, although every text begins as a blank page, for the writer as well as the reader, it does not remain that way for long. If the act of writing is a symbolic population of the desert, the act of reading also produces navigable terrain out of what began as a void of meaning: "The first glance, the first reading, sees it as impenetrable, there is no way in."[5] As we begin to recognize patterns, tropes, and references, however, we realize that our first impression of inscrutability was a product of our gaze, which was not yet adjusted to this textual landscape. Jitrik points out that all gazes are conditioned by visual memory, training, and culture, and that Sarmiento's gaze—informed by his faith in books and reason—was no exception.[6] The foundational myth of the desert as a senseless void is thus reframed as a failure of perception.

In what follows, I contend that beyond simply disarming the imperial gaze that seeks to order and domesticate the rural interior, Saer's fiction reveals it to be an untrained gaze. To Jeremy Blackwood, the pampa maintains its recalcitrant illegibility, but to the patient and observant reader (and perhaps to Jeramías?), the field of gray begins to resolve into something else, revealing that it only appeared empty to the uninitiated. I thus read Saer's much-discussed negative poetics—the use of avant-garde techniques to defamiliarize the familiar, to reflect on the limits of perception and communicability, and to keep the reader from closing in on a stable and totalizing interpretation—as coupled with the education of the reader's gaze.[7] Both within individual texts and throughout his intertextual oeuvre, Saer stages iterative encounters with the same places, the same characters, and the same scenes, thus challenging his reader to learn the lay of the land and to resolve what may at first seem an inscrutable textual landscape into one that is, if not fully intelligible, at least intimately familiar and pregnant with significance. In Saer's most experimental novel, *El limonero real* (1974), I will argue later in this chapter, the tedium and difficulty of the text safeguard against facile appropriation of its pastoral subject matter while demanding of the reader a deeper mode of engagement, one whose ultimate reward is not the ability to visually survey or rationally comprehend the world represented, but rather the ability to sense the temporal and affective depths the landscape enfolds for those who dwell there.

As I have suggested, a similar process plays out in "El viajero." As the story progresses (if we can describe its recursive movement as progression), we learn that Jeremy Blackwood has been wandering for days, that he has been separated from his horse, that he has been going in circles because he cannot identify a single reference point such as a ranch or a tree on the horizon, and that he cannot even navigate by the stars because of the incessant mist and drizzle veiling the sky. The reader's disorientation likely converges with Blackwood's in a moment when both the narrative and its protagonist return to where they have been. The story, which began with the line, "Rompió el reloj," takes us back to the moment immediately *before* this initial action:

> Un momento antes de romper el reloj la perplejidad creció un poco   descubrir que después de caminar dos días parándose únicamente de tanto en tanto para jadear más cómodo   se llegaba otra vez al punto en que la tregua de la llovizna había permitido encender una hoguera débil

> A moment before breaking the watch his perplexity grew a little   discovering that after walking for two days stopping only here and there to pant more comfortably   he arrived again to the point where the respite in the drizzle had permitted him to light a feeble fire[8]

Here, as in the first paragraph, the protagonist stumbles upon the ashes of his own campfire from days earlier, thereby realizing (again?) that he has been walking in circles. Narrative time, too, appears to be moving in circles, as the scene of breaking the watch is narrated *a second time*, as if the recognition of the familiar place has induced the memory of the original event or compelled its repetition:

> Está otra vez en el punto de la hoguera   sacó
> el reloj de su bolsillo   lo rompió   diseminó los
> pedacitos
> de vidrio sobre la ceniza   acuclillado

> Se paró y miró el horizonte   el pajonal
> no sabía que se llamaba así   se extendía
> hasta el horizonte gris parejo   monótono

He is again in the spot of the campfire   he took
the watch out of his pocket   he broke it   he
disseminated the little pieces
of glass on the ash   kneeling

He stood up and looked at the horizon   *el pajonal*
he didn't know it was called that   extended
to the gray, even monotonous   horizon[9]

In this second telling, the cause of Blackwell's disorientation becomes more apparent. Not even knowing the local term for the type of wetland he sees, the British traveler is incapable of distinguishing potential landmarks, and everywhere he looks, he sees only more of the same. Of course, none of this information is exactly new; as throughout Saer's fiction, the purpose of retelling is to make us recognize what we have already seen from a slightly different perspective and, thus, discern more than we saw the first time.

This short story is among other things a rewriting of the tradition of European travel narratives in Latin America. Saer parodies the triumphant tone of *cronistas* who report dominating the landscape by beholding it from a panoramic perspective or cutting a linear path of progress through it.[10] Here, as in *Grande sertão: Veredas* (discussed in chapter 3), there is no cartographic perspective from on high to be had; nor is the corresponding site of enunciation—that of an objective, scientific, and masterful outsider—available to the narrator, much less to the protagonist. Jeremy Blackwood is limited to his own bodily perceptions and irrelevant memories and visions of home. Moreover, as the narrative and the protagonist return again and again to the point where they began, the passage of time ceases to correspond with forward progress. The recursive temporality of the story draws dizzying circles around the protagonist and underscores the futility of his advancement. With every cycle, Jeremy Blackwood appears more doomed, and yet, with every cycle the reader has a better sense of his predicament, is better equipped to make sense of what Saer has been showing us all along. Though transparent, totalizing vision never becomes possible, the opacity of our experience of the text takes on new meaning.

I read "El viajero" as a metatextual fable for the experience of navigating Saer's fiction, particularly in infamously difficult texts such as *El limonero real* (1974), *La mayor* (1976), and *Nadie nada nunca* (1980).

The cyclical narrative structure and strangely opaque visual descriptions characteristic of "El viajero" are defining features of these texts, which collectively mark the most experimental phase of Saer's career. These are also the first works that Saer publishes from exile in France and the first that self-consciously anticipate an audience composed of outsiders to *la zona*, the regional world where Saer's fiction is set.[11] Not coincidentally, their composition spans one of the most turbulent and repressive eras in Argentine history, a period that includes the second presidency and subsequent death of Juan D. Perón, the coup that would put General Rafael Videla in power in 1976, and the so-called dirty war, in which upward of thirty thousand Argentinians were disappeared, tortured, and killed at the hands of the military junta. As Florencia Garramuño argues, the opacity of Saer's poetics in this phase of his career can be read as reflecting the senselessness and trauma of living through this historical moment.[12] For the reader of these texts, the accretion of concrete details—such as the texture of the broken glass falling on campfire ash in "El viajero"—creates a dense visual field, but this density, much like the incessant mist and drizzle that shroud the pampa in gray, obscures more than it reveals. One often has the sense when reading Saer's fiction from this period that nothing that matters can be seen, in spite of an abundance of visual information.

THE POLITICS OF OBSCURITY

How are we as readers to penetrate a world rendered in such vivid but thick, turbid detail? I would contend that this is the wrong question. Saer's pseudo-objectivist descriptions create deliberately opaque surfaces that detain the reader on the threshold of psychological and historical depths whose inaccessible presence they might nevertheless sense.[13] Importantly for my reading, as distinct from Garramuño's, the opacity of these descriptions does not merely reflect the impossibility of understanding experience but also leads us to approach experience differently. When narrative coherence and symbolic meaning become inaccessible, our attention is redirected to phenomenological perceptions. To be clear, it is not that immediate, private, sensorial experience (what Walter Benjamin called *Erlebnis*) compensates for the lost ability to accumulate and transmit social and historical experience (*Erfahrung*). Saer appears to share Theodor Adorno's pessimism regarding this possibility.[14] Nevertheless, the Adornian negativity that many readers have identified in Saer's approach does not foreclose the possibility of finding meaning in embodied interactions with the world.[15]

On the contrary, as Jason Baskin has argued, the anti-totalizing impulse of Adorno's thought itself reflects a phenomenological point of view.[16] Baskin draws a parallel between the awareness of negative spaces and unseen depths in one's perceptual field that Maurice Merleau-Ponty signals and the humbling recognition demanded by Adorno's negative dialectics: that our concepts do not exhaust the world but, rather, leave a remainder.[17] Because perception is an embodied activity, Baskin reminds us by way of Merleau-Ponty, one always sees from a situated perspective rather than a totalizing cartographic perspective. As such, any three-dimensional object whose surface we observe necessarily has depths that are not directly discernible from our vantage point. This does not mean that these depths are hidden, coded, or completely imperceptible to the viewer; on the contrary, our embodied interaction with the world depends on our being aware that there is an unseen backside to every frontside we see. According to Baskin's gloss of Merleau-Ponty, our phenomenological experience of the world is always already "thickened by the negativity of 'indeterminate presences' [. . .] aspects of the object that cannot be seen, but have a presence in the perceptual field."[18] It is hard to think of a better way to describe Saer's most experimental texts than "thickened by indeterminate presences." (In resonant terms, Beatriz Sarlo compares the political developments that silently underlie the evolution of Saer's *zona* as the reverse side of a tapestry, whose existence we can only infer from the side we do see.)[19] In Baskin's materialist account of late modernist literature, these "indeterminate presences" include social, historical, and economical processes. Baskin argues that rather than lying behind the surfaces we behold, awaiting hermeneutic excavation, these are immanent in the seemingly intransitive and opaque details we can directly observe in certain modernist texts.

The question that preoccupies Adorno—and Saer as well, I would argue—is how we might heighten our awareness of that which escapes the grasp of our direct perceptions and our conceptual systems. In order to perceive what is not immediately apparent, much less named, in Saer's narrative world, we must "habituate our eyes" to its opacity. This is a phrase that Saer uses in "Narrathon," an essay written in 1973, a grim moment for Latin American democracies.[20] Here Saer assigns the writer a specific role in times of repression. He describes the author's duty to inhabit the same blind, gray experience that his readers struggle to navigate: "Sharing with millions, hundreds of millions, the gray blindness, the dark night of oppression, the writer must try, as far as possible, to habituate his eyes to this darkness and to recognize it, and to make others recognize it."[21] There is a certain pessimism in this view, which confines the writer to teaching us to live with darkness rather than dispelling it with the light of truth, as would be the response of some of Saer's more militant contemporaries.[22] Still, these lines express commitment to the pedagogical function of literature: if not a weapon with which to fight oppression, it is at least a tool that can teach us to recognize the experience of oppression for what it is.

As Francine Masiello claims in her reading of *Nadie nada nunca*, training us to perceive our reality differently is the first step toward political awakening in a time of acute repression. *Nadie nada nunca* obliquely gestures to the disappearances, torture, and murder carried out by the state during Argentina's last dictatorship and conjures the mood of generalized fear, paranoia, and denial that accompanies the increased militarization of the country. Though a reader ignorant of the historical context could conceivably miss this backdrop, perceiving only the vague but ominous tone that hangs over the descriptions of banal actions, this novel takes on political subject matter more directly than any of Saer's other works written during the dictatorship. Masiello concludes that its political intervention does not consist simply of depicting and denouncing state violence; rather, "Saer teaches us different ways to be perceptive . . . to sense what is deeply wrong."[23]

This is, as many readers of Saer have noted, a negative project in the Adornian sense: the civic work of the reader begins with the realization that something is missing or "off" and takes the form of learning to perceive the shape of these negative spaces. David Oubiña describes the work of Saer's reader as learning to "see" more than what is present: "It's not about seeing only what is seen or seeing only beyond what is seen but, rather, seeing the emptiness in what is seen [. . .] then one understands that what representation does is precisely to allow absence to take place."[24] By attuning ourselves to the existence of what is not directly represented, what is unspeakable (because it is too traumatic, because it must be censored, or because it exceeds capture by language and concepts), we become aware of "the wrong state of things" that compels negative dialectics in the first place.[25] Just as importantly, we also become aware of still-opaque, indeterminate possibilities that have been excluded by this state of being. Therein lies the hope or futurity that is often missed in Adorno and Saer alike. For both, the value of negativity is that it gestures to a beyond, not just to that which has been irrecoverably lost but also to that which we may yet learn to perceive if we refuse to accept that currently available discourses exhaust the world.

This entryway into thinking about the political is indispensable for analyzing a body of work in which politics is extremely difficult to pin down. Saer insisted that his political commitment was immanent in his work and did not require explanation: "If you want to fully know my political position, *read me*."[26] Though he expressed aversion to any ideological dogma, he did believe in committed literature but understood it as an act of immersion in the world rather than explication of the world: "Commitment is precisely the result of immersion in a concrete situation. [. . .] The writer is not a tenor who enunciates generalities on a well-lit stage but a half-blind man who tries to see clearly in the blackness of history."[27] The obscurity of Saer's poetics is thus not at cross-purposes with his political commitment but integral to it.

In Saer's most experimental work, eschewing novelistic conventions— plot, intrigue, the totalizing vision of an omniscient narrator—becomes a way of resisting the commercialization of literature in the capitalist system and eluding the grip of the totalitarian state, threats that Saer sees as intertwined in Latin America during the period from the 1960s to the 1980s.[28] Saer sets out to subvert the qualities of prose that he claims have long made it "the instrument par excellence of the State": its clarity, coherence, efficiency, pragmatism, certainty, and commitment to the communicable.[29] It is through the formal difficulty of his works that Saer repudiates the commodification of Latin American culture in an increasingly globalized literary market and, specifically, the essentializing appropriations of the rural interior by national-populist discourses.[30]

FROM THE REGION AND THE NATION TO *LA ZONA*

Beyond reflecting what Garramuño calls the "opacity of experience during periods of state repression," Saer's negativity in his treatment of *las provincias* counteracts a regime of visibility that had long been deployed to domesticate and package regional difference. According to Jens Andermann, the consolidation of the modern Argentine nation has always depended on the state's ability to visualize the nation and, in particular, to render visible the least explored regions and most autochthonous cultures by way of maps, museum exhibits, *cuadros costumbristas*, and photography.[31] This last medium becomes the operative visual technology of populist states in the mid-twentieth century. In Argentina, Peronist propaganda, including photography and film, afforded a privileged position to the *campesino* in the discursive construction of *el pueblo*.[32] Far from the benign incorporation of alterity into an image of national unity, Gareth Williams argues, this rhetorical move is one of interpellation: the rural interior enters the nation as its subaltern other.[33] In the process, it is displaced into an archaic past. In fact, the disappearance and marginalization of rural figures such as the *gaucho* accompany their symbolic appropriation as figures in which to ground national identity.[34]

Saer's fiction actively resists the regime of visibility that leads to appropriation of the region by the nation. Though Saer has always proudly claimed affiliation with fellow Argentine writers such as Macedonio Fernández, Jorge Luis Borges, and Juan L. Ortiz, he consistently expresses an almost allergic aversion to discourses of nationalism and vociferously disavows any affiliation with regionalist literature, which he calls "a poor conception of literature."[35] Saer's cursory dismissal of regionalist literature risks making a straw man out of a complex and heterogeneous tendency in Latin American letters; nevertheless, his objections to the label are grounded in an astute critique: Saer alleges that overreliance on the category of "rural literature" posits a false binary between the local and the cosmopolitan, implying that those on the geographic peripheries do not participate in universal learned culture, and falsely suggesting that rural setting is aesthetically and thematically deterministic.[36] In the face of these stereotypes, Saer repudiates the ideological work regionalist literature has often been asked to perform—that of converting traditional ways of life into objects of folklore to be claimed as national patrimony—as well as the scourge of exoticism for which Saer criticizes prominent figures of the Latin American boom.[37]

In fact, Saer directly defies the expectations of foreign readers who seek in Latin American literature representations of local or national identity:

> I don't write to exhibit my supposed Argentineness, even if the expectations of many readers, especially non-Argentines, will be frustrated. I don't speak as an Argentine but as a writer. Narrative is not an ethnographic document nor a sociological document, nor is the narrator a middleman whose purpose is to represent the totality of a nation.[38]

I want to insist, however, that Saer's anti-nationalism—grounded in his experience with the populist rhetoric of the Perón regime and the authoritarianism and repression of the ensuing military dictatorships in Argentina—is not grounds for ignoring the profoundly local sense of belonging out of which his literature arises. On the contrary, it is precisely this aporia—of embracing the local as well as the global, while rejecting the construct of the nation—that makes Saer a critical regionalist.

Saer's vast and intertextual oeuvre famously coheres around what he calls "unidad de lugar" ("unity of place"): all his texts take place in *la zona*, a fictional version of the author's native Santa Fe province. Much like Honoré de Balzac's Paris, William Faulkner's Yoknapatawpha County, Mississippi, or Juan Carlos Onetti's Santa María de Buenos Aires, Saer's *zona* is populated by a cast of recurring characters. Many readers have noted that, far less totalizing than Balzac's *comédie humaine*, Saer's *zona* is fragmented and riddled with negativity.[39] Sarlo, for example, remarks that "the fictions present themselves, frequently, as versions and attempts to surround from different angles a totality which, by definition, cannot be completely represented."[40] The anti-totalizing nature of Saer's *zona* actively subverts the role regionalist literature has historically been assigned in nationalist discourses. Saer's essays make clear that writing (and incessantly rewriting) *la zona* allows him to carve out a space for the local apart from the nation-state. He has called the nation "a conspiracy against the individual," and the tradition of national literature a tool the totalitarian state uses to enforce its hegemony.[41] By in large, however, the most direct targets of Saer's critique are not Argentina's consecrated literary heroes, but rather those of his contemporaries whom he saw as exploiting regional culture for ideological or market motives.[42] For example, in *Lo imborrable* (1993), the character Carlos Tomatis writes a scathing review of a regionalist novel turned bestseller written by Walter Bueno, an opportunistic writer who also writes propaganda for the dictatorship.[43]

In short, Saer's *zona* decidedly resists being read as a metonym for the nation. As Ricardo Piglia has argued, *la zona* is located *beyond* the nation, offering a space from which the nation can be critiqued: "From this local space the nation is seen as a foreign territory, land occupied by official culture. The artist resists in his *zona* and establishes a direct link between his region and global culture."[44] In effect, *la zona* bypasses the nation as it shuttles back and forth between the local and the universal, configuring what Luigi Patruno calls "an extranational space."[45] It is in this vein that I read Saer's *zona* as anticipating Gayatri Chakravorty Spivak's notion of critical regionalism as a way of going "over and under the nation" to find new ways of articulating collective identity.[46]

Following the likes of Piglia, Patruno, and Laura Demaría, I see Saer as engendering through his fiction a *zona* that is *not* coterminous with the nation, a literary space that resists geographic or ideological definition and, instead, opens itself up as a site for aesthetic experience. Echoing Adorno, Saer insists that such work is urgently necessary in a totalitarian age:

> Preserving the illuminating capacity of poetic experience, its specificity as an instrument of anthropological knowledge, this is, it seems to me, the work that any rigorous writer should set himself. This position, which might seem aestheticizing or individualist, is on the contrary eminently political. In our age of ideological reduction, of repressive planning, aesthetic experience, which is one of our last freedoms, is constantly threatened. The principal function of the artist is then to safeguard its specificity.[47]

The politics of Saer's work must then be understood in negative terms: wresting *la zona* away from the certainty of ideology and returning it to the necessarily fragmentary and unstable epistemologies of fiction, memory, and subjective experience.

It is along these lines that Sarlo first reclaimed Saer as a committed author: his literature acts as a weapon against authoritarian discourse not by dealing with political subject matter but, rather, by insisting on the autonomy, the multiplicity, and the irreducibility of the worlds it creates.[48] In direct opposition to the way the rural interior has been coded alternately as *barbarie* and national heartland by intellectuals from Sarmiento to Leopoldo Lugones to Ricardo Rojas, Saer's work refuses to sacrifice the dynamic, temporally animate *experience* of place for the sake of producing legible national narratives.[49] This is a point to which I will return at the end of the chapter, but first it is necessary to emphasize that Saer's experimental poetics do not simply shut down overdetermined ways of knowing the region; they also open up alternative ways of knowing.

BEYOND NEGATIVITY

> The world is difficult to perceive. Perception is difficult to communicate. The subjective is unverifiable. Description is impossible.[50]

Saer describes a lot for someone skeptical of the practice. The dominant trend in the reception of Saer's work is to follow the author's cue and emphasize the difficulty, if not the impossibility, of arriving at the world through our perceptions and of transmitting our perceptions through writing. Sarlo, for example, reads Saer's narrative techniques in his most experimental phase as interrogating the possibility of perceiving, much less representing the materiality of the world, which is never stable but always caught in the flux of time.[51] In a related vein, Oubiña argues that Saer inverts the notion of description as a tool of positivism by emphasizing reality's way of escaping "the microscope of its perception": "Description here is not an instrument of capture but rather an operation that witnesses how the object slips and irredeemably escapes."[52] Psychoanalytic approaches, such as those of Garramuño and Julio Premat, put similar emphasis on negativity and failure. Premat reads Saer's undoing of vision as expressing an impossible, melancholic longing to recuperate a presymbolic oneness with the real, with the other, with the materiality of the world.[53] The fragmentation, opacity, and unintelligibility of the resulting narratives convey the futility of the endeavor: "The past is unnarratable (the story is out of reach), the world is not representable or nameable."[54] Premat sees this aesthetic as expressing a despondency that traverses several planes: personal melancholy, metaphysical despair at our inability to know our world, metaliterary preoccupation with how texts approach (or distance us from) reality, and collective social trauma related to Argentina's history of military dictatorship.[55]

Homing in on the relevance of this last point, Garramuño argues that the breakdown of meaning in Saer's experimental poetics expresses a specific, historical crisis, rather than the generalized estrangement from experience in aesthetic modernism. It is not simply that experience (*Erfahrung*) has become impossible to transmit through art but, rather, that experience itself has become opaque and unfathomable during the dictatorship, ceasing to be "a place of knowledge" and becoming instead "a site of ignorance and trauma."[56] Whereas she sees modernist art as highlighting the loss of experience through negative poetics *and* compensating for this loss by turning away from representation toward abstraction, she insists that Saer's poetics turn *toward* the world, through obsessive but never transparent attempts at realistic representation, thus repeating the senselessness and trauma of modern life rather than compensating for it or analyzing it.[57] In Garramuño's reading of Saer's negativity as a reaction to Argentina's last military dictatorship, then, unintelligibility becomes both a form of reproducing a world that no longer makes sense and a way of distancing literature from the rational discourses of the state.

I am proposing a different approach, one that does not take Saer at his word when he proclaims the utter impossibility of perception and description. Instead, I read Saer's incessant attempts to bring his *zona* into being in literature as testifying to his reluctance to abandon what would seem to be an impossible undertaking: wresting the ephemeral experience of everyday life away from abstraction and ideology without forgoing its communicability. In other words, I am interested in how we can read Saer's negative aesthetic as doing more than foreclosing the quest for meaning and the transmissibility of experience. How does it also bring us back to the phenomenological experience of dwelling?

As we began to see in "El viajero," what one learns by reading Saer is how to recognize recurrences and how to build a sense of place, a sense of meaning based on iterative encounters. Even in the absence of proper names, events, and landmarks, the reader recognizes from one text to another the sensorial qualities of *la zona*: its heat in the summer, its mist in the morning, its expansion across vast rivers and vaster plains. This "unidad de lugar" forged by returning to the same landscapes again and again is one of the lessons Saer learned from the poet Juan L. Ortiz, whom he claimed as a friend and mentor.[58] Ortiz, who filled volumes with poems about his native Entre Ríos province, uses intertextual repetition—the revisiting of the same riverbanks, the same trees, the same fields—not as a means of consolidating a totalizing vision of the landscape but, rather, as a means of revealing its temporality and emphasizing the singularity of each moment it enfolds: a field observed at dawn in the winter is not the same as a field observed in summer, in the afternoon, in the rain, and so on. In keeping with the accumulative logic of Ortiz's poetic oeuvre, it is the thickening of the same spaces with different times that teaches the reader of Saer's work how to discern an intelligible narrative world by moving between scenes that, when taken individually, may seem inconsequential or even devoid of meaning,

To further examine this phenomenon, we might turn to one of the most extreme and most frequently cited examples of how Saer dissolves the link between perception and knowledge: the short story "La mayor," published in the collection of the same name (1976). The story is a Proustian parody in which the unnamed first-person protagonist takes a bite of moistened cracker and finds that he remembers nothing at all. The refrain, "Otros, antes, podían" ("Others, before, used to be able to"), gestures to a lost capacity to recover the past through memory, to arrive at a totality from fragments, and to abstract meaning from perceptions. This story has been central to a range of readings that focus on the negativity and melancholia of Saer's poetics, including the above-cited work of Sarlo, Oubiña, Premat, and Garramuño.

"La mayor" puts particular emphasis on the opacity of vision. The protagonist's gaze "interrogates" but finds that the objects it beholds "don't show anything."[59] Most of the text is given over to disconnected descriptions of the protagonist's material surroundings: a folder and some blurry photographs on a desk, a Van Gogh print on the wall, the nighttime cityscape beheld from the terrace. This last image evokes Paris at dusk as beheld by Rastignac at the end of Balzac's *Père Goriot*,[60] but whereas that panoramic view of the lights coming on across the city has a totalizing effect in keeping with the exhaustiveness of Balzac's realist project, Saer's narrative gaze does not synthesize the images it takes in to form a coherent vista. Instead, it registers the city as a list of fragmentary images: "las casas, los árboles, las terrazas, las calles que se entrecortan cada cien metros, los edificios blanqueados, como huesos, por la luna, los parques negros, los ríos, los bares sucios, todavía abiertos" ("the houses, the trees, the terraces, the streets that intersect every hundred meters, the buildings whitened, like bones, by the moon, the black parks, the rivers, the dirty bars, still open").[61] As Oubiña observes, the crises of vision, meaning, and memory staged in this story are reflected on the level of the sentence: when vision can no longer aggregate disparate images into a panorama and when narrative can no longer weave isolated events into an order governed by causality or teleology, we are left with enumeration and parataxis.[62] In "La mayor," as elsewhere in his most experimental work, Saer's form of vision is opaque in that it cannot penetrate the surfaces it beholds and myopic in that it cannot generalize based on the particular.

Nevertheless, Saer's experimental visual poetics do more than dismantle (or bemoan the loss of) the link between seeing and knowing, between perceiving and understanding. Without returning to the compensatory model of literature with which Garramuño's reading breaks (that literature redeems the brokenness or senselessness of the modern world), I contend that drawing attention to the lost ability to know by looking—to construct sweeping panoramas out of the fragmentary and particular, and to find knowledge of the real in such overviews—is only part of Saer's contrapuntal or dialectical poetic project. The other part lies in teaching the reader to perceive what Benjamin has called the *opti-*

cal unconscious: what is invisible beyond the frame or behind the visual surface. This includes temporal depths, affective moods, and social, economic, and political relations. If the nineteenth-century Latin American *costumbrista* novel aspired to convey the whole of a society through a series of photographically rendered vignettes, Saer appears to parody this aesthetic by taking it to such extremes that visual information starts to become meaningless. The visual *cuadros* Saer renders are often so minute that they tell us nothing. Nevertheless, the first impression of unintelligibility is not the end of the story. Each time we reencounter a previously narrated scene, we see more, both because Saer adds new sensorial details and because, reading between discontinuous iterations, we begin to perceive what Saer has not directly shown us.

To return to the example of "La mayor," even though the narrator has lost the ability to resolve fragmentary images into visual totality or narrative coherence, the astute reader is equipped to come away with more than isolated splotches of color. Premat's and Garramuño's own analyses demonstrate this point. Grasping the indirect references to Van Gogh and Proust (neither one is named in the story), for example, allows us to read into Saer's story a reflection on aesthetic modernism. A reader versed in Saer's *zona* will recognize the unnamed protagonist as Carlos Tomatis, one of Saer's most frequently recurring characters, because Saer has made reference elsewhere to the Van Gogh print framed on Tomatis's wall. These clues, gleaned intertextually, do not restore the totality or coherence of the world evoked, but they do give the reader an active role to play, one whose primary mode is not interpretation but recognition, not the construction of an overview but the cultivation of familiarity. Instead of *el saber* (knowledge per se), what we glean is *el conocimiento* (a necessarily imperfect translation might give us "acquaintance").[63]

Perhaps we can no longer do what "otros, antes, podían," but through his experimental poetics, Saer insists that we can and must cultivate other ways of knowing our world and of transmitting it through literature.[64] As my reading of *Grande sertão: Veredas* in chapter 3 suggests, these other ways of knowing may prove less objectifying and imperialistic than the totalizing panorama and linear plot that critical regionalist authors like Guimarães Rosa and Saer reject. I thus join critics such as Masiello and Rafael Arce, who have begun to call for an approach to reading Saer that moves beyond negativity. In Arce's words, "The insistence on the negative work of Saer's narrative in criticism impedes recognizing this tension, which correlates to a positive quest:

one that attempts to *inscribe* something of the material experience of the world."[65] Arce proposes that Saer's negativity is the dialectical counterpoint to an earnest effort to make the experience of his *zona* transmissible. Masiello, in turn, makes explicit that Saer's negative poetics serve a pedagogical-political mission, one that she claims Garramuño has overlooked in her reading of *Nadie nada nunca*:

> What [Garramuño] misses is the education of the senses that follows in this elliptical break. In this interstitial zone, Saer teaches us how to assemble a story that leads to eventual critique. [. . .] Here, he signals a path of learning that leads to political awareness. With it, we come to value description and to discern what lies beyond it; we learn to detain the flow of time in order to learn how to feel. This, then, is an education of the senses that takes place in Argentina.[66]

In Masiello's analysis, the negativity, the breaks in narration, and the opaque descriptions are there to slow us down, to make us *feel*, so that we might learn to perceive a veiled and silenced political reality. The emphasis on embodied experience of place in this recent turn in the reception of Saer's work dovetails naturally with the theoretical framework that I, drawing on the work of Tim Ingold, have elaborated as the dwelling perspective.

As I emphasized in chapter 3, the dwelling perspective entails not only spatial immanence but also a peculiar temporal mode of engagement. Differentiating the dwelling perspective from the cartographic perspective, in which the totality of the landscape is simultaneously disclosed through the illusion of a view from nowhere, Ingold emphasizes the sedimented temporality of perception for the dweller: one comes to know one's environment through the accumulation of situated encounters with it over the course of a lifetime. The landscape is thus progressively disclosed through embodied interaction with it.[67] As I have argued throughout this book, there is an ethical dimension to cultivating the dwelling perspective in literature, which is related to what Édouard Glissant calls *poetics of duration*. Whereas making the world instantaneously perceptible in "lightning flashes" pretends to deliver it in its totality, disclosing the world through "the accumulation of sediments" makes a different demand on the reader; it "urges on those who attempt to live this totality."[68] In Saer, discerning what a given scene means is not a matter of zooming out to an impossible bird's-eye perspective or zooming in to microanalyze details but, rather, of repeatedly encountering it in different contexts, different points in the narration, and, often, in different texts. This is how the reader might come to *live* (over time) a totality that cannot be grasped but that must instead perpetually be imaginatively assembled by aggregating disparate moments and different views.

My focus on vision thus far foregrounds the (impossible) construction of a spatial totality, but as the allusion to Proust in "La mayor" reveals, this story is principally about how we reconstruct the past, or more precisely, how sensorial experience in the present conjures the past through involuntary memory. This capacity has not been lost, neither in this story nor in Saer's world more generally. Saer's objectivist descriptions may conjure a timeless present or a discontinuous series of stills (as in Oubiña's insightful reading of Saer's visual aesthetics as chronophotographic).[69] What the inculcated reader learns to perceive, however, is that each ostensibly suspended moment is animated by the presence of past and future times, which become perceptible to those who know how to look. What is more, knowing how to look is not an innate quality available to some readers and not others; it is a learnable skill that the text endeavors to impart.

A GAZE THAT GATHERS TIME

Saer appears to theorize the temporal depth and animation of the dweller's gaze in a passage in one of his preliminary sketches for the opening of *El limonero real*. Wenceslao, the fisherman protagonist of the novel, describes the experience of looking at the familiar face of his wife:

> Yo miro pensativo su cara, que a medida que ella recoge el tenso pelo hacia la nuca, se hace un nítido óvalo oscuro, color tierra, trabajado por el tiempo y el aire; hago algo más que mirar: porque si solamente mirara, vería un rostro y no el tiempo, el sufrimiento, y la lluvia. Vería menos que una cara. Vería ojos, y piel, y esa boca desdentada, y mandíbulas, y nariz, y orejas, no lo que puedo reunir mediante el recuerdo y llamar su rostro.

> Thoughtful, I look at her face, which, as she collects her taut hair toward her nape, forms a sharp, dark, earth-colored

oval, worked over by time and by the air; I do something more than look: because if I only looked, I would see a face and not time, suffering, and rain. I would see less than a face. I would see eyes, and skin, and that toothless mouth, and jaws, and a nose, and ears, not what I can gather through memory and call her face.[70]

This meditation does not appear in the final version of the novel, the majority of which is narrated in the third person. Nevertheless, I read the novel as a whole as aspiring to more-than-look on the narrated world with the temporal fullness with which Wenceslao contemplates his wife's face in this passage. Just as Wenceslao sees this familiar face not simply as the collection of shapes and colors that appears before him in the present moment but, instead, as a temporal composition, one that has been shaped by time, suffering, and rain, so too does the novel seek to show the world it narrates not simply as it might appear in a snapshot of the present but, rather, as a time-bound way of life that has been and continues to be shaped by the cyclical rhythms of work, weather, and hardship. This world only acquires depth and meaning when beheld by a gaze that (re)collects other times, both past and future. As is evident in this example, this mode of perception—animated by memory and affect—is not only more intimate; it also reveals more than would be revealed by an objective, analytic gaze that would break the face into its component parts and end up seeing "menos que una cara" ("less than a face").

For Saer, recollecting the past in this way is indistinguishable from the act of sensorial perception in the present. As Arce emphasizes, what makes Saer's treatment of the past different from memory per se is that the past is evoked in the form of sensations rather than narratives.[71] The visual tableaux Saer describes—landscapes, faces, quotidian scenes—do not simply trigger involuntary memories; *they already contain* them. In this way, Saer's world demands to be read as Ingold suggests the archeologist and the "native dweller" alike read the landscape:

> The landscape tells—or rather is—a story. It enfolds the lives and times of predecessors who, over the generations, have moved around in it and played their part in its formation. To perceive the landscape is therefore to carry out an act of remembrance, and remembering is not so much a matter of calling up an internal image, stored in the mind, as of engag-

ing perceptually with an environment that is itself pregnant with the past.[72]

In a similar fashion, the reader of *El limonero real* must learn to more-than-look in order to perceive a story that will not be directly related. Instead, it has been incorporated into the materiality of the landscape and the bodies that inhabit it.

El limonero real describes one day in the lives of peasant families living on remote islands in the Río Paraná. The novel begins over and over again, each time breaking off to recommence with the identical refrain: "Amanece. Y ya está con los ojos abiertos" ("Dawn breaks. And his eyes are already open"). The cycle repeats eight times (nine counting the last line of the novel), with each iteration progressing slightly further into the day than the last. Much as we saw in the cyclical structure of "El viajero," each retelling revisits previously narrated scenes from a slightly different perspective, making it extremely difficult for a first-time reader to tell if one is making narrative progress or reading in circles. One of the most remarkable features of this novel is that the narration of one day reveals through an obscured form of vision a story of much greater duration and consequence: the loss of a way of life as the rural community depicted becomes economically unviable and the younger generation leaves for the city.

Relatively little takes place during the day narrated: a family celebrates the new year by gathering, preparing and consuming food, drinking, conversing, and dancing late into the night. Yet, through the layering of recursive narrative fragments, frequently interrupted by flashbacks and visions, the novel slowly saturates the minute and the quotidian (the petting of a dog, the washing of a face, the paddling of a canoe, the deboning of a fish, etc.) with deeply emotional human drama: the tragic loss of a son who fell to his death from an urban construction site, a wife still immobilized by grief years later, an alcoholic brother-in-law (Agustín) who has lost his daughters to sex work in the city, and the ever-present contrast between these devastated families and the comparatively intact nuclear family of Wenceslao's other in-laws (Rosa and Rogelio).

The recursive temporal structure of *El limonero real* involves the reader in the process of re-collecting scattered moments in order that we might begin not only to follow the story that spans them but to perceive the affective charge they collectively carry. As in "El viajero," with every iteration, we become better equipped to recognize the recurring landmarks in the narrative, to discern the clues that we have returned to a familiar scene. We learn, for example, to draw connections between discontinuous scenes that are linked by the same temporal and seasonal markers: saturated with midday sun, illuminated by the full moon, muted by fog, and so on. Importantly, orienting ourselves to this world is not a matter of transcending it, of achieving an elevated point of view that allows us to separate ourselves from the landscape and contemplate its totality. Instead, in the process of reading we undergo a form of *apprentissage*, what James Gibson calls an "education of attention."[73] This is how Ingold argues we learn to dwell, whether we are natives to the environment or outsiders being inducted into it.[74] Neither a lesson to be received passively nor one that is ever complete and mastered, this form of education amounts to the active, ongoing, cumulative practice of inhabiting *la zona*.

In the interest of illustrating this phenomenon with a concrete example, let's take a set of scenes (in truth, multiple iterations of the same scene) that take place under the punishing midday sun: Wenceslao and his brother-in-law Rogelio are making their way on foot to a local bar when Wenceslao perceives a mirage on the horizon. The mirage appears at high noon, when the sun gives the illusion of holding still at the apex of its arc and when the staggering midday heat makes movement feel impossible. This image first appears in the form of a visual premonition of sorts, projected from an earlier moment when the day is still new and cool:

> A mediodía el sol calcinará el aire, lo hará polvo; la arena de la costa se pondrá blanca, la tierra parecerá cocida y después como encalada, y cruzando el río y a una hora de a pie desde la otra orilla, el camino de asfalto que lleva a la ciudad se llenará de espejismos de agua.

> At midday the sun will scorch the air, it will turn it to dust; the sand of the coast will become white, the earth will seem cooked and later as if whitewashed, and crossing the river and an hour on foot from the other bank, the asphalt road that leads to the city will fill with mirages of water.[75]

The transition to the future tense, a technique used intermittently throughout the novel, allows the narrator's gaze to project itself forward in time (to midday) and in space (to the paved road that is still an hour's walk distant from Wenceslao). The second iteration also employs the future tense and this time thickens the image of the mirage with additional details:

> A mediodía estará en lo alto del cielo, porque sube despacio, sometiendo a las sombras a una reducción lenta; por un momento permanecerá inmóvil en lo alto, el disco al rojo blanco y lleno de destellos paralelo a la tierra y sus rayos verticales chocando contra las cosas, penetrando con incisión sorda la materia que cambia en reposo aparente; la luz llevará por el aire el reflejo de los ríos y de los esteros y lo proyectará sobre el camino de asfalto que corre liso hacia la ciudad creando ante los ojos de los viajeros espejismos de agua.

> At midday it will be at the top of the sky, because it rises slowly, submitting the shadows to a slow reduction; for a moment it will remain immobile at the top, a red-white disk full of sparkles parallel to the earth and its vertical rays crashing into things, penetrating with deaf incision the material that changes in apparent repose; the light will carry the reflection of the rivers and estuaries through the air and will project it on the asphalt road that runs smooth toward the city creating before the eyes of travelers mirages of water.[76]

This version lingers on the sun's momentary immobility as well as the continual changes undergone by material "in apparent repose," introducing the tension between mobility and stillness, which runs throughout the novel. It also introduces to the scene the unnamed travelers (at once Wenceslao and his brother-in-law and the archetypical travelers fatally misled by mirages of water in the desert).

The same scene of the mirage is later related in Wenceslao's voice, that of an uneducated peasant who describes what he sees without recourse to literary allusions or even the vocabulary "espejismo":

> Yo veía adelante el camino blanco y derecho, y al fondo el calor subiendo desde la tierra y enturbiando que le dicen el horizonte. Más avanzábamos más nos costaba avanzar. No va que llega un momento en que me parece que casi no avanzo más.

I saw ahead the white and straight road, and at the end the heat rising from the earth and clouding what they call the horizon. The more we advanced the harder it was for us to advance. Won't there come a moment when it seems to me that I almost don't advance anymore.[77]

Here the apparition of the mirage coincides with the disorientating illusion of not making progress. Just as the sun *appears* to briefly pause at the top of its arc, and just as narrative time *appears* to be suspended in this moment, Wenceslao perceives that he has ceased moving forward, even though his ability to keep pace with Rogelio illustrates that the feeling of suspension is only in his head, an effect of exhaustion in the intense midday heat.

Finally, this scene echoes another scene set under the midday sun: an oneiric episode that might be interpreted as a premonition (it follows an abrupt break in the narration after Wenceslao dives into the river). In the first person, Wenceslao narrates his collapse from heatstroke while walking up a path at midday years after the day when the majority of the novel takes place. He blames his fall on the midday sun: "Por el sol, por el sol cayendo a pique en pleno mediodía que ha de ser seguro lo que me tumbó" ("Because of the sun, because of the sun falling in shafts in the very middle of the day, that must surely be what knocked me down").[78] The narrator becomes increasingly incoherent as he is brought indoors and laid down in bed, and his speech gives way to inarticulate sounds and finally the silence of a black box on the page. This scene appears to be that of Wenceslao's death, particularly in light of one of the final retellings of the episode. In the saccharine tone of a children's religious fable, we are told that Wenceslao is greeted by the archangel Gabriel and climbs up to heaven to be reunited with his father and his son at midday on a sunny summer's day. The suggestion that Wenceslao eventually dies under the midday sun imbues the scene of his exhaustion on the path when the mirage appears with a sense of foreboding, intensified by the use of the future tense in the first two iterations.

Reading between a cluster of scenes tied together by recurring images and sensations such as the embodied memory of struggling to walk under the midday sun, it becomes possible to perceive that Wenceslao's fear that there will arrive a moment when "no avanzo más" reflects not only the fear of falling behind Rogelio but also the fear of death amplified by the impossibility of carrying on his line now that his only child is dead. With no living heir, Wenceslao cannot pass on the skills and traditions he has inherited from his father. The apparition of the mirage thus evokes the end of Wenceslao's line and way of life.

The fact that the mirage appears on the paved road to the city is significant in a novel where the city is viewed as a source of dangerous and illusory promises, luring the youth from the coast away from their traditional way of life, and, in the case of Wenceslao's son, leading him to his death. This road figures prominently in the only scene of the novel where the city is described from the older generation's point of view. After lunch, Wenceslao recalls a trip he and Rogelio once took to sell a crop of watermelons at the market in the middle of a violent storm. Thwarted by the rain, the mud, and the slipperiness of wet asphalt under the unshod hooves of the horse pulling their cart, the two brothers-in-law arrive late to the market, which is already glutted with watermelons, and are forced to unload their crop at discount prices. This episode dispels the illusion of progress and prosperity promised by the paved road to the city, at least for the traditional farmers and fishers of the coast. When real water (as opposed to mirages), covers this road, which has been paved to benefit motor traffic, it becomes hazardous to those relying on more traditional modes of transport. The city proves an equally hostile place: the brothers-in-law are disrespectfully dismissed by the other merchants. The disastrous attempt to participate in the exchange economy cements Wenceslao's disillusionment with the promise of financial gain to be had in the city.[79] For Wenceslao, then, the mirages on the road to the city are understated reminders of the siren songs of urban, capitalistic culture to which the younger generation is always at risk of succumbing.

This reading is not available from within any one iteration of the scene; it is only by gathering together a multiplicity of scenes linked by the presence of the midday sun or the road to the city that we come to recognize the depth and complexity of affect carried by the mirage, which evokes on the one hand Wenceslao's mistrust of the path toward modernization and, on the other, his fear of immobility, stagnation, and mortality. The process through which we become literate in this world—building a vocabulary in which words like "espejismos," "camino de asfalto" or "inmóvil" are pregnant with affective connotations and past and future narrative events—is not akin to looking words up in a dictionary and lighting upon a one-to-one relation between signified and signifier. Instead, it resembles learning a language through immersion, through repeated exposure to the ever-expanding contexts that give these words meaning. As Adorno emphasizes, this "open intellectual experience" yields knowledge that is less precise but far more nuanced.[80] It is through this kind of education—active, immersive, disorienting—that Saer approximates for the reader the challenge of learning to dwell in an initially unfamiliar place.

THE ELUSIVE FLUIDITY OF *LA ZONA*

What is at stake for Saer in disclosing his *zona* only in indirect, accretive fashion? As we have seen in "El viajero," emphasizing the opacity or illegibility of this landscape to the unindoctrinated eye underscores the folly of the outsider who, blinded by his ambitions or expectations, fails to train his gaze to the local landscape. Jeremy Blackwood, a representative of European capitalism, experiences the pampa as empty and meaningless because instead of learning to perceive what is actually there, he projects scenes of his homeland onto the *llanura* as if it were a blank screen. Saer's pampa is similarly confounding to Bianco, the European protagonist of *La ocasión*. Bianco is drawn to this space both for the chance to enrich himself and because the land's very emptiness makes it an ideal metaphor for his anti-materialist philosophy: he imagines it as a blank page that will not resist being populated with ideas.[81] The tragic disappointment of each foreigner echoes Ezequiel Martínez Estrada's depiction of the conquest as an act of quixotic projection doomed to collide with the material reality of a land that, rather than containing riches to be looted and dragons to be slayed, demands the same dwelling activities as any other land: "He needed not to conquer but to populate; he needed not to reap but to sow."[82] As a space whose potential wealth (in agricultural and cattle production) literally depends on cultivation—on dwelling in the sense of weathering the seasons and staying with cyclical rhythms—the pampas are a barren wasteland to those who come as conquerors to reap riches or tourists to reap exotic images of local color.[83] Similarly, Saer's *zona* reveals itself only to the patient reader who is willing to stay with the confusion and tedium of his recursive narrative and continually revisit his opaque descriptions.

Another effect of this technique is that when *la zona* does come into focus for the reader, it does so fleetingly, thus resisting ossification under their gaze. Saer's predilection for intertextual repetition is one of the ways he keeps his *zona* in flux, as if it were forever being created and re-created. Readers—from Mirta Stern to Piglia to Sarlo to Montaldo and Premat—have noted the way Saer incessantly re-writes his zona, maintaining it in a state of perpetual incompletion. Premat observes that Saer's novels "are not written, but being written, always to be written."[84] Montaldo sees this process of interminable rewriting as an expression of "mistrust of narration and writing, which requires that all that is written must be narrated again."[85] If this principle structures Saer's oeuvre writ large, it also underlies the formal construction of *El limonero real*, which recommences narrating the same day eight different times. "El viajero," "La mayor," and *Nadie nada nunca* follow similarly recursive structures. This technique suggests that the narration of any one day, of any one moment, could be infinitely elaborated, infinitely thickened with new perspectives and new details and still not be complete.

Though most of Saer's narratives are more linear and plot driven than *El limonero real*, when taken together, they create a similar effect: *la zona* cannot be conceived as a finite territory, but rather, must be imagined as an inexhaustibly rich web of experiences awaiting narrative elaboration and, inevitably, reelaboration. Each new intervention in *la zona* may demand that we reread everything we have read in a new light, leaving indefinitely open the possibility of returning to the version of events we think we know "to test its most diverse possibilities."[86] Saer thus refuses to treat the story of the rural interior as a fait acompli, rejecting its reification in nationalist myths as well as its displacement into a primitive past. These characteristics make Saer a critical regionalist in the classical, cultural-studies sense.

The implications of Saer's treatment of his *zona*—that the interior is not a fixed and stable referent of realist representation but, instead, always in the process of being discursively formed—would constitute subversive political gesture at any time. Argentina, like many American nations, has a long history of shoring up its national identity on literary versions of its rural heartland. If, as Montaldo has argued, literary discourses of the rural serve as a way of reinventing the nation's past in order to authorize a given version of the present and the future, then both the populist state and the authoritarian state seek to mystify this process and naturalize the foundational myth in keeping with the regime's ideological needs.[87] The authoritarian state, Sarlo reminds us, is by definition antagonistic to any pluralistic interpretation or reworking of history.[88] By revealing the possibility and the necessity of opening up the rural to reelaboration in the present, Saer challenges the master narrative of the national experience. For example, Premat reads *La oca-sión*, set in the nineteenth century and depicting the pampa in flux, as an intervention that destabilizes populist rhetoric eager to claim this iconic landscape as a bedrock for national identity.[89]

Saer's commitment to undermining the authority of any one discursive construction of his *zona* is most explicit in his nonfiction. In *El río sin orillas* (1991), which was commissioned as an expository piece about the Río de la Plata, Saer underscores the limits of the documentary genre and redirects his reader to the modest wisdom of fiction over the illusory authority of fact. Giving his work the subtitle "tratado imaginario" ("imaginary treatise"), Saer discards all pretense of offering an objective portrait of the region, and produces instead a pastiche of *crónicas*, travel writing, and cultural history, liberally sprinkled with his own personal experience. Saer's version of this river includes his biography (his emotionally loaded return visits from France), politics (scathing remarks about Perón and omnipresent references to the horrors of the most recent dictatorship), and literary tastes (Lugones is ridiculed; Ortiz is upheld as *the* poet of the Río de la Plata). The author acknowledges that these personal "asides"—so prolific they cease to be asides and become the substance of the book—are unconventional in a documentary work. Nevertheless, he insists that the form he has chosen is the only possible means of representing the region because there is no definitive version of the Río de la Plata: "There are as many Ríos de la Plata as there are discourses uttered about it."[90] These myriad discourses course through the historical strata of the region, destabilizing any single, crystalized version of it. As Demaría concludes, the version of the provinces that comes into being in this text "is not a reified, exterior, and immutable object."[91] Instead, evading the demands of the commission, Saer proliferates versions of *la zona* that cannot be fixed in a cartographic or sociological gaze. It is in Saer's fiction where this gesture gathers its full force and where, moreover, one might find alternative ways of knowing *la zona*. In Saer's intertextual, genre-spanning oeuvre, such *conocimiento* is accumulated iteratively and is by definition never complete.

To know the fluvial landscape of Saer's *zona* is to know it not just in its current form, nor as a cartographer would have drawn it at any given point in history. Rather, it is to know it simultaneously in the infinitely many forms that the riverbanks have taken over the last five hundred years. Acquiring such knowledge demands that one attempt to contemplate this landscape through the perspectives of the Indigenous populations that were eliminated from it through acts of genocide (*El entenado*), the European settler colonialists and capitalists who arrived to make it their own (*La ocasión*, "El viajero"), the fishermen who continue to live off of it (*El limonero real*), and the poets and intellectuals who write about it from within and from exile (the vast majority of Saer's novels). When we begin to look at this landscape through the archeological lens of what Ingold calls the *dwelling perspective*, to read its present configuration as embodying all the different paths its rivers have cut, all the different trails its inhabitants have walked, all the footprints, campfires, and fish bones left behind in the course of their daily activities, and when we add to this the intertextual web in which it exists—all the *crónicas*, poems, essays, and novels written about it—the legibility and synchronicity of the map gives way to an impossibly dense palimpsest of experiences and stories superimposed in space. Far from yielding a singular and coherent version of the national heartland, this figuration of *la zona* is extremely difficult to decipher. The illegibility of *la zona* is not, however, the result of its being a desert that resists inscription but, rather, the result of its having incorporated a myriad of daily dwelling activities over the course of centuries.

REFRAMING THE OUTSIDER'S GAZE:
OPACITY AS A RESOURCE

It is not only *la zona* that eludes singular identities and fixed categories in Saer's work; the subjectivity through which it is conjured proves equally fluid and multifaceted. Recent critical studies by Luigi Patruno and Demaría have underscored this point. Patruno claims that Saer denounces nationalistic essentialism by adopting "the carefree gaze of travelers."[92] However, if the gaze of the nation is overdetermined, the gaze of the foreign traveler is equally problematic. In fact, the two gazes share a fetishizing relationship to the region that is inherited from colonial travel narratives. Just as Mary Louise Pratt reminds us that the gaze of the foreign tourist is continuous with that of the colonizer, Adolfo Prieto points out that in Argentina, the gaze of the nation also imitates that of the colonial *cronista*. Many of the authors who shaped Argentine national literature in the nineteenth century (Alberdí, Echevarría, Marmol, Sarmiento) were influenced by British travel narratives (Humboldt, Head, Andrews, Darwin, Fitz-Roy).[93] It is the structural similarity between the imperialist gaze of the European traveler-cum-colonizer and that of the state that Saer recognizes when he announces that "nationalism and colonialism are thus two aspects of the same phenomenon."[94] Both discourses of European colonialism and of internal colonialism aspire to use a totalizing visual perspective to domesticate the unruliness of the rural interior while at the same time separating themselves from it.[95]

In the previous chapter, I suggested that in critical regionalist texts such as *Grande sertão: Veredas*, this domesticating, ordering gaze is projected onto the outsider-reader at the same time as its violence is revealed and subverted. When the would-be conqueror begins to take on the dwelling perspective, however, things begin to change. As my reading of "El viajero" suggests, when the foreigner is immersed in the local landscape, when he is forced to renounce the distance of the overview, other possibilities emerge. It is the myopia of the traveler engaged in what Guimarães Rosa calls the *travessia*—the blind act of traversing rather than contemplating from without—that Saer, too, finds worth exploring. In fact, as Demaría observes: "For Saer, vision from above immediately becomes opaque," redirecting the reader instead toward "an intimate gaze of one's own."[96] Like Guimarães Rosa and Arguedas, then, Saer's primary commitment is to conjuring *la zona* from deep within, requiring that the reader learn to relate to *la zona* not as a complete foreigner (*un extranjero*) but rather as an outsider who is nevertheless intimately connected to this place: what Demaría calls a *forastero*.

Saer is one of the authors who for Demaría epitomizes Carlos Mastronardi's sense of the *forastero* who, similarly to a flaneur (but in a nonurban context), casts a defamilarized gaze on the provinces, thus articulating "a world and an aesthetic not conditioned by geographic, national, or state determinisms."[97] It is worth emphasizing that this internally divided position, at once "inside and outside, a home and an exile," "in which we are located but to which we do not belong," is not reached only upon physical exile.[98] On the contrary, this destabilizing, anti-nationalistic stance seems to have always defined Saer's sense of place. The author himself has written of his exile: "The distance already existed before the going away, the rupture before the separation."[99] What is more, despite spending the first decades of his career eschewing the literary scene of Buenos Aires and consorting with an intimate circle of local intellectuals, Saer never lived an insular provincial existence. The son of Syrian immigrants and a consummate reader, translator, and critic of literature from around the world, he always participated in cosmopolitan intellectual culture and saw national and regional labels as stifling.[100]

In her uptake of Mastronardi's concept of the *forastero*, Demaría valorizes the "ajenidad" ("foreignness" or "otherness") that allows the outsider to perceive *la provincia* free from overdetermined discourses about it; such an enunciatory position liberates the authors and narrators of regionalist literature from the ontological status of "ser de provincia" ("being from the provinces"), allowing them instead to occupy the dynamic position of "estar en provincia" ("being in the provinces"). Nevertheless, Demaría gestures toward, without fully exploring, the possibility that *un extranjero* (an absolute foreigner with no relationship to or literacy in the local) might also come to occupy the intermediary positionality of the *forastero*, characterized by "a halfway belonging," through a process of "acercamiento" ("coming near").[101] In her discussion of César Aira, Demaría ends up questioning the binary she has set up between the two kinds of outsiders, *forasteros* and *extranjeros*:

> Isn't it perhaps necessary [. . .]to partially lose one's "foreignness" in order to make a home, insert oneself, participate in, and, from a distance, belong to this way of being in which one is located even though one does not squarely belong? And if this is the case, if the opening up of foreignness is necessary, wouldn't this "foreigner" [*extranjero*] be an "outsider" [*forastero*]?[102]

Such a transformation—losing a degree of one's foreignness (but not completely going native) in the process of gaining greater literacy in the local—is precisely what the character Maxwell in Arguedas's *El zorro de arriba y el zorro de abajo* brags of having undergone (see my discussion in chapter 2). Perhaps it is also what happens to Jeremy Blackwood when he becomes Jeramías. It is, furthermore, what I have argued the narrator of *Grande sertão: Veredas* entreats the reader to do (see chapter 3). It is what is demanded of the reader if they are to learn to dwell.

Demaría goes as far as to suggest that "all of us are, in some way "outsiders" ("forasteros") and, therefore, members of "a community to come," one that "couldn't be defined from a closed and fixed, authentic and immemorial identity, but that is articulated, invented daily in the cadences of a way of being marked by a close distance or a distant closeness."[103] The emergence of such a critical regionalist community represents the utopic horizon of the texts analyzed in this book. Nevertheless, Demaría puts much more emphasis on the value of *lejanía* (distance) as a tool for undoing restrictive notions of the region than learned, affective *cercanía* (closeness) as a way of remaking community once essentialist identity categories have been undone.

Though it is the centrifugal energy of critical regionalism—the urge to deterritorialize belonging and shake off deterministic narratives—that Demaría and many critical regionalists working in the deconstructivist tradition privilege, I believe a close reading of Saer (as well as of Arguedas and Guimarães Rosa) compels us to also heed its centripetal energy, which has often been read in the key of melancholia: the impossible desire to return to a state of belonging to and oneness with the region but to do so on different terms. The dialectic proper to critical regionalist poetics as I define it entails moving back and forth between these two urges, one that refuses to see hailing from the provinces as what Demaría calls "una fatalidad" and one that refuses to throw a sense of loyalty and belonging to the region out with the bathwater in the act of destabilizing discourses of local identity.

The turn beyond negativity in the reception of Saer's work, which I have been championing in this chapter, entails attending to the lingering (though revised) Heideggerianism in the author's work in addition to the destabilization of the region as imagined in nationalistic discourses. Saer navigates the tension between these two seemingly contradictory impulses by recasting belonging as a matter of sensorial participation and affective loyalty rather than identity or ideology. Belonging ceases to be a birthright or a "fatalidad" and becomes a contingent relationship, a status that is earned through the way one inhabits space, the way one perceives and participates in the local landscape. As Demaría suggests, this possibility may be available to all of us.

The question of what it means to be loyal to *la zona* without participating in discourses that reify it (which would constitute a betrayal on par with or worse than severing ties altogether) comes up in the short story "Discusión sobre el término zona" (Discussion about the term *zona*) (*La mayor*, 1976). The discussion or argument takes place between Lalo Lescano and Pichón Garay, two friends born and raised in the same small city. The question of how to retain his allegiance and connection to *la zona* from afar is a pressing one for the character Garay, who in 1967, when the story is set, is preparing to depart for Europe, as well as for Saer, whose exile in France would begin the following year. Garay is preoccupied with how he will relate to his homeland from afar: "La discusión comienza cuando Garay dice que va a extrañar y que un hombre debe ser siempre fiel a una región, a una zona" ("The argument begins when Garay says that he will miss it and that a man must always be loyal to a region, to a zone").[104] Lescano responds that one cannot be loyal to a region because there is no such thing: because it is impossible to delineate the border between two contiguous regions like *la costa* and *la pampa*, he argues, regions do not exist. For Lescano, deep familiarity with a place is precisely what blurs the neat boundaries drawn by cartographers and politicians: "Pero cualquiera de nosotros sabe muy bien, porque ha nacido aquí y ha vivido aquí" ("But any one of us knows very well, because he has been born here and has lived here").[105] Lescano recognizes that a term like "la costa" is meaningless if it refers only to an arbitrary shape on a map and that it gleans its true meaning from the forms of dwelling with which it is associated in common usage. It refers to places where the earth is a certain color, where certain crops (cotton, tobacco, rice) grow better than others, where certain people (poorer *criollos* rather than wealthy immigrants) live.

To this argument, Garay responds simply, "No comparto" ("I don't share this view"), leaving the reader to infer that the foundation for his loyalty to *la zona* cannot be argued on Lescano's terms, or perhaps cannot be *argued* (*discutido*) in abstract, discursive terms at all.[106] For Garay, who speaks while staring into the river, and who prefers the restaurant where he is sitting because it was once frequented by the local literary *vanguardia*, loyalty does not require a mappable, geographic region to which to adhere; on the contrary, it is an affective connection based on lived experience and shared history. The question of how to maintain this connection from afar without producing discourses of identity for export is one Saer will attempt to resolve formally in his most experimental phase. It is an aesthetic question but also a deeply personal ethical preoccupation.

As we have seen in the previous two chapters, narrating as an outsider, *un forastero*, is not an achievement to be unambivalently celebrated for these authors. Casting off the stigma of being branded a *provinciano* and writing from an exterior, cosmopolitan, or "universal" position may be upheld as a victory in the prevailing culture environment (hence Arguedas's admitted envy of "los cortázares" and Guimarães Rosa's acclaim as the Brazilian James Joyce), but it is felt in the novels I have analyzed as a loss and a betrayal. Arguedas is fixated on the problems posed by his own outsider status in Chimbote, and even Guimarães Rosa's *sertanejo* narrator Riobaldo questions whether he truly belongs to the *sertão* and whether he has, in trying to see it from without, betrayed it. Likewise, at stake in Saer is how literature might help us find our way back to the experience of the local, even as it as it remains committed to subverting the version of *las provincias* upheld by the grand narratives of the nation. Undoubtedly, Saer's own proclamations on the region and regionalism, the state and national identity, and realism and literary autonomy all support reading his self-imposed exile and his concurrent turn away from representational literature as a form of escape. Yet both the region and the real appear in his work as objects of melancholic loss.[107] In Saer's work of the 1970s onward, this loss is in part the result of the author's exile; however, it also reflects the predicament that Carlos J. Alonso claims regionalist literature has always had to confront: even the most authentic regionalist writer necessarily writes from a place of exteriority.[108] This inescapable estrangement often produces a melancholic register and a sense of betrayal, as in Alonso's reading of *Don Segundo Sombra* and mine of *Grande sertão: Veredas*. Nevertheless, for Saer, the exogenous status to which any lettered subject is condemned when writing about "rustic" subject matter also provides an opportunity.

As Demaría's and Patruno's readings underscore, Saer embraces the estrangement of the outsider's vantage point. I want to propose, however, that beyond providing critical distance, such a gaze is generatively limited: it can, like a camera, register the opaque surfaces of regional life but not penetrate them. Allowing the reader to encounter *la zona* only through such a gaze safeguards its opacity and shields it from the reader's projections. Equally importantly, this aesthetic strategy also draws to the forefront the process of *apprentissage* through which one must be inducted into a local world. In Heideggerian fashion, this world does not disclose itself immediately; it is only through the protracted and iterative process of dwelling that one might begin to perceive all that it contains: its sensorial richness and temporal depth, the iterative rhythms of daily life that animate it, and the relations that bind us all to it. Achieving such a perspective necessarily reanimates the regional world depicted, thus saving it from ossification in ideological or memorialist discourses, as many of Saer's readers recognize. But I am equally interested in how the opacity or exteriority of the *forastero*'s narrative gaze might serve as an ethical resource. How might it check the novel's historical propensity for granting the reader access to the interiority of its characters, and how might this buffering gesture be particularly important when these characters are humble peasants?

Nicolás Lucero reads *El limonero real* as being largely about negotiating this very problem, noting that while most of Saer's novels center on a circle of writers and intellectuals, Saer's most objectivist novel takes on peasant life.[109] Though the privileging of phenomenological perceptions over psychological depths is a defining feature of the *nouveau roman*, this shift has rarely been considered a mechanism for negotiating cultural and experiential differences between author, reader, and literary subjects. This blind spot reflects the way that, as Doris Sommer points out, "the study of rhetoric has generally assumed cultural continuity" between these figures.[110] If, however, following the lead of thinkers such as Pratt and Glissant, we view texts written in and about (neo)colonial contact zones as self-consciously negotiating the challenges, risks, and limitations of transmitting cultural and locational particularity to outside audiences, the stakes of such formal experimentation change. I propose in what remains of this chapter that Saer's objectivist technique, which is taken to extremes in this novel anomalously centered on peasant life, cannot be read independently of his anxieties surrounding how marginalized experiences on the brink of extinction are represented, assimilated, and circulated.

Unlike in *El zorro de arriba y el zorro de abajo* or in *Grande sertão: Veredas*, concerns over the position from which one narrates and reads *la zona* are rarely explored explicitly by the narrators of Saer's fiction. One notable exception is *El entenado*, which is set during the Spanish colonial invasion of the Río de la Plata. The retrospective narrator, who as a youth spent ten years living with an Amerindian tribe, reflects at length on the challenges of conveying this experience—colored as it is by the cosmovision of his hosts/captors—to a European audience. A full discussion of *El entenado* is beyond the scope of this chapter, but as Premat points out, the reader is, like the narrator, positioned as an insider-outsider to the Colastiné tribe.[111] The word for this role in Saer's version of the Colastiné language is "def-ghi," which is approximated in the title of the novel. "El entenado" translates to "stepchild" or "witness": one who has been adopted by, dwells in, registers, and represents a community to which he does not fully belong.[112] More directly than any of Saer's other works, then, *El entenado* draws attention to the narrator's—and by extension, the reader's—position as an outside observer to the world narrated and to the inescapable colonial dimensions of the quest to understand alterity. The violence of this power dynamic might be mitigated only by the witness adopting a seemingly impossible site of enunciation: narrating from a position of complete immersion in local forms of life that are foreign to him.

Much as I have argued of Guimarães Rosa's narrator in chapter 3, the narrator of *El entenado* finds attaining narrative coherence from this immanent position to be an overwhelming and impossible task. The versions of the Colastiné he does communicate to a European audience no longer belong to the dwelling perspective. This is in part because they are elegiac (by this point the tribe has been eliminated in an act of genocide itself made possible by information shared by the narrator) and in part because they are immediately appropriated by Eurocentric discourses. When the narrator relays his experience to Padre Quesado, (a figure for Bartolomé de las Casas), the latter rewrites it in the vein of the *buen salvaje*. When the narrator creates a commercially successful play based on his adventures, it is farcical: pandering to the expectations of the European audience, he treats the Colastiné as caricatured barbarians. He later disavows it and attempts, once again, to give proper form to his experience by writing it down in the form of the novel. *El entenado* thus reflects on the inevitable betrayals that accompany moving from the dwelling perspective to a sufficiently exogenous perspective to enable narration. A parable in the vein of Borges's "The Ethnographer," the novel suggests the ethical and epistemological limits of both ethnography and art as ways of transmitting lived experience across cultural, linguistic, and temporal gaps.[113]

The text I have examined in most detail in this chapter, *El limonero real*, lays out similar problems in the absence of a self-reflexive narrator. With no intermediary figure, what Rama would call a *transculturator*, within the world of the text to help orient them, the reader must learn directly from their own immersive yet partially opaque experience with *la zona*. In other words, rather than voicing anxieties about the task of representing cultural difference, in *El limonero real*, Saer uses the formal difficulty of the text to mark the limits of what the reader can know. In one of the novel's most avant-garde formal gestures—the moment when language dissolves into incoherent babel and, finally, a black box on the page—the reader's tenuous, incomplete, and opaque access to the world narrated becomes unavoidable.[114] Pénelopé Laurent reads this moment as reflecting the indescribable, unnarratable presence of alterity in the text.[115] This black box eventually gives way to a rebirth of language followed by an origin myth related in the voice of an oral storyteller, suggesting that, throughout the novel, the autochthonous perspective resides as a negative presence, immanent if illegible in the opaque surfaces we have been contemplating. The omnipresent imagery of the river, whose surface is traversed by canoes and whose depths are plumbed only in oneiric passages difficult to assimilate into any chronological narrative, further emphasizes that invisible, unfathomable worlds are latent in everything that meets the eye, whether these be banal objects and actions or impenetrable yet animated (undulating, scintillating, sometimes reflective) surfaces.

Between the narrator and the characters of *El limonero real*, Lucero writes, there is "an opaque, dense, and porous border."[116] Though this opaque barrier gradually becomes more translucent through cumulative encounters with Saer's world, the inner lives of the peasant subjects of *El limonero real* remain largely inaccessible to the narrator and therefore to the reader. As Montaldo observes, scenes of quotidian life are related "by an exterior but not foreign consciousness."[117] Neither explaining and translating the reality observed in the mode of the ethnographer or travel writer, nor privileging certain events and actions over others as one who participated in this daily reality would, the narrator perceives this world with a camera-like objectivist gaze.[118]

THE PARADOX OF SAER'S VISUAL POETICS

Though invoking photographic and filmic languages in literature has been common since the historic avant-gardes of the early twentieth century, Saer does so in a way that is not as celebratory of visual technologies as it might first appear. In an age when the visual media of photography and cinema pervade the cultural imaginary, Saer dwells on the elements of experience that elude visual apprehension. Arce observes that despite frequently being compared to the objectivism of the French *nouveaux romanciers*, Saer emphasizes all that is missed by the gaze of the camera: "It is not that novelistic narration displays the impossibilities that filmic storytelling would come to solve; it is the opposite, the possibilities of writing mark a certain appearance of things that is irreducible to the visual."[119] The irony is that Saer draws on the technique of ekphrasis to stage his critique of visual representation. His dense yet opaque visual descriptions gesture to a beyond that cannot be perceived with the eyes alone.

In other words, Saer takes visual description to its breaking point, parodying rather than duplicating the positivism of description in the natural sciences, *costumbrismo*, and the realist regionalist novel.[120] This exercise reveals the paradoxical nature of verbal ekphrasis, which Ricardo Padrón has observed cannot escape the intrinsic "temporal unfolding of language" to deliver the world to the optical regime, that is, to make it "available, in synchronous matter, to the gaze of the reader."[121]

As I have argued elsewhere, this is the point: Saer's descriptions refuse to produce still lifes by incessantly reinserting his visually rendered *cuadros* into the flux of time.[122] Saer's descriptions thus resist reifying *la zona* precisely because they reveal language's incapacity to make good on the promises of photographic documentation: objectivity, or, the illusion of the world reproduced through a mechanical rather than subjective gaze, and timelessness, or, the illusion of a still life plucked from history and social processes. Though many late modernist authors took inspiration from cinema in their attempts to reanimate literary description, in Saer's case, it is the writer's formation as a poet, as much as his training as a filmmaker, that enables his critique of the reification of the rural in images of local color.[123]

In addition to claiming the poet Juan L. Ortiz as his *padre literario* and being a reader and translator of poetry, Saer was himself a poet, although he is much better known for his narrative works. In 1977, he published a collection of poems written over the previous two decades, titled *El arte de narrar* (The art of narrating). As this title suggests, Saer was deeply preoccupied with the relationship between narrative and poetry, and far from being simply a secondary literary pursuit, poetry offered him a way of revitalizing the form of the novel. In a conversation with Ricardo Piglia, he expresses hope that "the relationship between lyric and narration" might offer "a way to overcome certain dead ends within the novelistic tradition."[124] In his notebooks, Saer theorized at length a hybrid genre he called *la novela poética*, which would be written in a language whose rhythm varied only subtly from regular prose. Its distinguishing feature would be its temporal concentration: the entire novel would take place in the span of one or two days.[125] Intriguingly, only several notebook pages after his meditations on *la novela poética*, Saer begins his first draft of the novel that would become *El limonero real*, which famously takes place in a single day.

If we read *El limonero real* as Saer's *novela poética*, what are we to make of the fact that his most poetic novel is also his most cinematic? I would argue, following Arce, that this convergence underscores the impossibility of capturing *la zona* in purely visual terms.[126] In the spirit of Adornian negativity, the opacity of the objectivist gaze redirects us to poetic ways of knowing as a dialectical counterpoint to visual representation. Despite the many ways Saer's prose in *El limonero real* appears to emulate cinematic language, this objectivism is always in tension with another project that we might describe as slowly saturating the landscape with affect. Describing this novel, Saer writes that

Wenceslao "goes about filling the material world" with his memories and internal universe.[127] The affective texture of Wenceslao's world is not narrated so much as captured cinematically by a gaze that opaquely registers more than the narrator (or the reader) can fully decipher, as if the camera were located "in the eye or in the mind of the characters to capture those meanings that the narrator cannot access, be it due to his intention to introspectively show other points of view, or due to his geocultural distance from the cosmovision of that region."[128] Though we may not have direct access to Wenceslao's interiority, we have the opportunity to perceive from a vantage point of intimate proximity a world that, rather than existing independently of him, *is* the material accretion of his dwelling activities, memories, ancestry, and fears about the future. This is why, as Arce claims, a literal, mechanical camera could never capture the landscapes Saer gives us in his poetic descriptions.[129]

This surprisingly subjective take on objectivist description testifies to the depth of Ortiz's influence on Saer. The latter praises the poet's renunciation of the ambition to objectively document space or catalog local color; instead, Saer observes with admiration, Ortiz treats the landscape as always already colored by the poet's subjectivity.[130] As Andermann points out, Ortiz's form of knitting together place and its human inhabitants is profoundly ecological: "Poetry inscribes the environment in the body and vice versa."[131] Following Ingold, we might substitute "inscribes" with "incorporates," as the forms of the landscape and the subjectivities of their (human and non-human) inhabitants are mutually constitutive.[132] In foregrounding this relationality, which defies subject-object relations, Ortiz and Saer alike contest the reification of lived territory in discourses that would reduce it to a source of natural resources or politically instrumental tropes and symbols.

In sum, Saer avails himself of the opacity and exteriority of the camera's gaze to curtail projection onto and appropriation of the landscapes of his *zona*, even as he slowly, iteratively discloses the way these are always already subjectively colored for those who dwell there. Much like viewers of unedited, uninterpreted ethnographic footage, or for that matter, of Lisandro Alonso's early films, which I discuss in the coda that follows, readers of *El limonero real* are aware of looking in on a foreign world from an intimate vantage point. From this perspective, remarkably similar to that of the narrator of *El entenado*, who does not speak the language of the community in which he dwells, we are humbly aware that we lack the tools to fully make sense of the world we are witnessing, but this does not mean we cannot learn something from attending to its movements, following its cyclical patterns. Coming to know Saer's *zona* in this way demands that we live with its alterity rather than domesticate it to our insufficient conceptual understanding. This lesson is the legacy Saer, like Arugedas and Guimarães Rosa before him, leaves to today's critical regionalist storytellers: it is by practicing, though never mastering, the exercise of perceiving the sensory, affective, and temporal texture of another way of dwelling that we might enter into intimate relation with alterity without demanding that it surrender its opacity.

Coda

In Lisandro Alonso's 2006 film, *Fantasma*, an unexpressive man sits down in a nearly empty movie theater to watch himself on-screen. This man is Argentino Vargas, the nonprofessional actor who stars in Alonso's earlier film, *Los muertos* (2004). *Fantasma* takes place during a screening of *Los muertos* in Teatro San Martin, an art theater in Buenos Aires. The footage that Vargas sees—and that the viewer of *Fantasma* also sees in between shots of Vargas's face in the flickering light of the projector—shows him navigating a densely forested river in a canoe. The shot is saturated with green and exemplifies Alonso's signature style: long takes that privilege repetitive, embodied movement and ambient sound over plot development, dialogue, or psychological interiority. This style, which bears an explicit debt to Juan José Saer's *El limonero real*,[1] also characterizes *Fantasma*, with one important difference: whereas most of Alonso's films are known for their remote natural settings (the pampa in *La libertad*, the forest of Corrientes in *Los muertos*), the landscape featured in *Fantasma* is the seemingly vast and labyrinthine modernist cinematheque. Though this landscape is composed largely of grays rather than greens, of geometric rather than organic forms, of mechanical sounds and footsteps on linoleum rather than birdsongs and branches cracking underfoot, it is given similar prominence in the composition of the film as natural landscapes are in the previous films.

In short, if in Alonso's first feature-length films, *La libertad* (2001) and *Los muertos*, the filmmaker (and by extension the viewer) was an outsider observing the "native dwellers" of rural spaces, in *Fantasma* the tables have been turned. Now Vargas and Misael Saavedra, the non-professional actor who stars in *La libertad*, explore Teatro San Martin as an exotic landscape. This inversion is reflected formally in the relative stasis of the camera. In *Fantasma*, the camera sometimes pans to follow the movement of the actors as they explore an unfamiliar landscape, but it does not explore the landscape independently of them as in the unnerving traveling shots in *La libertad* and *Los muertos*. This change underscores the agency of Saavedra and Vargas, who become the principal observers and explorers of the film, rather than merely objects of curiosity for the camera's gaze. As he wanders in and out of various backstage spaces—locker rooms, kitchens, dressing rooms, and so on—Saavedra exhibits boyish curiosity, peering into corners and drawers, handling various objects he encounters. At one point, he steps out onto a balcony, from which he takes in his urban surroundings. These include a woman sleeping inside her apartment in an adjacent building, emphasizing the voyeurism of Saavedra's gaze. Although Saavedra still plays himself in *Fantasma*, casting him in the role of one who visually surveys the novelty of an urban landscape inverts the pseudoethnographic paradigm that governs Alonso's preceding films. The effect of showing Vargas as a cinematic spectator is similar.

Fantasma thus endeavors to turn the gaze of the camera back on to filmmaking and exhibition as a form of labor rendered equivalent to the labor foregrounded in the earlier films: harvesting lumber, skinning and cooking an animal, traveling by canoe, and such. The local color or ethnographic subjects in this world include the ticket taker, the usher, and the security guard, who are shown not only performing their workplace duties but also absorbed in mundane tasks like eating and reading the newspaper. In this way, Alonso acknowledges the suitability of any life, including the urban lives of those in the film industry, as the object of ethnographic fascination. Bringing Saavedra and Vargas into this landscape also underscores the contemporaneity of their lives; they do not exist only in a distant time and place but also in Alonso's.[2] Might this film, which simultaneously draws the viewer into the phenomenological experience of inhabiting a specific place and self-reflexively calls attention to its own mediation, be considered an example of critical regionalist poetics? What of Alonso's earlier films, in which pseudoethnographic footage of rural life is coupled with subtly estranging camerawork and jarring extradiegetic music? For that matter, Alonso is representative of a larger trend in Latin American cinema at the turn of the millennium: a boom in slow-paced indie films set in nonurban locations.[3] What might the films of Lucrecia Martel, Paz Encina, Carlos Reygadas, and others have to tell us about the forms critical regionalist poetics takes in the twenty-first century and in cinema? Might their long takes and sensorially immersive aesthetics convey the temporal and embodied dimensions of dwelling as only cinema can?

*

Given that my aim in this book has not been to delimit a particular literary movement or style but, rather, to explore new ways of imagining affiliative communities born out of shared ethical commitments and aesthetic affinities, it is only fitting to conclude by opening the concept of critical regionalist poetics out, exploring the ways it might extend beyond the texts in my corpus and their historically situated projects. Thus far, I have elaborated critical regionalist poetics as a set of experimental literary techniques that engage the reader's senses to re-create the immersive, embodied, and temporal experience of dwelling, even as they introduce elements of negativity, opacity, and self-reflexivity that check the illusion of immediacy and remind the reader of that which escapes capture. I have argued, moreover, that these formal strategies, which are not uncommon in literary modernism, serve a particular ethical and political function in texts that represent so-called regional spaces to audiences presumed to be outsiders.

In the historical context on which I have focused—mid-twentieth-century Latin America—the outside readers hailed by critical regionalist texts include domestic audiences, such as the elite classes of the coastal cities, as well as international audiences, such as the growing readership for Latin American literature in the Global North in the wake of the Latin American boom. Half a century or more later, how have these dynamics changed? Might these same texts (and others directly or indirectly inspired by their poetics) now reach broader and more diverse audiences? As *Fantasma* playfully suggests, might these audiences include not only urbanites but also those who literally dwell in the regional spaces depicted?

If we are to contemplate what critical regionalist poetics looks like in the twenty-first century, we might also ask: How has it evolved in response to the era of full-fledged global neoliberalism, escalating environmental crises, and the emergence of a more diverse media landscape in which literature plays but a minor role? To what degree did Cold War–era critical regionalists already anticipate these turns, and what do they still offer to writers, artists, and filmmakers who seek forms of transnational solidarity with marginalized communities, ways of attending to the specificities of local lifeways, and spaces of resistance to the neoliberal order? How might ongoing focus on the critical regionalist ethos bring into view transhistorical aesthetic continuities and modes of intermedial intertextuality that would otherwise be missed? I do not have room to fully answer these questions (nor do easy answers exist), but I hope they can be taken up by scholars working on contemporary experimental filmmaking, ecopoetry, and evocations of place in other media.[4]

In other words, though I stand by the case I have made for the aesthetic, geopolitical, and historical continuities that unite the midcentury novels I have analyzed, I do not feel the need to jealously guard the limits of critical regionalist poetics as a regionally, historically, or media specific concept. Like critical regionalist scholars before me who have deterritorialized the framework, adapting it to disciplinary, regional, and historical contexts beyond those of its origins (in US architectural theory of the early 1980s), I take the inherently fluid and migratory nature of the critical regionalist project to be an asset. My understanding of critical regionalism remains anchored in the theoretical, aesthetic, and political conversations that informed Kenneth Frampton's original articulation of the term, including Heideggerian phenomenology, Frankfurt School critiques of modernity, and a wariness of placeless aesthetics and unbridled cosmopolitanism that is an outgrowth of both. Nevertheless, I have made the case that critical regionalist poetics was being practiced under other names and in other places and other media for decades before Frampton coined the term. In short, this concept is useful to me insofar as it renders visible a constellation of ostensibly anomalous literary achievements that share an ethos and a set of strategies for manifesting it in literary form. To the extent that it is useful for rendering visible the afterlives of this moment in cultural production— the heirs that never were to Arguedas, Guimarães Rosa, and Saer—I embrace the continued expansion of the term.

Moreover, conceiving of critical regionalist poetics beyond literature would seem to offer a way out of one of the central paradoxes of *Dwelling in Fiction*: that extremely difficult literary texts are by their nature elitist, selecting for a small audience of educated readers and categorically excluding anyone who is illiterate or alienated by literary language. This may have once meant that there was little overlap between the audiences such texts reached and the communities they represented. This is not necessarily the case anymore, however, given the increased access to education in areas beyond Latin America's major cities as well as the widespread legacy of critical regionalist texts, which encompasses commemorative events and places designed for the public (museums, parks, public readings, etc.) as well as an ever-growing intertextual web that includes film and the visual and performing arts.[5]

In fact, I have suggested in chapter 1 that the texts that make up my primary corpus may have telepoetically invited more diverse future audiences, thus anticipating a world where more readers identify simultaneously as regional dwellers and as lettered subjects looking in on their homes—their mother tongues, the places and traditions with which they affectively identify—as outsiders. We might think, for example, of Riobaldo's ambivalent position as both a *jagunço* and a narrator who guiltily (and deliberately unsuccessfully?) packages his own story for the outsider's consumption. Most readings of *Grande sertão: Veredas* assume the reader will identify with O Doutor, the urban intellectual who serves as Riobaldo's interlocutor, but what of readers who identify with Riobaldo and his longing to continue to dwell in a world he fears he has betrayed and abandoned even as he struggles to contemplate it from an exterior perspective? I would argue that the text offers at least as much to this reader. While *jagunço letrado* may remain a rarified category, its modern corollary—the educated subject from a marginalized background who must grapple with what belonging means when one contemplates one's own community from the metropolitan center or from the academe—is increasingly common. It would seem, then, that critical regionalist poetics might be a valuable tool in navigating intercultural and diasporic experience.

It follows that the question at the heart of Alonso's *Fantasma*—what does Argentino Vargas see when he seems himself on-screen?—is central to twenty-first-century critical regionalist poetics. This class of question is not entirely new. At one point in *El limonero real*, for example, the characters pose for a picture taken by a visitor from the city, and this prompts them to self-consciously contemplate their own images from an exterior position. They are described as nervously fidgeting before the camera: "Seguirán moviéndose, buscando la actitud adecuada, como si quisiesen poner en la fotografía lo mejor de sí mismos, o lo que esperan que los otros perciban de ellos, o lo que ellos mismos esperan reconocer de sí mismos tiempo después, cuando se reencuentren en la imagen" ("They will keep moving, looking for the appropriate attitude, as if putting into the photograph the best of themselves, what they hope others will perceive of them, or what they themselves hope to recognize in themselves in later times when they reencounter themselves in the image").[6] In Saer's account, the rural family is not the passive object of the gaze of the tourist's camera; instead they actively create a version of themselves for an outside audience, which, they intuit, could one day include themselves as well.

The ability of such subjects to view themselves from an outside perspective does not depend on visual technologies such as photography and cinema—O Doutor and his pen serve much the same function for Riobaldo in *Grande sertão*—but the proliferation and democratization of such technologies in the late twentieth and early twenty-first centuries have presented new opportunities for self-representation and added new layers to questions surrounding the vantage point from which images of rural life are crafted and consumed. Might such technologies resolve some of the problems that I have argued are endemic to literary representations of the regional?

One of the unspoken questions that haunts all the texts analyzed in *Dwelling in Fiction* is whether the written word is really the best way to capture, transmit, and re-create the experience of dwelling. In fact, the incessant gesturing beyond themselves to embodied experience of place is one of the most salient features uniting the texts examined here, making them examples of what Natalia Brizuela, drawing on the vocabulary of Jacques Rancière, calls "literatura fora de si."[7] In *El zorro de arriba y el zorro de abajo*, Arguedas grounds his authority to narrate Andean life in tactile and, above all, aural knowledge. Likewise, in *Grande sertão*, Guimarães Rosa insists that the *sertão* can truly be known only through the immersive act of traversing it. These texts conjure folk songs and oral conversation and storytelling as alternative media that might be better equipped than writing to convey what Arguedas calls "la materia de las cosas" ("the substance of things").[8] In *El limonero real* photography and cinema appear as implicit intermedial interlocutors: Saer stages scenes of photography and emulates the cinematic gaze in his pseudo-objectivist prose.[9] These technologies thus serve as an implicit foil for the author's literary project. Though such visual technologies are products of Western modernity, what they have in common with oral means of transmitting culture is that they do not require literacy nor passage through abstract signs.[10] To paraphrase Arguedas's foxes, words are imprecise because they fragment the world, introducing distance between the planes of sensorial experience and meaning.

Cinema, in contrast, has often been celebrated for bypassing the indirection of linguistic signification.[11] Its indexical and sensory nature confront the viewer with the materiality of the profilmic world with a directness toward which literary language can only aspire. In fact, for Laura U. Marks, film excels at creating experiences in which the pro-filmic world is "sensuously remade in the body" of the viewer.[12] One might ask, then, if a different medium can offer a way out of the double binds of critical regionalist poetics.

*

Though there are many places we might look for examples of critical regionalist poetics in cinema, I am particularly interested in experimental films that blur the boundary between documentary and fiction to represent a specific place or place-specific lifeway. What Scott MacDonald calls *Avant-Docs* have long been a privileged means of conjuring place and landscape.[13] Wenceslao Machado de Oliveira Jr., who writes about film's unique capacity to affect the perception of space, is likewise drawn to films in which documentary and fictional structures interpenetrate each other and notes a boom in such films around the turn of the millennium.[14] This genre-defying mode of filmmaking includes experimental documentaries and video installations, as I go on to discuss, but also feature films. The early films of Alonso might fall into this category. Despite being works of fiction, their hyperrealist aesthetics, including long takes of nonprofessional actors performing everyday tasks, align them with the conventions of ethnographic filmmaking.

The same might be said of the films of Paz Encina, who is surely one of the masters of critical regionalist poetics in cinema. The extreme temporal dilation and minimal narrative diegesis of her first feature film, *Hamaca paraguaya* (2006), which is set in a remote region of Paraguay in 1935, demands that the viewer dwell with the sights and sounds of the forest over the long duration. Meanwhile, the selective legibility of the rural world represented is underscored by the exclusive use of Guaraní as the language of dialogue, requiring most viewers to rely on the subtitles. What makes this film remarkable (and, for me, clearly an instantiation of critical regionalist poetics) is the way that history is negatively inscribed in the landscape represented on-screen. Though all we see are the mundane actions of an elderly couple, Ramón and Cándida, who are waiting for their son to return from the war, as Jens Andermann observes, the world off-screen permeates these actions without ever being directly depicted.[15] Most of the sounds we hear, including the nonsynchronous dialogue between the two protagonists and the incessant chirping of birds, issues from sources that are not shown.[16] The absence of the couple's son, who has been killed in the Chaco War, epitomizes the devastating capacity for the world beyond the frame to penetrate and reshape the extremely local world in which Ramón's and Cándida's lives play out. In this way, notes Andermann, "The temporality of the nation and of war" violently shoots through "the local temporality" governed by agricultural rhythms.[17] Though remote, Ramón and Cándida's world is no untouched Arcadia.

The inevitable ways in which history and politics penetrate seemingly insular spaces—the remote, the rural, the domestic—is also a central theme of Encina's next feature film, *Ejercicios de memoria* (2016). Here, too, an asynchronous audio track is overlaid on slow, sensorially rich footage. There is pronounced dissonance between what we see— tranquil, beautifully filmed scenes evoking an idyllic rural childhood— and what we hear: a narrative voice-over about state violence and interviews with the adult children of Agustin Goiburú, a member of the resistance to the Stroessner dictatorship who was disappeared and murdered for his militarism.[18] Like *Hamaca paraguaya*, then, *Ejercicios de memoria* teaches the viewer to perceive more than what meets the eye, to linger on seemingly banal objects and scenes until the historical forces (and historical violence) latent in them become apparent. This film, which incorporates images and recordings from Paraguay's Archives of Terror (the records kept by the Stroessner regime), epitomizes the blurring of the line between documentary, fiction, and poetic storytelling characteristic of many of the most compelling Latin American films about place made in the first decades of the twenty-first century.

Another relevant example is Marília Rocha's *Aboio* (2005), which was partially inspired by Guimarães Rosa and makes use of avant-garde form to document cowboys who practice an ancient form of cattle calling in the remote parts of the Brazilian *sertão*.[19] Rocha combines color and black-and-white footage, and digital and Super 8 film, to evoke different temporalities—the past, when the now-elderly cowboys came of age and learned the art of the *aboio*, and the present, when overland herding has been replaced with trucking and the *aboio* is becoming a folk tradition rather than a part of working life. Rather than juxtaposing these two moments, however, Rocha's editing weaves them together, suggesting the way that, for the cowboys, the past is not simply recollected—it lives in the body as embodied memory called up by the *aboio* songs.

Aboio evokes the ethnographic tradition by filming rural subjects engaged in physical labor and traditional cultural practices but distances itself from this tradition in its indifference to providing information, context, or interpretation. The interviews with the cowboys, where we might look for such framing, are far more performative—highlighting the oral arts of storytelling and singing—than informative.[20] Rather than holding steady on the face of these subjects in medium close-up, as is typical in documentary interviews, the camera zooms in, emphasizing the way one's throat moves with song, or cuts away to motion-blurred traveling shots filmed from horseback. Such nonrepresentational evocations of the multisensory, temporally deep experiences the *aboio* songs carry for the cowboys convey to the viewer significance that far surpasses the message of the words spoken, and which may not be fully intelligible to the viewer. At least, this meaning cannot be grasped with the intellect alone. In the case of *Aboio*, as I have argued elsewhere, the stakes of representing regional traditions in sensorial terms include forestalling the reification of regional lifeways in ethnographic discourse and foregrounding instead the fluidity of relations with the past and with the nonhuman world that characterize the experience of dwelling in the *sertão*.[21]

A similar exercise takes on more personal dimensions in Cecilia Vicuña's "documentary poem," *Kon Kon* (2010). Here, the ecofeminist poet, artist, and activist appears before the camera, introducing the beach near Valparaíso, Chile, where she played as a child through a combination of song, spoken word, performance art, and archival footage. The subject matter of this film in many ways echoes that of Arguedas's *El zorro de arriba y el zorro de abajo*: the transformation of a fishing community and coastal ecosystem on the Pacific Ocean with the arrival of industrialization and capitalistic greed in the 1960s. Beyond simply denouncing the ecological and social damage wrought (the disappearance of the clams, the construction of a refinery on an ancient cemetery, the "war on the dunes, on connection"), however, Vicuña's film emphasizes the ongoing, if attenuated ties between humans and nature, past and present, land and sea. It foregrounds, moreover, the role of traditional Andean rituals—and Quechua musical traditions specifically—in nourishing such relations and keeping them in view. Vicuña describes, for example, the tradition of carrying seashells to the mountaintop as a way of recognizing the water cycle, the way the mountain rivers are always in conversation with the sea. Whereas Arguedas laments in his last novel the need for such dialogues between above and below to pass through (written, Spanish) words, which divorce meaning from place and sound, Vicuña makes use of the audiovisual medium of film to let these personified waterways accompany her musical performance. As she sings about the fertility engendered by their confluence and their tradition of "looking at one another," the viewer sees close-ups of water flowing and of Andean wetland flowers. They hear ever more complex harmonies between voices, instruments, and natural sounds. This chorus culminates during the closing credits, when the sound of water droplets keeps time for a concert of human voices and instruments. The image we see of the poet walking over the undulating dunes appears choreographed to its rhythm. The editing of the film, including the overlay of multiple sound recordings, thus *creates* the delicate but vital harmonies of which the poet speaks and sings.

Much like *Aboio*, *Kon Kon* engages with memorialist discourses.[22] Both are, at the end of the day, about place-bound lifeways condemned to extinction by modernization, but neither falls into binary models of before and after. Instead, they foreground how embodied art forms can foment connection to place and engender belonging and connectivity *in the present*. True to Heidegger's insistence that poetic thought can still bring us into dwelling, such films stage performances that demonstrate how the rhythms, dialogues, and affective webs constitutive of emplaced belonging might be restored. Though they demand patience and tolerance for dissonance and incomprehension, for being thrown by avant-garde form, both films can be understood as inducting the viewer into extremely local modes of perception, thus proving that these have not been completely lost, that they can still be practiced.

These examples might seem to affirm that the sensory languages of the filmic medium offer a solution to the problems faced by critical regionalist writers struggling against the limitations of the written word. Suggesting that perhaps cinema can more fully realize the original project of Frampton's critical regionalism, Marks describes the way "local sensuous experience" can be created in film as a way to resist "the tide of the commodification and genericization of sense experience" and the proliferation on nonplaces in late capitalism.[23] Moreover, cinema, and especially films that communicate primarily through the senses, have the potential to reach much wider audiences than literary texts can. To be clear, however, the experimental films discussed here are by no means mainstream; they are more likely to be screened at film festivals than at your local theater. As such, the communities from which their subjects and nonprofessional actors hail are unlikely to make up their viewership. Alonso's *Fantasma* draws attention to this disconnect by bringing two nonprofessional actors into a Buenos Aires art theater. This gesture underscores that what one sees when one sees a film about rural life varies greatly based on the viewer's background and level of familiarity with the place and customs depicted.

In this vein, Marks reminds us that film does not fully resolve the problem of how to access the sensorium of another or offer an exit to the impasse of representing cultural difference.[24] If, as we saw in the case of Arguedas, literature's ability to mimetically conjure songs and landscapes that are by definition silent on and absent from the page depends on the reader's embodied memories, then film faces similar though not identical limitations. As Marks argues, the viewer's ability to mimetically remake the profilmic world in their own body will still vary according to their degree of familiarity with the sounds, smells, and textures conjured as well as their configuration of the sensory (the hierarchical or synesthetic relationships between different senses that they have learned from their culture and from lived experience).

In fact, Marks contends that evoking senses beyond the visual and the aural in intercultural cinema has the effect of confronting the viewer with the incommensurability of their sensory experience with that of the filmmaker or the subjects of the film: "Intercultural spectatorship is the meeting of two different sensoria which may or may not intersect. Spectatorship is thus an act of sensory translation of cultural knowledge."[25] This act of translation, both between cultures and between lived experience and filmic representation, is necessarily incomplete, introducing negativity—"a sense of what we are missing"—into the viewing experience.[26] For Marks, this negativity is crucial to the ethical work of intercultural cinema as well as its critique of ethnography, since films that communicate this sense of loss refuse to simply feed "the tourist's hungry gaze."[27] As I have argued throughout the book, this kind of negative dialectic—on the one hand hailing the reader or viewer as an embodied participant and, on the other, marking the limits of their sensory knowledge of local particularity—lies at the heart of critical regionalist poetics.

This negativity may take the form of the indifference toward the viewer's comprehension and identification with the characters that critics have observed in Alonso's filmmaking.[28] It may take the form of the dissonance and confusion produced by the different film stocks Rocha employs in *Aboio* or that of the viewer's awareness that they do not fully understand what they hear, whether it be the Guaraní language spoken in *Hamaca paraguaya* or the language in which Vicuña insists the sea speaks to her body in *Kon Kon*. (Though of course, some hypothetical viewers—those who grew up with the *aboio* songs, those who speak Guaraní, those who have dwelled intimately with the coastal waters—will hear these sounds differently, with more recognition and comprehension.) In critical regionalist filmmaking, I would propose, cinema's capacity to sensorially immerse the viewer, to literally engage their senses and train them in the patterns and rhythms of local lifeways with which they may not be familiar (or with which they may have lost touch), does not compensate for this negativity. Rather, the two exist in a dialectical relationship. In Adornian fashion, if critical regionalist poetics bring the viewer closer and closer to the experience of dwelling, this is not because impasses to access are progressively overcome or contradictions dialectically resolved but, rather, because the viewer becomes increasingly aware that their inability to fully comprehend forms part of the experience of the contact zone between disparate modes of dwelling.

I would argue that this is true, too, of the evolution of critical regionalist poetics across media. In other words, reading intertextually between critical regionalist literature and film suggests that the limitations an artist faces when it comes to imparting lessons in dwelling can never be entirely pinned on the medium. As such, technological innovation will never fully overcome these limitations. If the immediacy and reality promised by new technologies can never close the gap between regional life and the exterior position from which it is represented, such technologies *can* make us aware of their mediated nature in new ways. A key feature of critical regionalist poetics as I understand it is the imperative to show that aesthetic mediation is not only an impasse barring us from "authenticity" but also a tool for training one's attention, for rendering perceptible connections that would otherwise be missed.

In short, critical regionalist texts in any medium must acknowledge their limitations and point "to [their] own asymptotic, caressing relation to the real."[29] Yet they must not stop there. They must also embrace their obligation to teach, understood in the dual sense of offering the viewer the opportunity to hone new senses and new kinds of attention and of raising their awareness of the limits of what they can presume to know and how fully they can expect to dwell in a world encountered only through textual mediation. This is not, however, to fetishize the notion of immediate experience, for both in the world one literally, corporally inhabits and in the worlds one encounters in texts, one must, in Heidegger's words, "ever learn to dwell."[30] This learning is never complete, accomplished in the preterit tense, not even in the places and texts in which we feel most at home. Critical regionalist poetics merely centers this ongoing learning process, whereas in less experimental texts, as among places, languages, and conventions that feel familiar, it may slip from view.

Notes

INTRODUCTION

1. Heidegger, too, begins by questioning whether dwelling is "incompatible with the poetic" but concludes that, on the contrary, the former depends on the latter: "Poetry is what really lets us dwell." Perceiving this relationship requires recognizing that dwelling extends beyond "merely the occupying of a lodging" and that true poetry does not transcend the world we inhabit but, rather, brings it forth: "Poetry does not fly above and surmount the world in order to escape it and hover over it. Poetry is what first brings man onto the earth, making him belong to it, and thus brings him into dwelling." Martin Heidegger, "Poetically Man Dwells," in *Poetry, Language, Thought*, trans. Albert Hofstadter (New York: Harper & Row, 1971), 213, 215, 218.

2. This sense of remove is illusory. As Ericka Beckman argues, rural zones represented in classics of the Latin American regionalist tradition do not exist outside of modern capitalist relations but, rather, are deeply imbricated in them. Ericka Beckman, *Capital Fictions: The Literature of Latin America's Export Age* (Minneapolis: University of Minnesota Press, 2013).

3. As Anna Tsing points out, universality has long been attributed to the colonizers, while particularity is attributed to the colonized. Following Tsing, I do not seek to dismiss aspirations to universality as always problematic (as in a betrayal of the particular or a cover for imperial projects) but rather to move beyond this duality by recognizing that "the universal" is a horizon that is never completely reached, and that dialogues across difference are always full of friction. Anna Lowenhaupt Tsing. *Friction: An Ethnography of Global Connection* (Princeton, NJ: Princeton University Press, 2005), 9, 7.

4. Pablo Heredia notes that the boom produced the first Latin American literatures published primarily on other continents. Pablo Heredia, *El texto literario*

y los discursos regionales: Propuestas para una regionalización de la narrativa argentina contemporánea (Córdoba, Argentina: Ediciones Argos, 1994), 27.

5. For example, Paula Serafini is invested in exploring extractivism as at once a material and economic phenomenon and "a cultural phenomenon": "This means considering how cultural production can be extractive in its processes and can sustain the legitimacy of extractivism, but also how culture is a ground for contesting the very roots of extractivism, to weaken its hold in the social imaginary, and to allow the envisioning and enacting of other worlds." Paula Serafini, *Creating Worlds Otherwise: Art, Collective Action, and (Post)Extractivism* (Nashville, TN: Vanderbilt University Press, 2022), 33–34. See also Axel Pérez Trujillo Diniz, *Imagining the Plains of Latin America: An Ecocritical Study* (London: Bloomsbury Academic, 2021); Jens Andermann, *Entranced Earth: Art, Extractivism, and the End of Landscape* (Evanston, IL: Northwestern University Press, 2023). Amanda M. Smith, *Mapping the Amazon: Literary Geography after the Rubber Boom* (Liverpool: Liverpool University Press, 2021).

6. Charlotte Rogers notes that "sites of extractivism are generally far removed from the societies that enjoy the material benefits they provide." Charlotte Rogers, *Mourning El Dorado: Literature and Extractivism in the Contemporary American Tropics* (Charlottesville: University of Virginia Press, 2019), 7. Macarena Gómez-Barris emphasizes the importance of contesting "the extractive view," which "sees territories as commodities," by "perceiving otherwise," from "submerged perspectives" that "perceive local terrains as sources of knowledge, vitality, and livability." Macarena Gómez-Barris, *The Extractive Zone: Social Ecologies and Decolonial Perspectives* (Durham, NC: Duke University Press, 2017), 1, 5, 9.

7. On this point, I join Gisela Heffes, who claims that literary texts can reclaim "a sense of spatial and local belonging" and that this "is one of the most important features of ecocriticism, given that the relation we establish with a specific place determines our ways of being and acting." Gisela Heffes, *Políticas de la destrucción—poéticas de la preservación: Apuntes para una lectura eco-crítica del medio ambiente en América Latina* (Rosario, Argentina: Beatriz Viterbo, 2013), 59, 29. See also: Ursula K. Heise, *Sense of Place and Sense of Planet: The Environmental Imagination of the Global* (Oxford: Oxford University Press, 2008); Laura Barbas-Rhoden, *Ecological Imaginations in Latin American Fiction* (Gainesville: University of Florida Press, 2011).

8. This turn can be traced back to Jennifer French, *Nature, Neo-Colonialism, and the Spanish American Regional Writers* (Hanover, NH: Dartmouth College Press, 2005). It also includes Beckman, *Capital Fictions*; Rogers, *Mourning El Dorado*; Andermann, *Entranced Earth*.

9. See, for example, Jennifer Wenzel, *The Disposition of Nature* (New York: Fordham University Press, 2019).

10. Beginning in the 1980s, a wave of revisionist readings of early twentieth-century regionalism has called into question long-standing stereotypes about regionalist literature, such as the equation of historical regionalism with a naive faith in "straight," naturalistic representation and with unwitting complicity in nationalistic ideology and modernization projects. For example, Carlos J. Alonso has argued in relation to the *novelas de la tierra* of the Hispanic Ameri-

can tradition that it would be a mistake to treat these classical regionalist texts as simply vehicles for nationalistic ideology. Unlike most conventional documentary projects, even so-called traditional regionalist texts often reflect on their own representational practices and media specificity, thus anticipating the critical regionalist project I foreground in this book. Carlos J. Alonso, *The Spanish American Regional Novel: Modernity and Autochthony* (Cambridge: Cambridge University Press, 1990). Nevertheless, the myth of regionalist literature as retrograde has proved quite intractable. As French laments, in spite of the prominence and insightfulness of such revisionist readings, the *novelas de la tierra* continue to be viewed as "a literary precondition, hopelessly backward in their representational simplicity, their isolation from international literary developments, and their naïve political formulas." French, *Nature, Neo-Colonialism, and the Spanish American Regional Writers*, 8.

11. For example, these questions can be traced back to the historical avant-gardes of the 1920s. Fernando J. Rosenberg's analysis of the Latin American avant-gardes of the 1920s and '30s posits that the modern innovation of these texts lies primarily in their self-reflexivity on the predicament of being caught up in modernity from a geopolitical position that is perpetually seen as premodern. As Rosenberg has argued, beyond mediating between heterogeneous cultures and temporalities, intellectuals seeking to engage in cosmopolitan culture from its peripheries bear "an acute awareness of their position in the modern/colonial order." Fernando J. Rosenberg, *The Avant-Garde and Geopolitics in Latin America* (Pittsburgh: University of Pittsburgh Press, 2006), 19.

12. As I argue, the emancipatory politics of experimental neo-regionalist texts of this time is often missed, especially in their reception outside Latin America. This has to due in part with Cold War cultural politics, which all but guaranteed that novel aesthetics from Latin America such as magical realism would be celebrated in the academies of the Global North only when shorn of their political critique.

13. The second half of the twentieth century (1945 and later) saw the exponential expansion of railroads, highways, hydroelectric plants, and gas pipelines, as well as the introduction of air travel. It also produced unprecedented urban growth and, in at least one case (Brasília), the construction of a completely new city. This period, sometimes dubbed the Great Acceleration, brought a rapid increase in extractivism and the incorporation of remote parts of the South American continent into the capitalist economy. See Rogers, *Mourning El Dorado*, 15–16.

14. Ángel Rama, *Writing across Cultures: Narrative Transculturation in Latin America*, trans. David Freye (Durham, NC: Duke University Press, 2012).

15. There are, of course, significant regional differences in how and when national populism developed in Latin America. For example, the Andean case is anomalous both because of the prominence of the "Indigenous problem"—to speak of the peasant classes is to speak of the unassimilated Indigenous population—and because the middle class emerged later than in other parts of Latin America, which experienced bourgeois revolutions in the early twentieth century (most notably the Mexican Revolution of 1910 and university reform in Argentina in 1918). Nevertheless, national-populist rhetoric throughout

the region shares the propensity to interpellate the peasants in order to quell the threat of revolution as well as provide an authenticating myth of origins grounded in shared roots in the land and the working of the land. See chapter 1 for more detail.

16. Wenzel notes that "belowness involves not only *class position*, in the familiar idiom of subalternity, but *spatial position*: perspective and altitude in a literal sense." Wenzel, *Disposition of Nature*, 22.

17. Donna Haraway, "Situated Knowledges: The Science Question in Feminism and the Privilege of Partial Perspective," *Feminist Studies* 14, no. 3 (1988): 583–84.

18. The pedagogical function of literature is a frequent object of critique, from Marxist demystifications of the bourgeois novel's sentimental education to the "pedagogical or sentimental discourses that aim to teach, totalize, or enclose" targeted by deconstructive practices. Román de la Campa, *Latin Americanism* (Minneapolis: University of Minnesota Press, 1999), 61. As I go on to explain, I am using pedagogy differently, in line with what Gayatri Chakravorty Spivak calls *aesthetic education*. Gayatri Chakravorty Spivak, *An Aesthetic Education in the Era of Globalization* (Cambridge, MA: Harvard University Press, 2013).

19. José María Arguedas, *El zorro de arriba y el zorro de abajo* (Buenos Aires: Losada, 2011), 13; José María Arguedas, *The Fox from Up Above and the Fox from Down Below*, trans. Frances Horning Barraclough (Pittsburgh: University of Pittsburgh Press and Colección Archivos, 2000), 9. I have chosen to include the original (Spanish or Portuguese) as well as the English translation when citing my primary sources, as their language is idiosyncratic and difficult to fully capture in translation. What is more, the locatedness of these texts—in place, in local culture, and in the specificity of the language in which they were written—is central to my argument in this book.

20. João Guimarães Rosa, *Grande sertão: Veredas* (Rio de Janeiro: Nova Fronteira, 2014), 418; João Guimarães Rosa, *The Devil to Pay in the Backlands*, trans. James L. Taylor and Harriet de Onís (New York: Alfred A. Knopf, 1963), 328. Translation modified.

21. Luís Bueno cites the distinction Luiz Felipe Pondé draws between two kinds of outsiders: *turistas* (who come in barbarous hordes and do not truly relate to the place they visit) and *viajantes* (whose finer sensibilities allow them to perceive the beauty and spirituality of the place they visit), but he suggests the difference might not be tenable in the end—tourism is still a possible starting place "for the difficult contact with the other." He considers, moreover, that regionalist literature is a kind of literary tourism in the general sense of being driven by "interest in other lands and other peoples." Luís Bueno, "O intelectual e o turista: Regionalismo e alteridade na tradição literaria," *Revista do Instituto de Estudos Brasileiros*, no. 55 (2012): 114,118. Laura Demaría draws a parallel distinction between *extranjeros* and *forasteros* (categories that prove similarly mutable and porous in the end), which I discuss in more detail in chapters 1 and 4. Laura Demaría, *Buenos Aires y las provincias: Relatos para desarmar* (Rosario, Argentina: Beatriz Viterbo, 2014). Note that when not otherwise attributed, all translations are my own.

22. Whereas in *Being and Time*, Heidegger focuses on how to live with rather than overcome homelessness and alienation, by the writing of "Building Dwelling Thinking" and "Poetically Man Dwells," he has come around to understanding human existence as "ontologically secure" (to be human is to dwell, to be at home, to be safe) though most remain ignorant of this state of things. For this reason, it is still necessary to learn to dwell. Julian Young, "What Is Dwelling? The Homelessness of Modernity and the Worlding of the World," in *Heidegger, Authenticity, and Modernity: Essays in Honor of Hubert L. Dreyfus*, ed. Mark Wrathall and Jeff Malpas, vol. 1 (Cambridge, MA: MIT Press, 2000), 193.

23. Martin Heidegger, "Building, Dwelling, Thinking," in *Poetry, Language, Thought*, trans. Albert Hofstadter (New York: Harper Colophon, 1971), 146–49.

24. Klaus Benesch, "Space, Place, Narrative: Critical Regionalism and the Idea of Home in a Global Age," *Zeitschrift für Anglistik und Amerikanistik* 64, no. 1 (2016): 102.

25. Laura Bieger, "No Place like Home; or, Dwelling in Narrative," *New Literary History* 46, no. 1 (2015): 17.

26. In his translator's introduction, Albert Hofstadter explains, "The speech of genuine thinking is by nature poetic. It need not take the shape of verse; as Heidegger says, the opposite of the poem is not prose; pure prose is as poetic as any poetry." Heidegger, *Poetry, Language, Thought*, x. On the sense of *vieldeutig*, see Young, "What Is Dwelling?," 196.

27. Young, "What Is Dwelling?," 196.

28. Benesch, "Space, Place, Narrative," 102–3.

29. Bieger, "No Place like Home," 34.

30. One notable and highly relevant exception would be the critical reception of Arguedas's work by the likes of Ángel Rama, Martin Lienhard, and William Rowe. See chapter 2 for more detail.

31. For an example of such an account, see Mario Vargas Llosa, "Primitives and Creators," *Times Literary Supplement* 3481 (1968): 1287–88.

32. Jean Franco, *The Decline and Fall of the Lettered City: Latin America and the Cold War* (Cambridge, MA: Harvard University Press, 2002), 8.

33. Mariano Siskind, *Cosmopolitan Desires: Global Modernity and World Literature in Latin America* (Evanston, IL: Northwestern University Press, 2014), 84. For more on the aesthetic resources—namely temporal alterity—that underdeveloped rural orders contribute to high modernism, see Fredric Jameson, *A Singular Modernity: Essay on the Ontology of the Present* (London: Verso, 2002).

34. De la Campa, *Latin Americanism*, 4. See also Nelly Richard's critique of postmodernism. Nelly Richard, "Intersectando Latinoamérica con el latinoamericanismo: Saberes académicos, práctica teórica y crítica cultural," *Revista Iberoamericana* 63, no. 180 (1997): 345–61.

35. See Fredric Jameson, *The Modernist Papers* (London: Verso, 2016); Jessica Berman, *Modernist Commitments: Ethics, Politics, and Transnational Modernism* (New York: Columbia University Press, 2012); Eric Hayot and Rebecca Walkowitz, eds., *A New Vocabulary for Global Modernism* (New York: Colum-

bia University Press, 2016); Andrew Reynolds, *Behind the Masks of Modernism: Global and Transnational Perspectives* (Gainesville: University of Florida Press, 2016); Joe Cleary, *Modernism, Empire, World Literature* (Cambridge: Cambridge University Press, 2021).

36. David Viñas, "Pareceres y digresiones en torno a la nueva narrativa latinoamericana," in *Más allá del boom: Literatura y mercado.*, ed. David Viñas (Mexico City: Marcha, 1981), 22. See also Ángel Rama, "El 'boom' en perspectiva," in *Más allá del boom: Literatura y mercado*, ed. David Viñas (Mexico City: Marcha, 1981), 51–129; Siskind, *Cosmopolitan Desires*.

37. Franco, *Decline and Fall of the Lettered City*, 41.

38. Vargas Llosa, "Primitives and Creators," 1287.

39. Ulises Juan Zevallos Aguilar, *Las provincias contraatacan: Regionalismo y anticentralismo en la literatura peruana del siglo XX* (Lima, Peru: Universidad Nacional Mayor de San Marcos, 2009), 18.

40. Vargas Llosa, "Primitives and Creators," 1288.

41. Ligia Chiappini, "Regionalismo(s) e regionalidade(s) num mundo supostamente global, 21," in *Memórias da Borborema 2: Internacionalização do Regional*, ed. Diógenes André Vieira Maciel (Campina Grande, Brazil: Abralic, 2014), 41.

42. For more on the relationship between Candido and Rama, see Gabriel dos Santos Lima, "A teoria desenvolvimentista do 'super-regionalismo' em Antonio Candido e o caso Arguedas," *Criação & Crítica* 26 (2020): 40–54.

43. Lima, "A teoria desenvolvimentista," 44.

44. Lima, "A teoria desenvolvimentista," 46.

45. Rama, *Writing across Cultures*, 15.

46. Rama, *Writing across Cultures*, 26.

47. Rama, *Writing across Cultures*, 32–33

48. Rama, *Writing across Cultures*, 84.

49. The term *transculturation* was originally introduced by Cuban intellectual Fernando Ortiz as an alternative to *acculturation*, which according to Rama implies "acquiring another culture" and "necessarily involves the loss or uprooting of a previous culture, which could be defined as a deculturation." Rama, *Writing across Cultures*, 19, 46.

50. Quoted in Lima, "A teoria desenvolvimentista," 48.

51. Lima, "A teoria desenvolvimentista," 47.

52. Lima, "A teoria desenvolvimentista," 48. For more on how *desarrollismo* was overtaken by dependency theory in Argentina and Brazil, see Nicolas Allen and Pablo Nicotera, "Del desarrollismo al dependentismo en el ensayo socioeconómico: Celso Furtado / Raúl Prebisch—Fernando Henrique Cardoso / Juan José Sebreli," in *Historia comparada de las literaturas argentina y brasileña. Tomo V: Del desarrollismo a la dictadura, entre privatización, boom y militancia (1955–1970)*, ed. Marcela Croce (Villa María, Argentina: Editorial Universitaria Villa María, 2018), 275–301.

53. Lima, "A teoria desenvolvimentista," 50.

54. Mariana Miggiolaro Chaguri, "O norte e o sul: Região e regionalismo em meados do século XX," *Sociologia & Antropologia* 4, no. 1 (2014): 185.

55. Franco, *Decline and Fall of the Lettered City*, 51.

56. For example, Julio Prieto argues that Mariátegui's reading of Vallejo's *Trilce* as a form of "indigenismo vanguardista" emphasizes the identitarian and revolutionary aspects of Vallejo's most experimental text without closely engaging with its poetic innovations. Julio Prieto, *La escritura errante: Ilegibilidad y políticas del estilo en Latinoamérica* (Madrid and Frankfurt: Iberoamericana and Vervuert, 2016), 100–101.

57. See Vargas Llosa, "Primitives and Creators"; Mario Vargas Llosa, "José María Arguedas: Entre ideología y la arcadia," *Revista Iberoamericana* 47 (1981): 33–46.

58. According to Gareth Williams, Perón didn't need the intellectuals because he disseminated his cultural messaging through newer technologies such as radio, film, and photography. Gareth Williams, *The Other Side of the Popular: Neoliberalism and Subalternity in Latin America* (Durham, NC: Duke University Press, 2002), 53.

59. Oscar Terán, *Nuestros años sesentas: La formación de la nueva izquierda intelectual argentina, 1956–1966* (Buenos Aires: Siglo Veintiuno, 2013), 22.

60. For more on the intellectual climate of the 1960s, and particularly the fracturing of the left in response to Peronism, see Terán, *Nuestros años sesentas*.

61. Terán, *Nuestros años sesentas*,128. While avant-garde aesthetics were seen as politically suspect in Argentina in the years leading up to the military dictatorship, in Brazil, where most of the 1960s were lived under authoritarian rule, they offered a refuge. According to Herasmo Braga de Oliveira Brito, the Left gravitated toward antirealist and fantastic works in the second half of the century in reaction to the "vigilance of political regimes that rigidly promoted censorship." Herasmo Braga de Oliveira Brito, *Neoregionalismo brasileiro: Análises de uma nova tendência da literatura brasileira* (Teresina, Brazil: Gráfico do Povo, 2017), 37. During Brazil's dictatorship, which was established by a US-backed coup in 1964 and lasted until 1985, dissident political views could not be expressed directly in realist works. In other words, the referentiality and local particularity characteristic of the politically committed regionalists of the 1930s and '40s were abandoned by many writers not only because they were dubbed aesthetically retrograde but also because they became politically dangerous. The shift away from regionalist subject matter and realist style began before the dictatorship, however, during the rapid urbanization and industrialization of the 1950s.

62. Many of these claims were echoed by Juan Carlos Onganía, who used the alleged infiltration of the universities by Marxists to justify his 1966 coup. Terán, *Nuestros años sesentas*, 217.

63. Terán, *Nuestros años sesentas*, 95.

64. Pablo Heredia, *El suelo: Ensayos sobre regionalismos y nacionalismos en la literatura argentina* (Córdoba, Argentina: Editorial Facultad de Filosofía y Humanidades Universidad Nacional de Córdoba / Universitas, 2005), 150–51.

65. Siskind, *Cosmopolitan Desires*, 96. See also Juan José Saer, "La espesa selva de lo real." Juan José Saer, *El concepto de ficción* (Mexico City: Universidad Iberoamericana, 1997), 259–63.

66. Heredia, *El texto literario y los discursos regionales*; Demaría *Buenos Aires y las provincias*.

67. See, for example, Edward W. Said, *Orientalism* (New York: Vintage, 2014); David Damrosch, *What Is World Literature?* (Princeton, NJ: Princeton University Press, 2003); Emily Apter, *The Translation Zone: A New Comparative Literature* (Princeton, NJ: Princeton University Press, 2006); Édouard Glissant, *Poetics of Relation*, trans. Betsy Wing (Ann Arbor: University of Michigan Press, 1997); Héctor Hoyos, *Beyond Bolaño: The Global Latin American Novel* (New York: Columbia University Press, 2015); Richard, "Intersectando Latinoamérica con el latinoamericanismo"; Spivak, *Aesthetic Education*.

68. For a discussion of the limits and risks of empathy "across national, cultural, racial and gender boundaries" and a critique of its appropriation by the neoliberal market, see Carolyn Pedwell, *Affective Relations: The Transnational Politics of Empathy* (New York: Palgrave Macmillan, 2014), xii.

69. Bieger, "No Place like Home," 23.

70. Spivak, *Aesthetic Education*, 112.

71. Spivak, *Aesthetic Education*, 113.

72. Spivak, *Aesthetic Education*, 19–24.

73. Spivak, *Aesthetic Education*, 98.

74. Spivak, *Aesthetic Education*, 98.

75. Spivak, *Aesthetic Education*, 4.

76. Spivak, *Aesthetic Education*, 27.

77. Spivak, *Aesthetic Education*, 114.

78. Spivak, *Aesthetic Education*, 2.

79. Pérez Trujillo Diniz, *Imagining the Plains*, 15, 96, 114.

80. Demaría, *Buenos Aires y las provincias*, 486–87.

81. I borrow the term *aesthetic frame* from Eugenio Di Stefano, who contrasts texts that attempt to vanish the frame that marks the distinction between art and life with those that thicken it by foregrounding their own constructedness as aesthetic artifacts. For the works in my corpus, as for those that interest Di Stefano, counterintuitively, the latter move proves more politically radical. See Eugenio Claudio Di Stefano, *The Vanishing Frame: Latin American Culture and Theory in the Postdictatorial Era* (Austin: University of Texas Press, 2018).

82. *Coevalness* is Johannes Fabian's term for contemporaneity that is denied ethnographic subjects as a condition of possibility for producing them as an object of anthropological knowledge. Johannes Fabian, *Time and the Other: How Anthropology Makes Its Object* (New York: Columbia University Press, 2006).

83. For more on the "perils of the contact zone," see Mary Louise Pratt, "Arts of the Contact Zone," *Profession (Modern Language Association)*, 1991, 33–44.

84. See Thomas L. Friedman, *The World Is Flat: A Brief History of the Twenty-First Century* (New York: Farrar, Straus and Giroux, 2005). For counterarguments, see Neil Smith, *Uneven Development: Nature, Capital, and the Production of Space* (Athens: University of Georgia Press, 2004), 4–5; Tsing, *Friction*, 11.

85. Walls are a recurrent metaphor in Arguedas's speech, "No soy un aculturado," which is discussed in chapter 2.

86. Davi Kopenawa and Bruce Albert, *The Falling Sky: Words of a Yanomami Shaman*, trans. Nicolas Elliot and Alison Dundy (Cambridge, MA: Belknap Press of Harvard University Press, 2013).

87. I do not mean literally untranslatable but rather, following Krista Brune's use of the term, difficult to translate and to market in translation. Krista Brune,

Creative Transformations: Travels and Translations of Brazil in the Americas (Albany: State University of New York Press, 2020).

88. Francine R. Masiello, *El cuerpo de la voz (poesía, ética y cultura)* (Rosario, Argentina: Beatriz Viterbo, 2013), 253.

89. Masiello, *El cuerpo de la voz*, 253.

90. Masiello, *El cuerpo de la voz*, 253.

91. Tsing, *Friction*, 4.

92. These topics are richly explored, though not in explicit conversation with critical regionalism, in scholarship including: Sara Ahmed, *Strange Encounters: Embodied Others in Post-Coloniality* (New York: Routledge, 2000); Glissant, *Poetics of Relation*; bell hooks, *Belonging: A Culture of Place* (New York: Routledge, 2009); Gómez-Barris, *Extractive Zone*.

93. As Sara Ahmed argues, the very idea of being at home depends on dividing the world into bodies that dwell and abject bodies that are not at home and not "liveable," and historically, white bodies are most often constructed as "at home" by virtue of nonwhite bodies being classified as strangers. Ahmed, *Strange Encounters*, 53. None of the texts focused on in this study fully examines how race, class, and gender differentially shape one's ability to dwell, to pursue at-homeness in the world. In fact, Arguedas is the only one of the three to center questions of race, and Guimarães Rosa is the only one to grapple in complex ways with gender. Arguedas's attempts to imagine female subjectivities tend to be discomforting, and Saer's treatment of women is ultimately objectifying and misogynistic. Guimarães Rosa, in contrast, writes from within a patriarchal frame wherein it is impermissible for a woman to dwell as a *jagunço* or for two men to dwell as lovers, but *Grande sertão: Veredas* throws the oppressiveness and violence of this frame into relief, making it the only text of my corpus to treat gender subversively (though there is still little attempt to introduce female perspective into its overwhelmingly masculine world).

94. See José Martí, *Nuestra América* (Jalisco, Mexico: Universidad de Guadalajara, 2002). Fernando Rosenberg points out that in many manifestos of the historical avant-gardes, including Andrade's *Manifesto antropófago* (1928), "America" signifies "a predicament that points back to the colonial encounter." Rosenberg, *Avant-Garde and Geopolitics*, 18. Rama refers to the transnational region spanned by his literary and cultural criticism as "América" or "el continente." As Rama's English translator David Frye suggests, the choice of this term belies his lifelong ambition to situate the writers he studies not only in their respective national contexts but also within the larger framework of literature of the Americas. Rama, *Writing across Cultures*, xi–xii.

95. Pérez Trujillo Diniz, *Imagining the Plains*.

96. Sarmiento's thought is a prime example. See Pérez Trujillo Diniz, *Imagining the Plains*.

97. Pérez Trujillo Diniz, *Imagining the Plains*, 3–4, 125.

98. Robert Patrick Newcomb, *Nossa and Nuestra América: Inter-American Dialogues* (West Lafayette, IN: Purdue University Press, 2012).

99. Florencia Garramuño, *Frutos estranhos: Sobre a inespecificidade na estética contemporânea*, ed. Paloma Vidal, trans. Carlos Nougué (Rio de Janeiro: Rocco, 2014), 28.

100. Garramuño, *Frutos estranhos*, 44–45. Judith Butler and Gayatri Chakravorty Spivak, *Who Sings the Nation-State? Language, Politics, Belonging* (London: University of Chicago Press, 2010).

101. Garramuño, *Frutos estranhos*, 45.

102. Given these intersections, Rulfo's absence from my corpus may strike some readers as conspicuous. Though Rulfo's experimental fiction shares many characteristics with the texts in my corpus—such as narrative fragmentation, sensorial evocation of local spaces, and skepticism toward national developmentalist agendas—one key component is missing: the presence of the outsider (a character or narrator who serves as a proxy for the reader) who is not bound to the region by filiation but who is nevertheless invited or challenged to learn to dwell there. Recall that in *Pedro Páramo*, Juan Preciado is a native son of Comala, and his eventual (eternal) residence there is presented as an inevitable inheritance, more a curse than an opportunity. Thought the texts I analyze are not necessarily more optimistic about the fate of their characters, the way they evoke learning to dwell as a possibility feels to me tonally, affectively different. Another reason that Rulfo does not fit well within my corpus is that he stopped writing on the eve of the period that interests me, defined by the Cuban Revolution and its aftermath.

103. Saer and Arguedas are rarely compared, but Demaría recognizes in Saer a commitment to writing from a site of enunciation "in the provinces," which she associates with Arguedas's reclaiming of the term *provinciano*. Demaría, *Buenos Aires y las provincias*, 52.

104. These factors will be discussed in more detail in chapter 1. See Heredia, *El suelo*; Demaría, *Buenos Aires y las provincias*.

105. As I have discussed, my use of this term is informed by Spivak's work on the role of aesthetic experience (reading literature in particular) in imparting ethical training for planetary citizenship in a postcolonial world. I also draw on Jacques Rancière's notion of the aesthetic as playing a role in determining and interrupting the distribution of the sensible—that is, what and whose experience is thinkable. Spivak, *Aesthetic Education*; Jacques Rancière, *The Politics of Aesthetics: The Distribution of the Sensible*, trans. Gabriel Rockhill (London: Bloomsbury Academic, 2006).

CHAPTER 1

1. See, for example: Alonso, *Spanish American Regional Novel*; French, *Nature, Neo-Colonialism, and the Spanish American Regional Writers*; Chiappini, "Regionalismo(s) e regionalidade(s)"; Brito, *Neoregionalismo brasileiro*; Hebe Beatriz Molina and María Lorena Burlot, "El regionalismo como problema conceptual," in *Regionalismo literario: Historia y crítica de un concepto problemático*, ed. Hebe Beatriz Molina and Fabiana Inés Varela (Mendoza, Argentina: Biblioteca Digital de la Universidad Nacional de Cuyo, 2018), 11–46; Zevallos Aguilar, *Las provincias contraatacan*; Heredia, *El texto literario y los discursos regionales*; Demaría, *Buenos Aires y las provincias*.

2. See the introduction for my discussion of the accounts of this shift provided by Mario Vargas Llosa, Antonio Candido, and Ángel Rama.

3. Mary Louise Pratt, *Planetary Longings* (Durham, NC: Duke University Press, 2022), 51.

4. Antonio Candido's *Formação da literatura brasileira* divides Brazilian regionalism into three distinct phases: the Romanticism of the founding national literatures (closely linked to *indianismo* and *sertanismo*), the exoticism and quaint local color of the turn of the twentieth century, and the politically committee d regionalism of the 1930s and 1940s. Candido grants aesthetic merit only to the last of these phases while dismissing the first two as "subliteratura" ("subliterature") excessively burdened by elaborating national identity and aesthetically limited to "o pitoresco" ("the picturesque"). Antonio Candido, *Formação da literatura brasileira (Momentos decisivos)* (São Paulo: Editora Itatiaia, 1975).

5. "Super-regionalismo" is Candido's term. Antonio Candido, "Literatura e subdesenvolvimento," in *A educação pela noite e outros ensaios* (São Paulo: Editora Ática, 1987), 10–22; Beatriz Sarlo describes Saer's regionalism as "regionalismo no regionalista." Molina and Burlot, "El regionalismo como problema conceptual," 29; "regionalismo no nostálgico" is from Friedhelm Schmidt-Welle, "Regionalismo abstracto y representación simbólica de la nación en la literatura latinoamericana de la región," *Relaciones* 130 (2012): 115–27.

6. See Mary Louise Pratt, *Imperial Eyes: Travel Writing and Transculturation* (New York: Routledge, 2008); Marta Penhos, *Ver, conocer, dominar: Imágenes de Sudamérica a fines del Siglo XVIII* (Buenos Aires: Siglo Veintiuno, 2005); Adolfo Prieto, *Los viajeros ingleses y la emergencia de la literatura argentina (1820–1850)* (Buenos Aires: Sudamérica, 1996); Jens Andermann, "State Formation, Visual Technology and Spectatorship: Visions of Modernity in Brazil and Argentina," *Theory, Culture & Society* 27, no. 7–8 (2010): 161–83.

7. Graciela Montaldo, *De pronto, el campo: Literatura argentina y tradición rural* (Rosario, Argentina: Beatriz Viterbo, 1993), 26.

8. As Estelle Tarica argues of the Andean context, for example: "Whenever indigenism moved from being an oppositional to a state discourse, *indigenistas* construed contemporary Indians, as opposed to their illustrious ancestors, as an obstacle to modernization. [. . .] Shoved firmly into the past, at the nation's origin, Indian identity became expressive, even in that prehistory, of the nation's distinct essence." Estelle Tarica, *The Inner Life of Mestizo Nationalism* (Minneapolis: University of Minnesota Press, 2008), 5.

9. Raymond Williams, *The Country and the City* (New York: Oxford University Press, 1973). For more on the role of early twentieth-century literature in this temporal displacement, see Alonso, *Spanish American Regional Novel.* One example of such a regionalist novel is Ricardo Güiraldes's *Don Segundo Sombra* (Buenos Aires: Emecé Editores, 2000).

10. On the periodization of populism, see Jorge Castañeda, *Utopia Unarmed: The Latin American Left after the Cold War* (New York: Random House, 1993), 44.

11. Williams, *Other Side of the Popular.*

12. Brazilian *modernismo* is not to be confused with Hispanic American *modernismo*. The former is an avant-garde movement that appears in São Paulo in the 1920s, and it is more akin to Hispanic American *vanguardismo* than Hispanic American *modernismo*, which has its roots in the late nineteenth century.

13. José Aderaldo Castello, *José Lins do Rêgo: Modernismo e regionalismo* (São Paulo: Edart, 1961), 19.

14. Aderaldo Castello notes that Freyre and Lins do Rego read and dialogued (often quite amicably) with *modernistas* such as Manuel Bandeira, Mário de Andrade, Carlos Drummond de Andrade, and Sérgio Buarque de Holanda, who shared an interest in Brazilian folklore and Indigenous and Afro-descendant cultures. Aderaldo Castello, *José Lins do Rêgo*, 33. Freyre also studied in the United States and traveled extensively Europe.

15. Gilberto Freyre, *Manifesto regionalista* (Recife, Brazil: Fundação Joaquim Nabuco, 1996), 95.

16. Maria Arminda do Nascimento Arruda, "Modernismo e regionalismo no Brasil: Entre inovação e tradição," *Tempo Social: Revista de Sociologia da USP* 23, no. 2 (2011): 201.

17. Arruda, "Modernismo e regionalismo no Brasil," 193.

18. Arruda, "Modernismo e regionalismo no Brasil," 193.

19. Though *Grande sertão: Veredas* is set in the *sertão*, it is set primarily in the lower *sertão* of Minas Gerais, not in the northeastern states of Bahia, Sergipe, Alagoas, Pernambuco, Paraíba, Rio Grande do Norte, and Ceará, which were the focus of regionalists of Freyre's generation.

20. Chiappini, "Regionalismo(s) e regionalidade(s)," 32.

21. Molina and Burlot, "El regionalismo como problema conceptual," 12–13.

22. Demaría, *Buenos Aires y las provincias*, 15.

23. Molina and Burlot, "El regionalismo como problema conceptual," 26.

24. Heredia, *El suelo*, 150–54.

25. Victoria Cohen Imach, *De utopías y desencantos: Campo intelectual y periferia en la Argentina de los sesenta* (Tucumán, Argentina: Universidad Nacional de Tucumán, Facultad de Filosofía y Letras, Instituto Interdisciplinario de Estudios Latinoamericanos, 1994), 476; Heredia, *El texto literario y los discursos regionales*, 27–28, 39.

26. Heredia, *El texto literario y los discursos regionales*, 35–45.

27. Guimarães Rosa as well as subsequent Brazilian neo-regionalists including Raimundo Carrero and Milton Hatoum have rejected the regionalist label for similar reasons. André Tessaro Pelinser and Márcio Miranda Alves, "A permanência do regionalismo na literatura brasileira contemporânea," *Estudos de Literatura Brasileira Contemporânea*, no. 59 (January 24, 2020): 1–13.

28. Juan José Saer, Notebook, n.d. Princeton University Library.

29. Julio Premat, *La dicha de Saturno: Escritura y melancolía en la obra de Juan José Saer* (Rosario, Argentina: Beatriz Viterbo, 2002), 301.

30. Heredia, *El texto literario y los discursos regionales*, 134–35.

31. Tarica, *Inner Life of Mestizo Nationalism*, 8–9.

32. Zevallos Aguilar, *Las provincias contraatacan*, 21

33. Tarica, *Inner Life of Mestizo Nationalism*, xii.

34. Tarica, *Inner Life of Mestizo Nationalism*, 4.

35. Zevallos Aguilar, *Las provincias contraatacan*, 10.

36. Tarica, *Inner Life of Mestizo Nationalism*, 2.

37. Zevallos Aguilar, *Las provincias contraatacan*, 29.

38. Tara Daly, *Beyond Human: Vital Materialisms in the Andean Avant-Gardes* (Lewisburg, PA: Bucknell University Press, 2019), 10.

39. Tarica, *Inner Life of Mestizo Nationalism*, xi.

40. Martin Lienhard, *Cultura andina y forma novelesca: Zorros y danzantes en la última novela de Arguedas* (Lima, Peru: Editorial Horizonte, 1990); Cohen Imach, *De utopías y desencantos*.

41. Tarica, *Inner Life of Mestizo Nationalism*, 25.

42. For example, Francine Masiello notes the impact of Merleau-Ponty's thought on the Argentine intellectuals associated with the journal *Contorno* in the 1950s, and José Eduardo Gonzáles has analyzed the influence of the Frankfurt School on Ángel Rama. See Francine R. Masiello, *The Senses of Democracy: Perception, Politics, and Culture in Latin America* (Austin: University of Texas Press, 2018), 181–85; José Eduardo Gonzáles, *Appropriating Theory: Ángel Rama's Critical Work* (Pittsburgh: University of Pittsburgh Press, 2017).

43. Jameson notes that Frampton's critical regionalism is inherently backward looking, or "rearguard": "A certain retrogression is built into the project itself where it is underscored by the slogan of an *arrière-garde* or rearguard action." The ensuing problem is both theoretical and political: "how to fashion a progressive strategy out of what are necessarily the materials of tradition and nostalgia? How to use the attempt to conserve in an actively liberatory and transformational way?" Fredric Jameson, *The Seeds of Time* (New York: Columbia University Press, 1994): 190–91, 202.

44. For example, see the way that Krista Comer recuperates the anthropological work of James Clifford and Mary Louise Pratt as already anticipating critical regionalism, or the way Randi Tanglen and Melina Vizcaíno-Alemán each turn back to earlier moments in Mexican cultural production to locate instances of critical regionalism. Krista Comer, "Exceptionalism, Other Wests, Critical Regionalism," *American Literary History* 23, no. 1 (2011): 159–73; Randi Lynn Tanglen, "Critical Regionalism, the US-Mexican War, and Nineteenth-Century American Literary History," *Western American Literature* 48, no. 1 (2013): 180–99; Melina Vizcaíno-Alemán, "What's So Critical about Critical Regionalism? The Case of Fray Angélico Chávez's New Mexico Triptych," *Western American Literature* 49, no. 2 (2011): 199–222.

45. This last turn gains momentum at the turn of the millennium. For more on how it plays out beyond the Latin American context, see: Sheila Jasanoff and Marybeth Long Martello, eds., *Earthly Politics: Local and Global in Environmental Governance* (Cambridge, MA: MIT Press, 2004); Ali Mirsepassi, Amrita Basu, and Frederick Stirton Weaver, eds., *Localizing Knowledge in a Globalizing World: Recasting the Area Studies Debate* (Syracuse, NY: Syracuse University Press, 2003); Roxann Prazniak and Arif Dirlik, eds., *Places and Politics in an Age of Globalization* (Lanham, MD: Rowman & Littlefield, 2001).

46. Rosenberg, *Avant-Garde and Geopolitics*, 40.

47. For more on cosmopolitan longing, see Siskind, *Cosmopolitan Desires*.

48. Jameson claims: "Critical Regionalism could be characterized as a kind of postmodernism of the global system as a whole (or at least of the semiperiphery if not the Third World), as opposed to the First World's own internal and external postmodernisms." Jameson, *Seeds of Time*, 194.

49. Alberto Moreiras, *Tercer espacio: Literatura y duelo en América Latina* (Santiago, Chile: Universidad Arcis, 1999).

50. Kenneth Frampton, "Towards a Critical Regionalism: Six Points for an Architecture of Resistance," in *The Anti-Aesthetic*, ed. Hal Foster (Seattle: Bay Press, 1983), 30.

51. Frampton, "Towards a Critical Regionalism," 31.

52. Jameson, *Seeds of Time*, 197.

53. For how spatial others ("not here") are recoded as temporal others ("not yet modern") in colonial narratives of modernity, see Dipesh Chakrabarty, *Provincializing Europe: Postcolonial Thought and Historical Difference* (Princeton, NJ: Princeton University Press, 2007). Challenging the Hegelian concept of teleological history is also a central tenet of dependency theory in the Americas, which informs theories of decoloniality as well as my use of critical regionalism. See Hosam Aboul-Ela, *Other South: Faulkner, Coloniality, and the Mariátegui Tradition* (Pittsburgh: University of Pittsburgh Press, 2007), 41; Walter D. Mignolo and Catherine E. Walsh, *On Decoloniality: Concepts, Analytics, Praxis* (Durham, NC: Duke University Press, 2018), 110–11.

54. Comer, "Exceptionalism, Other Wests, Critical Regionalism," 163.

55. Neil Campbell, *The Rhizomatic West: Representing the American West in a Transnational, Global, Media Age* (Lincoln: University of Nebraska Press, 2008), 71, 49.

56. Vizcaíno-Alemán, "What's So Critical about Critical Regionalism?," 201.

57. Chiappini, "Regionalismo(s) e regionalidade(s)," 52.

58. Chiappini, "Regionalismo(s) e regionalidade(s)," 53.

59. Demaría, *Buenos Aires y las provincias*, 492.

60. Demaría, *Buenos Aires y las provincias*, 420.

61. Ricardo J. Kalimán, "Un marco (no 'global') para el estudio de las regiones culturales," *Journal of Iberian and Latin American Research* 5, no. 2 (1999): 11–22.

62. See Walter Mignolo, "Posoccidentalismo: El argumento desde América Latina." In *Teorías sin disciplina (Latinoamericanismo, poscolonialidad y globalización en debate)*, ed. Santiago Castro-Gómez and Eduardo Mendieta (Mexico City: Miguel Ángel Porrúa, 1998); Richard, "Intersectando Latinoamérica con el latinoamericanismo"; Gómez-Barris, *Extractive Zone*, 11.

63. Douglas Reichert Powell, *Critical Regionalism: Connecting Politics and Culture in the American Landscape* (Chapel Hill: University of North Carolina Press, 2007), 66.

64. Powell, *Critical Regionalism*, 46.

65. According to Serafini, such ideologies underpin extractivism and must be understood as narratives, that is, as cultural products that can still be rewritten. Paula Serafini, *Creating Worlds Otherwise: Art, Collective Action, and (Post) Extractivism* (Nashville, TN: Vanderbilt University Press, 2022), 18.

66. "Submerged perspectives" is Macarena Gómez-Barris's term. Gómez-Barris, *Extractive Zone*.

67. Serafini, *Creating Worlds Otherwise*, 5.

68. Moreiras, *Tercer espacio*, 15.

69. Moreiras, *Tercer espacio*, 23.

70. Alberto Moreiras, *The Exhaustion of Difference: The Politics of Latin American Cultural Studies* (Durham, NC: Duke University Press, 2001), 67.

71. Alberto Moreiras, "Fragmentos globales: Latinoamericanismo de segundo orden," in *Teorías sin disciplina (latinoamericanismo, poscolonialidad y globalización en debate)*, ed. Santiago Castro-Gómez and Eduardo Mendieta (Mexico City: Miguel Ángel Porrúa, 1998).

72. Freyre, *Manifesto regionalista*, 75.

73. Humberto Hermenegildo de Araújo, "Leituras sobre regionalismo e globalização," *Imburana: Revista do Núcleo Câmera Cascudo de Estudos Norte-Rio-Grandenses/UFRN* 4, no. 7 (2013): 27–28.

74. Araújo, "Leituras sobre regionalismo e globalização," 30.

75. For example, such sentiments can be found in Freyre's and Candido's works.

76. For Moreiras, critical regionalism is a deconstructive, anti-identitarian project, whereas he alleges that transculturation relies on essentialist notions of identity. For a rejoinder to this critique, see Román de la Campa, who agrees that transculturation as an ideology of *mestizaje*, or racial synthesis, has lost its relevance but claims that Rama's original project was a structuralist theory all along, "an intricate web of dialogical relations with texts and other cultural forms." De la Campa, *Latin Americanism*, 26.

77. Adam Joseph Shellhorse, *Anti-Literature: The Politics and Limits of Representation in Modern Brazil and Argentina* (Pittsburgh: University of Pittsburgh Press, 2017), 29.

78. For more on the concepts of friction and opacity in neocolonial discourse, see, respectively, Tsing, *Friction* and Glissant, *Poetics of Relation*.

79. Prieto, *La scritura errante*, 30, 39.

80. Jane Bennett, *Vibrant Matter: A Political Ecology of Things* (Durham, NC: Duke University Press, 2010), 14.

81. Chiappini, "Regionalismo(s) e regionalidade(s)," 51.

82. Horst Nitschack notes that though novels such as *Don Segundo Sombra* might be considered Latin American bildungsromans, they invert Sarmiento's notion of education, which oppressively imposes a Western notion of civilization, by valorizing the natural world as that which might provide an alternative education or, perhaps, "antieducation." Horst Nitschack, "La refiguración latinoamericana de la bildungsroman: Ernesto Sabato y Antonio Callado," in *Historia comparada de las literaturas argentina y brasileña. Tomo V: Del desarrollismo a la dictadura, entre privatización, boom y militancia (1955–1970)*, ed. Marcela Croce (Villa María, Argentina: Editorial Universitaria Villa María, 2018), 185–86.

83. I am thinking here of Peter Brooks's argument in *Reading for the Plot*, which Clara Rowland discusses in her reading of *Grande sertão*. See chapter 3.

84. Alonso, *Spanish American Regional Novel*, 98–99.

85. Alonso, *Spanish American Regional Novel*, 103.

86. Alonso, *Spanish American Regional Novel*, 64.

87. Tim Ingold, *The Perception of the Environment: Essays on Livelihood Dwelling and Skill* (London: Routledge, 2000), 166–67.

88. See chapter 3 for a discussion of Collot and Benjamin on the immersive nature of reading.

89. Wolfgang Iser, "The Reading Process: A Phenomenological Approach," in *The Implied Reader*. (Baltimore: Johns Hopkins University Press, 1974), 233.

90. Susan Sontag, "Against Interpretation," in *Essays of the 1960's & 70's*, ed. David Rieff (New York: Library of the Americas, 2013), 20.

91. See Masiello, *El cuerpo de la voz*; Baskin, *Modernism*; Marília Librandi, *Writing by Ear: Clarice Lispector and the Aural Novel* (Toronto: University of Toronto Press, 2018).

92. Here we might discern echoes of Jameson's claim that critical regionalist aesthetics induce the synesthetic meeting of the senses in order to counter "the isolation of the individual sense that becomes the fundamental symptom of postmodern alienation, an isolation most often visual." Jameson, *Seeds of Time*, 198.

93. Ingold, *Perception of the Environment*, 227.

94. Arguedas, *El zorro de arriba y el zorro de abajo*, 20.

95. Donna Jeanne Haraway, "Situated Knowledges," 590.

96. Martin Jay, *Downcast Eyes: The Denigration of Vision in Twentieth-Century French Thought* (Berkeley: University of California Press, 1993).

97. There is a rich tradition of scholarship on this topic in Latin American studies. See the notes in chapter 3 for more detail.

98. See Mary Louise Pratt, *Imperial Eyes*; Jens Andermann, *The Optic of the State: Visuality and Power in Argentina and Brazil* (Pittsburgh: University of Pittsburgh Press, 2007).

99. Andermann suggests that it is only recently that twentieth-century "aesthetic propositions formerly relegated to the margins of the modernist archive become fully readable—as glimpses of the 'quake in being" that has thrown into crisis the modern western idea of nature." Jens Andermann, Lisa Blackmore, and Dayron Carillo Morell, eds., *Natura: Environmental Aesthetics after Landscape* (Zurich: Diaphnes, 2018), 12–13.

100. What Andermann calls "landscape"—a relationship to the natural world in which the viewing subject remains separate from it—I call "visual landscape" to distinguish it from Ingold's use of "landscape" to designate the environment in which one dwells, which is necessarily experienced phenomenologically. See chapter 3 for a more detailed discussion of this difference.

101. See Jens Andermann, *Tierra en trance: Arte y naturaleza después del paisaje* (Santiago, Chile: Metales Pesados, 2018); Andermann, *Entranced Earth*; Andermann, Blackmore, and Morell, *Natura*.

102. Andermann, *Tierra en trance*, 27.

103. Andermann, *Entranced Earth*, 10.

104. Andermann, *Entranced Earth*, 17.

105. Whereas Husserl's emphasis on "the reflective power of the transcendental ego" and Sartre's oppositional view of immanence and transcendence, objectivity and subjectivity each engenders a view of the phenomenological subject as separate and separable from the world, Merleau-Ponty emphasizes the reciprocal, chiasmatic relation between what we perceive and how we perceive it (noesis and noema). See Duane H. Davis, "The Phenomenological Method," in *50 Concepts for a Critical Phenomenology* (Evanston, IL: Northwestern Uni-

versity Press, 2020), 3; Shiloh Whitney, "Immanence and Transcendence," in *50 Concepts for a Critical Phenomenology*, 190; Lisa Guenther, "Critical Phenomenology," in *50 Concepts for a Critical Phenomenology*, 13. Closely related to his theory of embodied consciousness, Merleau-Ponty's ambiguous, mutually imbricated understanding of transcendence and immanence throws into question the possibility—and in fact the ethical desirability—of achieving a site of perception independent from the materiality of the world in which we dwell. See Whitney, "Immanence."

106. As Haraway writes, boundaries are indispensable to situated knowledges, and relativist approaches that pretend to sweep them away are, in truth, just the flip side of the coin of totalizing approaches that pretend to transcend them. Haraway, "Situated Knowledges" 584.

107. Ahmed, *Strange Encounters*, 119.

108. Ahmed, *Strange Encounters*, 119.

109. Apter, *Translation Zone*.

110. Laura U. Marks, *The Skin of the Film: Intercultural Cinema, Embodiment, and the Senses* (Durham, NC: Duke University Press, 2000).

111. Baskin, *Modernism*, 10.

112. I have found Aboul-Ela's gloss of the Mariátegui tradition particularly helpful in understanding rural underdevelopment in Latin America. In this model, underdevelopment is not a historical stage but a condition imposed by economic colonialism and imposed unevenly on different spaces. Just as the Global South writ large is economically colonized, maintained in a state of perpetual underdevelopment, so are specific intranational regions like the Andean highlands and the interior plains of Argentina and Brazil. One result is that in largely agrarian-based economies, class tensions are inextricable from regional tensions and that, more generally, in a postcolonial world, "the Other is not an individual but a space." Aboul-Ela, *Other South*, 16. See also Henri Lefebvre, *The Production of Space*, trans. Donald Nicholson-Smith (Oxford: Blackwell, 1984); Smith, *Uneven Development*.

113. Arguedas was influenced by the Marxist thought of José Carlos Mariátegui, the Peruvian journalist, sociologist, and political philosopher and activist. Guimarães Rosa and Saer were infamously recalcitrant about the political meaning of their writing, though rather than dismissing the idea of committed literature wholesale, each implied that the politics of his writing was immanent in its poetic function.

114. Willi Bolle, *Grandesertão.Br: O romance de formação do Brasil* (São Paulo: Livraria Duas Cidades, 2004), 148–49.

115. Theodor W. Adorno, *Negative Dialectics*, trans. E. B. Ashton (New York: Continuum, 2007), 28.

116. Héctor Hoyos, *Things with a History: Transcultural Materialism and the Literatures of Extraction in Contemporary Latin America* (New York: Columbia University Press, 2019), 23.

117. Hoyos, *Things with a History*, 38.

118. Andermann, *Entranced Earth*, 71.

119. Hoyos, *Things with a History*, 28.

120. For a definition of new ethics, see Dorothy Hale, "Aesthetics and the New Ethics: Theorizing the Novel in the Twenty-First Century," *PMLA* 124, no. 3 (2009): 896–905. For more on new formalism, see Ellen Rooney, "Form and Contentment," *Modern Language Quarterly* 61, no. 1 (March 2000): 17–40, and the special edition in which it appears.

121. Georg Lukács, "Narrate or Describe," in *Writer and Critic and Other Essays*, trans. Arthur Kahn (London: Merlin Press, 1970), 110–48.

122. Theodor W. Adorno, *Aesthetic Theory*, trans. Robert Hullot-Kentor (Minneapolis: University of Minnesota Press, 1996), 237.

123. Adorno concedes that this critical practice becomes retrograde when practiced undialectically, as in some veins of New Criticism, which leads, in turn, to an impoverished understanding of the aesthetic: "Today it is already evident that immanent analysis, which was once a weapon of artistic experience against philistinism, is being misused as a slogan to hold social reflection at a distance from an absolutized art. Without social reflection, however, the artwork is not to be understood in relation to that of which it constitutes one element, nor is it to be deciphered in terms of its own content." Adorno, *Aesthetic Theory*, 180.

124. Adorno, *Aesthetic Theory*, 6.

125. Adorno, *Aesthetic Theory*, 230.

126. Rooney, "Form and Contentment," 36.

127. Jason M. Baskin, "Soft Eyes: Marxism, Surface, Depth," *Mediations* 28, no. 2 (2015): 7.

128. Terán, *Nuestros años sesentas*, 31.

129. Terán, *Nuestros años sesentas*, 31, 162.

130. Ramsey McGlazer, *Old Schools: Modernism, Education, and the Critique of Progress* (New York: Fordham University Press, 2020), 13.

131. Hale, "Aesthetics and the New Ethics," 900.

132. Judith Butler, "Values of Difficulty," in *Just Being Difficult? Academic Writing in the Public Arena*, ed. Jonathan Culler and Kevin Lamb (Stanford, CA: Stanford University Press, 2003), 214.

133. Spivak, *Aesthetic Education*, 197.

134. Frampton writes: "The liberative importance of the tactile resides in the fact that it can only be decoded in terms of *experience* itself: it cannot be reduced to mere information, to representation or to the simple evocation of a simulacrum substituting for absent presences." Frampton, "Towards a Critical Regionalism," 32.

135. Doris Sommer, "Slaps and Embraces: A Rhetoric of Particularism," in *The Latin American Subaltern Studies Reader*, ed. Ileana Rodríguez (Durham, NC: Duke University Press, 2001), 175–90.

136. See Shellhorse, *Anti-Literature*; Prieto, *La escritura errante*.

137. Prieto, *La escritura errante*, 25.

138. Bennett, *Vibrant Matter*, 15.

139. Spivak, *Aesthetic Education*, 290–91.

140. Spivak, *Aesthetic Education*, 290.

141. Martin Jay, *Songs of Experience* (Berkeley: University of California Press, 2005), 360.

142. William Rowe, "Reading Arguedas's Foxes," in *The Fox from Up Above and the Fox from Down Below*, ed. Julio Ortega (Pittsburgh: University of Pittsburgh Press and Colección Archivos, 2000), 283.

143. Dylan Robinson, *Hungry Listening: Resonant Theory for Indigenous Sound Studies* (Minneapolis: University of Minnesota Press, 2020), 25.

144. Glissant, *Poetics of Relation*, 154.

145. Haraway, "Situated Knowledges," 586.

146. Demaría, *Buenos Aires y las provincias*; Haraway, "Situated Knowledges," 591.

147. Haraway, "Situated Knowledges," 590.

148. Gayatri Chakravorty Spivak, *Death of a Discipline* (New York: Columbia University Press, 2005).

149. Jay, *Songs of Experience*, 143.

150. Baskin, *Modernism*, 26.

151. Butler and Spivak, *Who Sings the Nation-State?*, 94.

152. Butler and Spivak, *Who Sings the Nation-State?*, 49.

153. Frampton, "Towards a Critical Regionalism," 27.

154. It is also worth noting that Heidegger was famously hostile to modern literature and therefore unlikely to endorse my linkage of the experimental novel with poetics of place. For all of these reasons, it is necessary to specify that it is a heavily revised Heideggerianism that informs my notion of dwelling. Benesch, "Space, Place, Narrative," 99–100, 102.

155. Bieger, "No Place like Home," 32–33.

156. Heidegger, "Building, Dwelling, Thinking," 161, 151; Martin Heidegger, "Introduction to 'Building, Dwelling, Thinking,'" in *Basic Writings*, ed. David Farrell Krell (New York: Harper & Row, 1977), 321–22.

157. Günter Lorenz, "Diálogo com Guimarães Rosa," *Coleção Fortuna Crítica* 6 (1987): 65–66.

158. For more on Guimarães Rosa's use of *Heimatschriftsteller*, see Pelinser and Alves, "A permanência do Regionalismo."

159. Bieger, "No Place like Home," 33.

160. Bieger, "No Place like Home," 17–18.

161. Bieger, "No Place like Home," 18.

162. Bieger, "No Place like Home," 33.

163. Shannon Sullivan, "Introduction: Doing Philosophy from Southern Standpoints," in *Thinking the US South: Contemporary Philosophy from Southern Perspectives*, ed. Shannon Sullivan (Evanston, IL: Northwestern University Press, 2021), 1–13, 4–5.

164. In addition to national socialism in Germany, we might consider the reactionary tendencies of the Southern Agrarians in the US South as well as the problematic dimensions of Freyre's thought. See *I'll Take My Stand: The South and the Agrarian Tradition* (New York: Harper & Brothers, 1930); Freyre, *Manifesto regionalista*.

165. Rob Nixon, "Environmentalism and Postcolonialism," in *Postcolonial Studies and Beyond*, ed. Anita Loomba et al. (Durham, NC: Duke University Press, 2005), 233–51.

166. Glissant, *Poetics of Relation*, 148.

167. Glissant, *Poetics of Relation*, 150.

168. Elizabeth DeLoughrey and George B. Handley, eds., *Postcolonial Ecologies: Literatures of the Environment* (Oxford: Oxford University Press, 2011), 28.

169. Ahmed, *Strange Encounters*, 87.

170. Ahmed, *Strange Encounters*, 88.

171. Benesch, "Space, Place, Narrative," 105.

172. Val Plumwood, *Environmental Culture: The Ecological Crisis of Reason* (London: Routledge, 2002), 233.

173. Samir Gandesha, "Leaving Home: On Adorno and Heidegger," in *The Cambridge Companion to Adorno*, ed. Thomas Huhn (Cambridge: Cambridge University Press, 2004), 103.

174. Gandesha, "Leaving Home," 119.

175. Gandesha, "Leaving Home," 107–9.

176. Gandesha, "Leaving Home," 120.

177. According to Gandesha, this is "the task of the materialist philosopher." Gandesha, "Leaving Home," 112.

178. Theodor W. Adorno, *Minima Moralia: Reflections from Damaged Life*, trans. E. F. N. Jephcott (London: Verso, 2005), 39.

179. Gandesha, "Leaving Home," 122.

180. Cheryl Temple Herr, *Critical Regionalism and Cultural Studies: From Ireland to the American Midwest* (Gainesville: University Press of Florida, 1996), 20.

181. Herr, *Critical Regionalism and Cultural Studies*, 22.

182. Adorno, *Minima Moralia*, 74.

183. Adorno, *Minima Moralia*, 74.

184. Mariano Siskind, "The Globalization of the Novel and the Novelization of the Global: A Critique of World Literature," *Comparative Literature* 62, no. 4 (2010): 357.

185. Hoyos, *Beyond Bolaño*, 11, 23.

186. Chiappini, "Regionalismo(s) e regionalidade(s)," 56–57.

187. Glissant understands the right to opacity as the right to difference and the right "not to become cornered in any essence." Glissant, *Poetics of Relation*, 189–90, 192.

188. Glissant, *Poetics of Relation*, 193.

189. Ahmed, *Strange Encounters*, 168.

190. Chiappini, "Regionalismo(s) e regionalidade(s)," 53.

191. Chiappini, "Regionalismo(s) e regionalidade(s)," 53.

192. Chiappini, "Regionalismo(s) e regionalidade(s)," 54.

193. Chiappini, "Regionalismo(s) e regionalidade(s)," 55.

194. Chiappini, "Regionalismo(s) e regionalidade(s)," 58.

195. Wenzel, *Disposition of Nature*, 8.

196. See, for example, Antonio Cornejo Polar, "Mestizaje e hibridez: Los riesgos de las metáforas. Apuntes," *Revista Iberoamericana* 63, no. 200 (2002): 867–70.

197. Chiappini, "Regionalismo(s) e regionalidade(s)," 58.

198. Chiappini, "Regionalismo(s) e regionalidade(s)," 60.

199. Haraway, "Situated Knowledges," 590.

200. Chiappini, "Regionalismo(s) e regionalidade(s)," 59.

201. Walter Benjamin, "One-Way Street," in *One-Way Street and Other Writings*, trans. J. A. Underwood (London: Penguin, 2008), 52. Bolle is among those who have compared the mode of narration in *Grande sertão: Veredas* to Benjamin's figure of the pedestrian who walks along the road as opposed to surveying it from above like the air traveler. Bolle, *Grandesertão.Br*, 76.

CHAPTER 2

1. Arguedas, *El zorro*, 360; *The Fox*, 270.

2. In 1967, Cortázar published an open letter to Roberto Fernández Retamar in *Casa de las Américas*, in which he objected to Latin American authors being classified in national and regional terms. Beyond suggesting that his own sensibility was placeless, reflecting the cosmopolitan setting of his exile in Paris rather than the Peronist nationalism that predominated at the time in his homeland, Argentina, Cortázar suggests living abroad as a means of overcoming narrow provincialism. Arguedas responded in 1968, in a piece he published in the journal *Amaru* and also included in the first diary of *El zorro de arriba y el zorro de abajo*, identifying with and defending those whom Cortázar had pejoratively called "los provincianos." Cortázar published a searing and sarcastic response in *Life en español*, to which Arguedas responded in turn in *El Comercio de Lima*. Arguedas's response, which he includes in the third diary of *Los zorros*, makes clear that Cortázar's sharp and personal attack in *Life* delivered a harsh blow and interfered with his ability to continue working on his novel. Many consider the escalation of this polemic and the humiliating terms in which Arguedas was treated a decisive factor in his deteriorating mental health and eventual suicide. See Mabel Moraña, "Territorialidad y foresterismo: La polémica Arguedas/Cortázar revisitada," in *María Arguedas: Hacia una poética migrante*, ed. Sergio R. Franco (Pittsburgh: Instituto Internacional de Literatura Iberoamericana and University of Pittsburgh Press, 2006), 103–20; Fernando Rivera, *Dar la palabra: Ética, política y poética de la escritura en Arguedas* (Madrid and Frankfurt: Iberoamericana and Vervuert, 2011), 28–30. This polemic and the way it shaped Arguedas's perception of the contemporary literary scene and his place in it will be taken up in more detail at the end of this chapter.

3. *Misti* is the Quechua word for *mestizo*, or a person of Spanish (often in addition to Indigenous) descent.

4. Barraclough translates *indio* as "Indian," but I have opted for "Indigenous" in most cases, due to the pejorative and colonial connotations the word "Indian" carries when referring to Indigenous peoples of the Americas. Though Peru is home to over fifty Indigenous peoples, Arguedas focuses on and identifies with the Quechua. Following Arguedas's lead, I use "Andean," "serrano," "Quechua," and "Indigenous" more or less synonymously in this chapter, although I realize these terms are not always coextensive. "Andean," of course, can refer to a vast region spanning from Ecuador to northern Argentina, but within Peru "lo andino" often refers to "a specific region, of the altiplano near Lake Titicaca and the southern sierra of Peru." Erick D. Langer, "Periodos y

regiones: Una perspectiva histórica," in *Memorias de JALLA Tucumán 1995* (Tucumán, Argentina: Proyecto "Tucumán en el contexto de los Andes Centro-meridionales," Instituto de Historia y Pensamiento Argentinos de la Facultad de Filosofía y Letras de la Universidad Nacional de Tucumán, 1997), 2:10–22. It is in this latter sense that Arguedas and scholars of his work tend to use the term.

5. Arguedas, *El zorro*, 359; *The Fox*, 269.

6. Gareth Williams refers to Rama's transculturation as "tamed." *Other Side of the Popular*, 27.

7. William Rowe argues that the text anticipates such a reader. Rowe, "Reading Arguedas's Foxes," 238.

8. Kenneth Frampton, "Towards a Critical Regionalism," 23.

9. José Eduardo Gonzáles's research on this topic foregrounds Rama's engagement with Walter Benjamin, and to a lesser extent, Theodor Adorno, Max Horkheimer, and Georg Lukács. Gonzáles argues that Rama's debt to the Frankfurt School in *Transculturación narrativa* goes nearly unacknowledged precisely because hanging his theory from a framework generated in Europe did not suit the politics of Rama's project. It is for this reason, Gonzáles conjectures, that Rama chooses to highlight the Latin American genealogy of his thought, citing his debt to Fernando Ortiz, even though Gonzáles surmises that Rama had fully developed his theory of transculturation before reading the Cuban anthropologist and appropriating his terminology. Gonzáles, *Appropriating Theory*, 6.

10. In fact, Rama purportedly learned German in order to have greater access to Benjamin's untranslated works. In 1972, he published an article called "La literatura hispanoamericana en la era de las máquinas," which dialogues directly with Benjamin's "Art in the Age of Mechanical Reproduction" (1935). Gonzáles, *Appropriating Theory*, 4.

11. Paul Ricoeur, "Universal Civilizations and National Cultures," in *History and Truth* (Evanston, IL: Northwestern University Press, 1965), 282.

12. Gonzáles, *Appropriating Theory*, 66.

13. Gonzáles, *Appropriating Theory*, 115.

14. Gonzáles, *Appropriating Theory*, 118.

15. De la Campa, *Latin Americanism*, 76.

16. See Cornejo Polar, "Mestizaje e hibridez," 867–70; Silvia Spitta, "Traición y transculturación: Los desgarramientos del pensamiento latinoamericano," in *Ángel Rama y los estudios latinoamericanos*, ed. Mabel Moraña (Pittsburgh: Instituto Internacional de Literatura Iberoamericana, 1997): 173–92.

17. Cornejo Polar, "Mestizaje e hibridez," 876.

18. Antonio Cornejo Polar, *Writing in the Air: Heterogeneity and the Persistence of Oral Tradition in Andean Literatures*, trans. Lynda J. Jentsch (Durham, NC: Duke University Press, 2013), 59–60.

19. Williams, *Other Side of the Popular*, 5. For more on this periodization, see Castañeda, *Utopia Unarmed*, 44.

20. Williams, *Other Side of the Popular*, 26.

21. Williams, *Other Side of the Popular*, 27.

22. Cornejo Polar, "Mestizaje e hibridez," 867.

23. Spitta, "Traición y transculturación," 179.

24. Ángel Rama, *La transculturación narrativa en América Latina* (Buenos Aires: El Andariego, 2008), 141, 132, 133.

25. Tsing, *Friction*, 5.

26. Spitta, "Traición y transculturación," 174.

27. For readings of the novel as an aesthetic failure or an incomplete work, see Julio Ortega, "Itinerario de José María Arguedas: Migración, peregrinaje y lenguaje en *El zorro de arriba y el zorro de abajo*," in *José María Arguedas: Hacia una poética migrante*, ed. Sergio R. Franco (Pittsburgh: Instituto Internacional de Literatura Iberoamericana, 2006), 81–102; Vargas Llosa, "José María Arguedas: Entre ideología y la arcadia"; Eduardo J. Pantigoso, "La rebelión contra el indigenismo y la afirmación del pueblo en el mundo de José María Arguedas," *Chasqui* 12, no. 1 (1982): 82–85. For complications of such readings, see Dara Sales, "Introducción: José María Arguedas, Wiñaq," in *José María Arguedas: Quepa Wiñaq . . . siempre literatura y antropología* (Madrid and Frankfurt: Iberoamericana and Vervuert, 2009), 11–55; Catalina Ocampo, "La agonía de José María Arguedas y la palabra trágica," in *José María Arguedas: Hacia una poética migrante*, 121–42; Prieto, *Escritura errante*.

28. Moreiras, *Exhaustion of Difference*.

29. Lienhard, *Cultura Andina y forma novelesca*.

30. Lienhard, *Cultura Andina y forma novelesca*, 22–23.

31. William Rowe, "El nuevo lenguaje de Arguedas en *El zorro de arriba y el zorro de abajo*," *Texto Crítico*, no. 11 (1978): 199–200.

32. Moreiras, *Exhaustion of Difference*, 193.

33. Moreiras, *Exhaustion of Difference*, 190.

34. Moreiras, "Fragmentos globales," 225–26, 218.

35. Moreiras, *Exhaustion of Difference*, 204.

36. Rama, *Writing across Cultures*, 68.

37. Rama, *Writing across Cultures*, 121.

38. From *gamonal*, meaning "large landowner." José Carlos Mariátegui denounced the system as a vestige of feudalism that exploited the Indigenous people and, in response, called for a Socialist revolution. José Carlos Mariátegui, *Siete ensayos de interpretación de la realidad peruana* (Havana: Casa de las Américas, 1973), 170. Though the economic underpinnings of the system were eroded in the mid-twentieth century, it was not until 1969, the year of Arguedas's suicide, that Peru would begin to see agrarian reform, following the 1968 coup that brought Juan Velasco Alvarado to power.

39. Rodrigo Montoya Rojas, *100 años del Perú y de José María Arguedas* (Lima, Peru: Editorial Universitaria, 2011), 38.

40. Rivera, *Dar la palabra*, 30. Arguedas vehemently resisted the label "indigenista," which he believed marginalized what was in fact a central question of Peruvian identity: the Indigenous experience. See Montoya Rojas, *100 años*, 55. As I note in chapter 1, *indigenismo* has taken on different meanings at different points in time: originally associated with its colonialist function as an orientalist "discourse by non-Indians about Indians," it was subsequently reclaimed by José Carlos Mariátegui as a socially progressive, even revolutionary brand of thought aimed at benefiting and empowering the Indigenous community. See

Tarica, *Inner Life of Mestizo Nationalism*, vi-xi. Arguedas embraced the spirit of Mariátegui's *indigenismo* but continued to feel the stigma of the label.

41. Montoya Rojas, *100 años del Perú*, 51, 55.

42. Tarica, *Inner Life of Mestizo Nationalism*, xvi.

43. Tarica, *Inner Life of Mestizo Nationalism*, xvii.

44. Ortega, "Itinerario de José María Arguedas," 86.

45. Rowe's recent work on *Los zorros* proposes breaking with the national framework in which Arguedas has often been read. See "'No hay mensajero de nada': La modernidad andina según los zorros de Arguedas" in *Revista de Crítica Literaria Latinoamericana* 36, no. 72 (2010): 71.

46. Arguedas, *El zorro*, 332; *The Fox*, 233.

47. Arguedas, *El zorro*, 313; *The Fox*, 235–36.

48. José Luis Rouillón reads Maxwell as a heroic avatar for Arguedas: as one who has been purified by the world above, he is tasked with battling the chaos of down below. See "La luz que nadie apagará: Aproximaciones al mito y al cristianismo en el último Arguedas," in *El zorro de arriba y el zorro de abajo*, ed. Eve Marie Fell (Madrid: CISIC, 1990), 344.

49. He accuses Alejo Carpentier as being someone who "considers our Indigenous things to be an excellent element or [raw] material to work with," mocks the furious, industrial pace at which Carlos Fuentes writes, and dismisses commercial displays of folklore as "cosas que son fabricaciones de los 'gringos' para ganar plata" ("gringo fabrications for making money"). Arguedas, *El zorro* 20, 22; *The Fox* 14–15.

50. Prieto, *La escritura errante*, 156.

51. The "yo" of the diary sections quite obviously refers to Arguedas in many respects: in addition to reflecting at great length on the difficulty of completing the work in front of him, he identifies himself as the author of *Todas las sangres*, as the intellectual embroiled in a polemic with Julio Cortázar, as the psychiatric patient of Dr. Laura Hoffman, and as the man who has recently attempted suicide. Nevertheless, numerous readers have pointed out that these similarities should not impede us from reading the author figure as a fictional character or the inclusion of the diaries as a literary strategy.

52. Arguedas has been criticized, most prominently by Mario Vargas Llosa, for constructing and disseminating autobiographical myths including the image of himself as a Quechua-speaking *indio*. See Mario Vargas Llosa, "José María Arguedas." (Arguedas's claims that he spoke only Quechua until adolescence have been largely debunked.) Tarica proposes that much of the autobiography with which Arguedas's literature is infused ought to be understood as rhetorical positioning aimed at establishing him as a privileged insider to the world he represents, rather than as fact. See Tarica, *Inner Life of Mestizo Nationalism*, 83. Along similar lines, Cornejo Polar suggests we should read Arguedas's "modern Quechua" identity as his chosen site of enunciation for his literature: "Like any writer, Arguedas constructs the identity through which he utters his discourse. It is senseless to ask whether it corresponds or not to his 'real' biography." See Cornejo, *Writing in the Air*, 146, 145.

53. Arguedas, *El zorro*, 119–20; *The Fox*, 87.

54. Rivera, *Dar la palabra*, 294.

55. As Cornejo Polar has argued, the Andean literary tradition he traces from Vallejo to Arguedas assumes "that the authenticity of language resides in the spoken word" and alternately expresses nostalgia for this "lost orality" and attempts to recuperate it in writing. See Cornejo Polar, *Writing in the Air*, 165, 172. This is notably different from Derrida's expansion of the definition of writing to encompass all semiotic systems (arche-writing) and ensuing argument that writing has always been part of human thought.

56. Arguedas, *El zorro*, 358–59. Prominent in this tradition is Lévi-Strauss's account of the "writing lesson," from which he concludes that writing serves primarily as a tool for exploitation rather than enlightenment. See Claude Lévi-Strauss, *Tristes Tropiques*, trans. John Weightman (New York: Penguin, 2012), 299.

57. Rama, *Writing across Cultures*, 172.

58. Tarica, *Inner Life of Mestizo Nationalism*, 105.

59. William Rowe, *Ensayos arguedianos*, ed. Maruja Martínez (Lima, Peru: Centro de Producción Editorial de la Universidad Nacional Mayor de San Marcos, 1996), 51.

60. Rowe, *Ensayos arguedianos*, 17.

61. Rowe, "El nuevo lenguaje," 22.

62. Rama has analyzed the centrality of the *huaynos* in *Los ríos profundos*, and Rowe has argued that Arguedas engages these songs not only as intercalated texts but as a structural component that imbues the novel with "a paradigm of Andean knowledge." See Rama, *Writing across Cultures*, 240; Rowe, *Ensayos arguedianos*, 15.

63. Arguedas, *El zorro*, 105; *The Fox*, 78.

64. Jean-Luc Nancy defines voice as "sounds from a human throat without being language, which emerges from an animal gullet or from any kind of instrument, even from the wind in the branches: the rustling toward which we strain or lend an ear." See Nancy, *Listening*, trans. Charlotte Mandell (New York: Fordham University Press, 2007), 22.

65. Masiello, *El cuerpo de la voz*.

66. Cornejo Polar, *Writing in the Air*, 172.

67. Catalina Ocampo describes *Los zorros* as attempting to recapture "an epiphanic, poetic, magic language." Ocampo, "La agonía," 136. Sara Castro-Klaren claims that Arguedas attempted to use language shamanistically—conjuring the sacred and the affective—throughout his career, but that translating shamanistic texts in *Dioses y hombres de Huarochirí* provided him a new framework for understanding this process. Sara Castro-Klaren, "'Como chancho, cuando piensa': El afecto cognitivo en Arguedas y el con-verter animal," *Revista Canadiense de Estudios Hispánicos* 26, no. 1/2 (2001/2002): 34. Cornejo Polar compares this operation to alchemy. Cornejo Polar, *Writing in the Air*, 152.

68. Arguedas, *El zorro*, 13; *The Fox*, 9.

69. In addition to the infamous polemic with Julio Cortázar, *Todas las sangres* was harshly critiqued at a 1965 roundtable in which acclaimed social scientists alleged that Arguedas did not understand Peru's contemporary reality.

70. Arguedas, *El zorro*, 71; *The Fox*, 52–53.

71. Arguedas, *El zorro*, 73; *The Fox*, 54.

72. Arguedas, *El zorro*, 74; *The Fox*, 55.

73. See Arguedas, *El zorro*, 110–11.

74. Jannine Montauban, "El olfato como forma de conocimiento," in *Un universo encrespado: Cincuenta años de El zorro de arriba y el zorro de abajo*, ed. Enrique E. Cortez (Lima, Peru: Editorial Horizonte, 2021), 124.

75. Arguedas, *El zorro*, 74; *The Fox*, 55.

76. Adorno, *Negative Dialectics*, 5.

77. Baskin, *Modernism*, 21.

78. I am thinking both of Arguedas's noteworthy use of "nosotros" and of Adorno's sense of the "aesthetic We" as the "nonexistent social whole" anticipated by art: "The antagonisms of society are nevertheless preserved in it. Art is true insofar as what speaks out of it—indeed, it itself—is conflicting and unreconciled. [. . .] Paradoxically, art must testify to the unreconciled and at the same time envision its reconciliation; this is a possibility only for its nondiscursive language. Only in this process is its We concretized." Such a "we" does not presume universality or coherence but rather preserves its specificity as the product of "forces and relations of an epoch" as well as the conflictive heterogeneity of society. See Adorno, *Aesthetic Theory*, 168.

79. Moreiras, "Fragmentos," 69.

80. Moreiras, *Exhaustion of Difference*, 200, 202–3.

81. Moreiras, *Exhaustion of Difference*, 204.

82. Prieto, *La escritura errante*, 129.

83. See chapter 1 for my references to the work of Édouard Glissant on opacity, Emily Apter on untranslatability, Judith Butler on the contemporary politics of Adorno's claims about formal difficulty in literature, and Adam Joseph Shellhorse on the stakes of difficulty and negativity in representing Latin American subaltern subjects specifically. Also see Catalina Ocampo's reading of silence and secrets in *Los zorros* as a "protective case" for sacred truths. Ocampo, "La agonía," 135.

84. Librandi, *Writing by Ear*, 38.

85. Librandi, *Writing by Ear*, 37.

86. Rowe, *Ensayos arguedianos*, 45.

87. Tsing, *Friction*, 3.

88. Aymará de Llano, "Crisis de lectura en el lector hispano: El caso Arguedas," in *Memorias de JALLA Tucumán 1995* (Tucumán, Argentina: Proyecto "Tucumán en el contexto de los Andes Centromeridionales," Instituto de Historia y Pensamiento Argentinos de la Facultad de Filosofía y Letras de la Universidad Nacional de Tucumán, 1997), 1:564.

89. Rama, *Writing across Cultures*, 141.

90. Rowe, "Reading Arguedas's Foxes," 283.

91. Rivera notes that Arguedas had long displayed a sophisticated notion of his audience. For example, according to the research of John Landrea, his song translations from Quechua to Spanish varied depending on intended audience. See Rivera, *Dar la palabra*, 230–31. Zevallos Aguilar observes that while most of Arguedas's novels were aimed at Spanish-speaking readers, his poem "Tupac Amaru" was written primarily for a Quechua listener and only secondarily for a bilingual reader. Zevallos Aguilar, *Las provincias contraatacan*, 100–101.

92. Arguedas, *El zorro*, 15–16; *The Fox*, 10–11.

93. Masiello, *Senses of Democracy*, 4.

94. Masiello, *Senses of Democracy*, 8.

95. Marks, *Skin of the Film*, 239.

96. Here, too, we might hear echoes of Laura Demaría's distinction between "estar en provincia" ("being in the provinces") and "ser de provincial" ("being from the provinces"). See Demaría, *Buenos Aires y las provincias*.

97. Marks, *Skin of the Film*, 196.

98. As Prieto points out, Bazalar has abandoned his roots in traditional Andean culture, but his commitment to the local community, his work as an organizer, and his expressed desire to one day cease to be a stranger in his natal land all suggest that his exile from this world need not be permanent; he too is learning to dwell. Prieto, *La escritura errante*, 142.

99. Borrowing the phrase from Arguedas, Tarica defines intimate indigenism as a way of thinking of ethnicity in terms of affinity rather than difference. Tarica, *Inner Life of Mestizo Nationalism*, xiii.

100. José María Arguedas, *Los ríos profundos* (Madrid: Cátedra, 2010), 398; *Deep Rivers*, trans. Frances Horning Barraclough (Austin: University of Texas Press, 1978), 186.

101. Arguedas, *Los ríos*, 398; *Deep Rivers*, 186.

102. This alienating difficulty is evincive of what Adorno calls *art's enigmaticalness*. In reference to music, Adorno writes, "Its enigmaticalness may in an elementary fashion confirm the so-called unmusical, who does not understand the 'language of music,' hears nothing but nonsense, and wonders what all the noise is about; the difference between what this person hears and what the initiated hear defines art's enigmaticalness. This is of course not restricted to music, whose aconceptuality makes it almost too obvious." See Adorno, *Aesthetic Theory*, 120. As I have argued in chapter 1, the difficulty of critical regionalist texts does not simply alienate; it also initiates.

103. De Llano, "Crisis de lectura," 559.

104. Masiello, *Senses of Democracy*, 213.

105. See, for example, Sales, "Introduction," 18.

106. Having earned a doctorate in ethnology from the Universidad de San Marcos in 1963, he taught at his alma mater and worked for the Museo Nacional. He went on to direct the sociology department at the Universidad Agraria la Molina until his death.

107. Montoya Rojas, *100 años del Perú*, 122.

108. Montoya Rojas, *100 años del Perú*, 145; Rowe, *Ensayos arguedianos*, 52.

109. Tarica, *Inner Life of Mestizo Nationalism*, 82.

110. Marks, *Skin of the Film*, 230.

111. Rivera, *Dar la palabra*, 289–90.

112. The sociological tradition greatly shaped *indigenista* literature in the Andes, as early indigenist literature, like the nineteenth-century Latin American novel in general, was largely mediated by discourses from the natural and social sciences. Rivera, *Dar la palabra*, 69, 37.

113. Rivera, *Dar la palabra*, 293, 218, 215.

114. Rivera, *Dar la palabra*, 300.

115. Librandi, *Writing by Ear*, 14.

116. Rivera, *Dar la palabra*, 321.

117. Rivera, *Dar la palabra*, 117.

118. Rivera, *Dar la palabra*, 112.

119. Arguedas, *El zorro*, 311; *The Fox*, 234.

120. Arguedas, *El zorro*, 310. My translation.

121. Arguedas, *El zorro*, 304–5; *The Fox*, 229.

122. Arguedas, *El zorro*, 316; *The Fox*, 238.

123. Castro-Klaren, "Como chancho," 30.

124. Arguedas, *El zorro*, 314; *The Fox*, 236.

125. The conflict between the two men first erupts in a brothel, where El Mudo is at home as his mother works there and where Maxwell attracts unusual attention, as foreigners do not normally come to the brothels frequented by the fishermen. The pursuit of embodied knowledge acquires a less innocent cast when it manifests as carnal knowledge, especially in a world where sexuality is associated almost exclusively with sex work and rape.

126. Arguedas, *El zorro*, 307; *The Fox*, 231.

127. Arguedas, *El zorro*, 311; *The Fox*, 234.

128. Demaría, *Buenos Aires y las provincias*, 481.

129. Demaría, *Buenos Aires y las provincias*, 486.

130. Demaría, *Buenos Aires y las provincias*, 484.

131. Moraña, "Territorialidad y foresterismo," 105.

132. Moraña, "Territorialidad y foresterismo," 105–7.

133. In Cortázar's defense, it should be noted that in spite of his intellectualism, he does not ignore or devalue embodied experience. See Masiello, *Senses of Democracy*, 180.

134. Arguedas, *El zorro*, 244; *The Fox* 182–83.

135. Rowe, "El nuevo lenguaje," 200.

136. Likewise, the shift Tarica observes from an *indigenismo* grounded in racial identity to an *indigenismo* grounded in a sense of local belonging demands reevaluating received notions of authenticity and who is authorized to represent Indigenous communities. Tarica, *Inner Life of Mestizo Nationalism*.

137. Arguedas, *El zorro*, 23, 20; *The Fox*, 16, 14.

138. Arguedas, *El zorro*, 20; *The Fox*, 14.

139. See, for example, Paulo Moreira, *Modernismo localista das Américas: Os contos de Faulkner, Guimarães Rosa, e Rulfo* (Belo Horizonte, Brazil: Editora UFMG, 2012).

140. Apter explains: "For if translation failure is acceded to too readily, it becomes an all-purpose expedient for staying narrowly within one's own monolingual universe. A parochialism results, sanctioned by false pieties about not wanting to 'mistranslate' the other. This parochialism is the flip side of a globalism that theorizes place and translates everything without ever traveling anywhere." Apter, *Translation Zone*, 91.

CHAPTER 3

1. Marli Fantini Scarpelli, for example, reads Riobaldo as a transculturator and as a figure for the diplomat-author skilled at navigating between worlds,

cultures, and languages. Marli Fantini Scarpelli, "Diálogos iberoamericanos: *Grande sertão: Veredas* entre regionalismo e vanguarda," *Revista Brasileira de Literatura Comparada* 33 (2018): 110–29.

2. I use "untranslatability" in the sense that Krista Brune has elaborated in dialogue with the work of Emily Apter and Barbara Cassin: difficult to translate "in the market sense" but for that very reason inviting "multiple interpretations, and, therefore, retranslations." Brune, *Creative Transformations*, 185.

3. At a moment when he is emerging from the fog of his most recent suicide attempt, the author figure of the diaries recalls his rape as a boy by the pregnant sex worker, Fidela. This traumatic episode is addressed in an intimate register to Guimarães Rosa: "Sí, queridísimo João Guimarães Rosa, te voy a contar de algún modo en qué consiste ese veneno mío" ("Yes, my dear João Guimarães Rosa, I'm somehow going to tell you what that poison of mine consists of"). Arguedas, *El zorro*, 32; Arguedas, *Fox*, 23.

4. *Grande sertão* was quickly translated into German, French, Italian, Spanish, and English. The Spanish edition was published in 1967 by Seix Barral, the Barcelona-based publisher that was a major driving force in the European circulation of Latin American literature in this period.

5. Piers Armstrong, "Rosa in Translation: Scrittore, Editore, Traduttore, Traditore," *Luso-Brazilian Review* 38, no. 1 (2001): 65.

6. Jacqueline Penjon, "The Reception of João Guimarães Rosa in France," in *Studies in the Literary Achievement of João Guimarães Rosa: The Foremost Brazilian Writer of the Twentieth Century*, ed. Ligia Chiappini, Marcel Vejmelka, and David Treece (New York: Edwin Mellen Press, 2012), 113.

7. Silviano Santiago, *Genealogía de la ferocidad: Ensayo sobre Gran sertón: Veredas, de Guimarães Rosa*, trans. Mary Luz Estupiñán (Santiago, Chile: Mimesis, 2018), 24.

8. *Grande sertão: Veredas* was, in critic Piers Armstrong's words, "translated very quickly and very widely." Armstrong, "Rosa in Translation," 56. Nevertheless, translators met with significant challenges including how to deal with the poetic features of Guimarães Rosa's language such as alliteration, rhyme, anaphora and "how to render Rosean neologisms, lexical items non-existent in the target language, and non-standard syntactic procedures." David Treece, "Translating Guimarães Rosa into English," in *Studies in the Literary Achievement of João Guimarães Rosa*, 30.

9. In my use of "enigma," I channel Theodor Adorno, for whom it "is not a glib synonym for 'problem'" to be solved like a puzzle but rather something that "remains a vexation." Adorno, *Aesthetic Theory*, 121.

10. Penjon, "Reception," 117.

11. Armstrong, "Rosa in Translation," 79.

12. Leopoldo M. Bernucci, "Guimarães Rosa para alunos norte-americanos," *Hispania* 91, no. 4 (2008): 744–47.

13. Rex Nielson's makes the case that the *sertão* has always been by definition a lacuna on the map. For Portuguese explorers, the term originally referred to "undiscovered lands" and "any cultural manifestation that was outside of European knowledge." It signifies not only a remote and wild (*selvagem*) interior territory but an epistemological void. Rex P. Nielson, "The Unmappable Sertão," *Portuguese Studies* 30, no. 1 (2014): 8, 10.

14. Saramago analyzes descriptions of the Brazilian *sertão* in accounts of Portuguese explorers and concludes that the word connotes remoteness, indeterminacy, difficulty of entry, emptiness, mystery, unknowability, and "unreachability." Victoria Saramago, "'Sertão Dentro': The Backlands in Early Modern Portuguese Writings," *Portuguese Literary and Cultural Studies* 27 (2015): 255, 258, 267. She notes elsewhere that the term is "rarely used in the region's everyday vocabulary"; its sense of "a vast nonurbanized area" implies a metropolitan perspective. Victoria Saramago, *Fictional Environments: Mimesis, Deforestation, and Development in Latin America* (Evanston, IL: Northwestern University Press, 2021), 60.

15. For example, Saramago argues that the difficulty and materiality of the book "mimetically embodies the environment of northwestern Minas Gerais," and this is "reinforced by a constant reflection on the possibilities and limits of narrating and reading." Victoria Saramago, "Birds, Rivers, Book: Material Mimesis in João Guimarães Rosa's *Grande Sertão: Veredas*," *Luso-Brazilian Review* 57, no. 1 (2020): 128.

16. Piers Armstrong, *Third World Literary Fortunes: Brazilian Culture and Its International Reception* (Lewisberg, PA: Bucknell University Press, 1999), 238.

17. Esther Gabara, *Errant Modernism: The Ethos of Photography in Mexico and Brazil* (Durham, NC: Duke University Press, 2008), 40, 47,79.

18. Bueno, "O intelectual e o turista," 118.

19. Bueno, "O intelectual e o turista," 120.

20. Bueno, "O intelectual e o turista," 121.

21. Bueno, "O intelectual e o turista," 124.

22. Bueno, "O intelectual e o turista," 124.

23. Chakrabarty, *Provincializing Europe*. See Aboul-Ela's discussion of the dependency theorists and how nonteleological views of history permeate literary production of the Global South. Aboul-Ela, *Other South*, 103–5.

24. Pérez Trujillo Diniz, *Imagining the Plains*, 122, 9.

25. Guimarães Rosa, *Grande sertão*, 590; *Devil to Pay*, 465.

26. Guimarães Rosa, *Grande sertão*, 418; *Devil to Pay*, 238. Translation modified. (I have occasionally supplemented or modified the Taylor and Onís translation when it leaves out or fails to capture the linguistic features I wish to analyze. This translation, the only English-language version of the text to date, omits entire phrases of Guimarães Rosa's language; these omissions cumulatively abridge the text by more than one hundred pages. In my work with the two versions of the text, I have found that the English translation also irons out much of the temporal ambiguity that is of interest to me in the original. Overcorrecting perhaps, in my own translations, I have leaned toward being as literal as possible in translating the idiosyncrasies of Guimarães Rosa's syntax and use of verb tense.)

27. Santiago points out that the initial reception of the novel focused largely on its unreadability; for example, the leftist literary bulletin *Leitura* (out of Río de Janeiro) featured a collection of testimonies from writers who had been unable to get through the text. Santiago claims it challenges the critic to tame it and perennially eludes (and shows up as arrogant) this "domesticating activity." Santiago, *Genealogía de la ferocidad* 18, 34.

28. A *sertanejo* is an inhabitant of the *sertão*; a *jagunço* is a cowboy-bandit who roams the *sertão*, usually on horseback and armed, sometimes loyal to a ranch owner who employs him but often loyal only to the leader of his errant band of *jagunços*. "O Doutor" is a generic title, akin to "Sir," used in rural Brazil to express respect for one of a higher cultural or economic status.

29. Guimarães Rosa, *Grande sertão*, 116; *Devil to Pay*, 83.

30. Dating back to colonial explorations of Latin America, the project of bringing order and "civilization" to the remote interior of the continent has been imagined as a process of visualization and, specifically, mapping. Ricardo Padrón defines mapping as "a form of cultural work" not limited to visual maps but also "carried out [. . .] by other kinds of texts in which we can identify a crucial cartographic dimension." Ricardo Padrón, *The Spacious Word: Cartography, Literature, and Empire in Early Modern Spain* (Chicago: University of Chicago Press, 2004), 26. Examples of such mapping practices include colonial *crónicas* in the sixteenth and seventeenth centuries as discussed by Padrón, as well as European travel writing, landscape painting, and natural science expeditions in the eighteenth and nineteenth centuries (Pratt, Penhos, Prieto), and projects of national consolidation carried out in a variety of media (literature, photography, displays in museums and world's fairs, etc.) in the nineteenth and twentieth centuries (Prieto, Andermann, Brizuela). As the diversity of this list suggests, mapping practices are far from monolithic and serve different forms of power (empire, capital, the nation-state, etc.) at different moments in history. They nevertheless share the common ends of organizing space and "optimizing its legibility and visibility" to facilitate its material exploitation and symbolic appropriation. Nielson, "Unmappable Sertão," 10. As a fundamental component of imperial ideologies, argues Padrón, mapping converts previously indominable terrain into discrete, apprehensible territories and domesticates the exotic, placing it within a system of rational knowledge. Padrón, *Spacious Word*, 3, 20. There is a rich tradition of scholarship critiquing the ideological work of (neo)colonial mapping practices, and this indicates that relying on mapping practices to make the interior of the continent known is problematic for three closely interrelated reasons: (1) mapping practices privilege the perspective of outsiders while erasing the presence of native dwellers; (2) they tend to imagine these remote regions as "natural," timeless, and outside history; and (3) they mystify their own status as tools of power. See, for example: Jordana Dym and Karl Offen, eds., *Mapping Latin America: A Cartographic Reader* (Chicago: University of Chicago Press, 2011); Pratt, *Imperial Eyes*; Andermann, *Optic of the State*; Natalia Brizuela, *Fotografia e império: Paisagens para um Brasil moderno* (São Paulo: Companhia das Letras, 2012); Penhos, *Ver, conocer, dominar*; Smith, *Mapping the Amazon*.

31. The *mãe-da-lua* is a nocturnal bird endemic to Central and South America, known in English as the *potoo*. A relative of the whippoorwill, this species is known for its mournful cries.

32. See Maria Cecilia de Moraes Leonel, "Imagens de animais no sertão rosiano," *Scripta* 6, no. 10 (2002): 286–98; Ana Luisa Martins Costa, "Diadorim, delicado e terrível," *Scripta* 5, no. 10 (2002): 38–52; Saramago, "Birds, Rivers, Book"; Marília Librandi, "Sertão, City, Saudade," in *The New Ruralism*:

An Epistemology of Transformed Space, ed. Joan Ramon Resina and William Viestenz (Madrid and Frankfurt: Iberoamericana and Vervuert, 2012), 61–75.

33. Guimarães Rosa, *Grande sertão*, 340; *Devil to Pay*, 269.

34. Guimarães Rosa, *Grande sertão*, 159; *Devil to Pay*, 121.

35. Riobaldo describes his memories as treasured possessions that he likes to keep nearby at all times and compares forgetting to losing money. At other times though, he wishes he could forget some of the evil he has witnessed. Guimarães Rosa, *Grande sertão*, 217, 423, 37, 408.

36. Alia Al-Saji, "Durée," in *50 Concepts for a Critical Phenomenology*, 99–106.

37. Walter Benjamin, "Theses on the Philosophy of History," in *Illuminations*, trans. Harry Zohn (New York: Schocken, 1968), 263.

38. For discussions of melancholia in *Grande sertão*, see Clara Rowland, *A forma do meio* (São Paulo: Editora da Universidade de São Paulo, 2011); Susana Kampff Lages, *João Guimarães Rosa e a saudade* (São Paulo: Ateliê, 2002); Patricia Carmello, *Memória e esquecimento no Grande sertão: Veredas: Travessia e melancolia* (Rio de Janeiro: Viveiros de Castro, 2013); Librandi, "Sertão, City, Saudade." It is important to note that the theories of melancholia and *saudade* that have most informed my reading do not equate looking backward simply with nostalgia for the past. Informed by queer theory, my understanding of the melancholic temporality of the novel is not reducible to a longing to return to the past; rather, it expresses an unwillingness to abandon cherished experiences to the past, as demanded by teleologically oriented narrative. See an expanded treatment of the topic in Ashley Brock, "The Queer Temporality of *Grande sertão: Veredas*," *Chasqui* 47, no. 2 (2018): 190–203.

39. João Adolfo Hansen, *O o: a ficção da literatura em Grande sertão: Veredas* (São Paulo: Hedra, 2000), 178.

40. Michel de Certeau, *The Practices of Everyday Life*, trans. Steven Rendall (Berkeley: University of California Press, 1984), 129.

41. See the discussion of Merleau-Ponty in chapter 1, as well as Whitney, "Immanence and Transcendence," 189–96; Gunther, "Critical Phenomenology," 11–16.

42. I am grateful to Marília Librandi for leading me to Ingold's work and helping me to see its relevance to Guimarães Rosa's literary universe; she has observed that Ingold's understanding of landscape fits this world "perfectly." Librandi, "Sertão, City, Saudade," 73.

43. De Certeau, *Practices of Everyday Life*, 108.

44. Tim Ingold, "The Temporality of the Landscape," *World Archeology* 25 (1993): 153.

45. Ingold, *Perception of the Environment*, 190, 198.

46. Ingold, "Temporality of the Landscape," 164.

47. Ingold, "Temporality of the Landscape," 159.

48. Ettore Finazzi-Agrò, *Um lugar do tamanho do mundo: Tempos e espaços da ficção em João Guimarães Rosa* (Belo Horizonte, Brazil: UFMG, 2001), 85–86.

49. Fantini Scarpelli, *Guimarães Rosa*, 164.

50. For all these thinkers, landscape is by definition that which is looked at (from without) rather than experienced by one who participates in it. For

Cosgrove, landscape is an instrumental and highly rational way of seeing whose underlying principles are continuous with those of mapmaking, land surveying, commerce, warfare, and, generally, "the practical appropriation of space." Its ideological work consists of "the control and domination over space as an absolute, objective entity, its transformation into the property of individual or state." It arises in the fifteenth and sixteenth centuries, a product of renaissance humanism, and employs the new technique of linear perspective to scientifically master space and position the sovereign eye of the beholder outside the scene beheld. Denis Cosgrove, "Prospect, Perspective and the Evolution of the Landscape Idea," *Transactions of the Institute of British Geographers* 10, no. 1 (1985): 19, 46, 48. Raymond Williams observes that landscape often means country life viewed from afar by one who surveys the land from a class-specific remove rather than one who works it. Williams, *Country and the City*. Both thinkers point out that the conventions of landscape painting serve to create an image of harmony, invisibilizing class tensions and conflicts between humans and the nonhuman environment. Mitchell goes yet a step further, calling landscape a means of framing space "tailor-made for the discourse of imperialism." W. J. T. Mitchell, ed., *Landscape and Power* (Chicago: University of Chicago Press, 1994), 17.

51. Andermann, *Entranced Earth*, 9.

52. Andermann, Blackmore, and Morell, *Natura*, 8.

53. Andermann, *Tierras en transe*, 10.

54. See Maurice Merleau-Ponty, *The Visible and the Invisible*, ed. Claude Lefort, trans. Alphonso Lingis, (Evanston, IL: Northwestern University Press, 1968). For more on the phenomenological turn in landscape studies, see Rachael Ziady DeLue and James Elkins, eds., *Landscape Theory*, vol. 6, *The Art Seminar* (New York: Routledge, 2007).

55. Though the phenomenological turn in landscape studies is a late twentieth-century phenomenon, the notion that written accounts can capture the experience of inhabiting space better than visual media is not new. See, for example, Oliver Lubrich's analysis of the written landscapes of Alexander Von Humboldt in the eighteenth century, which Lubrich describes as "multi-medial" in the sense of "at once optical and acoustic, pictorial and poetic." Humboldt describes "the education of his senses" at the hands of his Indigenous guides and his resulting aim "to convey the character of a place not solely as a vision, but also as a *symphony: landscape* as *soundscape*." According to Humboldt, landscape painting had yet to achieve such success in "approximat[ing] the experience of inhabiting the landscape." Oliver Lubrich, "Humboltian Landscapes," in *Natura: Environmental Aesthetics after Landscape*, ed. Jens Andermann, Lisa Blackmore, and Dayron Carillo Morell (Zurich: Diaphnes, 2018), 98, 97, 100.

56. Carmello, *Memória e esquecimento*, 59, 63.

57. Michel Collot, "Du sens de l'espace à l'espace du sens," in *Espace et poésie*, ed. Michel Collot and Jean-Claude Mathieu (Paris: Presse de l'École Normale Supérieure, 1987), 104.

58. See Benjamin's analogy of walking along a country road rather than surveying it from above in an airplane. Benjamin, "One-Way Street." Butler stresses the ethical importance of renouncing the ambition to grasp totality and instead

avowing the "limits of our own epistemological horizon." Butler, "Values of Difficulty," 206. Haraway, "Situated Knowledges."

59. For Gómez-Barris, the concept of submerged perspectives stands in opposition to "the extractive view," which "sees territories as commodities." Gómez-Barris, *Extractive Zone*, 5.

60. Smith, *Mapping the Amazon*, 10, 12.

61. Andermann, *Tierra en trance*.

62. Gómez-Barris, *Extractive Zone*, 3.

63. Gómez-Barris, *Extractive Zone*, 3.

64. Pérez Trujillo Diniz, *Imagining the Plains*, 4.

65. Andermann, *Entranced Earth*, 18.

66. Anne Whiston Spirn, *The Language of the Landscape* (New Haven, CT: Yale University Press, 1998), 22.

67. Guimarães Rosa, *Grande sertão*, 23; *Devil to Pay*, 3.

68. Significantly, this episode signals that "reading" sounds is a learned (and learnable) skill. Librandi writes that certain novels endeavor to train their readers as listeners, thus emulating what Mia Couto describes as the "learning process rural societies confer upon us": literacy not just in words but also in sounds and silences. Librandi has analyzed *Grande sertão: Veredas* as a metareflection on how a man from the city might learn to listen to the *sertão* and, in particular, its oral culture. She describes the novel as an example of "high 'illiterate' literature, a literature whose literary value has unlettered practices at its pulsating heart." Librandi, *Writing by Ear*, 45, 58.

69. Sommer, "Slaps and Embraces," 176.

70. Silviano Santiago, *The Space In-Between: Essays on Latin American Culture*, trans. Ana Lúcia Gazzola (Durham, NC: Duke University Press, 2001), 87.

71. Santiago, *Space In-Between*, 89.

72. Sommer, "Slaps and Embraces."

73. Walnice Nogueira Galvão notes the importance of Riobaldo being a lettered *jagunço* and being called "professor." She argues that Riobaldo's literacy disrupts the classical regionalist or anthropological model where there is a marked contrast between the intellectual and the native informant on the level of language: both because Riobaldo is educated and because the novel knows no outside to his language, it becomes impossible to see him as an exotic and folkloric type awaiting capture by the literary class represented by the writer. Walnice Nogueira Galvão, "Rapsodo do sertão: Da lexicogênese à mitopoese," *Cadernos de Literatura Brasileira* 20–21 (2006): 165.

74. Guimarães Rosa, *Grande sertão*, 42; *Devil to Pay* 19.

75. Santiago, *Genealogía de la ferocidad*, 20.

76. Guimarães Rosa, *Grande sertão*, 440; my translation.

77. Guimarães Rosa, *Grande sertão*, 506; *Devil to Pay*, 398.

78. Guimarães Rosa, *Grande sertão*, 161,165; *Devil to Pay*, 122,126.

79. See Brock, "Queer Temporality."

80. Adria Frizzi describes the text as dilatory in the sense of practicing "the infinite deferral of 'truth.'" She claims that the revelation of Diadorim's identity is the exception to this rule, but in other major matters such as the pact with the devil, the "delays of the answer (snares, equivocations, ambiguities, jammed

answers, etc.) endlessly succeed one another, teasing the reader with the never fulfilled promise of a disclosure." Adria Frizzi, "The Demonic Texture: Deferral and Plurality in 'Grande Sertão: Veredas,'" *Chasqui* 17, no. 1 (1988): 26, 28.

81. Guimarães Rosa, *Grande sertão*, 156; *Devil to Pay*, 118.

82. Guimarães Rosa, *Grande sertão*, 387; my translation.

83. Guimarães Rosa, *Grande sertão*, 92; *Devil to Pay*, 62.

84. Guimarães Rosa, *Grande sertão*, 144–45; *Devil to Pay*, 108.

85. Santiago, *Geneología de la ferocidad*, 47–48.

86. Santiago, *Geneología de la ferocidad*, 13. The Second Republic lasted from 1930 to 1937. The Third Republic, otherwise known as the Estado Novo or the Vargas dictatorship, lasted from 1937 to 1945. Kubitschek's *Plano de Metas* was an important part of his 1955 presidential campaign. It promised rapid industrialization, and its capstone was the construction of a new capital, Brasília, in the inland state of Goias, just west of the *sertão* traversed by Riobaldo and his men. This moment serves as the immediate historical context for the publication of *Grande sertão: Veredas*.

87. Guimarães Rosa, *Grande sertão*, 276; *Devil to Pay*, 217. As Antonio Candido points out, "desnortear" means to disorient but also "to de-North, or remove the quality belonging to the North." Antonio Candido, "O homem dos avessos," *Coleção Fortuna Crítica* 6 (1987): 299. Note that northern Brazil, much like the southern United States, bears a stigma of underdevelopment and backwardness.

88. Guimarães Rosa, *Grande sertão*, 407; *Devil to Pay*, 320.

89. Guimarães Rosa, *Grande sertão*, 305; my translation.

90. Guimarães Rosa, *Grande sertão*, 150; *Devil to Pay*, 113.

91. Perhaps the most infamous example of a text that seeks to domesticate the *sertão* by making it known is Euclides da Cunha's 1902 *Os sertões*, which documents the defeat by Republican troops of the settlement of *sertanejos* known as Canudos. Before turning to the war itself, Euclides's text draws on the techniques of ethnography and *costumbrismo* to depict daily life in the backlands. It thus parallels the military conquest he chronicles: whereas the government troops the journalist accompanied sought to subject the *sertão* to federal rule, his text seeks to subject the *sertão* to modern disciplines of knowledge. Cunha, *Os Sertões* (São Paulo: Brasiliense, 1985). For a more in-depth discussion see Brizuela, *Fotografia e império*; Walnice Nogueira Galvão, "Rebellion in the Backlands: Landscape with Figures," trans. Paulo Henriques Britto, *ABEI (The Brazilian Journal of Irish Studies)* 12 (2010): 91–97.

92. Hansen, *O 0*, 167.

93. Guimarães Rosa, *Grande sertão*, 41; *Devil to Pay*, 19.

94. Guimarães Rosa, *Grande sertão*, 187; *Devil to Pay*, 144.

95. João Guimarães Rosa, *Gran sertón: Veredas*, trans. Florencia Garramuño and Gonzalo Aguilar (Córdoba, Argentina: Adriana Hidalgo, 2009).

96. On Humboldt and Sarmiento, see Prieto, *Los viajeros ingleses*, 20. According to Nielson, the sertão-sea binary originates much further back in colonial mapmaking projects. Nielson, "Unmappable Sertão," 20. For more on this dualism and its reverberations in contemporary cultural production see Cláudio Cledson Novaes, "Euclides Da Cunha e 'o sertão vai virar mar,'" *O Eixo e a Roda: Revista de Literatura Brasileira* 8 (2002): 65–79. For the ways in which

Grande sertão might be considered a rewriting of *Os sertões*, see: Candido, "O homem dos avessos"; Bolle, *Grandesertão.Br*.

97. Bolle: *Grandesertão.Br*, 53–54, 75–85.

98. Bueno, "O intelectual e o turista," 121.

99. Bueno, "O intelectual e o turista," 121.

100. Bueno, "O intelectual e o turista," 122.

101. Virgulino Ferreira da Silva, known as Lampião, is the most iconic *cangaceiro*, or bandit, of the Brazilian *sertão*. He and his sizable band roamed the northeastern backlands throughout the 1920s and 1930s. Antônio Vicente Mendes Maciel, known as Antonio Conselheiro, was a late nineteenth-century religious leader who founded the religious community of Canudos and is immortalized in Euclides da Cunha's *Os sertões* (1902). *Luzia-Homem* (1903) is a naturalist novel by Domingos Olímpio. Set in the *sertão* of Ceará, it tells the story of Luzia, a woman who dresses as a man and works as a construction worker. For how the medieval myth of the woman warrior is transposed from the Iberian peninsula to Brazil and taken up by Guimarães Rosa specifically, see Joyce Rodrigues Ferraz Infante, "Revisitando o tema da donzela-guerreira em Grande sertão: Veredas," in *João Guimarães Rosa: Um exiliado do linguagem comum* (Salamanca, Spain: Universidad de Salamanca, 2017).

102. Guimarães Rosa, *Grande sertão*, 41–42; *Devil to Pay*, 19.

103. Guimarães Rosa, *Grande sertão*, 183; my translation.

104. The construction of Brasília, designed by modernist architects Lúcio Costa and Oscar Niemeyer, began in 1956, and is widely seen as marking the end of the *sertão* as a space "sparsely occupied by pastoral economic activities" and the inauguration of "the expansionist and developmentalist occupation of the *sertão* for soy plantation and other agribusiness in large scale." Marília Librandi, "Multiple Rumors: Recado and Conconversa in João Guimarães Rosa's Fiction," *Luso-Brazilian Review* 53, no. 2 (2016): 66.

105. Saramago goes as far as to suggest fiction such as that of Guimarães Rosa conserves disappearing natural landscapes much in the same sense that nature preserves do. Saramago, *Fictional Environments*, 16.

106. Hansen, *O o*, 162–64.

107. Deise Dantas Lima, *Encenações do Brasil rural em Guimarães Rosa* (Niterói, Brazil: Editora da Universidade Federal Fluminense, 2001), 115.

108. Carmello, *Memória e esquecimento*, 73.

109. Dantas Lima, *Encenações do Brasil*, 124.

110. Bolle, *Grandesertão.Br*, 29.

111. Bolle, *Grandesertão.Br*, 20.

112. Guimarães Rosa, *Grande sertão*, 325; my translation.

113. Bolle reads Euclides's text as expressing a planning, controlling "*esprit de géometrie*" evincive of the author's training as an engineer and social scientist and, more broadly, of man's claim to dominate nature through instrumental reason. Bolle, *Grandesertão.Br*, 76. Yet to what degree *Os sertões* succeeds in this "conquest" by mapping and to what degree it allows the *sertão* to escape its grasp is a topic open for debate. Natalia Brizuela, for example, reads da Cunha's text as a failed work of positivistic documentation in which the *sertão* remains partially opaque and unrepresentable. Brizuela, *Fotografia e império*, 179.

114. As I have argued elsewhere, this shame is inseparable from that of having internalized heteronormative narratives of development, which are similarly linear and teleological. Brock, "Queer Temporality."

115. Guimarães Rosa, *Grande sertão*, 80; *Devil to Pay*, 52.

116. Guimarães Rosa, *Grande sertão*, 51; *Devil to Pay*, 27.

117. At one point, as his narrative approaches the climatic final battle, Riobaldo instructs O Doutor to pull out a piece of paper and draw a map of the place he describes, claiming it is the only way to communicate the layout. Rosa, *Grande sertão*, 563. He also repeatedly checks to make sure O Doutor is writing down his story and counts the pages he has amassed. See Rowland on how the text resists the form of the book "as a figure for finished and apprehensible totality." Rowland, *O lugar do meio*, 11. See Bolle on how the text resists the rational and instrumental logic of cartography. Bolle, *Grandesertão.Br*, 76–78.

118. The most remarkable example is Riobaldo's decision to withhold the knowledge of Diadorim's female body until the moment in the narrative when he made this discovery (only a few pages before the novel's conclusion). The narrator emphasizes the need for O Doutor to discover Diadorim's secret along with the character Riobaldo. Guimarães Rosa, *Grande sertão*, 615.

119. Bolle, for example, compares Guimarães Rosa's text to a labyrinth, which he contrasts with the map. Bolle, *Grandesertão.Br*, 85. Although it is possible (and common) to represent labyrinths from above (e.g., the bird's-eye view of a hedge maze), Ivan Almeida argues that the ontological status of the labyrinth is immanence. Ivan Almeida, "Borges, o los laberintos de la inmanencia," in *Borges: Desesperaciones aparentes y consuelos secretos*, ed. Rafael Olea Franco (Mexico City: El colegio de México, 1999): 35–59.

120. Guimarães Rosa, *Grande sertão*, 624; *Devil to Pay*, 492.

121. Guimarães Rosa, *Grande sertão*, 285; *Devil to Pay*, 224.

122. Kampff Lages, *João Guimarães Rosa e a saudade*, 87.

123. Kampff Lages, *João Guimarães Rosa e a saudade*, 87.

124. Guimarães Rosa, *Grande sertão*, 611; my translation.

125. Carmello, *Memória e esquecimento*, 175.

126. Rowland, *O lugar do meio*, 57.

127. Rowland, *O lugar do meio*, 15.

128. Rowland, *O lugar do meio*, 119.

129. Guimarães Rosa, *Grande sertão*, 590; *Devil to Pay*, 465.

130. Guimarães Rosa, *Grande sertão*, 325; *Devil to Pay*, 257. Emphasis mine.

131. Guimarães Rosa, *Grande sertão*, 156; *Devil to Pay*, 118.

132. See Al-Saji, "Durée," 102.

133. Santiago concludes, "If there is a crime in *Grande sertão: veredas*, it is that of the lover outliving the beloved." Santiago, *Geneología de la ferocidad*, 81. Bolle, in turn, describes Riobaldo's story as that of one who has "let die" the love of his life, but beyond being structured by the guilt and mourning provoked by this personal sacrifice, this narrative is according to Bolle both a self-recrimination and a discourse of legitimization for a subject who has risen from the subaltern position of *jagunço* to a member of the landed class. In this reading, the supernatural pact is what allows for this social mobility, which would have been improbable in the historical *sertão*. Bolle, *Grandesertão.Br*,

258, 184, 288. On the difference between submerged and extractive views, see Gómez-Barris, *Extractive Zone*.

134. Walnice Nogueira Galvão, "'O certo no incerto: O pactário,'" *Coleção Fortuna Crítica* 6 (1987): 419.

135. Galvão, "O certo no incerto," 411.

136. Guimarães Rosa, *Grande sertão*, 591; *Devil to Pay*, 466.

137. Guimarães Rosa, *Grande sertão*, 611; *Devil to Pay*, 482; translation modified.

138. Hansen, *O o*, 171.

139. Bolle, *Grandesertão.Br,* 173.

140. Alonso, *Spanish American Regional Novel*, 103.

141. Leo Bersani, "I Can Dream, Can't I?," in *Thoughts and Things* (Chicago: University of Chicago Press, 2015), 68.

142. Guimarães Rosa, *Grande sertão*, 546; my translation.

143. Santiago, *Geneología de la ferocidad*, 68.

144. Armstrong, "Rosa in Translation," 67–68.

145. Bolle, *Grandesertão.Br*, 215.

146. Andermann, *Entranced Earth*, 30.

147. Kathrin H. Rosenfield, "Devil to Pay in the Backlands and João Guimarães Rosa's Quest for Universality," *Portuguese Literary and Cultural Studies* 4/5 (2000): 197–205, 198.

148. Pratt, "Arts of the Contact Zone," 37.

149. Fantini Scarpelli, *Guimarães Rosa*, 176, 180.

150. Fantini Scarpelli, *Guimarães Rosa*, 209.

151. For example, Finazzi-Agrò draws the connection between the suspension of the *travessia* and the suspension of the *terceira margem* and sees both as expressions of hybridism prevalent in Guimarães Rosa's texts. He points to Diadorim (both man and woman, both amorous and diabolical) and Hermógenes (whose name derives from Hermaphrodes) as figures of hybridity and to the hybrid nature of Guimarães Rosa's language. Finazzi-Agrò, *Um lugar do tamanho do mundo*, 47–56.

152. Finazzi-Agrò, *Um lugar do tamanho do mundo*, 114, 113.

153. The critique of critical distance extends to Guimarães Rosa's thoughts on literary criticism: he has said that a good critic "should be part of the literature," thus ceasing to be a critic "in the proper sense." He has little tolerance, moreover, for the critic who aspires to "vingar-se da literatura" ("take revenge on literature"), which we might, following Santiago, recognize as the Zé-Bebelo model of irascibility. Lorenz, "Diálogo com Guimarães Rosa," 75–76.

CHAPTER 4

1. Juan José Saer, *La mayor* (Buenos Aires: Seix Barral, 2005), 164.

2. Saer, *La mayor*, 171.

3. Gabriela Nouzeilles, "The Iconography of Desolation: Patagonia and the Ruins of Nature," *Review: Literature and Arts of the Americas* 40, no. 2 (2007): 252–62.

4. Montaldo, *De pronto, el campo*, 180.

5. Noé Jitrik, "La extensión," *Revista del Centro de Letras Hispanoamericanas* 24, no. 29 (2015): 24.

6. Jitrik, "La extensión," 23.

7. In truth, vision is but one of many senses that Saer's experimental poetics endeavors to educate. As Rafael Arce points out, *El limonero real* conjures a largely auditory world and *Nadie nada nunca* a tactile world. Rafael Arce, *Juan José Saer: La felicidad de la novela* (Santa Fe, Argentina: Universidad Nacional del Litoral, 2015), 37.

8. Saer, *La mayor*, 165.

9. Saer, *La mayor*, 166.

10. See Pratt, *Imperial Eyes*; Penhos, *Ver, conocer, dominar*.

11. In 1968, during the dictatorship of Juan Carlos Onganía, Saer departed for Paris to accept a grant to study the *nouveau roman*. He resided in France until his death in 2005.

12. Florencia Garramuño, *La experiencia opaca: Literatura y desencanto* (Buenos Aires: Tierra Firme, 2009).

13. Saer's formal experimentations in this phase of his career are widely acknowledged to be influenced by the French *nouveau roman*, which eschews plot and character in favor of objectivist descriptions, rendering the world as if through the mechanical gaze of the camera. Jitrik suggests that Saer was first inspired by Antonio di Benedetto's use of objectivist description. Noé Jitrik, "Entre el corte y la continuidad: Hacia una escritura crítica," *Revista Iberoamericana* 68: 200 (2002): 729–36. Jitrik and Arce both emphasize that Saer's adaptation of the technique laces it with negativity (focusing on what escapes positivistic capture), thus distinguishing it from the true objectivism associated with the *nouveau roman*. See Jitrik, "Entre el corte," 734; Arce, *Juan José Saer*, 40.

14. At least in his early writings, Benjamin expressed hope that the very poverty of experience in the modern era may yield traces of a more immediate experience that is always already lost to symbolic discourses, a position Adorno critiqued as contradictory if not untenable. Jay, *Songs of Experience*, 331–36.

15. In addition to Garramuño's reading, see David Oubiña, *El silencio y sus bordes* (Buenos Aires: Tierra Firme, 2011); Rafael Arce, "La imagen novelesca," *Revista Hispánica Moderna* 66, no. 2 (2013): 109–20; Cecilia Policsek, "The Poetics of Negativity as a Form of Seeing Literature: *The Witness*," *Neophilogus* 97, no. 1 (2013): 1–8; María Teresa Gramuglio, "Un postmodernismo crítico," *Punto de Vista* 15, no. 42 (1992): 27; Beatriz Sarlo, "El saber del texto," *Punto de Vista* 9, no. 26 (1986): 6–7; Beatriz Sarlo, "Una mirada política," *Punto de Vista* 3, no. 8 (1985): 1–4.

16. Baskin, "Soft Eyes," 5–18. For more on the relationship between Adorno and phenomenology, see Gandesha, "Leaving Home," 101–28.

17. Adorno, *Negative Dialectics*, 5.

18. Baskin, "Soft Eyes," 9.

19. Beatriz Sarlo, "La política, la devastación," in *Glosa y El entenado: Edición crítica*. Ed. Julio Premat. (Paris: Archivos, 2010), 770.

20. This was the year of Augusto Pinochet's coup in Chile. In Argentina, it marked Perón's return from exile and anticipated the Videla coup by three

years. The neighboring countries of Brazil and Paraguay were already under military dictatorships.

21. Saer, *El concepto de ficción*, 144.

22. We might think of Heraldo Conti, Juan Gelman, and Roldolfo Walsh. The last is the paradigmatic example of a writer who found fiction to be an insufficient tool with which to fight oppression: he denounced the military dictatorship directly in his *Carta abierta a la junta militar* (1977) and was disappeared in 1977 for his militarism. Saer, in contrast, never felt that dedicating himself to literature was an abdication of political responsibility: "Writing is a much more political act than many channels self-defined as political." Saer, Notebook. He did, however, acknowledge that literature was not the tool called for to remedy acute situations of injustice: "It is evident that state terrorism, the exploitation of one man by another, the use of political power against the popular classes and against the individual demand immediate and absolute change of social structures; unfortunately it is not literature that can bring this about." Saer, *El concepto de ficción*, 262.

23. Masiello, *Senses of Democracy*, 205.

24. Oubiña, *El silencio y sus bordes*, 111.

25. J. M. Bernstein, "Negative Dialectic as Fate: Adorno and Hegel," in *The Cambridge Companion to Adorno*, ed. Thomas Huhn (Cambridge: Cambridge University Press, 2004), 11.

26. Saer, Notebook.

27. Juan José Saer, "Sartre: Contra entusiastas y detractores," *Punto de Vista* 3, no. 9 (1980): 11–12.

28. Pénélope Laurent, "Melancolía de lo sagrado en la obra de Juan José Saer," *Revista Iberoamericana* 84, no. 263 (2018): 442–43.

29. Juan José Saer, "La cuestión de la prosa," in *La narración objeto* (Buenos Aires: Seix Barral, 1999), 57.

30. For more on how regional cultures were instrumentalized to forge a national-populist identity under Peronism, see Heredia, *El suelo*.

31. Jens Andermann, *Mapas de poder: Una arqueología literaria del espacio argentino* (Rosario, Argentina: Beatriz Viterbo, 2000).

32. For a discussion of the role of photography in Perón's Argentina, see Iliana Cepero, "Photographic Propaganda under Peronism, 1946–55: Selections from the Archivo General de La Nación Argentina," *History of Photography* 40, no. 2 (2016): 193–214; Natalia Brizuela, "Grete Stern, Horacio Coppola and the Question of Modern Photography in Argentina," *Journal of Latin American Cultural Studies* 24, no. 2 (2015): 243–65; Andermann, "State Formation."

33. Williams, *Other Side of the Popular*.

34. Montaldo, *De pronto el campo*.

35. Juan José Saer and Ricardo Piglia, *Diálogo* (Santa Fe, Argentina: Universidad Nacional del Litoral, 1990), 65.

36. Saer insists on putting "rural" and "urban" literature in quotation marks, claiming that he finds these distinctions of little use or importance ("Interview with Gabriel Saad," Notebook).

37. See "Un reportaje," Notebook. Saer has also written, "As in the golden age of colonial exploitation, the majority of Latin American writers procure for

the European reader certain products that, as the experts claim, are rare in the metropole and recall the raw materials and the tropical fruits that the European climate cannot produce: exuberance, freshness, strength, innocence, return to sources." Saer, *El concepto de ficción*, 266.

38. Saer, *El concepto de ficción*, 260.

39. See, for example, Saer and Piglia, *Diálogo*, 16; Julio Premat, *Héroe sin atributos: Figuras de autor en la literatura argentina* (Buenos Aires: Tierra Firme, 2009), 192; Arce, *Juan José Saer*, 49.

40. Sarlo, "El saber del texto," 7.

41. Saer, Notebook.

42. One notable exception is Leopoldo Lugones (1874–1938), a poet and public intellectual who came to embody Argentina's nationalist Right. Saer caustically ridicules him in *El río sin orillas*, and as Julio Premat argues, Saer's philosophical elaboration of the role of the writer as a negative figure "sin atributos" seems to be conceived as the antipode to Lugones's mythical status. Premat, *Héroe sin atributos*, 10.

43. Saer also lambastes Gabriel García Márquez and Mario Vargas Llosa for writing retrograde novels masquerading as avant-garde creations, claiming that they peddle in nostalgia. Saer, Notebook.

44. Saer and Piglia, *Diálogo*, 38.

45. Luigi Patruno, *Relatos de regreso: Ensayos sobre la obra de Juan José Saer* (Rosario, Argentina: Beatriz Viterbo, 2015), 27.

46. Butler and Spivak, *Who Sings the Nation-State?*, 94.

47. Saer, *El concepto de la ficción*, 282.

48. Sarlo, "El saber del texto," 7.

49. For more on the history of Argentine regionalism and Saer's relation to it, see the introduction as well as Heredia, *El texto literario y los discursos regionales*.

50. Juan José Saer, "Razones," in María Teresa Gramuglio, *Juan José Saer por Juan José Saer* (Buenos Aires: Celtia, 1986), 17.

51. Beatriz Sarlo, "Narrar la percepción," in *Escritos sobre literatura argentina* (Buenos Aires: Siglo Veintiuno, 2007), 285.

52. Oubiña, *El silencio y sus bordes*, 83–85.

53. Premat, *La dicha de Saturno*, 432–33.

54. Premat, *La dicha de Saturno*, 255.

55. Premat, *La dicha de Saturno*, v, 33.

56. Garramuño, *La experiencia opaca*, 118.

57. Garramuño, *La experiencia opaca*, 128.

58. "Unidad de lugar" is also the title of Saer's first collection of short stories. I follow Rafael Arce's assertion that the unity of Saer's discontinuous *zona* is rooted in the phenomenological experience of the narrator. Arce, *Juan José Saer*, 49. For more on Ortiz's influence, see Juan José Saer, "Juan," in *Juan L. Ortiz: Obra completa* (Santa Fe, Argentina: Universidad Nacional del Litoral, 1996), 11–14.

59. Saer, *La mayor*, 19.

60. I am grateful to Natalia Brizuela for drawing my attention to this connection.

61. Saer, *La mayor*, 16.

62. Oubiña, *El silencio y sus bordes*, 98.

63. Often translated as "knowledge," "consciousness," or "familiarity," *conocimiento* implies firsthand experience. I choose "acquaintance" in part because *conocer* rather than *saber* is always used in reference to knowing people and in part because of the connotations of "acquaintance" evoked by Dora Zhang in her discussion of modernist description. For Zhang, acquaintance is "a form of knowing" grounded in sensory perceptions that "yields no knowledge of truths." It is often presented as ineffable and unshareable not because it is too strange but because it is too familiar: it is "what we know *too* well for words." Dora Zhang, "Naming the Indescribable: Woolf, Russell, James, and the Limits of Description," *New Literary History* 45, no. 1 (2014): 57, 58, 54.

64. María Teresa Gramuglio reads "La mayor" in a similar vein, arguing that new forms of writing beyond what used to be possible might compensate for "the dispossession of the world." Gramuglio, *Juan José Saer*, 7–8.

65. Arce, *Juan José Saer*, 41.

66. Masiello, *Senses of Democracy*, 213.

67. Ingold, *Perception of the Environment*, 60.

68. Glissant, *Poetics of Relation*, 33.

69. See Oubiña, *El silencio y sus bordes*.

70. Juan José Saer, *Papeles de trabajo: Borradores inéditos*, ed. Julio Premat (Buenos Aires: Seix Barral, 2012), 121–22.

71. Arce, *Juan José Saer*, 61.

72. Ingold, "Temporality of the Landscape," 152–53.

73. Ingold, *Perception of the Environment*, 167.

74. Ingold, *Perception of the Environment*, 190.

75. Juan José Saer, *El limonero real* (Buenos Aires: Seix Barral, 2010), 23.

76. Saer, *El limonero real*, 60.

77. Saer, *El limonero real*, 166.

78. Saer, *El limonero real*, 141.

79. In an early draft of the novel, Saer includes passages that explicitly treat the resentment Wenceslao feels toward the exploitative city economy, as represented by the fish wholesalers who buy from him. Saer, *Papeles de trabajo*, 122. In the final version of the novel, however, the reader is given scant direct access to Wenceslao's interiority and only isolated glimpses of the social and economic totality in which his way of life is bound. During the watermelon episode, he remarks simply: "Maldita la hora que arrendamos y nos pusimos a sembrar" ("Damn the moment we rented the land and started to plant it"). Saer, *El limonero real*, 103.

80. Theodor W. Adorno, "The Essay as Form," in *Notes to Literature*, vol. 1, trans. Rolf Tiedmann (New York: Columbia University Press, 1991), 13.

81. Julio Premat, "El cataclismo de los orígenes: La pampa histórica de Juan José Saer," *Cambio y Permanencia en las Culturas del Río de la Plata* 17–18 (1997): 691.

82. Ezequiel Martínez Estrada, *Radiografía de la pampa* (Paris: Archivos, 1991), 9.

83. Martínez Estrada writes that the conquerors "did not arrive forewarned of the very simple and poor reality of America. They already had it populated

with monsters, difficulties, and riches. America was, upon landing, a sudden disappointment." Martínez Estrada, *Radiografía*, 5. Recalling Alexander Von Humboldt's advice that the painter Johann Moritz Rugendas skip the pampa because there was nothing to see there, Graciela Silvestri reminds us that this visual landscape has long been regarded as paling in comparison to the more "vibrant" and exotic tropical landscapes to be found farther north. Silvestri points to "the scarcity of iconography before the nineteenth century": "Brambilla and Rugendas are among the few travelers who bequeathed works of aesthetic quality about the Rioplatense landscape: there wasn't much of interest to see here." Graciela Silvestri, *El lugar común: Una historia de las figuras de paisaje en el Rió de La Plata* (Buenos Aires: Edhasa, 2011), 42–43.

84. Premat, *Héroe sin atributos*, 171.

85. Graciela Montaldo, *Juan José Saer: El limonero real* (Buenos Aires: Hachete, 1986), 24.

86. Marta Stern, "Introduction," in *El limonero real*, by Juan José Saer (Buenos Aires: Centro Editor de América Latina, 1981), iv. The most dramatic example may be the disappearance of El Gato and Elisa by the military dictatorship, which takes place but is never narrated in *Nadie nada nunca* (1980). It is only after reading a proleptic revelation of their fate in *Glosa* (1985) and a description of their abandoned house in *La pesquisa* (1994) that we are able to be sure of what happened. This information casts novels written years earlier into a new light and directly confronts the reader with the political violence that runs throughout Saer's work as a silenced subtext. Sarlo writes of this phenomenon: "A single phrase in *Glosa* obliges me to reread *Nadie nada nunca* in a way that I didn't imagine I could reread it before: to see what was there in that past, in that month of February in which the novel takes place, but which I didn't see, which Saer probably didn't hide but didn't say either." Beatriz Sarlo, "La condición mortal," in *Escritos sobre literatura argentina*, 294.

87. Montaldo, *De pronto el campo*, 12.

88. Sarlo, "El saber del texto," 6.

89. Premat, *La dicha de Saturno*, 322–23.

90. Juan José Saer, *El río sin orillas* (Madrid: Alianza, 1991), 24.

91. Demaría, *Buenos Aires y las provincias*, 462.

92. Patruno, *Relatos de regreso*, 42.

93. Prieto, *Los viajeros ingleses*.

94. Saer, *El concepto de ficción*, 261.

95. In her discussion of the relationship between visual apprehension, knowledge, and domination in late eighteenth-century travel writing, Marta Penhos enumerates the techniques through which travel writers create the illusions of totalizing vision and of temporal stillness. Penhos identifies a variety of narrative techniques borrowed from the visual arts and cartography, which conspire to produce these illusions, thereby domesticating nature as a visible and traversable landscape. These include the aggregation of spatial perspectives to create a totalizing bird's-eye view, the preference for the static and impersonal perspective of an objective outsider over the dynamic perceptions of one who participates in the landscape, and the use of high and distant perspective to make a scene bustling with daily activity appear as a static and timeless visual

landscape. Together with a Baconian faith in visualization, as a means to understanding, these techniques give the foreign observer and reader a sense of mastery over spaces whose expansiveness, wildness, and foreignness would otherwise render them indomitable and threatening. Penhos, *Ver, conocer, dominar.*

96. Demaría, *Buenos Aires y las provincias,* 447.

97. Demaría, *Buenos Aires y las provincias,* 462.

98. Demaría, *Buenos Aires y las provincias,* 481. See also Sylvia Molloy, who reminds us: "It is clear that physical distance cannot assure the aesthetic autonomy necessary to produce the missing gaze that subverts the regularity of the nation, nor can presence in the country guarantee cultural belonging." Sylvia Molloy, "A modo de introducción. Back home: Un posible comienzo." In *Poéticas de la distancia: Adentro y afuera de la literatura argentina,* ed. Sylvia Molloy and Mariano Siskind (Buenos Aires: Grupo Editorial Norma, 2006), 10.

99. Juan José Saer, "Experiencia y lenguaje II: Dos ensayos de Juan José Saer," *Punto de Vista* 18, no. 51 (1995): 7.

100. In his essays, Saer often insists that Latin American intellectuals, such as Borges and Guimarães Rosa, can and should be read within the cultural filiation of the great European masters. Saer, *Trabajos* (Buenos Aires: Seix Barral, 2006), 77. He attests, moreover, that books by the likes of Joyce, Kafka, Proust, Faulkner, Neruda, Vallejo, Pound, Eliot, Pessoa, and Woolf were available in his small town. Saer, Notebook.

101. Demaría, *Buenos Aires y las provincias,* 484–86.

102. Demaría, *Buenos Aires y las provincias,* 486.

103. Demaría, *Buenos Aires y las provincias,* 489, 491.

104. Saer, *La mayor,* 126.

105. Saer, *La mayor,* 127–28.

106. Saer, *La mayor,* 128.

107. For example, see Premat, *La dicha de Saturno;* Laurent, "Melancolía de lo sagrado," 439–54.

108. Alonso, *Spanish American Regional Novel.*

109. Nicolás Lucero, *La vuelta incompleta: Saer y la novela* (Buenos Aires: Santiago Arcos, 2017), 132.

110. Sommer, "Slaps and Embraces," 180.

111. Premat, *Héroe sin atributos,* 445.

112. *Entenado* is a synonym of *hijastro,* "stepchild," but Margaret Jull Costa's English translation of the novel is titled *The Witness.* The narrator eventually discovers that the Colastiné take prisoners like him so that outsiders might bear witness to, remember, and represent their way of life.

113. Patruno has also drawn this comparison with Borges but focuses primarily on the narrator's status as an outsider to European culture once he returns. Patruno, *Relatos de regreso.*

114. Lucero, *La vuelta incompleta,* 148.

115. Laurent, *Melancolía,* 451.

116. Lucero, *La vuelta incompleta,* 136.

117. Montaldo, *Juan José Saer: El limonero real,* 31.

118. Montaldo, *Juan José Saer: El limonero real,* 57.

119. Arce, "La imagen novelesca," 115

120. For examples of how critics have emphasized the contrast between Saer's visual poetics and the trappings of regionalism—*pintoresquismo, color local, costumbrismo*, and so on, see Sarlo, "El saber del texto"; Gramuglio, "Juan José Saer."

121. Padrón, *Spacious Word*, 94.

122. Ashley Brock, "Algo Más Que Mirar: More-Than-Looking at Regional Life in Juan José Saer's *El Limonero Real*," *Revista de Estudios Hispánicos* 52, no. 1 (2018).

123. Saer had a truly multimedia formation. He claims to have learned from poets, painters, and musicians in Santa Fé and speculates that he became a novelist largely out of fear of failing as a poet. See Saer, Notebook. His training also included collaborations with Fernando Birri, the so-called father of El Nuevo Cine Latinoaméricano, at the Instituto de Cinematografía at the Universidad Nacional del Litoral in Santa Fe, where Saer would go on to teach history of cinematography. Saer joined the Instituto de Cine in 1962 and collaborated on the award-winning screenplay to *Las veredas de Saturno* (1986). He also collaborated with Nicolás Sarquís on the film adaptation of *Palo y hueso*.

124. Saer and Piglia, *Diálogo*, 11–12.

125. Saer, *Papeles de trabajo*, 114.

126. Arce, *Juan José Saer*, 40.

127. Saer, Notebook.

128. Heredia, *El texto literario y los discursos regionales*, 137.

129. Arce, "La imagen novelesca," 114.

130. Saer, "Juan," 113.

131. Andermann, *Entranced Earth*, 247.

132. Ingold, "The Temporality of the Landscape," 162.

CODA

1. In a 2011 interview with *Cineaste*, Alonso conjectures that the greatest influence on his treatment of time was *El limonero real*. See Dennis West and Joanne M. West, "Cinema beyond Words: An Interview with Lisandro Alonso," *Cineaste* 36, no. 2 (2011): 33. For more on this intertextuality, see Ashley Brock, "Lisandro Alonso's *La libertad* and the Objectivist Tradition of Juan José Saer," *FORMA: A Journal of Latin American Criticism & Theory* 3, no. 1 (2023).

2. Jens Andermann, *New Argentine Cinema* (London: I. B. Tauris, 2012), 92.

3. Andermann calls this trend a form of neoregionalism. Andermann, *Tierra en trance*, 380. It might be said to form part of global trend that Tiago de Luca calls "sensory realism," which is characterized by the hyperbolically long take, which creates "a sensuous viewing experience anchored in materiality and duration." Tiago de Luca, *Realism of the Senses in World Cinema: The Experience of Physical Reality* (London: I. B. Tauris, 2014), 1. Beyond simply expressing a tendency for longer-than-average shot length, this style's telltale features include a predilection for stillness and silence and the use of nonprofessional actors. Tiago de Luca and Nuno Barradas Jorge, *Slow Cinema* (Edinburgh: Edinburgh University Press, 2015), 5–6.

4. Ecopoetry is not a well-defined concept, but attempts to codify it have been made in recent years. See John Elder, *Ecopoetry: A Critical Introduction*, ed. J. Scott Bryson (Salt Lake City: University of Utah Press, 2002); Angela Hume and Gillian Osborne, eds., *Ecopoetics: Essays in the Field* (Iowa City: University of Iowa Press, 2018). For more on *ecopoesía* in the Latin American context, see the database compiled by Odile Cisneros: "Ecopoesia," https://eco poesia.com/en/home/about.

5. *Grande sertão: Veredas* has been adapted to film and stage many times, including a popular miniseries produced by Rede Globo, and spurred the creation of parks and preserves such as the Grande Sertão Veredas National Park. See Saramago, *Fictional Environments*. *El limonero real* was adapted to film in 2016 by Gustavo Fontán, and as part of a celebration of Saer's legacy, the full text of the novel has been read over mobile loudspeakers in Rosario, the capital of the author's native province.

6. Saer, *El limonero real*, 87.

7. For Brizuela, this phrase describes literary texts that either include photographs or re-create photographic ways of seeing in order to gesture beyond themselves. She understands this drive—both self-destructive and self-renovating—to seek the outside of the work of art as expressive of Adornian negativity. Natalia Brizuela, *Depois da fotografia: Uma literatura fora de si*. Rio de Janeiro: Rocco, 2014, 87–89.

8. Arguedas, *El zorro*, 113; *The Fox*, 9.

9. Brock, "Algo Más Que Mirar."

10. For more on this connection and its anti-colonial dimensions, see Silvia Rivera Cusicanqui, *Sociología de la imagen: Miradas ch'ixi desde la historia andina* (Buenos Aires: Tinta Limón, 2015).

11. Laura U. Marks argues that film far outstrips literature in this regard: "Cinema, by virtue of its richer and muddier semiotic relationship to the world, is all the more an agent of mimesis and synthesis than writing is." See Marks, *Skin of the Film*, 214.

12. Marks, *Skin of the Film*, 141

13. Scott MacDonald, *The Garden in the Machine: A Field Guide to Independent Films about Place* (Berkeley: University of California Press, 2001).

14. Wenceslao Machado de Oliveira Jr., "Lugares geográficos e(m) locais narrativos: Um modo de se aproximar das geografias de cinema," in *Qual o espaço do lugar? Geografia, epistemologia, fenomenologia* (São Paulo: Perspectiva, 2012), 127.

15. Andermann, *Tierra en trance*, 380.

16. Andermann, *Tierra en trance*, 380.

17. Andermann, *Tierra en trance*, 380.

18. For more on the implications of this dissonance, see Ashley Brock, "Reanimating the Domestic Still Life," *CR: The New Centennial Review* 20, no. 1 (March 1, 2020): 51–74.

19. Rocha first encountered the *aboio* in literature, including Guimarães Rosa's stories, and set out into the *sertão* with her crew to see if it was still practiced anywhere. Multiple critics have remarked on the film's intertextuality

with *Grande sertão: Veredas*. See Luciano Barisone, "Os últimos: Dois filmes de Marília Rocha," n.d., teia.art.br/br/textos.

20. Paulo Antonio Paranaguá, "Aboio: Marília Rocha, Brasil, 2005," n.d., teia.art.br/br/textos.

21. Ashley Brock, "The Ethnographic Pastoral Re-Imagined: Embodiment and Inhabitation in *Aboio* and *Sweetgrass*," *Journal of Cinema and Media Studies* (forthcoming).

22. In one moment, Vicuña incorporates photographs of disappeared and disappearing things, such as ancestral cemeteries, the *fiesta de los chinos*, and the dunes, into her composition of yarn on the beach, explicitly evoking the use of photographs by the mothers of the disappeared during the Pinochet dictatorship.

23. Marks, *Skin of the Film*, 245.

24. In fact, as Rafael Arce argues, Saer's pseudo-objectivist poetics actually underscores the regards in which literature surpasses film in conveying the subjective experience of time and place. Arce, "La imagen novelesca," 155.

25. Marks, *Skin of the Film*, 153.

26. Marks, *Skin of the Film*, 153.

27. Marks, *Skin of the Film*, 232.

28. Andermann observes, in relation to *Los muertos*, that the unexpressive acting of Alonso's solitary and laconic protagonists along with his preference for medium shots keep the viewer at a remove. Andermann, *Tierras en trance*, 382. Bernhard Chappuzeau notes that rebuffing the viewer's desire for identification in this way has an alienating, abrasive effect: "Alonso was always criticized for not respecting his audience by denying them empathy with his characters." Chappuzeau, "La imagen lejana y el impulse de tocarla: La recepción afectiva de *Liverpool* (Lisandro Alonso, 2008) en el extranjero," in *Cine argentino contemporáneo: Visiones y discursos*, ed. Bernhard Chappuzeau and Christian Von Tschlilischke (Madrid: Iberoamericana, 2016), 280.

29. Marks, *Skin of the Film*, 192.

30. Heidegger, "Building, Dwelling, Thinking," 161.

Bibliography

Aboul-Ela, Hosam. *Other South: Faulkner, Coloniality, and the Mariátegui Tradition*. Pittsburgh: University of Pittsburgh Press, 2007.

Aderaldo Castello, José. *José Lins do Rêgo: Modernismo e regionalismo*. São Paulo: Edart, 1961.

Adorno, Theodor W. *Aesthetic Theory*. Translated by Robert Hullot-Kentor. Minneapolis: University of Minnesota Press, 1996.

———. "The Essay as Form." In *Notes to Literature*. Vol. 1, translated by Rolf Tiedmann, 3–23. New York: Columbia University Press, 1991.

———. *Minima Moralia: Reflections from Damaged Life*. Translated by E. F. N. Jephcott. London: Verso, 2005.

———. *Negative Dialectics*. Translated by E. B. Ashton. New York: Continuum, 2007.

Ahmed, Sara. *Strange Encounters: Embodied Others in Post-Coloniality*. New York: Routledge, 2000.

Alegría, Ciro. *Los perros hambrientos*. Madrid: Ediciones Cátedra, 1996.

Allen, Nicolas, and Pablo Nicotera. "Del desarrollismo al dependentismo en el ensayo socioeconómico: Celso Furtado / Raúl Prebisch—Fernando Henrique Cardoso / Juan José Sebrèli." In *Historia comparada de las literaturas argentina y brasileña. Tomo V: Del desarrollismo a la dictadura, entre privatización, boom y militancia (1955–1970)*, edited by Marcela Croce, 275–301. Villa María, Argentina: Editorial Universitaria Villa María, 2018.

Almeida, Ivan. "Borges, o los laberintos de la inmanencia." In *Borges: Desesperaciones aparentes y consuelos secretos*, edited by Rafael Olea Franco, 35–59. Mexico City: El colegio de México, 1999.

Alonso, Carlos J. *The Spanish American Regional Novel: Modernity and Autochthony*. Cambridge: Cambridge University Press, 1990.

Alonso, Lisandro, dir. *Fantasma*. 2006; 4L, Fortuna Films, Slot Machine, Intermedio.

———. *La libertad*. 2001. 4L, Fortuna Films, Slot Machine, Intermedio.

———. *Los muertos*. 2004. 4L, Fortuna Films, Slot Machine, Intermedio, Arte France cinéma.

Al-Saji, Alia. "Durée." In *50 Concepts for a Critical Phenomenology*, 99–106. Evanston, IL: Northwestern University Press, 2020.

Andermann, Jens. *Entranced Earth: Art, Extractivism, and the End of Landscape*. Evanston, IL: Northwestern University Press, 2023.

———. *Mapas de poder: Una arqueología literaria del espacio argentino*. Rosario, Argentina: Beatriz Viterbo, 2000.

———. *New Argentine Cinema*. London: I. B. Tauris, 2012.

———. *The Optic of the State: Visuality and Power in Argentina and Brazil*. Pittsburgh: University of Pittsburgh Press, 2007.

———. "State Formation, Visual Technology and Spectatorship: Visions of Modernity in Brazil and Argentina." *Theory, Culture & Society* 27, no. 7–8 (2010): 161–83. https://doi.org/10.1177/0263276410384749.

———. *Tierra en trance: Arte y naturaleza después del paisaje*. Santiago, Chile: Metales Pesados, 2018.

Andermann, Jens, Lisa Blackmore, and Dayron Carillo Morell, eds. *Natura: Environmental Aesthetics after Landscape*. Zürich: Diaphnes, 2018.

Andrade, Oswaldo de. "Manifesto Antropófago." *Revista de Antropofagia* 1 (1928): 3, 7.

Apter, Emily. *Against World Literature: The Politics of Untranslatability*. London: Verso, 2013.

———. *The Translation Zone: A New Comparative Literature*. Princeton, NJ: Princeton University Press, 2005.

Araújo, Humberto Hermenegildo de. "Leituras sobre regionalismo e globalização." *Imburana: Revista do Núcleo Câmera Cascudo de Estudos Norte-Rio-Grandenses/UFRN* 7 (2013): 23–31.

Arce, Rafael. *Juan José Saer: La felicidad de la novela*. Santa Fe, Argentina: Universidad Nacional del Litoral, 2015.

———. "La imagen novelesca." *Revista Hispánica Moderna* 66, no. 2 (2013): 109–20.

Arguedas, José María, trans. *Dioses y hombres de Huarochirí: Narración Quechua recogida por Francisco de Ávila*. Lima, Peru: Universidad Antonio Ruiz de Montoya, 2009.

Arguedas, José María. *Deep Rivers*. Translated by Frances Horning Barraclough. Austin: University of Texas Press, 1978.

———. *El zorro de arriba y el zorro de abajo*. Buenos Aires: Losada, 2011.

———. *The Fox from Up Above and the Fox from Down Below*. Translated by Frances Horning Barraclough. Pittsburgh: University of Pittsburgh Press and Colección Archivos, 2000.

———. *Los ríos profundos*. Edited by Ricardo Gonzáles Vigil. Madrid: Cátedra, 2010.

Armstrong, Piers. "Rosa in Translation: Scrittore, Editore, Traduttore, Traditore." *Luso-Brazilian Review* 38, no. 1 (2001): 63–87.

————. *Third World Literary Fortunes: Brazilian Culture and Its International Reception*. Lewisberg, PA: Bucknell University Press, 1999.

Arruda, Maria Arminda do Nascimento. "Modernismo e regionalismo no Brasil: Entre inovação e tradição." *Tempo Social: Revista de Sociologia da USP* 23, no. 2 (2011): 191–212.

Bakhtin, M. M. *The Dialogic Imagination: Four Essays*. Edited by Michael Holquist. Translated by Caryl Emerson. Reprint edition. Austin: University of Texas Press, 1983.

Barisone, Luciano. "Os últimos: Dois filmes de Marília Rocha," N.d. teia.art.br/br/textos.

Barbas-Rhoden, Laura. *Ecological Imaginations in Latin American Fiction*. Gainesville: University of Florida Press, 2011.

Baskin, Jason M. *Modernism beyond the Avant-Garde: Embodying Experience*. Cambridge: Cambridge University Press, 2019.

————. "Soft Eyes: Marxism, Surface, Depth." *Mediations* 28, no. 2 (2015): 5–18.

Beckman, Ericka. *Capital Fictions: The Literature of Latin America's Export Age*. Minneapolis: University of Minnesota Press, 2013.

Benesch, Klaus. "Space, Place, Narrative: Critical Regionalism and the Idea of Home in a Global Age." *Zeitschrift Für Anglistik Und Amerikanistik* 64, no. 1 (2016): 93–108.

Benjamin, Walter. "One-Way Street." In *One-Way Street and Other Writings*, translated by J. A. Underwood, 46–115. London: Penguin, 2008.

————. "Theses on the Philosophy of History." In *Illuminations*, translated by Harry Zohn, 253–64. New York: Schocken, 1968.

————. "The Work of Art in the Age of Mechanical Reproduction." In *Illuminations*, translated by Harry Zohn, 217–51. New York: Schocken, 1968.

Bennett, Jane. *Vibrant Matter: A Political Ecology of Things*. Durham, NC: Duke University Press, 2010.

Berman, Jessica. *Modernist Commitments: Ethics, Politics, and Transnational Modernism*. New York: Columbia University Press, 2012.

Bernstein, J. M. "Negative Dialectic as Fate: Adorno and Hegel." In *The Cambridge Companion to Adorno*, edited by Thomas Huhn. Cambridge: Cambridge University Press, 2004.

Bernucci, Leopoldo M. "Guimarães Rosa para alunos norte-americanos." *Hispania* 91, no. 4 (2008): 744–47.

Bersani, Leo. "I Can Dream, Can't I?" In *Thoughts and Things*, 58–76. Chicago: University of Chicago Press, 2015.

Bhabha, Homi K. *The Location of Culture*. London: Routledge, 1994.

Bieger, Laura. "No Place like Home; or, Dwelling in Narrative." *New Literary History* 46, no. 1 (2015): 17–39.

Bolle, Willi. *Grandesertão.Br: O romance de formação do Brasil*. São Paulo: Livraria Duas Cidades, 2004.

Bourdieu, Pierre. *Outline of a Theory of Practice*. Translated by R. Nice. Cambridge: Cambridge University Press, 1997.

Brito, Herasmo Braga de Oliveira. *Neoregionalismo brasileiro: Análises de uma nova tendência da literatura brasileira*. Teresina, Brazil: Gráfico do Povo, 2017.

Brizuela, Natalia. *Depois da fotografia: Uma literatura fora de si*. Rio de Janeiro: Rocco, 2014.

———. *Fotografia e império: Paisagens para um Brasil moderno*. São Paulo: Companhia das Letras, 2012.

———. "Grete Stern, Horacio Coppola and the Question of Modern Photography in Argentina." *Journal of Latin American Cultural Studies* 24, no. 2 (2015): 243–65.

Brock, Ashley. "Algo Más Que Mirar: More-Than-Looking at Regional Life in Juan José Saer's *El limonero real*." *Revista de Estudios Hispánicos* 52 (2018): 27–49.

———. "The Ethnographic Pastoral Re-Imagined: Embodiment and Inhabitation in *Aboio* and *Sweetgrass*." *Journal of Cinema and Media Studies* (forthcoming).

———. "Lisandro Alonso's *La libertad* and the Objectivist Tradition of Juan José Saer." *FORMA: A Journal of Latin American Criticism & Theory* 3, no. 1 (2023).

———. "The Queer Temporality of *Grande sertão: Veredas*." *Chasqui* 47, no. 2 (2018): 190–203.

———. "Reanimating the Domestic Still Life." *CR: The New Centennial Review* 20, no. 1 (March 1, 2020): 51–74.

Brooks, Peter. *Reading for the Plot: Design and Intention in Narrative*. Cambridge, MA: Harvard University Press, 1992.

Brune, Krista. *Creative Transformations: Travels and Translations of Brazil in the Americas*. Albany: State University of New York Press, 2020.

Bueno, Luís. "O intelectual e o turista: Regionalismo e alteridade na tradição literária." *Revista do Instituto de Estudos Brasileiros*, no. 55 (2012): 111–26.

Butler, Judith. "Values of Difficulty." In *Just Being Difficult? Academic Writing in the Public Arena*, edited by Jonathan Culler and Kevin Lamb, 199–215. Stanford, CA: Stanford University Press, 2003.

Butler, Judith, and Gayatri Chakravorty Spivak. *Who Sings the Nation-State? Language, Politics, Belonging*. London: University of Chicago Press, 2010.

Campa, Román de la. *Latin Americanism*. Minneapolis: University of Minnesota Press, 1999.

Campbell, Neil. *The Rhizomatic West: Representing the American West in a Transnational, Global, Media Age*. Lincoln: University of Nebraska Press, 2008.

Candido, Antonio. *Formação da literatura brasileira (momentos decisivos)*. São Paulo: Editora Itatiaia, 1975.

———. "Literatura e subdesenvolvimento." In *A educação pela noite e outros ensaios*, 10–22. São Paulo: Editora Ática, 1987.

———. "O homem dos avessos." *Coleção Fortuna Crítica* 6 (1987): 294–309.

Carmello, Patricia. *Memória e esquecimento no Grande sertão: Veredas: Travessia e melancolia*. Rio de Janeiro: Viveiros de Castro, 2013.

Castañeda, Jorge. *Utopia Unarmed: The Latin American Left after the Cold War*. New York: Random House, 1993.

Castellanos, Rosario. *Balún-Canán*. Edited by Dara Sales. Madrid: Cátedra, 2004.

Castro-Klaren, Sara. "'Como chancho, cuando piensa': El afecto cognitivo en Arguedas y el con-vertir animal." *Revista Canadiense de Estudios Hispánicos* 26, no. 1/2 (2001/2002): 25–39.

Cepero, Iliana. "Photographic Propaganda under Peronism, 1946–55: Selections from the Archivo General de La Nación Argentina." *History of Photography* 40, no. 2 (2016): 193–214.

Chakrabarty, Dipesh. *Provincializing Europe: Postcolonial Thought and Historical Difference*. Princeton, NJ: Princeton University Press, 2007.

Chaguri, Mariana Miggiolaro. "O norte e o sul: Região e regionalismo em meados do século XX." *Sociologia & Antropologia* 4, no. 1 (2014): 185–206.

Chappuzeau, Bernhard. "La imagen lejana y el impulso de tocarla: La recepción afectiva de *Liverpool* (Lisandro Alonso, 2008) en el extranjero." In *Cine argentino contemporáneo: Visiones y discursos*, edited by Bernhard Chappuzeau and Christian Von Tschlilischke, 263–383. Madrid: Iberoamericana, 2016.

Chiappini, Ligia. "Regionalismo(s) e regionalidade(s) num mundo supostamente global, 21." In *Memórias da borborema 2: Internacionalização do regional*, edited by Diógenes André Vieira Maciel, 21–64. Campina Grande, Brazil: Abralic, 2014.

Cisneros, Odile. "Ecopoesia." Accessed January 6, 2023. https://ecopoesia.com/en/home/about.

Cleary, Joe. *Modernism, Empire, World Literature*. Cambridge: Cambridge University Press, 2021.

Clifford, James. "On Ethnographic Allegory." In *Writing Culture: The Poetics and Politics of Ethnography*, edited by James Clifford and George E. Marcus, 98–121. Berkeley: University of California Press, 1986.

Cohen Imach, Victoria. *De utopías y desencantos. Campo intelectual y periferia en la Argentina de los sesenta*. Tucumán, Argentina: Universidad Nacional de Tucumán, Facultad de Filosofía y Letras, Instituto Interdisciplinario de Estudios Latinoamericanos, 1994.

Collot, Michel. "Du sens de l'espace à l'espace du sens." In *Espace et poésie*, edited by Michel Collot and Jean-Claude Mathieu. Paris: Presse de l'École Normale Supérieure, 1987.

Comer, Krista. "Exceptionalism, Other Wests, Critical Regionalism." *American Literary History* 23, no. 1 (2011): 159–73.

Cornejo Polar, Antonio. "Mestizaje e hibridez: Los riesgos de las metáforas. Apuntes." *Revista Iberoamericana* 63, no. 200 (2002): 867–70.

———. *Writing in the Air: Heterogeneity and the Persistence of Oral Tradition in Andean Literatures*. Translated by Lynda J. Jentsch. Durham, NC: Duke University Press, 2013.

Cosgrove, Denis. "Prospect, Perspective and the Evolution of the Landscape Idea." *Transactions of the Institute of British Geographers* 10, no. 1 (1985): 19.

Cunha, Euclides da. *Os sertões*. São Paulo: Brasiliense, 1985.

Daly, Tara. *Beyond Human: Vital Materialisms in the Andean Avant-Gardes*. Lewisburg, PA: Bucknell University Press, 2019.

Damrosch, David. *What Is World Literature?* Princeton, NJ: Princeton University Press, 2003.

Dantas Lima, Deise. *Encenações do Brasil rural em Guimarães Rosa*. Niterói, Brazil: Editora da Universidade Federal Fluminense, 2001.

Davis, Duane H. "The Phenomenological Method." In *50 Concepts for a Critical Phenomenology*, 3–9. Evanston, IL: Northwestern University Press, 2020.

de Certeau, Michel. *The Practices of Everyday Life*. Translated by Steven Rendall. Berkeley: University of California Press, 1984.

DeLoughrey, Elizabeth, and George B. Handley, eds., *Postcolonial Ecologies: Literatures of the Environment*. Oxford: Oxford University Press, 2011.

de Luca, Tiago. *Realism of the Senses in World Cinema: The Experience of Physical Reality*. London: I. B. Tauris, 2014.

de Luca, Tiago, and Nuno Barradas Jorge. *Slow Cinema*. Edinburgh: Edinburgh University Press, 2016.

DeLue, Rachael Ziady, and James Elkins, eds. *Landscape Theory*. Vol. 6, *The Art Seminar*. New York: Routledge, 2007.

Demaría, Laura. *Buenos Aires y las provincias: Relatos para desarmar*. Rosario, Argentina: Beatriz Viterbo, 2014.

Di Stefano, Eugenio Claudio. *The Vanishing Frame: Latin American Culture and Theory in the Postdictatorial Era*. Austin: University of Texas Press, 2018.

Dym, Jordana, and Karl Offen, eds. *Mapping Latin America: A Cartographic Reader*. Chicago: University of Chicago Press, 2011.

Elder, John. *Ecopoetry: A Critical Introduction*. Edited by J. Scott Bryson. Salt Lake City: University of Utah Press, 2002.

Encina, Paz, dir. *Ejercicios de memoria*. 2016; Constanza Sanz Palacios Films, Silencia Cine, MPM Film, Autentica Films, and Torch Films.

———. *Hamaca paraguaya*. 2006; Wanda Distribución de Films.

Fabian, Johannes. *Time and the Other: How Anthropology Makes Its Object*. New York: Columbia University Press, 2006.

Fantini Scarpelli, Marli. "Diálogos iberoamericanos: *Grande sertão: Veredas* entre regionalismo e vanguarda." *Revista Brasileira de Literatura Comparada* 33 (2018): 110–29.

———. *Guimarães Rosa: Fronteiras, margens, passagens*. São Paulo: Senac and Ateliê, 2004.

Ferraz Infante, Joyce Rodrigues. "Revisitando o tema da donzela-guerreira em *Grande sertão: Veredas*." In *João Guimarães Rosa: Um exiliado do linguagem comum*. Salamanca, Spain: Universidad de Salamanca, 2017.

Finazzi-Agrò, Ettore. *Um lugar do tamanho do mundo: Tempos e espaços da ficção em João Guimarães Rosa*. Belo Horizonte, Brazil: UFMG, 2001.

Foucault, Michel. *The Order of Things: An Archeology of the Human Sciences*. New York: Vintage Books, 1994.

Frampton, Kenneth. "Towards a Critical Regionalism: Six Points for an Architecture of Resistance." In *The Anti-Aesthetic*, edited by Hal Foster, 17–34. Seattle: Bay Press, 1983.

Franco, Jean. *The Decline and Fall of the Lettered City: Latin America and the Cold War*. Cambridge, MA: Harvard University Press, 2002.

French, Jennifer. *Nature, Neo-Colonialism, and the Spanish American Regional Writers*. Hanover, NH: Dartmouth College Press, 2005.

Freyre, Gilberto. *Manifesto regionalista*. Recife, Brazil: Fundação Joaquim Nabuco, 1996.

Friedman, Thomas L. *The World Is Flat: A Brief History of the Twenty-First Century*. New York: Farrar, Straus and Giroux, 2005.

Frizzi, Adria. "The Demonic Texture: Deferral and Plurality in 'Grande sertão: Veredas.'" *Chasqui* 17, no. 1 (1988): 25–29.

Gabara, Esther. *Errant Modernism: The Ethos of Photography in Mexico and Brazil*. Durham, NC: Duke University Press, 2008.

Galvão, Walnice Nogueira. "'O certo no incerto: O pactário.'" *Coleção Fortuna Crítica* 6 (1987): 408–21.

———. "Rapsodo do sertão: Da lexicogênese à mitopoese." *Cadernos de Literatura Brasileira* 20–21 (2006).

———. "Rebellion in the Backlands: Landscape with Figures." Translated by Paulo Henriques Britto. *ABEI (The Brazilian Journal of Irish Studies)* 12 (2010): 91–97.

Gandesha, Samir. "Leaving Home: On Adorno and Heidegger." In *The Cambridge Companion to Adorno*, edited by Thomas Huhn, 101–28. Cambridge: Cambridge University Press, 2004.

Garramuño, Florencia. *Frutos estranhos: Sobre a inespecificidade na estética contemporânea*. Edited by Paloma Vidal. Translated by Carlos Nougué. Rio de Janeiro: Rocco, 2014.

———. *La experiencia opaca: Literatura y desencanto*. Buenos Aires: Tierra Firme, 2009.

Glissant, Édouard. *Poetics of Relation*. Translated by Betsy Wing. Ann Arbor: University of Michigan Press, 1997.

Gómez-Barris, Macarena. *The Extractive Zone: Social Ecologies and Decolonial Perspectives*. Durham, NC: Duke University Press, 2017.

Gonzáles, José Eduardo. *Appropriating Theory: Ángel Rama's Critical Work*. Pittsburgh: University of Pittsburgh Press, 2017.

Gramuglio, María Teresa. "Juan José Saer: El arte de narrar." *Punto de Vista* 2, no. 6 (1979): 3.

———. *Juan José Saer por Juan José Saer*. Buenos Aires: Celtia, 1986.

———. "Un postmodernismo crítico." *Punto de Vista* 15, no. 42 (1992): 27.

Guenther, Lisa. "Critical Phenomenology." In *50 Concepts for a Critical Phenomenology*, 11–16. Evanston, IL: Northwestern University Press, 2020.

Guimarães Rosa, João. "A terceira margem do rio." In *Primeiras estórias*. Rio de Janeiro: José Olympio, 1967.

———. *The Devil to Pay in the Backlands*. Translated by James L. Taylor and Harriet de Onís. New York: Alfred A. Knopf, 1963.

———. *Gran sertón: Veredas*. Translated by Florencia Garramuño and Gonzalo Aguilar. Córdoba, Argentina: Adriana Hidalgo, 2009.

———. *Grande sertão: Veredas*. Rio de Janeiro: Nova Fronteira, 2014.

Güiraldes, Ricardo. *Don Segundo Sombra*. Buenos Aires: Emecé Editores, 2000.

Hale, Dorothy J. "Aesthetics and the New Ethics: Theorizing the Novel in the Twenty-First Century." *PMLA* 124, no. 3 (2009): 896–905.

Hansen, João Adolfo. *O o: A ficção da literatura em Grande sertão: Veredas*. São Paulo: Hedra, 2000. https://doi.org/catalog.hathitrust.org/Record/101022318.

Haraway, Donna Jeanne. "Situated Knowledges: The Science Question in Feminism and the Privilege of Partial Perspective." *Feminist Studies* 14, no. 3 (1988): 575–99.

Hayot, Eric, and Rebecca Walkowitz, eds. *A New Vocabulary for Global Modernism.* New York: Columbia University Press, 2016.

Heffes, Gisela. *Políticas de la destrucción—poéticas de la preservación: Apuntes para una lectura eco-crítica del medio ambiente en América Latina.* Rosario, Argentina: Beatriz Viterbo, 2013.

Heidegger, Martin. "Building, Dwelling, Thinking." In *Poetry, Language, Thought,* translated by Albert Hofstadter, 143–62. New York: Harper Colophon, 1971.

———. "Introduction to 'Building, Dwelling, Thinking.'" In *Basic Writings,* edited by David Farrell Krell, 319–22. New York: Harper & Row, 1977.

———. "Poetically Man Dwells." In *Poetry, Language, Thought,* translated by Albert Hofstadter, 211–229. New York: Harper & Row, 1971.

Heise, Ursula K. *Sense of Place and Sense of Planet: The Environmental Imagination of the Global.* Oxford: Oxford University Press, 2008.

Heredia, Pablo. *El suelo: Ensayos sobre regionalismos y nacionalismos en la literatura argentina.* Córdoba, Argentina: Editorial Facultad de Filosofía y Humanidades Universidad Nacional de Córdoba / Universitas, 2005.

———. *El texto literario y los discursos regionales: Propuestas para una regionalización de la narrativa argentina contemporánea.* Córdoba, Argentina: Ediciones Argos, 1994.

Herr, Cheryl Temple. *Critical Regionalism and Cultural Studies: From Ireland to the American Midwest.* Gainesville: University Press of Florida, 1996.

hooks, bell. *Belonging: A Culture of Place.* New York: Routledge, 2009.

Hoyos, Héctor. *Beyond Bolaño: The Global Latin American Novel.* New York: Columbia University Press, 2015.

———. *Things with a History: Transcultural Materialism and the Literatures of Extraction in Contemporary Latin America.* New York: Columbia University Press, 2019.

Hume, Angela, and Gillian Osborne, eds. *Ecopoetics: Essays in the Field.* Iowa City: University of Iowa Press, 2018.

I'll Take My Stand: The South and the Agrarian Tradition. New York: Harper & Brothers, 1930.

Ingold, Tim. *The Perception of the Environment: Essays on Livelihood Dwelling and Skill.* London: Routledge, 2000.

———. "The Temporality of the Landscape." *World Archeology* 25 (1993): 152–74.

Iser, Wolfgang. "The Reading Process: A Phenomenological Approach," in *The Implied Reader,* 274–94. Baltimore: Johns Hopkins University Press, 1974.

Jameson, Fredric. *The Modernist Papers.* London: Verso, 2016.

———. *The Seeds of Time.* New York: Columbia University Press, 1994.

———. *A Singular Modernity: Essay on the Ontology of the Present.* London: Verso, 2002.

Jasanoff, Sheila, and Marybeth Long Martello, eds. *Earthly Politics: Local and Global in Environmental Governance.* Cambridge, MA: MIT Press, 2004.

Jay, Martin. *Downcast Eyes: The Denigration of Vision in Twentieth-Century French Thought*. Berkeley: University of California Press, 1993.

———. *Songs of Experience*. Berkeley: University of California Press, 2005.

Jitrik, Noé. "Entre el corte y la continuidad: Hacia una escritura crítica." *Revista Iberoamericana* 68, no. 200 (2002): 729–36.

———. "La extensión." *Revista del Centro de Letras Hispanoamericanas* 24, no. 29 (2015): 19–35.

Kalimán, Ricardo J. "Un marco (no 'global') para el estudio de las regiones culturales." *Journal of Iberian and Latin American Research* 5, no. 2 (1999): 11–22.

Kampff Lages, Susana. *João Guimarães Rosa e a saudade*. São Paulo: Ateliê, 2002.

Kopenawa, Davi, and Bruce Albert. *The Falling Sky: Words of a Yanomami Shaman*. Translated by Nicolas Elliot and Alison Dundy. Cambridge, MA: Belknap Press of Harvard University Press, 2013.

Langer, Erick D. "Periodos y regiones: Una perspectiva histórica." In *Memorias de JALLA Tucumán 1995*, 210–22. Tucumán, Argentina: Proyecto "Tucumán en el contexto de los Andes centromeridionales," Instituto de Historia y Pensamiento Argentinos de la Facultad de Filosofía y Letras de la Universidad Nacional de Tucumán, 1997.

Laurent, Pénélope. "Melancolía de lo sagrado en la obra de Juan José Saer." *Revista Iberoamericana* 84, no. 263 (2018): 439–54.

Lefebvre, Henri. *The Production of Space*. Translated by Donald Nicholson-Smith. Oxford: Blackwell Publishing, 1984.

Lévi-Strauss, Claude. *Tristes Tropiques*. Translated by John Weightman. New York: Penguin, 2012.

Librandi, Marília. "Multiple Rumors: Recado and Conconversa in João Guimarães Rosa's Fiction." *Luso-Brazilian Review* 53, no. 2 (2016): 62–83.

———. "Sertão, City, Saudade." In *The New Ruralism: An Epistemology of Transformed Space*, edited by Joan Ramon Resina and William Viestenz, 61–75. Madrid and Frankfurt: Iberoamericana and Vervuert, 2012.

———. *Writing by Ear: Clarice Lispector and the Aural Novel*. Toronto: University of Toronto Press, 2018.

Lienhard, Martin. *Cultura andina y forma novelesca: Zorros y danzantes en la última novela de Arguedas*. Lima, Peru: Editorial Horizonte, 1990.

Lima, Gabriel dos Santos. "A teoria desenvolvimentista do 'super-regionalismo' em Antonio Candido e o Caso Arguedas." *Criação & Crítica* 26 (2020): 40–54.

Limón, José E. "Border Literary Histories, Globalization, and Critical Regionalism." *American Literary History* 20, no. 102 (2008): 160–82.

Llano, Aymará de. "Crisis de lectura en el lector hispano: El caso Arguedas." In *Memorias de JALLA Tucumán 1995*, 1:559–65. Tucumán, Argentina: Proyecto "Tucumán en el Contexto de Los Andes Centromeridionales," Instituto de Historia y Pensamiento Argentinos de la Facultad de Filosofía y Letras de la Universidad Nacional de Tucumán, 1997.

Lorenz, Günter. "Diálogo com Guimarães Rosa." *Coleção Fortuna Crítica* 6 (1987): 62–97.

Lubrich, Oliver. "Humboltian Landscapes." In *Natura: Environmental Aesthetics after Landscape*, edited by Jens Andermann, Lisa Blackmore, and Dayron Carillo Morell, 73–110. Zurich: Diaphnes, 2018.

Lucero, Nicolás. *La vuelta incompleta: Saer y la novela*. Buenos Aires: Santiago Arcos, 2017.

Lukács, Georg. "Narrate or Describe." In *Writer and Critic and Other Essays*, translated by Arthur Kahn, 110–48. London: Merlin Press, 1970.

MacDonald, Scott. *The Garden in the Machine: A Field Guide to Independent Films about Place*. Berkeley: University of California Press, 2001.

Machado de Oliveira Jr., Wenceslao. "Lugares geográficos e(m) locais narrativos: Um modo de se aproximar das geografias de cinema." In *Qual o espaço do lugar? Geografia, epistemologia, fenomenologia*, 119–54. São Paulo: Perspectiva, 2012.

Mariátegui, José Carlos. *Siete ensayos de interpretación de la realidad peruana*. Havana: Casa de las Américas, 1973.

Marks, Laura U. *The Skin of the Film: Intercultural Cinema, Embodiment, and the Senses*. Durham, NC: Duke University Press, 2000.

Martí, José. *Nuestra América*. Jalisco, Mexico: Universidad de Guadalajara, 2002.

Martínez Estrada, Ezequiel. *Radiografía de la pampa*. Paris: Archivos, 1991.

Martins Costa, Ana Luisa. "Diadorim, delicado e terrível." *Scripta* 5, no. 10 (2002): 38–52.

Masiello, Francine R. *El cuerpo de la voz (poesía, ética y cultura)*. Rosario, Argentina: Beatriz Viterbo, 2013.

———. *The Senses of Democracy: Perception, Politics, and Culture in Latin America*. Austin: University of Texas Press, 2018.

McGlazer, Ramsey. *Old Schools: Modernism, Education, and the Critique of Progress*. New York: Fordham University Press, 2020.

Merleau-Ponty, Maurice. *The Phenomenology of Perception*. Translated by Colin Smith. London: Routledge, 2002.

———. *The Visible and the Invisible*. Edited by Claude Lefort. Translated by Alphonso Lingis. Evanston, IL: Northwestern University Press, 1968.

Mignolo, Walter. "Posoccidentalismo: El argumento desde América Latina." In *Teorías sin disciplina (latinoamericanismo, poscolonialidad y globalización en debate)*, edited by Santiago Castro-Gómez and Eduardo Mendieta. Mexico City: Miguel Ángel Porrúa, 1998.

Mignolo, Walter D., and Catherine E. Walsh. *On Decoloniality: Concepts, Analytics, Praxis*. Durham, NC: Duke University Press, 2018.

Mirsepassi, Ali, Amrita Basu, and Frederick Stirton Weaver, eds. *Localizing Knowledge in a Globalizing World: Recasting the Area Studies Debate*. Syracuse, NY: Syracuse University Press, 2003.

Mitchell, W. J. T., ed. *Landscape and Power*. Chicago: University of Chicago Press, 1994.

Molina, Hebe Beatriz, and María Lorena Burlot. "El regionalismo como problema conceptual." In *Regionalismo literario: Historia y crítica de un concepto problemático*, edited by Hebe Beatriz Molina and Fabiana Inés Varela, 11–46. Mendoza, Argentina: Biblioteca Digital de la Universidad Nacional de Cuyo, 2018.

Molloy, Sylvia. "A modo de introducción. Back home: Un posible comienzo." In *Poéticas de la distancia: Adentro y afuera de la literatura argentina*, edited by Sylvia Molloy and Mariano Siskind, 15–23. Buenos Aires: Grupo Editorial Norma, 2006.

Montaldo, Graciela. *De pronto, el campo: Literatura argentina y tradición rural*. Rosario, Argentina: Beatriz Viterbo, 1993.

———. *Juan José Saer: El limonero real*. Buenos Aires: Hachete, 1986.

Montauban, Jannine. "El olfato como forma de conocimiento." In *Un universo encrespado: Cincuenta años de El zorro de arriba y el zorro de abajo*, edited by Enrique E. Cortez, 123–39. Lima, Peru: Editorial Horizonte, 2021.

Montoya Rojas, Rodrigo, ed. *100 años del Perú y de José María Arguedas*. Lima, Peru: Editorial Universitaria, 2011.

Moraes Leonel, Maria Cecilia de. "Imagens de animais no sertão rosiano." *Scripta* 6, no. 10 (2002): 286–98.

Moraña, Mabel. "Territorialidad y foresterismo: La polémica Arguedas/Cortázar revisitada." In *María Arguedas: Hacia una poética migrante*, edited by Sergio R. Franco, 103–20. Pittsburgh: Instituto Internacional de Literatura Iberoamericana and Pittsburgh University Press, 2006.

Moreira, Paulo. *Modernismo localista das Américas: Os contos de Faulkner, Guimarães Rosa, e Rulfo*. Belo Horizonte, Brazil: Editora UFMG, 2012.

Moreiras, Alberto. *The Exhaustion of Difference: The Politics of Latin American Cultural Studies*. Durham, NC: Duke University Press, 2001.

———. "Fragmentos globales: Latinoamericanismo de segundo orden." In *Teorías sin disciplina (latinoamericanismo, poscolonialidad y globalización en debate)*, edited by Santiago Castro-Gómez and Eduardo Mendieta. Mexico City: Miguel Ángel Porrúa, 1998.

———. *Tercer espacio: Literatura y duelo en América Latina*. Santiago, Chile: Universidad Arcis, 1999.

Nancy, Jean-Luc. *Listening*. Translated by Charlotte Mandell. Annotated edition. New York: Fordham University Press, 2007.

Newcomb, Robert Patrick. *Nossa and Nuestra América: Inter-American Dialogues*. West Lafayette, IN: Purdue University Press, 2012.

Nielson, Rex P. "The Unmappable Sertão." *Portuguese Studies* 30, no. 1 (2014): 5–20.

Nitschack, Horst. "La refiguración latinoamericana de la bildungsroman: Ernesto Sabato y António Callado." In *Historia comparada de las literaturas argentina y brasileña. Tomo V: Del desarrollismo a la dictadura, entre privatización, boom y militanica (1955–1970)*, edited by Marcela Croce, 179–99. Villa María, Argentina: Editorial Universitaria Villa María, 2018.

Nixon, Rob. "Environmentalism and Postcolonialism." In *Postcolonial Studies and Beyond*, edited by Ania Loomba, Kaul Survir, Matt Bunzl, Antoinette Burton, and Jed Etsy, 233–51. Durham, NC: Duke University Press, 2005.

Nouzeilles, Gabriela. "The Iconography of Desolation: Patagonia and the Ruins of Nature." *Review: Literature and Arts of the Americas* 40, no. 2 (2007): 252–62.

Novaes, Cláudio Cledson. "Euclides Da Cunha e 'o sertão vai virar mar.'" *O Eixo e a Roda: Revista de Literatura Brasileira* 8 (2002): 65–79.

Ocampo, Catalina. "La agonía de José María Arguedas y la palabra trágica." In *José María Arguedas: Hacia una poética migrante*, edited by Sergio R. Franco, 121–42. Pittsburgh: Instituto Internacional de Literatura Iberoamericana and Pittsburgh University Press, 2006.

Olímpio, Domingos. *Luzia-Homem*. Rio de Janeiro: VirtualBooks, 2017.

Ortega, Julio. "Itinerario de José María Arguedas: Migración, peregrinaje y lenguaje en *El zorro de arriba y el zorro de abajo*." In *José María Arguedas: Hacia una poética migrante*, edited by Sergio R. Franco, 81–102. Pittsburgh: Instituto Internacional de Literatura Iberoamericana, 2006.

Oubiña, David. *El silencio y sus bordes*. Buenos Aires: Tierra Firme, 2011.

Padrón, Ricardo. *The Spacious Word: Cartography, Literature, and Empire in Early Modern Spain*. Chicago: University of Chicago Press, 2004.

Pantigoso, Eduardo J. "La rebelión contra el indigenismo y la afirmación del pueblo en el mundo de José María Arguedas." *Chasqui* 12, no. 1 (1982): 82–85.

Paranaguá, Paulo Antonio. "Aboio: Marília Rocha, Brasil, 2005," n.d., teia.art.br/br/textos.

Patruno, Luigi. *Relatos de regreso: Ensayos sobre la obra de Juan José Saer*. Rosario, Argentina: Beatriz Viterbo, 2015.

Pedwell, C. *Affective Relations: The Transnational Politics of Empathy*. New York: Palgrave Macmillan, 2014.

Pelinser, André Tessaro, and Márcio Miranda Alves. "A permanência do regionalismo na literatura brasileira contemporânea." *Estudos de Literatura Brasileira Contemporânea*, no. 59 (January 24, 2020): 1–13. https://doi.org/10.1590/2316–4018593.

Penhos, Marta. *Ver, conocer, dominar: Imágenes de sudamérica a fines del siglo XVIII*. Buenos Aires: Siglo Veintiuno, 2005.

Penjon, Jacqueline. "The Reception of João Guimarães Rosa in France." In *Studies in the Literary Achievement of João Guimarães Rosa: The Foremost Brazilian Writer of the Twentieth Century*, edited by Ligia Chiappini, Marcel Vejmelka, and David Treece, 110–24. New York: Edwin Mellen Press, 2012.

Pérez Trujillo Diniz, Axel. *Imagining the Plains of Latin America: An Ecocritical Study*. London: Bloomsbury Academic, 2021.

Plumwood, Val. *Environmental Culture: The Ecological Crisis of Reason*. London: Routledge, 2002.

Policsek, Cecilia. "The Poetics of Negativity as a Form of Seeing Literature: *The Witness*." *Neophilogus* 97, no. 1 (2013): 1–8.

Powell, Douglas Reichert. *Critical Regionalism: Connecting Politics and Culture in the American Landscape*. Chapel Hill: University of North Carolina Press, 2007.

Pratt, Mary Louise. "Arts of the Contact Zone." *Profession (Modern Language Association)*, 1991, 33–44.

———. *Imperial Eyes: Travel Writing and Transculturation*. New York: Routledge, 2008.

———. *Planetary Longings*. Durham, NC: Duke University Press 2022.

Prazniak, Roxann, and Arif Dirlik, eds. *Places and Politics in an Age of Globalization*. Lanham, MD: Rowman & Littlefield, 2001.

Premat, Julio. "El cataclismo de los orígenes: La pampa histórica de Juan José Saer." *Cambio y Permanencia en las Culturas del Río de la Plata* 17–18 (1997): 689–700.

———. *Héroe sin atributos: Figuras de autor en la literatura argentina*. Buenos Aires: Tierra Firme, 2009.

———. *La dicha de Saturno: Escritura y melancolía en la obra de Juan José Saer*. Rosario, Argentina: Beatriz Viterbo, 2002.

Prieto, Adolfo. *Los viajeros ingleses y la emergencia de la literatura argentina (1820–1850)*. Buenos Aires: Sudamérica, 1996.

Prieto, Julio. *La escritura errante: Ilegibilidad y políticas del estilo en Latinoamérica*. Madrid and Frankfurt: Iberoamericana and Vervuert, 2016.

Rama, Ángel. "El 'boom' en perspectiva." In *Más allá del boom: Literatura y mercado*, edited by David Viñas, 51–129. Mexico City: Marcha, 1981.

———. "La literatura hispanoamericana en la era de las máquinas." *Revista de la Universidad Nacional Autónoma de México* 26, no. 6–7 (1972): 15–18.

———. *La transculturación narrativa en América Latina*. Buenos Aires: El Andariego, 2008.

———. *Writing across Cultures: Narrative Transculturation in Latin America*. Translated by David Freye. Durham, NC: Duke University Press, 2012.

Ramos, Graciliano. *Vidas secas*. Rio de Janeiro: Editora Record, 1989.

Rancière, Jacques. *The Politics of Aesthetics: The Distribution of the Sensible*. Translated by Gabriel Rockhill. London: Bloomsbury Academic, 2004.

Reynolds, Andrew. *Behind the Masks of Modernism: Global and Transnational Perspectives*. Gainesville: University of Florida Press, 2016.

Richard, Nelly. "Intersectando Latinoamérica con el latinoamericanismo: Saberes académicos, práctica teórica y crítica cultural." *Revista Iberoamericana* 63, no. 180 (1997): 345–61.

Ricoeur, Paul. "Universal Civilizations and National Cultures." In *History and Truth*, 271–85. Evanston, IL: Northwestern University Press, 1965.

Rivera Cusicanqui, Silvia. *Sociología de la imagen: Miradas ch'ixi desde la historia andina*. Buenos Aires: Tinta Limón, 2015.

Rivera, Fernando. *Dar la palabra: Ética, política y poética de la escritura en Arguedas*. Madrid and Frankfurt: Iberoamericana and Vervuert, 2011.

Robinson, Dylan. *Hungry Listening: Resonant Theory for Indigenous Sound Studies*. Minneapolis: University of Minnesota Press, 2020.

Rocha, Glauber, dir. *Deus e o diabo na terra do sol*. Brighton, UK: Mr. Bongo Films, 1964.

Rocha, Marília, dir. *Aboio*. TEIA, 2005.

Rogers, Charlotte. *Mourning El Dorado: Literature and Extractivism in the Contemporary American Tropics*. Charlottesville: University of Virginia Press, 2019.

Rooney, Ellen. "Form and Contentment." *Modern Language Quarterly* 61, no. 1 (March 2000): 17–40.

Rosenberg, Fernando J. *The Avant-Garde and Geopolitics in Latin America.* Pittsburgh: University of Pittsburgh Press, 2006.

Rosenfield, Kathrin H. "Devil to Pay in the Backlands and João Guimarães Rosas's Quest for Universality." *Portuguese Literary and Cultural Studies* 4/5 (2000): 197–205.

Rouillón, José Luis. "La luz que nadie apagará: Aproximaciones al mito y al cristianismo en el último Arguedas." In *El zorro de arriba y el zorro de abajo*, edited by Eve Marie Fell, 341–59. Madrid: CISIC, 1990.

Rowe, William. "El nuevo lenguaje de Arguedas en *El zorro de arriba y el zorro de abajo*." *Texto Crítico*, no. 11 (1978): 198–212.

———. *Ensayos arguedianos.* Edited by Maruja Martínez. Lima, Peru: Centro de Producción Editorial de la Universidad Nacional Mayor de San Marcos, 1996.

———. "'No hay mensajero de nada': La modernidad andina según los zorros de Arguedas." *Revista de Crítica Literaria Latinoamericana* 36, no. 72 (2010): 61–96.

———. "Reading Arguedas's Foxes." In *The Fox from Up Above and the Fox from Down Below*, edited by Julio Ortega, 283–89. Pittsburgh: University of Pittsburgh Press and Colección Archivos, 2000.

Rowland, Clara. *A forma do meio.* São Paulo: Editora da Universidade de São Paulo, 2011.

Rulfo, Juan. *Pedro Páramo.* Madrid: Cátedra, 1983.

Saer, Juan José. *El arte de narrar.* Buenos Aires: Seix Barral, 2011.

———. *El concepto de ficción.* Mexico City: Universidad Iberoamericana, 1997.

———. *El entenado.* Buenos Aires: Seix Barral, 2012.

———. *El limonero real.* Buenos Aires: Seix Barral, 2010.

———. *El río sin orillas.* Madrid: Alianza, 1991.

———. "Experiencia y lenguaje II: Dos ensayos de Juan José Saer." *Punto de Vista* 18, no. 51 (1995).

———. "Juan." In *Juan L. Ortiz: Obra completa*, 11–14. Santa Fe, Argentina: Universidad Nacional del Litoral, 1996.

———. "La cuestión de la prosa." In *La narración objeto*, 55–61. Buenos Aires: Seix Barral, 1999.

———. *La mayor.* Buenos Aires: Seix Barral, 2005.

———. *La ocasión.* Barcelona: Destino, 1988.

———. *Lo imborrable.* Madrid: Alianza, 1993.

———. *Nadie nada nunca.* Buenos Aires: Seix Barral, 1994.

———. *Notebook*, n.d. Princeton University Library.

———. *Papeles de trabajo: Borradores inéditos.* Edited by Julio Premat. Buenos Aires: Seix Barral, 2012.

———. "Razones." In *Juan José Saer por Juan José Saer*, edited by María Teresa Gramuglio. 9–24. Buenos Aires: Celtia, 1986.

———. "Sartre: Contra entusiastas y detractores." *Punto de Vista* 3, no. 9 (1980).

———. *Trabajos.* Buenos Aires: Seix Barral, 2006.

Saer, Juan José, and Ricardo Piglia. *Diálogo.* Santa Fe, Argentina: Universidad Nacional del Litoral, 1990.

Said, Edward W. *Orientalism*. New York: Vintage, 2014.

Sales, Dara. "Introducción: José María Arguedas, Wiñaq." In *José María Arguedas: Quepa Wiñaq . . . siempre literatura y antropología*, 11–55. Madrid and Frankfurt: Iberoamericana and Vervuert, 2009.

Santiago, Silviano. *Genealogía de la ferocidad: Ensayo sobre Gran sertón: Veredas, de Guimarães Rosa*. Translated by Mary Luz Estupiñán. Santiago, Chile: Mimesis, 2018.

———. *The Space In-Between: Essays on Latin American Culture*. Translated by Ana Lúcia Gazzola. Durham, NC: Duke University Press, 2001.

Saramago, Victoria. "Birds, Rivers, Book: Material Mimesis in João Guimarães Rosa's *Grande sertão: Veredas*." *Luso-Brazilian Review* 57, no. 1 (2020): 125–49.

———. *Fictional Environments: Mimesis, Deforestation, and Development in Latin America*. Evanston, IL: Northwestern University Press, 2020.

———. "'Sertão Dentro': The Backlands in Early Modern Portuguese Writings." *Portuguese Literary and Cultural Studies* 27 (2015): 254–72.

Sarlo, Beatriz. "Aventuras de un médico filósofo." In *Escritos sobre literatura argentina*, 304–5. Buenos Aires: Siglo Veintiuno, 2007.

———. "El saber del texto." *Punto de Vista* 9, no. 26 (1986): 6–7.

———. "La condición mortal." In *Escritos sobre literatura argentina*, 289–95. Buenos Aires: Siglo Veintiuno, 2007.

———. "La política, la devastación." In *Glosa y El entenado: Edición crítica*. Ed. Julio Premat, 762–78. Paris: Archivos, 2010.

———. "Narrar la percepción." In *Escritos sobre literatura argentina*, 281–85. Buenos Aires: Siglo Veintiuno, 2007.

———. "Una mirada política: Defensa del partidismo en el arte." *Punto de Vista* 3, no. 8 (1985): 1–4.

Sarmiento, Domingo F. *Facundo: Civilización y barbarie*. Madrid: Cátedra, 2001.

Serafini, Paula. *Creating Worlds Otherwise: Art, Collective Action, and (Post) Extractivism*. Nashville, TN: Vanderbilt University Press, 2022.

Schmidt-Welle, Friedhelm. "Regionalismo abstracto y representación simbólica de la nación en la literatura latinoamericana de la región." *Relaciones* 130 (2012): 115–27.

Shellhorse, Adam Joseph. *Anti-Literature: The Politics and Limits of Representation in Modern Brazil and Argentina*. Pittsburgh: University of Pittsburgh Press, 2017.

Silvestri, Graciela. *El lugar común: Una historia de las figuras de paisaje en el Río de la Plata*. Buenos Aires: Edhasa, 2011.

Siskind, Mariano. *Cosmopolitan Desires: Global Modernity and World Literature in Latin America*. Evanston, IL: Northwestern University Press, 2014.

———. "The Globalization of the Novel and the Novelization of the Global: A Critique of World Literature." *Comparative Literature* 62, no. 4 (2010): 336–60.

Smith, Neil. *Uneven Development: Nature, Capital, and the Production of Space*. Athens: University of Georgia Press, 2008.

Smith, Amanda M. *Mapping the Amazon: Literary Geography after the Rubber Boom*. Liverpool: Liverpool University Press, 2021.

Sommer, Doris. "Slaps and Embraces: A Rhetoric of Particularism." In *The Latin American Subaltern Studies Reader*, edited by Ileana Rodríguez. 175–90. Durham, NC: Duke University Press, 2001.

Sontag, Susan. "Against Interpretation." In *Essays of the 1960's & 70's*, edited by David Rieff, 10–20. New York: Library of the Americas, 2013.

Spirn, Anne Whiston. *The Language of the Landscape*. New Haven, CT: Yale University Press, 1998.

Spitta, Silvia. "Traición y transculturación: Los desgarramientos del pensamiento latinoamericano." In *Ángel Rama y los estudios latinoamericanos*, edited by Mabel Moraña, 173–92. Pittsburgh: Instituto Internacional de Literatura Iberoamericana, 1997.

Spivak, Gayatri Chakravorty. *An Aesthetic Education in the Era of Globalization*. Cambridge, MA: Harvard University Press, 2013.

———. *Death of a Discipline*. New York: Columbia University Press, 2005.

Stern, Marta. "Introduction." In *El limonero real*, by Juan José Saer. Buenos Aires: Centro Editor de América Latina, 1981.

Sullivan, Shannon. "Introduction: Doing Philosophy from Southern Standpoints," in *Thinking the US South: Contemporary Philosophy from Southern Perspectives*, edited by Shannon Sullivan, 1–13. Evanston, IL: Northwestern University Press, 2021.

Tanglen, Randi Lynn. "Critical Regionalism, the US-Mexican War, and Nineteenth-Century American Literary History." *Western American Literature* 48, no. 1 (2013): 180–99.

Tarica, Estelle. *The Inner Life of Mestizo Nationalism*. Minneapolis: University of Minnesota Press, 2008.

Terán, Oscar. *Nuestros años sesentas: La formación de la nueva izquierda intelectual argentina, 1956–1966*. Buenos Aires: Siglo Veintiuno, 2013.

Treece, David. "Translating Guimarães Rosa into English." In *Studies in the Literary Achievement of João Guimarães Rosa: The Foremost Brazilian Writer of the Twentieth Century*, edited by Ligia Chiappini, Marcel Vejmelka, and David Treece, 31–48. New Haven, CT: Edwin Mellen Press, 2012.

Tsing, Anna Lowenhaupt. *Friction: An Ethnography of Global Connection*. Princeton, NJ: Princeton University Press, 2005.

Vargas Llosa, Mario. "José María Arguedas: Entre ideología y la arcadia." *Revista Iberoamericana* 47 (1981): 33–46.

———. "Primitives and Creators." *Times Literary Supplement* 3481 (1968): 1287–88.

Vicuña, Cecilia, dir. *Kon Kon.* 2010; Estudio Flotantes Chimuchina Records, Las Canteras.

Viñas, David. "Pareceres y digresiones en torno a la nueva narrativa latinoamericana." In *Más allá del boom: Literatura y mercado*, edited by David Viñas, 13–50. Mexico City: Marcha, 1981.

Vizcaíno-Alemán, Melina. "What's So Critical about Critical Regionalism? The Case of Fray Angélico Chávez's New Mexico Triptych." *Western American Literature* 49, no. 2 (2011): 199–222.

Wenzel, Jennifer. *The Disposition of Nature*. New York: Fordham University Press, 2019.

West, Dennis, and Joan M. West. "Cinema beyond Words: An Interview with Lisandro Alonso." *Cineaste* 36, no. 2 (2011): 30–38.

Whitney, Shiloh. "Immanence and Transcendence." In *50 Concepts for a Critical Phenomenology*, 189–96. Evanston, IL: Northwestern University Press, 2020.

Williams, Gareth. *The Other Side of the Popular: Neoliberalism and Subalternity in Latin America*. Durham, NC: Duke University Press, 2002.

Williams, Raymond. *The Country and the City*. New York: Oxford University Press, 1973.

Young, Julian. "What Is Dwelling? The Homelessness of Modernity and the Worlding of the World." In *Heidegger, Authenticity, and Modernity: Essays in Honor of Hubert L. Dreyfus*, edited by Mark Wrathall and Jeff Malpas, 1:187–204. Cambridge, MA: MIT Press, 2000.

Zevallos Aguilar, Ulises Juan. *Las provincias contraatacan: Regionalismo y anticentralismo en la literatura peruana del siglo XX*. Lima, Peru: Universidad Nacional Mayor de San Marcos, 2009.

Zhang, Dora. "Naming the Indescribable: Woolf, Russell, James, and the Limits of Description." *New Literary History* 45, no. 1 (2014): 51–70.

Index

Aboio (Rocha), 212–13, 215, 262n19
Aboul-Ela, Hosam, 68, 233n112, 246n23
acculturation, 57, 93–94, 222n49
Adorno, Theodor, 74–75, 78, 82–84, 234n123, 255n14; aesthetic We, 242n78; critical regionalist poetics and, 68; difficulty and, 242n83; on enigmaticalness of art, 243n102, 245n9; *Grande sertão: Veredas* (Rosa) and, 135; Heidegger and, 81–82; negative dialectics, 58–59, 67, 81, 107–8, 171–72; phenomenology and, 255n16; Rama and, 238n9; Saer and, 170–72, 176, 189; theory of avant-garde formal experimentation, 90; *El zorro de arriba y el zorro de abajo* (Arguedas) and, 107–8, 127. *See also* Benjamin, Walter; negativity
aesthetic education, 21, 34–35, 72, 76, 220n18; Schillerian, 75
aesthetic experience, 7, 58–59, 66, 71, 74–75, 78, 80, 176; politics of, 64; role of, 226n105
aesthetics, 11, 13, 19, 80, 207; antirepresentational, 73; avant-garde, 223n61; critical regionalist, 22, 51, 232n92; dwelling and, 79; hyperrealist, 211; from Latin America, 219n12; nonurban, 38; placeless, 50, 208; politics and, 4, 32; postmodernist, 47; Saer's visual, 182
Ahmed, Sara, 66, 81, 83, 225n93
Alegría, Ciro, 45; *Los perros hambrientes*, 39
alienation, 9, 90, 161, 221n22; postmodern, 232n92
Alonso, Carlos J., 23, 60–61, 160, 197, 218n10, 227n9
Alonso, Lisandro, 202, 215, 261n1; *Fantasma*, 205–7, 209, 214; *La libertad*, 205–6; *Los muertos*, 205–6, 263n28
alterity, 23, 28, 34, 72–73, 82, 89, 116, 129, 133, 174; cultural, 58; *El entenado* (Saer) and, 198; in *El limonero real* (Saer), 199, 203; radical, 20; temporal, 221n33; untranslatable, 127
Amado, Jorge, 41, 151
Américo de Almeida, José, 41, 60
Andermann, Jens, 65–66, 161, 173, 232n99; ecocriticism and, 22; on *Hamaca paraguaya*, 211–12; landscape, 141, 143, 232n100;

Andermann, Jens (*continued*)
mapping practices and, 247n30;
on *Los muertos* (Alonso), 263n28;
neoregionalism and, 261n3; on
Ortiz, 202; on regionalist literature
and thought, 69
Andrade, Oswaldo de, 30, 132;
Manifesto antropófago, 66, 225n94
apprentissage, 60–61, 127, 144, 185,
197
Apter, Emily, 22, 67, 83, 127,
244n140; on untranslatability,
242n83, 245n2
Arce, Rafael, 180–81, 183, 200–202,
255n7, 255n13, 257n58, 263n24
architecture, 3, 51, 65;
postmodernist, 50
Argentina, 4, 181; avant-garde
aesthetics in, 223n61; *capital*
versus *provincias* dichotomy in,
34, 43; Cortázar and, 237n2;
dependency theory in, 222n52;
dictatorship in, 172, 175, 177,
191, 223n61, 255n11; gaze of
the nation in, 192; indigeneity in,
31; inland plains of, 5, 233n112;
lettered elite in, 18; modernization
in, 16; national identity and,
190; neo-regionalism in, 53;
northern, 237n4; regionalism in,
34, 43; regionalist literature in, 44;
university reform in, 219n15. *See
also* Buenos Aires; pampa/pampas
Arguedas, José María, 4, 8, 14,
32, 34, 64, 96–97, 111–12, 195,
208, 215, 241n55; bilingualism
of, 76, 88, 130, 242n91; on
Carpentier, 240n49; Cortázar
and, 19, 88, 123–26, 196,
237n2, 240n51, 241n69; critical
regionalism and, 49; *Dioses y
hombres de Haurochirí*, 96, 118,
241n67; on Fuentes, 240n49;
indigenismo and, 46–47, 239n40,
243n99; Indigenous words and,
58; Mariátegui and, 233n113;
narrative transculturation and,

57; nosotros, 242n78; "No soy
un aculturado . . . ," 87–89, 95,
224n85; Quechua people and,
237n4; race and, 225n93; Rama
and, 17, 221n30; regionalism and,
40, 43, 45–47; regionalist literature
and, 37; regional particularity and,
30; *Los ríos profundos*, 93, 103,
114, 116, 193, 241n62; Rosa and,
33, 98, 124, 126, 129–30, 133,
162–64, 245n3; Rulfo and, 33, 126,
133; Saer and, 226n103; sonority
and, 93, 102, 107, 110; suicide of,
88, 109, 118, 237n2, 239n38; as
transculturator, 92; Vargas Llosa
and, 240n52; *Yawar Fiesta*, 97. *See
also* Rowe, William; *zorro de arriba
y el zorro de abajo, El*
assimilation, 18, 91, 100, 111, 120
audience, 8, 198, 207, 209, 214;
Alonso and, 263n28; Arguedas
and, 46, 88, 101, 107, 111–12,
242n91; boom and, 7; critical
regionalism and, 76; critical
regionalist poetics and, 208;
Grande sertão: Veredas (Rosa)
and, 136, 161–62; metropolitan,
58; neo-regionalist literature and,
4; regionalism and, 60; Saer and,
170, 210
authenticity, 52–53, 133, 144, 216,
244n136; clichés of, 84; European
avant-gardes and, 41; identity-
based notions of, 125; of language,
241n55; of Latin American
intellectuals, 124
autochthony, 27, 53, 61; fetishization
of, 41
autonomy, 41, 176; aesthetic,
260n98; artistic, 12, 17, 70;
literary, 197
avant-garde form, 17, 27, 46, 93,
212, 214
avant-gardes, 15, 18, 49; European,
41; historical, 11, 45, 55, 200,
225n94; international, 57; Latin
American, 219n11

Balzac, Honoré de, 175, 179
barbarie, 52, 150, 153, 163, 176
Baskin, Jason, 22, 63, 67–68, 70–71, 171
belonging, 3, 9–10, 47–48, 61, 77, 79–81, 195, 209, 214; being present without, 53; collective, 78; cultural, 260n98; dwelling and, 76; halfway, 194; Heideggerian sense of, 35; literature and, 175; local, 5, 17, 25–26, 52, 218n7, 244n136; regional, 29, 40, 49, 78; Los ríos profundos (Arguedas) and, 114, 116; travessia and, 163; El zorro de arriba y el zorro de abajo (Arguedas) and, 89, 96, 116, 126–27
Benjamin, Walter, 63, 85, 90, 138, 142, 249n58, 255n14; Erlebnis, 170; Grande sertão: Veredas (Rosa) and, 237n201; on immersive nature of reading, 231n88; optical unconscious, 179–80; Rama and, 238nn9–10
Bennett, Jane, 59, 74
Bieger, Laura, 9, 20, 79
Bolle, Willi, 159, 252n113; on Grande sertão: Veredas (Rosa), 69, 137, 153–54, 161–62, 237n201, 253n117, 253n119, 253n133; on Os sertões (Cunha), 150, 153
boom, 5, 7, 12, 32–34, 43, 55, 129–30, 217n4; Arguedas and, 96, 100; bestsellerismo of, 19, 130; Global North and, 207; modernist techniques and, 45; Saer and, 174
Borges, Jorge Luis, 13, 174, 260n100, 260n113; "The Ethnographer," 199
Brasília, 125, 219n13, 251n86, 252n104
Brazil, 4, 31, 132, 153, 233n112, 247n28; avant-garde aesthetics in, 223n61; o ciclo nordestino, 38; class tension in, 161–62; critical regionalism in, 55–56; dependency theory in, 222n52; dictatorship in, 251n86, 256n20;

First Republic, 138; Grande sertão: Veredas (Rosa) and, 130; intellectual tradition of, 56; litoral-sertão dichotomy in, 150; mapping practices in, 137; military regime in, 16; modernization and, 16, 153; Northeast, 17, 131; northern, 251n87; regionalism in, 40, 42, 47, 59, 79, 84; woman warrior myth in, 252n101. See also sertão
Brazilian modernismo, 41, 227n12
Brito, Herasmo Braga de Oliveira, 23, 42, 223n61
Brizuela, Natalia, 210, 247n30, 251n91, 252n113, 262n7
Brooks, Peter, 156, 231n83
Brune, Krista, 224n87, 245n2
Bueno, Luís, 9, 23, 42, 50, 132–33, 145, 150, 220n21
Buenos Aires, 5, 31, 43; elite of, 18; literary scene of, 193
Burlot, María Lorena, 43, 56
Butler, Judith, 22, 47, 72, 78, 83, 126, 142, 242n83, 249n58

Campbell, Neil, 22, 47, 52
campesino, 5, 40, 174
Candido, Antonio, 14–17, 22, 42, 48, 132, 222n42, 226n2, 231n75; desnortear, 251n87; Formação da literatura brasileira, 38, 227n4. See also super-regionalismo
capital, 6, 54, 68, 247n30; circulation of, 8; cultural, 28; global, 34, 98
capital cities, 5, 15, 34, 43, 46, 53
capitalism, 26, 52, 56, 72–73, 80, 214; extractive, 5, 23, 69; European, 189; global, 12, 28; international, 96; landscape and, 141
Carmello, Patricia, 153, 156
Carpentier, Alejo, 4, 123, 126, 240n49
cartography, 65, 142, 253n117, 259n95
Castro-Klaren, Sara, 120, 241n67
Chakrabarty, Dipesh, 133, 230n53

Chiappini, Ligia, 14, 23, 42, 50, 53, 55, 59, 83–84
cinema, 3, 64–65, 200–201, 210, 262n11; Cinema Novo, 143; critical regionalism and, 214; critical regionalist poetics and, 207, 211; experimental, 30; intercultural, 215; Latin American, 206
civilization, 46, 52, 147, 153, 163, 231n82, 247n30; universal, 90
Clifford, James, 52, 229n44
Cohen Imach, Victoria, 43, 46, 56
Cold War, 15, 28, 32, 38, 55; cultural, 13, 219n12; dualism of, 19, 49; rhetoric of, 19; socialist revolution and, 40
collectivity, 49, 65, 78, 108, 126
Collot, Michel, 63, 142, 231n88
colonialism, 23, 31, 39, 66, 72; economic, 233n112; internal, 6, 9, 46, 193; landscape and, 141; legacy of, 109; violence of, 158
Comer, Krista, 22, 52, 229n44
commodification, 19, 28, 34, 100, 173, 214
community, 35, 47–48, 72, 79, 91, 120, 141, 209; aesthetic experience and, 78; affective, 64, 73; affiliative, 67, 114; alternative forms of, 19; Arguedas and, 94–95, 102, 107–8, 112, 126–27; critical regionalist, 32, 126–27, 194; critical regionalist poetics and, 77; El entenado (Saer) and, 198, 202; Quechua speaking, 113; remaking, 195; rural, 184; to come, 194; transnational, 36
comparative literature, 22, 35, 84–85; critical regionalism and, 50; Reinhard's definition of, 33
Conti, Heraldo, 43, 256n22
Cornejo Polar, Antonio, 23, 56, 104, 109; on Arguedas, 240n52, 241n55, 241n67; on heterogeneity, 47, 91; on transculturation, 91–92
Cortázar, Julio, 4, 13, 130, 244n133; Arguedas and, 19, 88, 123–26,

237n2, 240n51, 241n69; Rayuela, 131
Cosgrove, Denis, 141, 249n50
cosmopolitanism, 10, 16, 41, 55, 57, 208; critical, 49
costumbrismo, 14, 38, 43, 200, 251n91, 261n120
critical regionalism, 19, 22–23, 28, 47–56, 90, 195, 208, 214, 225n92, 229nn43–44; Adorno and, 58–59, 82; Bueno and, 132; Butler and, 78, 126; collectivity and, 108; dependency theory and, 230n53; dwelling and, 78–79; literary studies and, 83, 85; Moreiras and, 22, 49, 54–56, 231n76; narrative transculturation and, 33; new Andean regionalist literature as, 47; postnationalist, 78; Spivak and, 75, 78, 126, 175; Tarica and, 114; El zorro de arriba y el zorro de abajo (Arguedas) and, 46, 94, 98. See also Frampton, Kenneth
critical regionalist poetics, 7, 10, 20–21, 23, 26–30, 32–35, 50, 67–68, 84, 129, 207–9, 216; community and, 77; critical cosmopolitanism and, 49; dialectic of, 195, 215; difficulty and, 71; double binds of, 211; dwelling and, 216; embodiment and, 51; Encina's films and, 211; Fantasma (Alonso) as example of, 206; negativity of, 74; pedagogy of, 62, 64, 89; phenomenological subject and, 66; political project of, 74; reading and, 70–71, 73; right to opacity and, 83; self-interrogation and, 93; transculturation and, 58
Critical Theory, 22, 48, 90
crónicas, 39, 191–92, 247n30
Cuban Revolution, 13, 33, 40, 226n102
cultural studies, 22, 28, 84; critical regionalism and, 53, 55, 85, 190; Latin American, 30, 49; US, 47, 49

De Certeau, Michel, 139, 142
De la Campa, Ramón, 12, 91, 231n76
Demaría, Laura, 9, 19, 23, 176; critical regionalism and, 50, 56, 195; *extranjero*, 25, 122–23, 194, 220n21; *forastero*, 122–23, 193–94, 220n21; on *provincias/* provinces, 43, 53, 76, 84, 191, 226n103, 243n96; on Saer, 192–93, 197, 226n103
Derrida, Jacques, 102, 241n55
developmentalism, 4, 16, 49; dependency theory and, 222n52; Latin American, 12
difficulty, 74–75, 177, 243n102; of *apprentissage*, 144; critical regionalist texts and, 76; formal, 7, 23, 26, 28, 57, 67, 71–73, 75, 100, 242n83; of *Grande sertão: Veredas* (Rosa), 129–30, 132, 137, 246n15; of *El limonero real* (Saer), 167, 199; of Saer's language, 24, 173
dislocation, 48, 78, 82
dwelling, 3–4, 6–10, 20, 23, 27–30, 34–35, 58, 62–64, 77, 81; activities, 140, 189, 192, 202; alterity and, 203; Arguedas and, 109, 115, 196; cinema and, 207, 213–14; critical regionalist poetics and, 216; ethos of, 126; habitability and, 74; Heideggerian concept of, 78–80, 82, 217n1, 235n154; Ingold's notion of, 68; multisensory experience of, 52; phenomenology and, 85, 89, 95, 178; in Saer's work, 19, 197; time-space of, 141
dwelling perspective, 7, 23, 62, 67, 181, 199; in *Grande sertão: Veredas* (Rosa), 64, 133–34, 139, 143–44, 155, 158–60, 164, 193; Saer's *zona* and, 192. *See also travessia*

ecocriticism, 22, 218n7
ekphrasis, 64–65, 200

embodiment, 22, 51, 63, 67, 102
Encina, Paz, 207; *Hamaca paraguaya*, 211–12, 215; *Ejercicios de memoria*, 212
essentialism, 7, 49, 132; critique of, 95; nationalistic, 192
ethics, 119; of reading *Grande sertão: Veredas* (Rosa), 145; Levinasian, 82–83; literature and, 20; new, 70, 234n120; of *El zorro de arriba y el zorro de abajo* (Arguedas), 77
ethnography, 44, 53, 117, 199, 251n91; critique of, 215; nineteenth-century, 29
exile, 48, 76, 82, 243n98; of Cortázar, 124, 126, 237n2; of Perón, 18, 255n20; of Saer, 77, 170, 192–93, 195, 197
experimentalism, 49; formal, 11, 19, 58; of *indigenismo*, 47
experimentation: avant-garde, 18; formal, 4, 6, 69, 90, 198; linguistic, 93; Saer's, 255n13
exteriority, 9, 163–64, 197; in *El limonero real* (Saer), 25, 202; refusal of, 133
extraction, 30, 65; capitalist, 28, 143; zones of, 5, 39, 142–43
extranjero, 25, 122–23, 193–94, 220n21

Fantini Scarpelli, Marli, 141, 162–63, 244n1
Faulkner, William, 4, 11, 126, 175, 260n100
Finazzi-Agrò, Ettore, 141, 163, 254n151
forastero, 115, 122–23, 193–94, 196–97, 220n21
Frampton, Kenneth, 47, 54, 57–58, 78, 80; architectural theory of, 22, 52; critical regionalism of, 50–51, 56, 85, 90, 94, 208, 214, 229n43; tactile and, 72, 234n134
Franco, Jean, 12, 17
French, Jennifer, 22, 56, 218n8, 219n10

Freyre, Gilberto, 40–41, 50, 55, 84, 228n14, 228n19, 231n75, 235n164
Fuentes, Carlos, 13, 123, 240n49

Galvão, Walnice Nogueira, 157–59, 250n73
Gandesha, Samir, 81, 236n177, 255n16
García Márquez, Gabriel, 4, 14, 130, 257n43
Garramuño, Florencia, 32–33, 150, 170, 173, 177, 179–81, 255n15
gaucho, 5, 40, 60–61, 174
Gibson, James, 62–63, 185
Glissant, Édouard, 52–53, 80, 83, 181, 198, 236n187, 242n83. See also opacity
globalization, 21, 28, 32, 47, 49, 57, 80, 97
Global North, 21, 28, 53, 55, 98, 207, 219n12
Global South, 21, 75, 143, 233n112; aesthetic markers of, 28; comparative literature and, 50; critical regionalism and, 49, 53; cultural production from, 73; cultures of, 29; experimental aesthetics from, 13; literary production of, 246n23; perspectives from, 19
Gómez-Barris, Macarena, 22, 53, 142–43, 218n6, 230n66, 250n59. See also submerged perspectives
Gonzáles, José Eduardo, 90, 94, 229n42, 238n9
Gramuglio, María Teresa, 19, 258n64
Güiraldes, Ricardo, 60–61; Don Segundo Sombra, 60, 227n9
Grande sertão: Veredas (Rosa), 7–8, 17, 62, 129–39, 145–64, 169, 180, 198, 209; Aboio (Rocha) and, 262n19; adaptations of, 262n5; Cuban Revolution and, 33; divided subjectivity in, 77, 160–61; difficulty and, 23, 28, 129, 135; domesticating gaze and, 193; dwelling perspective and, 139; Don Segundo Sombra (Güiraldes) and, 60–61, 197 (see also Alonso, Carlos J.); ethics and, 144–45; forastero and, 194; gender and, 225n93; landscape and, 64; melancholia in, 248n38; Os sertões (Cunha) and, 252n96; reading and, 145, 250n68; regionalist literature and, 37; self-reflexivity in, 25, 129, 210; super-regionalismo and, 42; Third Republic (Estado Novo) and, 251n86; translations of, 131, 245n4, 245n8, 246n26. See also audience; Bolle, Willi; difficulty; dwelling perspective; jagunço; Rowland, Clara; Santiago, Silviano; travessia

Hansen, João Adolfo, 138, 149, 153, 159–60
Haraway, Donna, 7, 22, 29, 64, 76, 142, 233n106. See also situated knowledges
Heffes, Gisela, 22, 218n7
Heidegger, Martin, 3, 9–10, 214, 216, 221n22, 221n26; Adorno and, 81–82; modern literature and, 235n154; nativist politics of, 78; ontology of, 79, 81; Poetry, Language, Thought, 9, 79, 217n1. See also belonging; dwelling; phenomenology
Heredia, Pablo, 19, 23, 43–44, 56, 217n4
Herr, Cheryl Temple, 22, 58, 81–82
heterogeneity, 47, 58, 89, 163, 242n78; cultural, 49, 91–92, 98, 110
historiography, 44; literary, 32, 55
Hoyos, Héctor, 22, 69, 83
Humboldt, Alexander Von, 150, 192, 249n55, 251n96, 259n83
humility, 28, 72, 110
hybridity, 47–48, 84, 90, 129, 141, 163, 254n151

identity, 43, 61, 133, 194, 244n136; American, 38; Argentine national, 46, 174, 190–91; authenticity and, 125; autochthonous, 31; Brazilian national, 131; collapse of, 94; collective, 175; differential, 81; essentialist notions of, 97, 195, 231n76; ethnic, 44–45, 48, 114, 123, 126; for export, 196; group, 67; Indian, 227n8; local, 53, 80, 195; modern Quechua, 240n52; national, 5, 32, 37, 39, 48, 75, 114, 132, 197, 227n4; national-populist, 256n30; Peruvian, 239n40; place and, 140; politics, 54; regional, 6, 19; transculturation and, 91, 108
indigenismo, 14, 44–47, 97, 239n40, 244n136; Mariátegui's, 240n40; *vanguardista*, 223n56
Indigenous communities, 39, 119–20, 239n40, 244n136; in Peru, 45
Indigenous peoples, 96, 237n4
indio, 5, 97, 237n4
indio culture, 88, 101
infrastructure, 6, 20, 138, 147, 166
Ingold, Tim, 22, 62–64, 68, 70, 139–40, 181, 185, 192; landscape and, 139, 141–42, 151, 155, 183, 202, 232n100, 248n42. *See also* dwelling perspective
intertextuality, 208, 261n1; in *Grande sertão: Veredas* (Rocha), 262n19

jagunçagem, 142, 152, 157, 159–60
jagunço, 5, 40, 60, 135–36, 138, 146, 157–59, 209, 225n93, 247n28, 253n133; *letrado*, 77, 145, 160, 162, 209, 250n73
Jameson, Fredric, 22, 47, 49, 51, 54, 229n43, 229n48, 232n92
Jitrik, Noé, 43, 167, 255n13
Joyce, James, 11, 260n100

Kafka, Franz, 11, 260n100
Kalimán, Ricardo, 22, 50, 53, 56, 84
Kampff Lages, Susana, 153, 155

Kant, Immanuel, 20, 77
Kon Kon (Vicuña), 213–15, 263n22
Kubitschek, Juscelino, 16, 147, 251n86; government of, 152

landscape, 138–43, 178, 183, 185, 232n100, 248n42, 248n50, 259n95; Andean, 89, 95, 97, 103, 110, 112; Arguedas and, 114; cinema and, 211; *cronistas* and, 169; dwelling in a particular, 67; dwelling perspective and, 181; in *Fantasma* (Alonso), 205–6; in *Grande sertão: Veredas* (Rosa), 140, 143–44, 146–47, 150–52, 155, 158; in *El limonero real* (Saer), 184, 189, 201; local, 7, 88, 143, 189, 193, 195; media, 29, 207; Ortiz and, 202; regional, 65; regionalism and, 60; studies, 249nn54–55; *travessia* and, 133; in *El zorro de arriba y el zorro de abajo* (Arguedas), 95, 97, 103, 105, 107, 110, 112–13, 116–17, 119–20. *See also* Andermann, Jens; Cosgrove, Denis; Ingold, Tim; pampa/pampas; Saer, Juan José: *la zona* of; *sertão*; Williams, Raymond
Latin American literature, 4–5, 7–8, 14–17, 50, 73, 123, 132; readership of, 100, 162, 174, 207; Seix Barral and, 245n4. *See also* boom
Latin American studies, 5–6, 22, 47, 50, 54, 232n97
lettered city (*ciudad letrada*), 21–22, 46, 111
Levinas, Emmanuel, 10, 82
Librandi, Marília, 22, 63, 103–4, 110, 118, 248n42
Lienhard, Martin, 46, 93, 111, 221n30
lifeways, 34; local, 58, 208, 216; place-specific, 136, 211, 214; regional, 67, 213
Lima, 5, 31, 45, 96–98

Lima, Gabriel dos Santos, 15–17

Lins do Rego, José, 41, 151, 228n14

limonero real, El (Saer), 33, 69, 77, 182–88, 190, 197, 199–202, 255n7, 258n79; critical regionalist poetics and, 209; difficulty of, 23, 28, 167, 169, 199; film adaptation of, 262n5; landscape and, 192; L. Alonso and, 205, 261n1; photography and cinema in, 210; regionalism and, 37, 44; rural interior and, 7; self-reflexivity of, 25

Lispector, Clarice, 41, 133

literary criticism, 254n153; Argentine, 42; Latin American, 65; Marxist, 70

literary studies, 84; critical regionalism and, 28, 50, 55; phenomenology and, 142

literature, 9, 11, 13, 20–21, 51, 58, 180, 215, 226n105; aesthetics of belonging and, 80; of the Americas, 225n94; anti-literature, 73; Arguedas and, 88, 100, 110, 117; body and, 103; Brazilian, 41, 56, 132–33; cinema and, 262n11, 263n24; committed, 17, 173, 233n113; compensatory model of, 179; critical regionalist, 29, 216; critical regionalist poetics and, 207–8; difficulty in, 242n83; dwelling and, 3–4, 35; dwelling perspective in, 181; early twentieth-century, 227n9; ethical and political work of, 64; high, 13, 44; *indigenista*, 45–46, 118, 243n112; landscape and, 142; literary criticism and, 254n153; mapping and, 247n30; modern, 18, 235n154; modernist, 171; national, 175, 192, 227n4; pastoral nostalgia in, 61; pedagogical function of, 172, 220n18; Peruvian, 110; photographic and filmographic languages in, 200; postboom, 55; regional particularity and, 74; rural, 174, 256n36; Saer and,

196–97, 256n22, 256n36; study of, 27; subaltern experience and, 117–18; telepoetic creation of new collectivities and, 77; territory and, 33; unintelligibility and, 178; visual landscape and, 65. *See also* comparative literature, Latin American literature; neo-regionalist literature; regionalist literature; world literature

local, the, 22, 25–26, 29, 48–50, 52, 84, 129; critical regionalism and, 64, 175 (*see also* Saer, Juan José); dwelling in, 30, 82, 132; *extranjero* and, 194; *forastero* and, 122; literature and, 196; mediation and, 58, 90; rural literature and, 174; translation and, 90, 111

Lucero, Nicolás, 197, 200

Lugones, Leopoldo, 176, 191, 257n42

Lukács, Georg, 70, 238n9

magical realism, 12, 18; Latin American, 94, 219n12

Mariátegui, José Carlos, 45–46, 56, 223n56, 239n40; Arguedas and, 233n113; *gamonalismo* and, 239n38 tradition of dependency theory, 68, 233n112

Marks, Laura U., 64, 114, 117, 211, 214–15, 262n11

Martí, José, 30, 50, 56

Martínez Estrada, Ezequiel, 189, 258n83

Masiello, Francine, 22, 28–29, 63, 103, 113, 116, 180; on Merleau-Ponty, 229n42; on *Nadie nada nunca*, 172, 181

Mastronardi, Carlos, 193–94. *See also forastero*

materialism, 69; Adorno's, 59; historical, 67

McGlazer, Ramsey, 72

melancholia, 153, 179, 195, 248n38

Merleau-Ponty, Maurice, 63, 66–67, 71, 139, 142, 171, 229n42, 232n105 *mestizaje*, 92; ideology of, 84, 91, 231n76; politics of, 18

migration, 48, 52, 79–80, 82, 96–97; forced, 80, 84; mass, 78, 96; urban, 161

Mitchell, W. J. T., 141, 249n50

modernism, 11, 41, 108, 132; aesthetic, 177, 180; European, 12, 73; foreign, 15; high, 221n33; international, 13, 18; late, 19; literary, 26, 207

modernity, 30, 38–39, 49, 53, 79, 150, 152, 219n11; Brazilian, 153; of capital cities, 5; capitalist, 6, 8, 45, 56–57; colonial narratives of, 230n53; Eurocentric narratives of, 12; Frankfurt School critiques of, 208; Heidegger on, 10; literary, 14; of the rural poor, 34; urban, 16, 54; Western, 18, 124, 210

modernization, 5–6, 26, 48, 94, 188, 214, 218n10; in Brazil, 153–54; campaigns, 39, 143, 152; capitalist, 55, 91; critical regionalism and, 49; impact of, 41; indigenism and, 227n8; industrial, 90; of Latin American literature, 16–17; narratives, 31, 52, 134, 153–54; in Peru, 45; uneven, 98

Molina, Hebe Beatriz, 43, 56

Montaldo, Graciela, 39, 167, 190, 200

Moreiras, Alberto, 22, 47, 49, 54–56, 85, 93–94, 108–9, 231n76

multiculturalism, 21, 29

Nancy, Jean-Luc, 103, 241n64

nationalism, 10, 78, 174; colonialism and, 193; cultural, 75; *mestizo*, 45; neo-nationalism, 80; Romantic, 44

national patrimony, 31, 174

nativism, 10, 80

negative spaces, 71, 107–8, 110, 127, 171–72

negativity, 23, 55, 58, 62, 207, 215–16, 242n83; Adornian, 170, 201, 262n7; Adorno on,

108; Arguedas and, 107, 172; of avant-garde poetics, 57; of critical regionalist poetics, 74; of indeterminate presences, 171; narrative transculturation and, 92; *provincias* and, 53; Saer and, 172–73, 175, 177, 179–81, 195, 255n13; of *terceira margem*, 163; of *El zorro de arriba y el zorro de abajo* (Arguedas), 94, 109–10, 117

neoliberalism, 17; global, 55, 75, 207

neo-regionalism, 29, 38, 48; in Argentina, 53

neo-regionalist literature, 4, 42–43, 69

Niemeyer, Oscar, 51, 252n104

novela de la tierra, 37, 45, 59–61, 218n10

nueva narrativa latinoamericana, 11–12, 14–15, 32, 38, 42, 123, 132

Ocampo, Catalina, 241n67, 242n83

opacity, 23–25, 67, 74–75, 91, 110, 177, 207, 242n83; of experience, 169, 173; of (neo)colonial encounters, 58, 231n78; poetics of, 57; right to, 83, 236n187; of Saer's poetics, 170–71, 189, 197, 201–3; selective, 89; *sertão* and, 131; of translation, 7; of vision, 179

originality, 15, 41, 90–91

Ortiz, Fernando, 57, 222n49, 238n9

Ortiz, Juan L., 174, 178, 201–2, 257n58

Oubiña, David, 172, 177, 179

Padrón, Ricardo, 200; on mapping practices, 274n30

pampa/pampas, 30–31, 39, 44, 61, 150, 189; in "Discusión sobre el término zona," (Saer), 196; Humboldt on, 259n83; in *La libertad* (Alonso), 205; in *La ocasión* (Saer), 189, 191; in "El viajero" (Saer), 165–67, 170, 189

Patruno, Luigi, 175–76, 192, 197, 260n113

pedagogy, 89, 220n18; Adorno and, 59, 75; of aesthetic experience, 74; critical regionalist, 66; critical regionalist poetics as, 23, 59, 62; of perception, 70

Penhos, Marta, 247n30, 259n95

Pérez Trujillo Diniz, Axel, 22, 24, 30, 134, 143

Perón, Juan D., 16, 18, 170, 191, 223n58; regime of, 174; return from exile of, 255n20

Peronism, 18, 43, 223n60; nationalism and, 237n2; populism and, 34; regional cultures and, 256n30

Peru, 4, 16, 45, 47, 237n4; agrarian reform in, 239n38; Arguedas on, 87–88, 101, 112–13

phenomenology, 48, 70; Adorno and, 255n16; Heideggerian, 22, 79, 208; of Merleau-Ponty, 67, 71; of place, 107; Sartre's, 71

Piglia, Ricardo, 175–76, 190, 201

poetic, the, 3–4, 9–10, 19, 217n1

poetics, 10; boom, 207; of duration, 181; experimental, 17, 34, 176–77, 179–80, 255n7; negative, 167, 177, 181; of place, 235n154; of recalcitrance and opacity, 57; of relation, 83; Saer's, 170, 173, 176–77, 179–81, 255n7, 261n120, 263n24; textualist, 73; visual, 64, 179, 261n120. See also critical regionalist poetics

poetic thought, 3, 9, 214

political commitment, 11, 34, 45, 67; Arguedas's, 46; Saer's, 173

politics, 18–19, 173, 219n12, 233n113, 242n83; abdication of, 12, 70; of aesthetic experience, 64; aesthetics and, 4, 32, 47; class, 69; of difference, 94; Ejercicios de memoria (Encina) and, 212; of experimental form, 13, 17; Heidegger's nativist, 78; Heidegger's reactionary, 3, 10; identity, 54; literature and, 20;

radical, 11, 75; of Rama's project, 238n9; Saer's, 176, 191; of style, 73; of El zorro de arriba y el zorro de abajo (Arguedas), 93

populism, 4, 16, 40, 47; in Argentina, 18, 34; national, 45, 49, 91, 219n15; periodization of, 227n10

poverty, 31, 151

Powell, Douglas Reichert, 22, 47, 53

power relations, 54, 96, 117; (neo) colonial, 5

Pratt, Mary Louise, 38, 52, 162, 192, 198, 229n44, 247n30

Premat, Julio, 44, 177, 179–80, 190–91, 198, 257n42

Prieto, Julio, 58, 73–74, 100, 109, 223n56, 243n98, 247n30

provincialism, 84, 237n2

provincias/provinces, 23, 34, 43, 53, 65, 76, 194–97, 243n96; national culture in, 18; Saer and, 19, 173, 191, 193, 226n103

Quechua, 76, 98, 102, 106, 110, 112–14, 116, 121, 127, 240n52; Andean culture and, 88; folk songs, 24, 103, 242n91; speaker of, 111; words, 130

Rama, Ángel, 15–17, 30, 33, 50, 55–59, 80, 89–95, 226n2; on acculturation, 222n49; on América, 225n94; on Arguedas, 17, 221n30; Benjamin and, 90, 238nn9–10; Candido and, 15, 222n42; Frankfurt School and, 56, 90, 229n42, 238n9; on huaynos in Los ríos profundos (Arguedas), 241n62; on regional particularity, 6; La transculturación narrativa en América Latina, 15, 89, 92; on transculturators, 126, 129, 199; on El zorro de arriba y el zorro de abajo (Arguedas), 102, 107, 111. See also critical regionalism; regionalism; regionalist literature; transculturation

Ramos, Graciliano, 41–42, 151;
Vidas secas, 39
Rancière, Jacques, 64, 210, 226n105
realism, 44; regionalist literature
and, 38, 43; Saer on, 197; sensory,
261n3; Soviet, 13; turn away from,
12. See also magical realism
realist novels, 45, 60, 90, 135
regionalism, 11, 14–15, 17, 22, 30,
32, 47–48, 53, 154; of the Andes,
46; Argentine, 42–44, 257n49;
Brazilian, 41–42, 132, 227n4;
early, 39; Freyre and, 41, 84;
historical, 15, 38, 60, 132, 218n10;
Latin American, 31; in Latin
American studies, 6; literary, 38,
55; regionalismo no nostálgico, 38,
227n5; regionalismo no realista,
38, 227n5; rescuing, 79; Rosa
and, 41–42; Saer and, 34, 44, 197,
227n5, 261n120. See also critical
regionalism; neo-regionalism;
super-regionalismo
regionalist literature, 6, 13–15,
22, 37–40, 55–56, 59, 69, 84;
alienation in, 161; Argentine, 19,
44; avant-garde, 46; Brazilian,
42, 59, 132; C. Alonso on, 197;
Cortázar on, 123; critical, 216;
experimentalism of, 49; extractivist
models of development and, 5;
forastero and, 194; as literary
tourism, 220n21; new Andean,
47; Saer and, 174–75; stereotypes
about, 218n10. See also neo-
regionalist literature
regionalist novel, 14; Don Segundo
Sombra (Güiraldes) as, 227n9;
historical, 60; El limonero real
(Saer) as, 44; modernist, 20; realist,
200; twentieth-century, 5
regionalist writers, 4, 6, 41, 45, 59,
151; critical, 214
regional life, 68, 72, 97, 197, 216;
fetishization of, 7; ossification of,
27; reification of, 64; subsumption
of, 16

Richard, Nelly, 53; critique of
postmodernism by, 221n34
Ricoeur, Paul, 78, 80, 90
Rio de Janeiro, 5, 41, 161, 246n27
Rivera, Fernando, 101, 106, 117–19,
242n91
Rogers, Charlotte, 22, 218n6
Rosa, João Guimarães, 3–4, 8, 19,
24, 32–34, 37, 40–43, 45, 47, 58,
79, 129–30, 193, 195, 203; Aboio
(Rocha) and, 212; Andrade and,
132; archaeology of the surface
and, 141; Arguedas and, 33, 98,
124, 126, 130, 133, 162, 245n3;
as critical regionalist, 49, 132;
critical regionalist poetics and,
208; dwelling perspective and, 134;
narrative transculturation and, 57;
politics and, 233n113; regionalism
and, 228n27; regional particularity
and, 30; Saramago and, 252n105;
sertão and, 143, 150–51, 153, 210;
super-regionalismo and, 15, 17; "A
terceira margem do rio," 162–63;
translators and, 161–62; woman
warrior myth and, 252n101.
See also Grande sertão: Veredas;
travessia
Rosenberg, Fernando J., 49, 219n11,
225n94
Rowe, William, 76, 93–94, 102–3,
107, 110–12, 125, 221n30, 238n7,
240n45; on huaynos, 241n62
Rowland, Clara, 153, 156–57, 159,
231n83, 253n117
Rulfo, Juan, 4, 33, 43, 98, 124, 126,
133, 226n102
rural interior, 5, 7, 167, 176, 190,
193; indigeneity and, 31; national-
populist discourses and, 173–74

Saer, Juan José, 4, 8, 18–19, 32–
34, 47, 64, 174, 177, 256n37,
260n100, 261n123; Arguedas and,
226n103; as critical regionalist, 49;
critical regionalist poetics and, 208;
difficulty and, 24; "Discusión

Saer, Juan José (*continued*)
  sobre el término zona," 195–96;
  divided self of, 77; dwelling and,
  30; *El entenado*, 192, 198–99,
  202; experimental poetics of, 176–
  77, 180, 255n7, 255n13; exile of,
  255n11; García Márquez and,
  257n43; gender and, 225n93;
  Lo imborrable, 175; language
  of, 58; literature and, 256n22;
  Lugones and, 257n42; *La mayor*,
  169; "La mayor," 178–80, 182,
  190, 258n64; *Nadie nada nunca*,
  169, 172, 181, 190, 255n7,
  259n86; negative poetics of, 167,
  177, 181; neo-regionalism and,
  43; poetics of, 170, 173, 176–
  77, 179–81, 261n120, 263n24;
  political violence in work of,
  259n86; politics and, 233n113;
  pseudo-objectivist poetics of,
  263n24; regionalism and, 40, 44,
  227n5, 257n49; *El río sin orillas*,
  191, 257n42; rural literature
  and, 256n36; Vargas Llosa and,
  257n43; "El viajero," 165–70,
  178, 184, 189–90, 192–93; visual
  aesthetics of, 182; visual poetics
  of, 64, 179, 200–202, 261n120;
  la zona of, 170–71, 175–76, 178,
  180–81, 185, 189–93, 195–99,
  201–3, 257n58. *See also limonero
  real, El*
Santiago, Silviano, 147, 149,
  254n153; on *Grande sertão:
  Veredas* (Rosa), 130, 137, 144–45,
  160, 246n27, 253n133
São Paulo, 41, 161, 227n12
Saramago, Victoria, 246nn14–15,
  252n105
Sarlo, Beatriz, 19, 171, 175–77, 179,
  190, 227n5, 259n86
Sarmiento, Domingo F., 18, 150, 167,
  176, 192, 251n96; on education,
  231n82; *Facundo*, 166
Sartre, Jean Paul, 71, 232n105
saudade, 153, 248n38

Schmidt-Welle, Friedhelm, 38, 227n5
self-reflexivity, 22–23, 25, 27, 62, 93,
  207, 219n11; of *Grande sertão:
  Veredas* (Rosa), 129; *novelas de la
  tierra* and, 60; in *El zorro de arriba
  y el zorro de abajo* (Arguedas), 117
Serafini, Paula, 218n5, 230n65
sertão, 5, 17, 30–31, 131, 136–41,
  143–64, 210; *Aboio* (Rocha) and,
  212–13, 262n19; Brasília and,
  251n86, 252n104; descriptions of,
  245nn13–14; domestication of,
  251n91; dwelling perspective and,
  64, 133; inhabitants of, 134; life
  in, 61, 136; lower, 228n19; oral
  culture of, 250n68; regionalism
  and, 39, 42; sea and, 251n96. *See
  also Grande sertão: Veredas* (Rosa);
  jagunço; *Os sertões* (Cunha)
sertões, Os (Cunha), 143, 150,
  153, 251n91, 252n96, 252n101,
  252n113
Shellhorse, Adam Joseph, 58, 73,
  242n83
Siskind, Mariano, 12, 22, 83
situated knowledges, 7, 76, 85,
  233n106
Smith, Amanda M., 142; on mapping,
  247n30
social mobility, 39, 97, 253n133
Sommer, Doris, 73, 144–45, 198
sovereignty, 77, 143
Spirn, Anne Whiston, 142, 144
Spitta, Silvia, 92–93
Spivak, Gayatri Chakravorty, 22, 29,
  33, 47, 72, 75, 77, 83, 220n18; *An
  Aesthetic Education in the Era of
  Globalization*, 20–21; aesthetic
  experience and, 226n105; critical
  regionalism and, 126, 175; double
  bind, 21, 26, 30; *Who Sings
  the Nation State?*, 78. *See also*
  aesthetic education
submerged perspectives, 54, 142,
  218n6, 230n66, 250n59
super-regionalismo, 14–16, 38, 42,
  227n5

Tarica, Estelle, 23, 44, 56, 97, 102, 114, 117, 240n52; on indigenism, 227n8, 243n99, 244n136
testimonio, 11, 73, 101, 118
textuality, 10; literary, 21; thick, 70, 75
transculturation, 29, 55, 57–58, 89–95, 107–9, 127, 222n49, 231n76, 238n9; *Grande sertão: Veredas* (Rosa) and, 129; narrative, 15–16, 33, 56–57, 90–92, 163; tamed, 238n6. *See also* Moreiras, Alberto; Ortiz, Fernando; Rama, Ángel; *El zorro de arriba y el zorro de abajo* (Arguedas)
translation, 48, 180, 224n87; cultural, 83, 89, 110, 215; of difference, 92; failure of, 57, 73, 244n140; global, 83; *Grande sertão: Veredas* (Rosa) and, 131, 246n26; mediation and, 58; opacity of, 7; transculturation and, 91; zone, 127; *El zorro de arriba y el zorro de abajo* (Arguedas) and, 220n19. *See also* untranslatability
travel writing, 39, 132, 191; European, 247n30; late eighteenth-century, 259n95
travessia, 133–34, 139, 145, 153–63, 193, 254n151
Tsing, Anna, 29, 92, 111, 217n3

uncertainty, 160; of living, 159; of the *travessia*, 157–58
universalism, 17, 34, 53; abstract, 13; false, 54
untranslatability, 28, 67, 110, 129, 242n83, 245n2

Vallejo, César, 17, 49, 241n55, 260n100; *Trilce*, 223n56
vanguardismo, 18, 32, 45, 227n12
Vargas, Getúlio, 16, 147; dictatorship of, 251n86
Vargas Llosa, Mario, 4, 17–18, 130, 226n2; Arguedas and, 240n52; "Primitives and Creators," 14, 221n31; Saer and, 257n43
Videla, Rafael, 170, 255n20

Walsh, Rodolfo, 256n22; *Operación Masacre*, 101
Wenzel, Jennifer, 84, 220n16
Williams, Gareth, 91, 174, 223n58, 238n6
Williams, Raymond, 39, 61, 71, 141, 249n50
Woolf, Virginia, 11, 260n100
world literature, 19, 29, 83–84, 145; critiques of, 22; decolonial approaches to, 6

Zevallos Aguilar, Ulises Juan, 23, 45, 242n91
zorro de arriba y el zorro de abajo, El (Arguedas), 8, 23–24, 26, 33, 37, 46, 68, 76–77, 93–113, 116–27, 163, 237n2, 240n45, 240n48; critical regionalism and, 98; difficulty and, 28; dwelling and, 210; *forastero* and, 122–23, 194; habitability and, 74; *Kon Kon* (Vicuña) and, 213; "No soy un aculturado . . ." and, 88–89, 95; Ocampo on, 241n67, 242n83; Rosa and, 130, 162

FLASHPOINTS

1. *On Pain of Speech: Fantasies of the First Order and the Literary Rant*, Dina Al-Kassim

2. *Moses and Multiculturalism*, Barbara Johnson, with a foreword by Barbara Rietveld

3. *The Cosmic Time of Empire: Modern Britain and World Literature*, Adam Barrows

4. *Poetry in Pieces: César Vallejo and Lyric Modernity*, Michelle Clayton

5. *Disarming Words: Empire and the Seductions of Translation in Egypt*, Shaden M. Tageldin

6. *Wings for Our Courage: Gender, Erudition, and Republican Thought*, Stephanie H. Jed

7. *The Cultural Return*, Susan Hegeman

8. *English Heart, Hindi Heartland: The Political Life of Literature in India*, Rashmi Sadana

9. *The Cylinder: Kinematics of the Nineteenth Century*, Helmut Müller-Sievers

10. *Polymorphous Domesticities: Pets, Bodies, and Desire in Four Modern Writers*, Juliana Schiesari

11. *Flesh and Fish Blood: Postcolonialism, Translation, and the Vernacular*, S. Shankar

12. *The Fear of French Negroes: Transcolonial Collaboration in the Revolutionary Americas*, Sara E. Johnson

13. *Figurative Inquisitions: Conversion, Torture, and Truth in the Luso-Hispanic Atlantic*, Erin Graff Zivin

14. *Cosmopolitan Desires: Global Modernity and World Literature in Latin America*, Mariano Siskind

15. *Fiction Beyond Secularism*, Justin Neuman

16. *Periodizing Jameson: Dialectics, the University, and the Desire for Narrative*, Phillip E. Wegner

17. *The Practical Past*, Hayden White

18. *The Powers of the False: Reading, Writing, Thinking Beyond Truth and Fiction*, Doro Wiese

19. *The Object of the Atlantic: Concrete Aesthetics in Cuba, Brazil, and Spain, 1868–1968*, Rachel Price

20. *Epic and Exile: Novels of the German Popular Front 1933–1945*, Hunter Bivens

21. *An Innocent Abroad: Lectures in China*, J. Hillis Miller

22. *Form and Instability: East Europe, Literature, Postimperial Difference*, Anita Starosta

23. *Bombay Modern: Arun Kolatkar and Bilingual Literary Culture*, Anjali Nerlekar

24. *Intimate Relations: Social Reform and the Late Nineteenth-Century South Asian Novel*, Krupa Shandilya

25. *Media Laboratories: Late Modernist Authorship in South America*, Sarah Ann Wells

26. *Acoustic Properties: Radio, Narrative, and the New Neighborhood of the Americas*, Tom McEnaney

27. *The New Woman: Literary Modernism, Queer Theory, and the Trans Feminine Allegory*, Emma Heaney
28. *Civilizing War: Imperial Politics and the Poetics of National Rupture*, Nasser Mufti
29. *Late Colonial Sublime: Neo-Epics and the End of Romanticism*, G. S. Sahota
30. *Globalizing Race: Anti-Semitism, Empire, and the Politics of Scale in Modern French and European Culture*, Dorian Bell
31. *Domestications: American Empire, Literary Culture, and the Postcolonial Lens*, Hosam Mohamed Aboul-Ela
32. *Behold an Animal: Four Exorbitant Readings*, Thangam Ravindranathan
33. *Capital Letters: Hugo, Baudelaire, Camus, and the Death Penalty*, Ève Morisi
34. *Immaterial Archives: An African Diaspora Poetics of Loss*, Jenny Sharpe
35. *Figures of the World: The Naturalist Novel and Transnational Form*, Christopher Laing Hill
36. *Imperfect Solidarities: Tagore, Gandhi, Du Bois, and the Forging of the Global Anglophone*, Madhumita Lahiri
37. *Fictional Environments: Mimesis, Deforestation, and Development in Latin America*, Victoria Saramago
38. *How to Read a Moment: The American Novel and the Crisis of the Present*, Mathias Nilges
39. *Secondhand China: Spain, the East, and the Politics of Translation*, Carles Prado-Fonts
40. *New World Maker: Radical Poetics, Black Internationalism, and the Translations of Langston Hughes*, Ryan James Kernan
41. *The Idea of Indian Literature: Gender, Genre, and Comparative Method*, Preetha Mani
42. *Concepts of the World*, Effie Rentzou
43. *Traces of the Unseen*, Carolina Sá Carvalho
44. *Cannibal Translation: Literary Reciprocity in Contemporary Latin America*, Isabel C. Gómez
45. *Entranced Earth: Art, Extractivism, and the End of Landscape*, Jens Andermann